Paranormal Beliefs

A Sociological Introduction

Paranormal Beliefs
A Sociological Introduction

Erich Goode

State University of New York, Stony Brook

Prospect Heights, Illinois

For information about this book, write or call:
Waveland Press, Inc.
P.O. Box 400
Prospect Heights, Illinois 60070
(847) 634-0081

Acknowledgments

I owe a debt of gratitude to a number of people who assisted me in the preparation of this book. I would like to begin by thanking the students who were enrolled in my seminar on the sociology of the paranormal during the fall semester of 1998. Most of them shared with me their personal beliefs about the paranormal in the form of accounts, which appear as an appendix at the end of this book. I am grateful to these students for permitting me to print their essays here. Sociologists Bob Bartholomew, Nachman Ben-Yehuda, Ray Eve, and Marcello Truzzi read the manuscript and commented on the validity of its statements, its intellectual adequacy, and its pedagogy. I am grateful to them for their feedback.

Physicist Paul Grannis and biologist Elof Axel Carlson read the portions of the manuscript that pertained specifically to science; I appreciate their comments as well. I relied on Susan Losh, Andrea Tyree, Vincent Bruzzese, and James Davis and Clifford Young (of NORC) to help me track down an especially pesky and elusive table. Bennett Sims and Staci Newmahr chimed in with the occasional useful comment. And as always, my wife, Barbara Weinstein, provided me with the necessary emotional and intellectual support I needed to complete this book. Five or six paragraphs in this book were adapted from two of my previous publications: *Collective Behavior*, Harcourt Brace, 1992, and "Two Paranormalisms or Two and a Half?" *Skeptical Inquirer*, vol. 23, November/December, 1999. I am grateful for the right to reprint that material here. Above all, I would like to thank Neil Rowe and Carol Rowe of Waveland Press, without whose support this book would not have seen the light of day. In spite of all the help I have received, however, I am responsible for the book's flaws and inadequacies; I alone must bear the burden of whatever failures may befall it.

Contents

꿍乙쨩

Part One

Introduction

⚜

Angels, witches, extra-sensory perception, psychics, astrology, healing crystals, pyramid power, levitation, foretelling the future, living past lives, ghosts, communicating with the dead, the spiritual significance of coincidence, lucky numbers: these and other astounding phenomena are accepted as valid by a substantial proportion of the public. Who believes in them? Why? And with what consequences? Are any of these beliefs valid or true? Do phenomena or events such as these actually exist?

Many nineteenth-century intellectuals, philosophers, and social scientists had adopted a rationalistic view of human behavior. They argued that an increase in society's level of education and the dissemination of scientific knowledge would result in the disappearance of what they regarded as mysticism, occult beliefs, pseudoscience, and other superstitious nonsense (in their eyes, this included religious dogma). Such self-proclaimed rationalistic thinkers as August Comte (1798–1857), Karl Marx (1818–1883), and Herbert Spencer (1820–1903) would have been baffled to witness the persistence and vigor—even more so the resurgence—of late twentieth and early-twenty-first century faith in occult and paranormal belief.

Over a quarter-century ago, Marcello Truzzi (1972) pointed to an "occult revival" in popular culture. It turns out he was prophetic in predicting a trend that is now in full flower. The strength of extra-scientific belief has grown considerably since Truzzi's prognostication. A Yankel-

1

ovich poll, conducted for *USA Today*, compared the incidence of paranormal beliefs in 1997 with those of 1976 and found that nearly all the beliefs had grown in strength. For instance, in 1976 only 12 percent of the respondents in the survey said that they believed in spiritualism "to at least some degree"; in 1997 this had exploded to 52 percent. The comparable figures for those who believed in faith healing in 1976 and 1997 were 10 and 45 percent; for astrology, an increase from 17 to 37 percent; for reincarnation, from 9 to 25 percent; and for fortune telling, from 4 to 14 percent (Nisbet, 1998, p.9). While one might quibble about the size of the figures and the magnitude of the increases, the fact remains that these figures have grown substantially.

Over the past decade, thousands of books on paranormal themes have been published, many of them appearing on bestseller lists. More generally, belief in paranormal phenomena or events is a major feature of media fare. The two most popular recent paranormal themes are extraterrestrials and communication with angels. As we take leave of the second millennium, *The X-Files* and *Touched by an Angel* remain hugely popular television programs; the latter is frequently television's top-rated show.

According to a 1991 Roper Poll, 3.7 million Americans believe themselves to manifest four or more indications of having been abducted by aliens (Hopkins, Jacobs, and Westrum, 1991). The 1997 issue of *Books in Print* lists 256 titles on UFOs, extraterrestrials, and interplanetary aliens, the vast majority of which are supportive of the idea that "we are not alone." In 1994, John Mack, a Harvard psychiatrist, published *Abduction*, his testimony to the belief that his patients' stories of their abductions are literally true. Just under half the American population believes that UFOs are real and are extraterrestrial aircraft. According to a 1996 Gallup poll (1997), seven Americans out of ten (72 percent) say that they believe in the literal existence of angels.

Topics that invoke the power of spiritual forces are immensely appealing to the general public. According to the American Booksellers Association, roughly ten million copies of New Age books, proclaiming faith in everything paranormal, from crystal and pyramid power to communication with angels and extraterrestrials, have been sold each year in the mid-to-late 1990s. *Forbes*, a business magazine, estimates that close to $2 billion is now spent each year on New Age spiritual and dietary aids to promote well-being, most of which mainstream physicians would regard as ineffective hocus-pocus. In 1994, a Roper poll found that close to half (45 percent) of the American population says that meditation has given them "a strong sense of being in the presence of something sacred." About the same proportion of the public believes in strict biblical creationism.

It is entirely possible that a substantial segment of the public takes our entry into the third millennium as an omen of cosmic proportions. Beginning in 1999, two supermarket tabloids, the *Weekly World News* and the *Sun* (whose combined weekly circulations run into the millions of copies) devoted week-by-week stories on the significance of the arrival of the year 2000. The headline for one story in the February 2, 1999 issue of the *Weekly World News*, captured the hysteria surrounding the event—"1999: Are We on the Eve of Destruction?"

In spite of their immense popularity, paranormal beliefs have not received a great deal of sociological study. Sociologists (unlike anthropologists) have tended to shy away from the "far-out," the occult, the esoteric, the supernatural. They usually focus far more attention on the mainstream, the typical—that which they regard as being of major significance. Many sociologists would admit that paranormal belief systems may be widespread, but they do not impact upon or tell us very much about the central workings of the society. They are of no more consequence, some observers claim, than hobbies, fads, or fashion. Without challenging the importance of these other behaviors, I most emphatically question the marginality of paranormalism. In fact, paranormal beliefs are cognate with, or translate into, parallel or related beliefs or processes in a variety of other social institutions.

The belief that unidentified flying objects (UFOs) are extraterrestrial craft fits like a jigsaw puzzle piece into political conspiracy theories. For instance, consider the belief that the crash of a mysterious craft in the desert near Roswell, New Mexico, in 1947 was "covered up" by the American government. In fact, the belief that UFOs are real and the belief that the government is engaged in a gigantic, insidious plot against the public to cover up secrets its citizens have the right to know about seem to reinforce one another. As we will see, many conspiracy theories have a paranormal basis.

Many forms of paranormalism have direct relevance for the strategies social movement organizations use to achieve their goals: creationists attempt to influence the content of educational curricula; Native American myths on human origins have influenced museum policy and archaeological research. Militant, right-wing, white supremacist groups combine a justification of violence against the government with mystical theories about the coming apocalypse and the origin of the races. Some political regimes make use of or do battle with paranormal beliefs.

Belief in creationism clearly has a religious origin. Many paranormal beliefs are a substitute for more conventional religious expression; intertwine with or supplement traditional religious belief; are held with a fervent, dogmatic, religious-like quality; and/or have become the basis for religion-like cults or sects. (Witness the 1997 "Heaven's Gate" collective suicide.) Over the course of the last few decades, a variety of paranormal belief systems have become an alternative to, a substitute for, or even a supplement to, more conventional religions. Recently, some paranormal beliefs have blended into or melded with traditional religions, and vice versa.

The close relationship between dependence on the media for information and depictions of strange, unexplainable, or anomalous phenomena is relevant for studies of mass communications.

The fact that many paranormal beliefs are held with great emotional intensity and rise and fall quickly in popularity indicates their relevance for the field of collective behavior, which focuses primarily on fleeting, spontaneous, extra-institutional behavior (Goode, 1992).

The fact that some paranormal beliefs are regarded as unconventional, unacceptable, eccentric, offbeat, or not altogether respectable in most mainstream or traditional social circles indicates their relevance for the field of deviant behavior.

The fact that, for the most part, the mainstream educational institution discourages paranormalism, and yet these beliefs remain immensely popular, tells us a great deal about the limitations of the socialization process that takes place in school systems—indeed, more generally, in practically all social institutions.

In short, the fact that paranormal beliefs are accepted as valid by an enormous segment of the American public indicates that they are worthy of sociological attention. It is inconceivable that, given the widespread acceptance of paranormal thinking, it also does not have an impact on a range of social institutions. The fact that it overlaps with, touches on, influences, or is influenced by such a broad range of sociological topics indicates that its study should be incorporated into a sociological understanding of social life.

The central point of this book is that a sociological understanding of paranormalism can be accomplished. A paranormal belief system is generated as a result of identifiable cultural, social, and social-psychological forces; it is linked with identifiable social institutions in identifiable ways and has identifiable consequences. The explication of how paranormal beliefs are accepted or rejected yields a richer understanding of social structure and dynamics. Accepting one or more of the beliefs—or accepting a cosmology that rules them out of the realm of the possible—tells us a great deal about the believers and disbelievers as well as the society in which they live. Paranormal beliefs are not an esoteric, marginal sphere of human existence; they are absolutely central to social life. It is our job here to examine and understand them and the role they play in our society.

Chapter One

A SAMPLER OF PARANORMAL BELIEFS

Michel de Nostredame, known as Nostradamus, a sixteenth-century French court physician and astrologer (1503–1566), wrote a book of rhymed prophecies entitled *Centuries* that brought him lasting fame. Cast in the form of cryptic quatrains, in a mixture of Latin, French, Greek, Italian, and English, these writings are believed by many to have been accurate predictions of future events. Nostradamus thus has been dubbed "the man who saw tomorrow." For instance, in one famous quatrain, Nostradamus wrote:

> *Beasts wild with hunger will cross the rivers, the greater part of the battlefield will be against Hister. He will drag the great one in a cage of iron, when the child of Germany observes no law.*

Many people believe that this quatrain predicted Hitler, the Nazis, and World War II. "Hister" (the Latin word for the Danube River) is a code name for Adolph Hitler; Hitler's plan to conquer Europe depended on crossing rivers; and Nazi Germany was a bestial regime that observed "no law."

Another of Nostradamus' quatrains is thought by some observers to be equally prophetic:

> *The great man will be struck down in daytime by a thunderbolt. An evil deed, foretold by a bearer of a petition. According to the prediction another is struck at night. Conflict in Reims, London, pestilence in Tuscany.*

Some say that this stanza predicts the assassination of John F. Kennedy, who was "struck down in daytime" by a bullet that must have seemed very much like a "thunderbolt." Moreover, his brother, Robert, also assassinated, was "struck at night." The petitioner was psychic

Jeane Dixon, who supposedly tried to prevent the "evil deed" from happening by warning Kennedy to stay away from Dallas in the days immediately before his fatal trip to that city in November, 1963.

> *He will enter, wicked, unpleasant, infamous, tyrannizing over Mesopotamia. All friends made by the adulterous woman. The land dreadful and black of aspect.*

Some believe that this poem refers to the Gulf War, which broke out in 1991. Ancient Mesopotamia was located in what is now Iraq; the "wicked, unpleasant, infamous" man referred to is, of course, Saddam Hussein, who invaded Kuwait. His armies set fire to that country's oilfields, leaving the land "dreadful and black" with smoke; in spite of having lost the war, Saddam continues to tyrannize the region.

In a like fashion, Nostradamus is said to have predicted the French and Russian Revolutions, Napoleon's rise to power, troubles in the British royal family, the Balkan crisis, the coming of the AIDS epidemic, space travel, catastrophic earthquakes, and a variety of other major events. How were these amazing predictions accomplished? There isn't any doubt, some argue, that the man had psychic powers both vastly beyond those of ordinary mortals as well as outside the scope of anything science can explain. Nostradamus was a seer, a visionary, a time traveler, a prophet. In short, he had paranormal powers (Ward, 1997).

THE RHINE RESEARCH CENTER IS LOCATED JUST A SHORT WALK from Duke University's pleasant, leafy campus, in Durham, North Carolina. It employs four scientists whose job is to investigate psi, or psychic powers, including telepathy (mind reading), precognition (foretelling future events), clairvoyance (perception of objects outside the five senses), and psychokinesis (moving objects with the mind). Declares the Rhine Center's chief parapsychologist Richard Broughton, "I don't believe in psi." Pausing for effect, he adds, "It's not a matter of belief. It's a matter of data" (Miller, 1998, p.90).

The Rhine Center was founded by Joseph Banks Rhine in 1927. Five years before, Rhine and his wife, Louisa, decided to give up their careers in botany after hearing a lecture on spiritism by Arthur Conan Doyle, author of the Sherlock Holmes mystery series. The Rhines began the tradition of investigating psi in the laboratory, "complete with controlled experiments, statistical charts and peer-reviewed journals" (p.90). They coined the term "parapsychology" to refer to their discipline.

Reporter Kenneth Miller's eyes are covered with ping-pong ball halves. A reddish light floods the tiny room. Through headphones, a voice commands him to relax. Then he is asked to describe the images that appear in his mind. After a half-hour, he confers with a parapsychologist who attempted to transmit images to him through mental processes. They agree that her picture of several creatures with fuzzy legs corresponds with one of his. Miller took part in a "Ganzfeld" (in German, "whole field") experiment, the results of which demonstrate to some researchers that correspondences appear far more often than the rules of chance would predict. Perhaps there are forces that conventional psychology does not yet understand, they suggest (Miller, 1998). Or is there a more conventional explanation? one wonders.

IN THE LATE 1970S, CIRCULAR PATTERNS BEGAN TO BE FOUND IN agricultural fields south and west of London. The demarcation between the flattened pattern area and the rest of the field is sharp, abrupt, and dramatic. Since that time, thousands of similar patterns have appeared in Britain, the United States, Canada, and Australia. There is a remarkable variety of forms, including circles within circles, dumbbell shapes, ladder-like rungs, and, in one case, a pattern resembling a bicycle. These forms have come to be known as "crop circles," and their origin became the subject of heated debate.

Two explanations for the circles come to mind, one conventional and the other unconventional. The conventional explanation is that they are of human origin—specifically, a hoax designed to create an entertaining pseudo-mystery. The unconventional explanation is that they have origins for which science can't account.

One of the most common unconventional explanations of crop circles is that they were created by extraterrestrial visitors bent on communicating with humans; flying saucer "nests" have also been suggested. Other commentators argue for a strange force not understood by traditional science, which they refer to as "plasma vortices." Some envision the forces of the earth itself somehow reaching up and generating the circles. Fairies have been suggested as another possible source. One commentator argues that Stonehenge must have been built on a crop circle. Organizations have emerged to study the circles, including The Circles Phenomenon Research Group and the Center for Crop Circle Studies;

a journal, *The Cereologist*, publishes endorsements of unusual or unconventional origins for the circles (Clark and Pear, 1997, pp.450–460; Hoggart and Hutchinson, 1995, pp.53–61). While some crop circle hoaxes have been revealed or admitted, some believers remain convinced that "something strange" created a substantial number of the crop circles.

AT THE AGE OF 11, JANIE BEGAN, AS SHE SAYS, TO SENSE "THE presence of a large being above my head, watching over me when I went to sleep. The presence was so big that it took on the appearance of a large white canopy of light that enveloped the entire ceiling of my bedroom" (Howard, 1992, p.2). In those early years, she explains, "there was only an awareness between us. I could see the being, and I knew that the being could see me, but neither of us spoke" (pp.2–3). Eventually, it became clear that the being "was an angel, because in my child's perception it began to look just like the angels I had seen on Christmas cards" (p.3).

When she became a teenager, Janie sensed that her angel was by her side "at other times of the day, too, and it wasn't long before I began talking to it" (p.3). She acquired a reputation for talking to herself, she explains, but she was "only sharing" with her "angelic friend" what she was thinking and feeling. "Through this sharing and the help that I started receiving in return," she explains, "the angel became my closest confidant" (p.3). Before long, Jane realized that there was "an abundance of angels all around and that they wanted nothing more than to be able to help us all." As a result of this realization, Jane decided to dedicate her life to "teaching others about the angelic kingdom. . . . I have been communing with the angels ever since" (p.3).

SOON AFTER THEIR GRADUATION FROM COLLEGE, RICHARD AND Jennifer Helfinger, both 23 years old, got married and purchased an abandoned farmhouse. During the first week in their new home, they began fixing up the old place, only to find that all their repairs were in vain. "The walls, floors, even the kitchen counters began cracking," Richard said, as if "they were trying to open up." Soon after that, a "dark red, sticky ooze" resembling blood "began to seep out." At that point, a "constant screaming and shrieking started." When they complained about it to the realtor who had sold them the house, they were reminded that, after all, they had purchased an old, run-down building. Local police found it difficult to believe the Helfingers' story.

Finally, the exasperated couple sought help from a team of psychics, who urged them to leave the house at once, before they were seriously hurt. Before abandoning the farmhouse, however, Richard and Jennifer decided to do some research into the history of the place. They discovered a story in the local newspaper that read: "A family of eight was violently axed to death in their sleep" in the house. Only one person escaped, Rachel, a disfigured 11-year-old child who had been locked in the basement; it seems the killer was unaware that she was cowering down there. The little girl died two months later of malnutrition and a respiratory ailment. According to psychic "experts," it is Rachel's "restless spirit" that has roamed the house since her death, screaming and crying. Richard and Jennifer decided to move to California, but the tormented ghost followed the couple, continuing to haunt them in their new residence. Says Jennifer, "her hideous screams and sobs keep Richard and me awake at night" (Logan, 1998).

EVA DESCRIBES TO HER PSYCHIATRIST HER FIRST CONTACT with extraterrestrials. This happened when she was four or five. The aliens looked like midgets, and there were three of them, about three feet tall, with dark brown, wrinkled skin and triangular heads. They stood at the side of her bed and probed at her genitals with their fingers. Unable to move or scream, she felt helpless. Just as her mother was about to enter the room, the creatures walked through the closed door and disappeared. Her mom told her it was just a dream and that she should go back to sleep, but Eva didn't believe her. "I was scared," she said. "I was sure they were real. I saw them. Heard them. Felt them. . . . I know it's true," she explains, because, now, as she is recounting the story, she says, "I have goose bumps all over" (Mack, 1995, p.235).

An event took place three years after her initial experience, Eva reports, that convinced her that the extraterrestrials had implanted a tracking device in her head. She was doing somersaults in a playground and bumped her head "really hard" on a horizontal bar. She said that "something moved" inside her head, "something they could [use to] keep track of me," she insisted. When the psychiatrist asked how she knew it was a tracking device, she responded, "I just know. . . . They had their signal" from the accident, she said, and then they returned "and corrected it" (p.236).

Eva says she has had many experiences with aliens since then. Sometimes, she asks—begs—for an encounter with them. "I volunteered myself for their examination," she explained in one diary entry, "so they can further their knowledge about us earthlings." Feeling as though she's being "sucked into" a kind of "tornado," she realizes that her wish "was granted, and I didn't want it to stop." She sees or feels "a light-blue light encompassing me. . . . It was a soothing light, yet one that I know would lead me to greater knowledge. It was magnetic. It was the feeling I got from it that is beyond words. . . . When I felt/saw the light the dizziness/ twirling stopped. I went blank. . . . When I woke up in the morning I was so tired! As if I went on a journey all night long. I hope I did. And I wish that someday I will remember those journeys and all about them so I can use the knowledge to help mankind" (pp.237–238).

Eva has had many such experiences. She is convinced that she has been abducted by creatures from another planet. The aliens, she explains, come from another intelligence, another dimension, "a realm beyond the physical world." It is her mission to act as a communicator between this intelligence and earthlings so that we can improve life on earth. The problem is, humans think in terms of the traditional five senses. To believe that something is true, most of us need physical proof, she said, and the aliens have learned to transcend their physical existence. So far, she has not been able to tell even her husband or children about her global mission. She is relieved that her psychiatrist takes her stories seriously (Mack, 1995).

TWO PSYCHOLOGY PROFESSORS INTRODUCE A MAN TO SEVERAL of their classes. In one class, his "psychic" abilities are stressed. In another, they skeptically suggest that his performance is "probably" a result of magic tricks. In the third, they clearly and unequivocally state that he will perform stunts that resembled psychic phenomena but really are not. The man enters the classes wearing sandals, a purple robe, and a "gaudy medallion." He then performs several "old-hat magic tricks . . ., easy amateur tricks that have been performed for centuries and are even explained in children's books of magic" (Singer and Benassi, 1980–1981, p.19): bending a sturdy metal rod; "dematerializing" some ashes; perceiving objects through a blindfold; and making a compass needle twirl by passing his hand over it.

Roughly a fifth of the students who witnessed the performance explicitly expressed "fright and emotional disturbance. Most expressed awe and amazement." In the rod-bending trick, during which the performer asked the class to chant to augment his powers, "the class was in a terribly excited state. Students sat rigidly in their chairs, eyes glazed and mouths open. . . . When the rod bent, they gasped and murmured. After the class was dismissed, they typically sat in their chairs, staring vacantly [into space] or shaking their heads" or rushed up to the performer asking him how he did what he did. If he "had asked the students at the end of his performance to tear off their clothes, throw him money, and start a new cult, we believe some would have responded enthusiastically" (p.20).

Over three-quarters of the class who had heard the speech suggesting that the performer might be psychic (77 percent) thought that he actually did possess psychic ability. Roughly two-thirds of the class who heard the speech suggesting his performance was "probably" due to magic tricks (65 percent) thought he was psychic. And just under six in ten of the class who was told he definitely was a magician (58 percent) nonetheless believed that he possessed psychic powers. In replications of the same experiment, a majority of the students in every class who witnessed his act believed he had psychic powers (Benassi, Singer, and Reynolds, 1980).

THE AMERICAN FLAT EARTH MOVEMENT HAD BEEN ORGANIZED by the 1870s, but it was not until 1914 that it had its most articulate and vocal spokesperson in Wilbur Glenn Voliva (1870–1942). Voliva was the general Overseer of the Christian Catholic Apostolic Church of Zion, Illinois, from whose pulpit he delivered sermons on a variety of subjects, including astronomy. In one, delivered in 1914, Voliva thundered: "If the world is whirling around in space at the rate of a million five hundred thousand miles a day, how is the Lord going to light on it? Just tell me!" Elaborating on this theme a year later, he stated: "I believe this earth is a stationary plane; that it rests upon water; and there is no such thing as the earth moving, no such thing as the earth's axis or the earth's orbit. It's a lot of silly rot, born in the egotistical brains of infidels." In a final flourish, he stated: "Neither do I believe there is any such thing as the law of gravitation. I believe that is a lot of

rot, too. There is no such thing! I get my astronomy from the Bible"
(Kossey, 1994, p.76). Voliva denounced anyone who believed that the
earth was a globe as a "globularist."

Scriptural authority, Voliva believed, issues from statements such
as a passage in the book of Daniel that states he had a vision of a tree
so tall that everyone on earth could see it, an impossibility unless the
earth were flat. In 1922, Voliva became a radio broadcaster; he offered
$5,000 to anyone who could prove that the earth is a globe. To every one
of the globularist's objections he had a ready answer. To the objection
that a traveler could circumnavigate the earth, he said: "Take a silver dollar to represent the stationary, plane Earth. The center of the dollar is
the North Center. As you go toward the Center you are travelling north;
as you go from the Center to the edge you are travelling south. East and
west are simply at right angles to north and south. Start from a given
point and travel due east, and you will be compelled to come back to the
point of departure" (pp.76–77).

If someone objected that the sun is millions of miles away from the
earth, Voliva declared: "The idea of a sun millions of miles in diameter
and 91,000,000 miles away is silly. The sun is only 32 miles across and
not more than 3,000 miles from the Earth. It stands to reason it must
be so. God made the sun to light the Earth, and therefore must have
placed it close to the task it was designed to do. What would you think
of a man who built a house in Zion [Illinois] and put the lamp to light it
in Kenosha, Wisconsin?" (p.77).

Voliva died in 1942, but the idea of a flat earth did not die with him.
Today, The Flat Earth Society still exists. According to the organization's
leader, Charles Johnson, "the known inhabited world is Flat, Level, a
Plane World. . . . We PROVE earth Flat by experiment, demonstrated
and demonstrable. Earth Flat is a Fact, not a theory!" In the 1970s and
1980s, much of the society's publications were devoted to attacks on the
space program; in 1988, denouncing the "FAKE landing of the shuttle,"
Johnson wrote:

> It is impossible for Mr. Reagan [40th president of the United
> States, 1981–1988] to believe in God and the Space Shuttle [at the
> same time]. Is he not telling the truth? about WHICH? The shuttle
> or God? I leave it to you to figure out. . . . EARTH IS FLAT, GOD
> EXISTS. HE IS IN HEAVEN, A PLACE, THAT IS UP ABOVE
> EARTH, ABOVE THE USA. . . . AT DEATH OUR SOUL GOES TO
> HEAVEN ABOVE THIS FLAT EARTH! (P.78).

✳ ✳ ✳

KAIT DUNCAN WAS SHOT AND KILLED ON THE STREET; HER mother, Lois, yearned to track down her murderers. Kait's heart and lungs were donated to a young man, who described a "vivid dream" he had under anesthesia during the transplant. In the dream, the man reported, "a young blond girl was being chased in her car by a slightly-built, black-haired, dark-complected men who wanted to kill her." It seems, Lois surmised, "that Kait's memories have been transferred along with her heart" (Duncan and Roll, 1995, p.229)

The day after Kait's funeral, her sister, Robin, visited a psychic, Betty Muench. Kait's killers had been driving a low-rider, she said, two men in front and one in back. Although there were no eyewitnesses, Muench said, the killers would be arrested because they boasted about the murder. Six months later, tipsters called Crime Stoppers and named three Hispanic men whom they had heard bragging about having shot Kait. They had been driving a low-rider. The police force will be unwilling to investigate the crime, Muench told Robin; help will come from a newspaper reporter, Mike Gallagher, who will publicize the crime and embarrass the police. The key to the crime, Robin was told, was Kait's boyfriend, who had been involved in illegal enterprises that Kait was about to expose (p.230).

Lois Duncan contacted a psychic detective, Noreen Reiner, who requested an article of clothing the victim had been wearing at the time of her murder; Duncan sent her a cross. Reiner then sensed abdominal pain in the victim, the fact that she had recently moved, was angry at her boyfriend, and that she had been killed at night while driving—all of which were confirmed by her mother. Then Reiner sent two sketches of men who might be responsible for the murder, perhaps because Kait had seen one of them purchasing drugs (p.232). One of the sketches resembled the dustjacket artwork of the face of a fictional "hit" man for a novel Lois had written, published shortly before her daughter's death; the edition featuring that face was not available in the United States. Duncan and the psychic detective decided that the significance of the face was that, from her grave, Kait had sent them a message that she was not killed by a random act of violence; she was telling them: "I was killed by a professional hit man like the one in Mother's book!" (p.233).

Reiner also sent Lois a tape of a session in which she went into a trance, speaking words that Kait would have spoken. "I meet a man in a shopping center with a C in it. . . . We drive up the hill toward the north. . . . I shouldn't have gone! There was a very important man there that I wasn't supposed to see. They had to make sure I wouldn't talk. The crime committed against me was to silence me. . . . The police have fear. This is a very powerful man" (p.233).

To check on the accuracy of Reiner's mediumship, Lois consulted another psychic who "obtained her information through telepathy" (p.234). She confirmed what Reiner had said when she took on Kait's identity. Then Lois returned to Betty Muench, who turned to her computer to provide, through "automatic writing," answers to some remaining questions. Key details were supplied, including locales, actors, and motivation. Meanwhile, the Hispanic man who had originally confessed to pulling the trigger on Kait recanted his confession; the crime remains unsolved. Lois Duncan is convinced there will eventually be closure on the case and the conspiracy that resulted in Kait's death will be revealed. She believes the facts of her daughter's murder taught her about the power of parapsychology. We are all connected, she says, just as all of us are connected with our physical environment. The most important thing that parapsychology can do for us, she writes, "is to help us find ourselves in other people and in the physical environment" (p.239). If we hurt others, we hurt ourselves, and if we hurt ourselves, we hurt others. "How startling this is to know—and how wonderful!" (p.240).

✳ ✳ ✳

TWO MEN ARE SITTING AT A TABLE IN A BAR, DISCUSSING A VARIety of subjects. At one point, John asks Jim, "Do you believe in paranormal phenomena? I mean, like coincidences and other stuff? Do you think there's some *significance* to things happening together?"

Jim says, "Well, I'm not sure. Like, exactly what do you mean? Give me an example."

"I'll give you three," John says, "Here's the first one. Years ago, before I met Sally, I was sort of having an affair with a married woman, Nora. Nobody knew about it. We were at party—Nora, her husband, and I were there, and a bunch of our friends. Nora and I were sitting on the floor, in a corner, a bit away from the rest of the party. Somebody handed us a Tarot deck, and we decided to check it out. We opened up the box, took out the deck, put it on the floor, and turned over the card on top of the deck. Do you know what it was?"

"I have no idea," Jim responded.

"The Lovers. The card we turned over was The Lovers. We just looked at one another, put the card pack on the pile, and put the deck back in the box. That was *spooky.*"

"I guess," Jim responded. "The odds were against it, but they weren't astronomical. How many cards are in a Tarot pack? Sixty? Eighty? We're not talking about something that's beyond the laws of chance, are we? OK, what was the second thing that happened?"

"This wasn't exactly a coincidence; maybe it was parapsychological or something, the transference of what was in one person's mind to another person's mind. A couple years before the first incident, I was dating a woman named Ellen. We were talking about mind reading, and we decided we'd check out if it works. So I said, look, I'll concentrate really hard on something, a thing, a physical object, and you tell me what I'm thinking about. OK, so, I focused my mind completely on one thing, one object, I thought and thought and thought about this one thing. Ellen tried to focus in on what I was thinking about, right, and she said, a *car*. Then I said, that's *amazing*, it's not a car, but you're really, really close. Now you keep concentrating and I'll keep concentrating, and we'll see if you can get closer. All right, on the second try, Ellen guessed a *jeep*, you know, an army jeep. And I said, wow, that's really amazing! It's not an army jeep, but you got closer, much closer. Keep concentrating. And she did. On the third try, she said, a *tank*—an army tank. That's what it was! Out of all the objects in the world, she guessed the *very thing* it was! Now, is that amazing or what?"

"I'm not sure," Jim replies. "You guys must have been thinking along similar lines. Maybe a few hours before, there was something in the news about the military. Or maybe your friend just figured, you being a man, would think of a car or something along military lines. Anyway, what was the third thing?"

"This happened about ten years ago," John says, "when our daughter, Tara, was a toddler. She was, oh, fourteen–fifteen months old. She had barely learned to walk. Sally and I are sitting on the living room couch, talking about the old Brooklyn Dodgers. I mentioned *The Boys of Summer*, which is about the Dodgers' glory days in the forties and fifties. I tell Sally about one time when a bunch of players went down to Havana to visit Hemingway, and they're all in a bar acting like tough macho guys, drinking booze, getting drunk, and bragging about how tough they all are. Hemingway tries to prove he's the toughest guy in the bar, and he sucker-punches one of the players, I forget which one. Remember, he's, like, 20 years older than any of the players, and he's overweight and drunk, and so Hemingway gets punched back, and ends up on his rear end on the barroom floor. I couldn't remember some of the details like who knocked Hemingway on his ass, so I got up and walked over to the bookcase to find the book. There are three bookcases against that wall, and there's a total of maybe four or five hundred books on those three shelves. I looked for *The Boys of Summer* for around five minutes, and I just couldn't find it. Annoyed, I sat down and finished telling what I could of the story. OK, now, here's the really interesting part. Are you ready for this?"

Jim nods solemnly.

"*Tara* toddled over to the bookcase, pulled a book off the shelf, toddled back to me, and handed it to me. Do you know what that book was? It was *The Boys of Summer*. The *same* book I had looked for and couldn't find! I'm telling you, our one-year-old daughter pulled the *very* book I was talking about off the shelf and handed it to me! Out of *all* the books she could have put her hands on, she hands me *that* one!"

"Yeah, I'd say that's a coincidence. One out of five hundred anyway. It's remarkable, I'll give you that. But what does it *mean?*"

"I have no idea," John responded. "Maybe something. Maybe nothing. I'm not sure."

"Of course, we *remember* coincidences," Jim said, "they're interesting and striking; we forget about all the times when the laws of chance held up. In a lifetime, there are a lot of coincidental events that take place just because, well, a lot of things happen to all of us. There may be nothing at all to any of this."

"I'm telling you," John insisted, "there's something really *spooky* about all this. Surreal. Something not quite, I don't know, not quite *normal*. Like somehow the laws of nature sometimes don't apply, you know what I mean?"*

---

*The three events described by John are literally true and happened to someone known to the author. The conversation between John and Jim is a fictional composite of several conversations.

Chapter Two

WHAT IS PARANORMALISM?

"How to Tell if You've Been Raped by a Space Alien!"
"Baby Born with Angel Wings"
"Captured Alien Warns of Invasion from Space"
"Snake Tattoo Chokes Man"
"Orphan Ghost Tortures Couple"
"Half-human Half-fish Are Washing up in Florida!"
"Amazing Dog Levitates in Mid-Air"
"10,000-Year-Old UFO Found in Jungle"
"Brain Doc Cuts Man's Head Open and Removes Demon"
"Chernobyl Chicken Is 6 Ft. Tall"
"Real-Life Flying Nun Floats in the Air & Heals the Sick!"
"Cat Eats Parrot—Now It Talks"
"UFOs Found Hiding in Circus Freak Show"
"Robot Gives Birth to a Human Baby"
"Ants Are Aliens from Space!"
"Sex-Change Woman Makes Self Pregnant"
"Town Beamed Up by UFO"
"Guardian Angel's Halo Blinds Sniper Targeting Cop"
"Eleven People Disappear in Connecticut 'Time Tunnel'"
"Four Space Aliens Held by CIA at Secret Compound in Maryland!"
"Painting of Elvis Weeps Real Tears"
"Woman Goes to Heaven—And Comes Back with Handful of Gold!"

These are a few headlines from articles published recently in tab-loid newspapers. Each one makes a claim about events that scientists would say are improbable or all but impossible. While many people read these stories mainly as entertainment (Bird, 1992), a number of such claims are believed to be true by a sizeable proportion of the public. Events, phenomena, or powers that scientists regard as contrary to the laws of nature are referred to as "paranormal."

The prefix "para" is taken from ancient Greek and means "next to" (as in "paraprofessional," "paralegal," or "paramedical"); "similar to" (as in a reference to the police as a "paramilitary" force); or "outside of" or "beyond," which is where "paranormal" comes in. The dictionary defines *paranormal* as that which is "outside of," lies "beyond," or cannot be explained by, routine, ordinary, known, or recognized scientific laws or natural forces. Paranormal claims or stories invoke or make use of forces, factors, dynamics, or causes that scientists regard as inconsistent with a satisfying, naturalistic or materialistic, cause-and-effect explanation. Gray (1991, p.78) defines the paranormal as that which "apparently transcend the explanatory power of mainstream science and stem from unknown or hidden causes." Says Hines, what characterizes the paranormal "is a reliance on explanations for alleged phenomena that are well outside the bounds of established science" (1988, p.7). Terms that overlap but are conceptually distinct include the "occult," the "supernatural," "esoterica," "pseudoscience," and "fringe," "extraordinary," "eccentric," "anomalous," "deviant," "one-eyed," "pathological," and "unconventional" science.

I'd like to disagree with at least one of these parallels and make it clear that pseudoscience and paranormalism are not the same thing. They overlap, of course, but the overlap is far from perfect. Many beliefs are contrary to the conclusions scientists have reached, but they are not paranormal. For instance, thinking that strange, scientifically unrecognized monsters (such as Bigfoot, the Abominable Snowman, the Loch Ness Monster) exist is not a paranormal belief. In principle, such monsters *could* exist; it's just that scientists feel that the evidence to support their existence is far too slim, patchy, or contradictory to reserve a place for them in biology texts. Indeed, *if* they were found to exist, these texts would not have to be drastically rewritten; the *basis* of biology would not be overturned.

In contrast, evolution is the very foundation-stone of modern biology; if creationist theory is correct, nearly every page of almost every current college biology textbook would have to be scrapped and rewritten. Says Donald Kennedy: "Evolution is as basic to the rest of biology as atomic structure is to physics" (1998). Belief in creationism is a statement about how biology's mechanisms operate; indeed, it is contrary to its laws, its very first principles. Even more broadly, "an assault on evolutionary theory . . . constitutes an attack on the whole of science" (Kitcher, 1982, p.4).

In sum, belief in Bigfoot is a statement about *evidence*, not biological theories or explanations. Hence, belief in Bigfoot is pseudoscience, not paranormalism. In contrast, belief in creationism is both pseudoscience *and* paranormalism.

Do beliefs exist that are paranormal but not pseudoscientific? Practitioners of at least one field of paranormal investigation believe their methodology to be scientifically valid, yet they invoke a causal mechanism that transcends the mainstream scientific framework. (They would deny that it is paranormal, however.) I refer, of course, to parapsychology, the systematic, empirical study of "psi" or psychic powers. Many parapsychologists hold a Ph.D. in a recognized academic discipline (typically, either psychology or physics); conduct legitimate research, with rigorous research methods; publish in refereed journals; hold scientific meetings; and make up a scientific community whose members discuss the validity of work as it is made public. Indeed, at least one observer has argued that parapsychologists "require for themselves much tighter methodological controls than do sociologists or psychologists" (McClenon, 1984, p.10). In these senses, then, parapsychology would be scientific, *not* pseudoscientific, yet (by the lights of mainstream scientists) paranormal at the same time.

The term "pseudoscience" is biased, inherently pejorative. It implies that by their very nature, all paranormal beliefs, assertions, claims, or fields of study badly imitate the sciences. Once you've referred to a given statement as pseudoscientific, its validity is automatically dismissed. One need not take it seriously; the only relevant questions become: Who is deluded into believing it?; Why?; and How does one persuade these souls of the truth of real science?

In contrast, the term "paranormal" implies no such pejorative quality. It is a purely descriptive term. It states clearly what is factually the case: that the mechanisms of causality transcend what scientists regard as the natural order. Hence, I agree with Truzzi: "pseudoscience" is not an appropriate term for much of what we'll be looking at in this book (1977).

The word "paranormal" refers, first, to the subject matter itself, as in paranormal *phenomena*—the events or powers that are alluded to. Second, it refers to how paranormal claims are *approached*—that is, whether the validity of these events is accepted, validated, or believed. Thus, when we read a headline that a woman who ate cat food turned into a cat, this narrative or story or claim refers, first, to a paranormal *event* (a woman turning into a cat) and, second, to a paranormal *belief* (the conviction that this event actually took place). Paranormalism is *a non- or extra-scientific approach to a phenomenon*—a scientifically implausible event is believed to be valid and literally and concretely true. Thus, the hallucinations a person under the influence of a psychedelic drug experiences would not be a paranormal phenomenon, since these effects are pharmacological in origin. But believing these visions to be concretely and literally real might very well represent a form of paranormalism.

The definition of paranormalism I offer uses terms that are commonly understood to explain a concept that addresses events that fall outside the ordinary. Classic science is more frequently identified with linear causality—a mechanical view of the universe where observation reveals what action causes what reaction. This definition is based on what scientists *believe* or *judge* to be beyond the workings of nature. My definition of a scientist is a person with a doctorate in one of the natural sciences who conducts research that is or could be published in the professional journals in these fields. This definition rests squarely in the subjective realm or dimension. That is, it is based on what a sector of the society, scientists, *believe*. Society often assumes that science is objective, based on observable fact—that scientists can point to concrete reasons as to *why* a given assertion is paranormal and another one is not. However, what scientists *believe* is an assertion, not a fact. It is possible that their belief is wrong. One day their label of paranormal (as something outside the boundary of how nature works) may be rejected. Currently that label is a reality and has important sociological consequences.

Hence, to refer to a belief or assertion as paranormal does not automatically mean that it is wrong; to refer to a theory or observation as scientific does not automatically mean that it is right. Many claims that have been labeled by scientists as all but impossible have turned out to be true. And many explanations that have been accepted by mainstream scientists at one time have been disproven later. What if, at one time, scientists believe a given assertion is all but impossible, that it makes use of an explanation that is contrary to the laws of nature, and, a few years later, they change their mind and accept that assertion as true? Such a thing has happened many times in the history of the world. This does not contradict the definition I have laid out, however. Keep in mind I'm primarily interested in how claims are reacted to and by whom, not the truth or accuracy of the claims themselves. In sum, I define paranormalism as a realm that is *defined, constructed, regarded, perceived,* or *labeled* in a certain fashion by the members of the scientific community, not what that realm "really" or "truly" is in some objective or essential sense.

In the 1700s, farmers and peasants reported that stones fell from the sky. Scientists claimed that such a thing was impossible. The peasants were right. The "stones" did fall; of course; today, we call them meteorites (Westrum, 1978). As a sociologist, I am interested less in whether a given claim is true and more in the struggle to establish a given claim *as* true. Knowing that it is true (and keeping in mind the fact that science was not fully dominant in Western society in the 1700s), I nonetheless have no hesitation to refer to the assertion about stones falling from the sky *at that time* as paranormal, if such an event were to invoke forces or powers that scientists then regarded as a violation of nature's workings. What is thought to be paranormalism in one era can become mainstream science in another. My definition is relative to what scientists think at a given time, and scientists, being human, are fallible. I'll return to this issue a number of times throughout this book. Right now, I'd like to qualify these remarks very slightly.

Belief in the efficacy of powers or phenomena that Western scientists now say are improbable or extremely unlikely have been around since the dawn of humanity, of course. Anthropological textbooks are full of descriptions of religious and magical beliefs that are or were prevalent in nonliterate societies around the world. Does practicing witchcraft cause your enemy to get sick and die? Does the volcano that looms above the village erupt when the volcano god becomes angry? Does animal sacrifice keep the evil spirits away? Were all the stars in the heavens created by the tears of a love-sick wizard? Can examining chicken entrails predict whether an expectant mother will bear a girl or a boy? Most of us today would answer no to these questions; we would argue that science demonstrates them to be empirically or factually without foundation. Most of us believe science has far more valid explanations for these matters than those offered by tribal, ancient, or folk peoples. Does that make these earlier beliefs about how the universe operates examples of paranormalism?

The answer is, no, not quite, at least not as I've defined the term. Most researchers of the paranormal do not investigate the non-scientific beliefs of small, tribal, preliterate, or preindustrial societies—at least not *as* a form of paranormalism. They would insist that the concept of paranormalism is meaningful only when traditional science is established as the norm and it competes with non-scientific beliefs in the same society. Persons who grow up in a society that socializes them to believe that witches, wizards, gods, and spirits have special powers are not able to weigh the validity of such beliefs against a scientific alternative, since science does not exist in that society. Simply by being functioning members of Druid society 2,000 years ago, we would have believed that priestly prayers ensure an abundant crop. As an instance of paranormalism, at a time when science did not exist, the acceptance of non-scientific beliefs is not especially interesting, problematic, or even meaningful.

Paranormalism becomes an intellectual issue only in a society where the scientific method is *hegemonic*, that is, the dominant belief. In Druid society, Western science did not exist; hence, there was no perspective *then* that could have labeled its beliefs *as* paranormal. The same is not true of the modern world. Why do so many people in the world today embrace beliefs that modern science says are false? It is an interesting question, but it was not even a *meaningful* question 2,000 years ago. I'll be raising and attempting to answer similar questions throughout this book. Therefore, when I refer to paranormal beliefs, I do so only within the context of the modern world. I will refer to paranormalism only as a belief system that *contrasts* with what scientists believe is likely *within* a scientifically oriented society.

At what point in the history of the West did science become established as the dominant or hegemonic belief system? When did it obtain the approval and support of the political institution, that is, the government? When did a scientific view of things become the major perspective in the public school system, as well as in higher education? In the mainstream or most authoritative media?

Science became more or less fully institutionalized in the western world roughly a century ago. There is no way of measuring this precisely, but in 1873, authorities at Johns Hopkins University announced that evolution would henceforth be taught as the valid interpretation of the origin of species. Within a few decades, this perspective became the dominant perspective in biology courses. A second date, 1910, is important. In this year the Flexner Report, which was a major step in the professionalization of medical education in the United States, was published. It announced the dominance of Western science in the field of medicine and established medicine as a scientific discipline. For good or ill, and whether their version of reality was valid or not, by some time at the beginning of the twentieth century, mainstream, positivistic Western science and medicine became legitimate, institutionalized, dominant, and hegemonic.

Once again, notice that I am not focusing on the issue of whether Western science or paranormalism is right or wrong. Instead, I am interested in a hegemonic versus a counter-hegemonic view of reality. How does an alternative interpretation of reality become established, legitimated? Given that it runs contrary to the dominant perspective, how does it get its message across? To which segments of the society does it appeal? This approach raises a host of important implications, which I'll explore throughout this book.

THE POPULARITY OF PARANORMAL BELIEFS

This book is a sociological investigation into paranormal beliefs—the view that under certain circumstances what are regarded by traditional scientists as the laws of nature can be bent, broken, suspended, violated, superseded, or subsumed under entirely different principles. A few examples of paranormalism include belief in the truth, reality, or validity of: psychics, occult prophecies, tarot cards, "automatic" writing, parapsychology, ESP (extrasensory perception), remote viewing or clairvoyance (seeing objects outside one's line of vision), time travel, a flat earth, a hollow earth, King Tut's "curse," weeping icons and statues, ancient astronauts, ghosts, seances, hauntings, spiritism (communication with the dead), telepathy (communicating with someone else, living or dead, without the aid of the five senses), precognition and retrocognition (the ability to "see" or intuit the past or to predict the future with one's mind alone, without the assistance of relevant data), channeling (speaking with the voice of a dead person's soul or spirit), spiritual possession, faith healing, dowsing (using a forked stick to determine where water or minerals are located in the ground), witches and witchcraft, angels, the devil as a material-world being, out-of-body experiences, past lives, reincarnation, karma, teleportation, PK (psychokinesis, or moving physical matter with the power of one's mind), lucky numbers, astral projection, unaided voyages to distant places, the physical appearance or earthly manifestation of dead people, miracles, Scientology, dianetics, theosophy, spontaneous combustion, seeing visions of physically nonexistent phenomena, immortality, synchronicity (coincidence, or the special significance or meaning of the appearance of related phenomena above and beyond the laws of chance), the occult origin of crop circles, pyramid power, crystal power, the "Bermuda Triangle," plant perception, astrology, the "lunar" effect (the belief that the position of the moon influences what happens on earth, beyond its gravitational pull), the "Mars" effect (the same for the position of Mars), the "Jupiter" effect (ditto for Jupiter), fairies, the transformation of humans or animals into fantastic creatures such as vampires and werewolves, UFOs as spaceships of extraplanetary origin, alien abductions, numerology (the special significance of certain sequences of numbers), and strict creationism.

Perhaps the most dramatic and memorable examples of paranormal assertions can be found in the pages of supermarket tabloids, of which the *Sun* and the *Weekly World News* are the most clear-cut examples. The headlines quoted at the beginning of this chapter were taken from these two tabloids. (Except for articles on astrology, miraculous healing, and psychic predictions, *The National Enquirer* has abandoned paranormal material and sticks pretty much to gossip about celebrities.) However, a substantial proportion (although far from all) the readers of these papers take these fantastic claims with a grain of salt and read them mainly for entertainment purposes.

Less dramatic but at least as revealing are the surveys taken by polling organizations on whether members of their samples hold paranormal beliefs. The Gallup poll is the most well-known of all polling organizations. In 1996, Gallup surveyed a nationally-representative sample of Americans on a number of paranormal beliefs (Gallup, 1997, pp.204–207). The results are quite illuminating. Nearly half the sample (48 percent) said that they believe in ESP; a third (35 percent) believed in telepathy; a third (33 percent) believed that houses "can be haunted"; three in ten (30 percent) believed in ghosts; a quarter (27 percent) believed in clairvoyance, "or the power of the mind to know the past and predict the future" and astrology (25 percent); and a fifth said that they believe in reincarnation (22 percent), mental communication with the dead (20 percent), psychokinesis (also called telekinesis, 17 percent), and witches (19 percent). Nearly half believed that UFOs are "something real" (48 percent), and have visited earth (45 percent). Over half (56 percent) believed in the reality of the devil, and four in ten (42 percent) believed that some people have been possessed by the devil. Just under three-quarters (72 percent) said they believe in the reality of angels. It is entirely likely that the size of nearly all of these beliefs have grown since these polls were conducted. (See also Gallup and Newport, 1991; Miller, 1987; Bainbridge and Stark, 1980). Other surveys on college students have turned up similar findings (for instance, Gray, 1995; Harrold and Eve, 1995; Goode, 1999).

Two things are noteworthy about the results of these surveys. First, all these assertions contradict what scientists argue is the way the universe works. And second, the percentage of respondents who believe these claims, both in the Gallup polls and in my survey among undergraduates, is substantial. Clearly, then, in the general population as well as in fairly well-educated segments of the public, paranormal beliefs are popular and extremely widespread.

Obviously, paranormal beliefs cover an immense territory. It is unlikely that a single explanation can account for all of them. However, their common thread is the fact that mainstream, conventional, or traditional science regards their existence or validity so improbable as to be all but impossible. In order to understand how paranormalism operates, therefore, it is necessary to understand the reasoning that undergirds its opposite—conventional or traditional science.

THE SCIENTIFIC APPROACH

Since paranormalism is defined by its contradiction with traditional science, it becomes necessary to say a few words about how scientists approach the world. (I'll expand on this subject in the next two chapters.) For now, two points should be sufficient. One, science is *empirical*. And two, science is *theoretical*. These two points might seem contradictory, but they are two sides of the same coin.

Empirical means that which is informed or guided by information derived from one or more of the five senses; empirical is sensory, what you can see, feel, smell, hear, or taste. To the empiricist, the senses determine what is true. Of course, there are times when you can't see or hear something directly; the senses sometimes need assistance. For instance, you may want to observe tiny pond creatures, but you can only see them with a microscope. If you want to see distant stars or areas of planets and the moon, you will need to use a telescope. Other types of observation may entail using certain chemicals, instruments (such as an electrocardiogram or an oscilloscope), or even questionnaires or interview schedules to find out what people say they have done or believe. Still others require examining the traces or remains of past events, such as fossils, shards of pottery, or ancient manuscripts. Thus, the "observation" that empiricists do may be indirect as well as direct; it may entail relying on what machines measure, what people say they did, or material that is left behind. (The demand that *all* events be *directly* observable is a fallacy; the pseudoscience on which it is based is referred to as "one-eyed" or "Baconian" science. It will assume importance in our discussion of creationism.) In short, observation (assisted by the necessary aids) is the watchword of the empiricist. "Observe and you shall know" is the empiricist's motto.

Being empirical isn't as easy as it sounds. The relevant information isn't always easy to observe. Sometimes it seems to be hiding in an inaccessible location. Very often, information is spotty, patchy, scattered; it comes in bits and pieces. Many of the things we might want to observe are not so homogeneous that they always appear the same way. We may observe certain things, but our observations may be flawed by the fact that we have seen only a small part of their reality. You've been told that John is a nasty person, but he's extremely nice to you. The Texas Grille has a reputation for efficient service, but the one time you ate at that restaurant you waited an hour to be served. You know it rains a lot in Seattle, but you stayed there for a week and didn't see a drop of rain. Your observations were empirical—you used the data of your senses. But they were very partial, very selective, and not a good cross-section of the things you observed. Scientific theories or explanations are a kind of "schematic diagram" of how reality operates; it is impossible for humans to take in and understand how all the details of a given phenomenon work simultaneously.

Scientists refer to evidence that is slanted or skewed as *biased*. When we use examples to tell us about the way something is, we ought to know that one or two examples are often biased. They may not look like or represent the whole of the thing we are talking about. You can always find one or two examples of almost anything. To scientists, the lesson of a few examples is not persuasive. They refer to evidence based exclusively on examples as "anecdotal." Instead of anecdotes, they say, we need *systematic* evidence—a good cross-section of what we are looking at. So, to determine John's character, we have to observe evidence of his relationships with a wide range of people, not just one. To find out if the service in the Texas Grille is good, we have to eat there a number of times, not just once. And to know about the rainfall in Seattle, we have to look at it year-round, not just during a single week.

Science does not just gather empirical information. Scientists would regard some facts, even if based on systematic observation, as useless. What would be the point of counting every grain of sand on a beach? It would be silly, even if the count were accurate. Scientists seek to tie their observations into an *explanatory* framework—a theory. It makes no difference to any theoretical framework that there are a trillion grains of sand on that beach or a trillion and one.

To many non-scientists, the word "theory" sounds like a guess, little more than wild speculation. Calling something a theory is to admit that it is unproven, as in "That's just a theory." To a scientist, a theory is not a guess, it is an *explanation* or *account* for a general class of phenomena. Why are things the way they are? A theory attempts to answer this question. Why did the dinosaurs die out? What causes AIDS? How did the universe begin? Theories are absolutely necessary in science. An explanatory or theoretical approach is precisely the opposite of mindless fact-gathering.

To a scientist, theories and facts are not opposites. Some theories are explanations that are empirically grounded—they are *facts*. Others are explanations that have not been confirmed; that is, they are theories but not yet regarded as facts. Still others have already been discarded because they were factually wrong. Theories may be wrong or right, they may have been confirmed or disconfirmed, but they, along with evidence, are the lifeblood of science.

Scientists argue that paranormal claims are false because they are not supported by plausible theories or explanations. This is more significant than the lack of evidence to support paranormal claims. Claims of levitation are always and automatically false, scientists would say, not *merely* because empirical observation of such an event is lacking or flawed, but because such an event would violate what is known about how the universe works. Claims that astrology can summarize people's character and predict their fate are false, not merely because the data to support such a claim are lacking but also because the claim cannot be supported by any plausible explanation. Scientists take evidence and theories equally seriously. If a claim violates the currently accepted theoretical framework, scientists become extremely suspicious of it. If the theory is wrong, the supposed data to support it must be flawed. On the other hand, if new evidence fit into a new theoretical scheme that articulates with established frameworks, scientists are likely to accept it. In other words, there is something of a dialectical tension between evidence and theories that often lead to a new synthesis.

Scientists have devised theories or explanatory accounts of how the world works that *exclude* or *prohibit* paranormal phenomena or events. Within the framework of traditional or conventional science, many of the events or phenomena that paranormalists say take place are all but impossible. Science has supplied accounts of how one factor or variable influences or causes another. Paranormalism supplies accounts that the universe works in a very different way. When someone claims that if a person lies underneath a pyramid-shaped structure, his or her intelligence will increase, scientists want to know *how* this process works. What are the precise *forces* or *mechanisms* that emanate from the pyramid to boost the intelligence of the person underneath it? What are the chemicals, the rays, or the molecules, that create the effect? Can they be detected, observed, measured? Where do they come from and how do they work? When such a claim is made, the scientist looks not only for empirical evidence or data relevant to the claim but also for a plausible account or explanation—a *theory*—of how it takes place. Anecdotal evidence that something has taken place more than once or twice is not enough. Without an explanatory theory, scientists inevitably remain unimpressed by paranormal claims. Some scientists go so far as to say, "I don't care *what* evidence you have! What you say is all but impossible!" Many non-scientists or paranormalists see this stance as closed-minded.

ABSOLUTES VERSUS PROBABILITIES

Science cannot definitively disprove the existence of paranormal forces. Scientists rarely use the word "impossible" when they refer to paranormal claims. (They may do so informally, but *as scientists*, they hardly ever do so.) They are more likely to use the phrase "highly unlikely" or perhaps "extremely improbable." Scientists refer to a claim as disconfirmed (but not absolutely disproven) when the evidence looks very strong against it. Scientists look for *degrees of probability*; they do not claim certainty. A critic can always come up with alternate explanations for why a given objection to a paranormal claim doesn't invalidate it.

Scientists do not make a claim to absolute, eternal truth. To a scientist, absolutes exist only in theology, logic, mathematics, political campaigns, and the popular mind. If a given proposition has been verified with extremely strong evidence, scientists say that it is true *beyond all reasonable doubt*. They grant that it is always possible for new and contradictory evidence to be dug up at some point in the future, but it is extremely unlikely. Once a given proposition is accepted as a fact, it has been "confirmed to such a degree that it would be perverse [or contrary] to withhold provisional assent. . . . I suppose that apples might start to rise tomorrow [instead of fall]," says biologist Stephen Jay Gould, "but the possibility does not merit equal time in the classroom" (1984, p.255). Scientists then move on to another issue. Even what are referred to as "paradigm shifts" do not toss out old theories so much as subsume them under more general principles. For instance, Newton's theories were not refuted but subsumed by Einstein's theory of relativity. Under specific and clearly stipulated conditions, scientists would say, apples *always* fall. But it's possible that conditions not yet conceived of may enter the picture, and scientists are willing to grant their power to change the picture.

WHAT IS TRUE VERSUS WHAT SCIENTISTS BELIEVE

Here's another point I'd like to reiterate: when I use phrases such as "scientists say," or "science would conclude" or "according to the scientific method," I am not claiming that whatever scientists believe to be true *is* true in some deep, fundamental, or absolute sense. With respect to paranormal beliefs, "rejected by the majority of scientists" does not mean that it is false in the objective, factual sense.

The first statement ("rejected by scientists") is descriptive; it refers to a belief or judgment held by a certain category or community—scientists. The second ("false") is a judgment or *conclusion* about a given assertion. When I say that paranormal beliefs are defined by the fact that scientists *regard* them as false, I mean what I say and no more: that scientists *do* believe that paranormal beliefs are contrary to the laws of nature. Their feeling that this is so is a fact. Whether this feeling is true or valid in some ultimate or absolute sense is a separate issue. Paranormalism is *defined* by its contrast with what the scientific community believes are the workings of nature. If scientists, taken as a whole, believe that a given assertion is true, then it is *not* an example of paranormalism.

Thus, when I refer to the beliefs of scientists, I imply nothing about their absolute truth, only that scientists do hold these beliefs. Their validity is a separate issue (and my feelings about them, likewise, are separate). The fact that some people reject what scientists hold to be true by holding paranormal beliefs is itself a sociologically interesting and important question. So, again, keep in mind that when I say, "scientists believe," I mean that and only that. I do not mean that if scientists believe something to be true, it is always automatically true, or that if someone believes something else, it is by its very nature false. In fact, as we'll see in the next chapter, scientists are often wrong. Science is defined not by the *content* of scientific beliefs but by the *method* by which evidence is gathered and their conclusions are reached. This method is often violated; even when followed, it sometimes produces incorrect results. There is nothing sacred about the views of scientists, but a study of their views, as well as the beliefs that contrast with them, is a sociologically interesting and important topic.

Another way of saying this is that the sociological study of both science and paranormalism are studies of *claims-making*. By that I mean that both science and paranormalism make claims about the nature of reality. Both assert that certain statements, and certain *kinds* of statement, are true. Our perspective does not automatically privilege one type of claim over another. Scientists and psychics are both in the business of convincing audiences that their assertions have validity. They describe the way things are, what the universe looks like, and how it behaves. While both make claims, they don't always make use of the same types of evidence, nor do they reason in the same way. Their audiences also differ in the type of evidence and reasoning processes they find convincing. All these things are sociologically and psychologically patterned, and must be understood as phenomena in their own right. Our interest is in the different approaches to reality. The conventional scientific approach and the paranormal approach make certain claims, use certain kinds of evidence and reasoning processes, and attract certain audiences. It is our job to understand how all this works.

SOCIOLOGISTS, SCIENTISTS, AND PARANORMALISTS

One last point: *the approach most sociologists use to study beliefs* is similar to the way traditional scientists gather evidence and draw conclusions. Sociologists of the paranormal are generally *empirical* in their approach; they ask questions, gather evidence, use science-like reasoning processes, make inferences, test theories, draw conclusions, and appeal to fairly traditional audiences. The sociologist's first response to claims that someone has levitated or communicated with the dead is to try to is to understand the sort of person who might make such a statement. But his or her *second* response is likely to be much the same as that of most natural scientists: "Show me the evidence."

I am a sociologist and an empiricist. I seek explanations for events in the social world that rely on cause-and-effect mechanisms. The way I do my intellectual work is not radically different from the way that traditional natural scientists conduct research. However, there are other aspects of my approach that diverge sharply from the conventional scientific perspective. I feel that the study of social behavior is not merely a scrutiny of the mechanical, cause-and-effect motions of a species of being, namely, humans. At least two things make the study of social life different from the study of the natural order.

One is that humans are thinking, reasoning, symbol-using creatures who devise beliefs and ways of life that must be understood in the context in which they were created. The fact that a given belief is accepted among a specific social circle must be understood in these terms. We need go no further than hormones, anatomy, and triggering environmental cues to understand why the bullfrog croaks. But when a survivalist in Idaho believes that United Nations troops are poised to invade and conquer the United States, that belief is an announcement about particular perceptions about the world, how it operates, and what it means. Beliefs both generate and represent meaning-systems; to understand them, we have to get inside them—in a way, *appreciate* them. The survivalist's world is *socially constructed* (Berger and Luckmann, 1966), and the nature of that construction process is the sociologist's stock-in-trade.

A second way in which the study of human behavior and belief is different from the study of natural phenomena is that social scientists are part of the world they study. Our social entanglements in the lives of the people we study are a factor in the way we view those lives. Political, ideological, and ethical considerations play a role in all investigation, scientific or otherwise, but they play a special role for sociologists. Will our research validate or discredit the groups we study? Will they support or harm a certain political cause? What if the publication of our study of a gang of drug dealers or delinquents results in their arrest? How will the social categories to which we belong (for instance, sex, race, age, socio-economic status) influence what we see and report? Is it right or proper to snoop into anyone's sex life? How much should we cooperate with the police? The government? The media? What if the people we study ask us to do things we feel are unethical or improper? Should we participate in the very behavior we study? These are very difficult questions, almost impossible to answer in a straightforward fashion. While the natural scientist is *sometimes* entangled in political, moral, and ideological issues (consider the subject evolutionists study), the social scientist *almost always* has to struggle with them, and this struggle is often painful.

A FEW CONCLUDING THOUGHTS

Many definitions of the paranormal are possible, and many have been proposed. I've defined paranormalism the non-scientific approach to a scientifically implausible event believed to be literally true. It is the operation of a principle or force that scientists say violates the laws of nature. Two camps or factions may object to this definition: traditional scientists and supporters of paranormalism.

Traditional scientists will argue that my definition relativizes science. To reiterate, notice that I do not say that paranormalism is a view that *violates* one or more laws of nature. Instead, I say that it is a view that violates what scientists *believe* are one or more laws of nature. I also insist that our definition is relative to *today*, not to 1600 or 1800; paranormalism is what scientists *now* regard as all but impossible. Remember, I am interested in how advocates of an alternative perspective (that is, paranormalism) struggle against a dominant perspective's interpretations and their consequences. Therefore, defining paranormalism relative to science in 1600 or 1800 is not entirely relevant. Why? Because science was not the dominant perspective in 1600, or even in 1800.

Many paranormalists, too, will object to my definition. Its point of departure is based on what scientists, not what paranormalists, believe. It is a negative definition, taking its meaning from the lack of correspondence with the mainstream, status-quo thinking. Why not define paranormalism positively, by how its advocates rather than its opponents think? After all, if we followed my definition, any heterodox or heretical scientific theory that is later accepted will be defined as paranormal.

It is not my job here to endorse one or another perspective, view, or theory. (Although, as I said, the very foundation of my thinking is more scientific than paranormal.) The question of the validity of one or another assertion about how nature works is not my primary interest here. I am *mainly* interested in how views of true and false are regarded, debated, and fought over. Science is currently the dominant view and its opposite, paranormalism, represents a deviation from the norm, whose proponents must struggle to achieve for it acceptance and legitimacy. How proponents of these two perspectives fight it out and to what conclusion is our central issue here. All good definitions apply *more or less* to the phenomena they define. None fit perfectly, all are fuzzy around the edges. If readers come up with a better definition of paranormalism than mine that is fairly airtight and addresses the issues with which I am concerned (centrality versus marginality, conventionality versus deviance, and the struggle to maintain dominance versus the struggle for acceptance), I would welcome the input.

Chapter Three

LOOKING AT PARANORMALISM

As a coat of many colors, there are many ways paranormalism can be approached or looked at. Someone who believes that paranormal phenomena exist or take place views reality differently from the traditional scientist who insists on particular forms of evidence. Social scientists, most of whom learned methods similar to those of scientists, may differ on some fundamental points. How then should we look at assertions of paranormal phenomena?

FOUR APPROACHES TO PARANORMAL BELIEFS

Four very different perspectives can be used to study paranormal beliefs: affirmation, radical skepticism, disbelief, and social constructionism. Each approach draws different conclusions about the validity or truth value of paranormalism.

Affirmation

The affirmer feels that paranormal events or phenomena *have* happened and *do* exist. Affirmers come in four subvarieties: the *violator, subsumer, deducer,* and *dimensionalizer.* In addition, combinations or blends of two or more of these belief systems can exist.

Affirmer-violator. Violators feel that paranormal events have taken place or continue to take place that demonstrate that scientific laws *can* be violated, broken, or suspended. Contrary to the laws of physics, under certain circumstances, people *can* float in the air without the aid of a device of any kind; they violate the law of gravity. Contrary to every law known to scientists, people's destiny *is* ruled by the stars, the planets, the sun, and the moon. Contrary to any known material reason, from time to time, some people have spontaneously burst into flames and are reduced to a small pile of ashes.

Violators believe that scientific laws are a bit like traffic laws: they can be violated. Principles entirely unknown to modern science *overwhelm*, *obliterate*, or *cancel out* its laws and produce phenomena and events that scientists simply cannot explain. Thus, to the violator, the weight of scientific evidence and theory is irrelevant. What counts is the fact that, under certain circumstances, science is simply set aside, and mysterious events take place. Scientists are simply *wrong* about many of their claims and assertions; what scientists imagine to be the laws of nature do *not* work everywhere or all the time.

Affirmer-subsumer. A second type of paranormal affirmer is the *subsumer*. Subsumers argue that the principles of science are fundamentally correct but incomplete. Scientists sometimes fail to draw the right conclusions by not taking note of broader or more general forces or factors that *subsume* or *enfold* their more specific principles. For instance, as we've seen, aspects of the mechanistic theories of Isaac Newton (1642–1727) were not refuted but subsumed by the more general theories of relativity advanced by Albert Einstein (1879–1955). The subsumer argues that many scientific observations and experiments are of this type. Scientists draw the boundaries of science too narrowly and thus refuse to accept anomalous phenomena or mechanisms—those that deviate from the norm—simply because they can't see far enough into the deep recesses of reality. Properly understood, the subsumer would say, some paranormal forces are consistent with the laws of nature, although they may contradict the conclusions of scientists at a given point in time.

Subsumers believe that there are forces or natural laws of which contemporary scientists are not yet aware. Some phenomena that scientists now label paranormal may actually obey the laws of nature, but they are based on principles that are currently unknown to science.

As was the case with Newton's findings, previously unknown principles have been incorporated into accepted frameworks. For thousands of years, humans believed that bats moved through the night air by means of mysterious, occult, or supernatural powers. Bats were thought to be mascots of evil, entities of the underworld. But it was not until the discovery and understanding of sound waves that it became clear how bats navigated so skillfully in the dark. The principles of sonar are neither mysterious nor supernatural.

When scientists make discoveries, many forces originally thought to be of paranormal origin may be found to have a perfectly natural agency. From today's scientific vantage point, the principles that make sound waves work can be "subsumed" under or are a special case of more general and widely accepted principles. Hence, the affirmer-subsumer says, it is reasonable to assume that forces now labeled as paranormal may also be a specific instance of more general scientific principles that scientists haven't yet discovered or don't yet understand. While most conventional scientists are willing to grant that such processes occur—indeed, will agree that they have occurred frequently in the history of science—they *deny* the validity of *most* of the forces that paranormalists argue subsume conventional science.

An excellent example of this is parapsychology. Many researchers in this field believe that, one day, the principles by which humans can move physical objects solely with the mind, communicate with one another solely with the power of the mind, see distant objects without the aid of devices of any kind (remote viewing), and picture or accurately imagine what will happen in the future will be discovered, and they will be consistent with the laws of physics, whether currently known or not yet known (Radin, 1997, pp.277–287). Another good example: the belief that many ufologists have that extraterrestrials have discovered scientific principles not yet known to, but entirely consistent with, earthly physics, chemistry, and biology (Mack, 1995, pp.16–18).

Affirmer-deducer. A third type of affirmer is the *deducer.* Like the subsumer but unlike the violator, the deducer accepts in principle the validity of scientific laws, but argues that scientists have drawn incorrect conclusions because they have read the evidence incorrectly or are prejudiced and refuse to take unconventional claims seriously. For instance, ufologists argue that traditional scientists—who conclude that creatures from other planets are not visiting the earth—are just not looking at the evidence with an open mind. The evidence, ufologists claim, is clear and points to the presence of extraterrestrials in our midst. (Ufologists are *also* subsumers in that they believe that extraterrestrials have figured out a scientifically viable means of traveling faster than the speed of light to get to earth.) In a like fashion, practitioners of "alternative" medicine believe that conventional medical scientists refuse to look at the evidence demonstrating the efficacy of their practices. Deducers believe that, unlike conventional scientists, *they* can read or interpret the available evidence with an open, unbiased mind and hence are more likely to reach correct conclusions.

Affirmer-dimensionalizer. The fourth type of affirmer is the *dimensionalizer*. Dimensionalizers argue that science is a perfectly valid dimension of reality, but it is limited. There is a spiritual *realm* or *dimension* in which entirely different principles operate. This dimension exists in a separate and distinct plane of existence and cannot be contradicted or refuted by empirical test. The paranormal dimensionalizer insists that the spiritual dimension can, but need not, manifest itself in concrete and tangible ways. When spiritual forces can't be seen or measured, this does not indicate that they are not there, it means that they are beyond the reach of the crude, materialistic instruments of science.

For instance, some spiritualists insist angels exist, although a videotape may not be capable of recording their presence. Only the believer will be capable of "seeing" them; the skeptic may miss their presence altogether. The "near-death" experiences described by many accident victims are regarded by many paranormalists as a kind of reality that exists on a plane of existence separate and different from that of the material world. Evidence cannot disprove the paranormalist's claim because the necessary evidence exists in a dimension of existence that lies beyond the limited world that scientists are capable of investigating.

Radical Skepticism

A second major type of approach to paranormal phenomena is that held by the *radical skeptic*. Also referred to as the "unlimited doubt" skeptic, this observer claims to keep a completely open mind; making no assumptions in advance about the truth of paranormal claims; taking each one separately, on a case-by-case basis. When encountering an assertion ("Archaeologist discovers 4,000-year-old cat in Pharoah's tomb"), the radical or "unlimited doubt" skeptic reacts by saying, let's look at the evidence. The radical skeptic does not foreclose the possibility of an anomalous or seemingly implausible claim being true simply because it seems to violate scientific laws. Perhaps there's something to it; perhaps it points to principles scientists don't yet understand. Radical skeptics sometimes refer to themselves as "true" skeptics, the only truly open-minded observers of reality. Critics refer to them as nihilists, solipsists, and negativists. The "unlimited doubt" skeptic obviously merges into the affirmer-subsumer. The difference between them is that the former remains open to the possibility of forces that scientists can't explain, while the latter has concluded that these forces have already been verified.

Disbelief

A third major approach to paranormal claims is held by *disbeliev-ers*. They argue that the laws of nature *cannot* be violated; hence, para-normal claims are *automatically* false by their very nature. Disbelievers come in two varieties.

Disbeliever-ignorer. The *ignorer* does not bother with an exami-nation of paranormal claims at all. Ignorers consider people who make such claims to be foolish and ignorant, and they sidestep the issue alto-gether. When someone asks them about a particular claim or assertion ("Don't you think there's some truth to astrology?"), they simply laugh and walk away, regarding the person who asked the question as a deluded fool. The laws of science are so firmly and robustly established, they feel, that it is a colossal waste of time to bother refuting each and every crackpot claim that comes along. All claims that violate science's basic facts or laws are based on ignorance, error, superstition, fraud, or humbuggery. The ignorer would say that a field's established knowledge reflects the workings of nature. Hence, violations of the laws of nature are so close to impossible that attempting to refute such claims is a fool's errand. All such claims, they feel, are automatically false.

Disbeliever-debunker. The second type of disbeliever is the *debunker*. Like the ignorer, debunkers agree that scientific laws cannot be violated; hence, any claim that seems to violate them is wrong by def-inition. Debunkers are disturbed that anyone would believe assertions contrary to scientific laws and attempt to use evidence to convince the public that paranormalism is invalid. They believe an audience will be convinced by the weight of their evidence and the force of their argu-ments. Debunkers are proselytizers for a cause; they see themselves as battling the evils of superstition and ignorance for the cause of scientific truth (Hines, 1988; Sagan, 1995).

Social Constructionism

The fourth and last approach to paranormal claims is that adopted by the author of this book. It is that of the *culturalist*, the *symbolic inter-actionist*, the *social constructionist*. The culturalist looks at the cus-toms, norms, beliefs, and values of the members of societies around the world; the symbolic interactionist adopts the theory that the meaning of a phenomenon is created by members of a society or social circle; the social constructionist argues that we ought to study how people define reality, not whether those definitions of reality are valid or invalid.

Holders of the social science or social constructionist position toward paranormal phenomena argue that the empirical truth or falsity of occult or extraordinary claims is either irrelevant or secondary. What is crucial about such assertions is that some people do believe them, that they fit into the lives of believers in interesting and important ways, and that they often have consequences for believers' lives, as well as for the collectivities into which they are integrated, and for the society as a whole.

How are such beliefs generated in an age in which science is supposedly the dominant paradigm or perspective? How are they transmitted from one believer to potential converts? How do believers formulate the plausibility of paranormal claims? (And how do debunkers put together *their* arguments rejecting such claims?) How are such beliefs sustained over time? Are they sustained by a more-or-less organized grouping of like-minded believers? Or by persons who are scattered here and there throughout the entire society? What sort of image does the mass media project of such beliefs and their believers? Jorgensen and Jorgensen (1982) say that the paramount sociological issue is not whether paranormal beliefs are valid within the canons of science, but how and why they are believed, and with what consequences.

As I said above, the social scientist, culturalist, or social constructionist sees the truth or falsity of paranormalist beliefs as either irrelevant or secondary. Actually, this spells out two positions, not just one. The position that sees the truth or falsity of paranormal claims as completely irrelevant might be referred to as that of a *radical* or *strict* constructionist or culturalist. The position that sees this issue as secondary could be termed that of a *moderate* constructionist or culturalist.

The radical constructionist. The "radical" constructionist or culturalist argues that issues of truth or falsity lie completely outside the scope of the social scientist; the only thing that counts is what people believe and act upon. Does magic cure people? Can a voodoo curse kill someone? Are extraterrestrial aircraft circling the earth at this very moment? Have aliens abducted or contacted thousands of earthlings and performed medical experiments on them? Can astrology predict our fate?

The radical culturalist would say that an answer to these questions is outside the scope of what the sociologist or social scientist is permitted to study. We can never answer them or any others like them. We must confine our attention to how such beliefs arise, who accepts them, what part they play in the lives of believers, and how they influence the society at large. If the sociologist or anthropologist were to get tangled up in the issue of truth value of assertions, this would represent a case of invading another discipline's turf—"ontological gerrymandering" (Woolgar and Pawluch, 1985). We ought to keep our perspectives pure and stick to an examination of social constructions, assumptions, or beliefs. Whether those constructions, assumptions, or beliefs happen to be true or false is *irrelevant* to the radical constructionist's task. It's not clear how the radical culturalist or strict constructionist would address an extreme issue such as the denial of the Nazi Holocaust, but their general or programmatic position is that delving into the facticity or empirical truth or falsity of claims is unacceptable.

Table 1.1 Approaches to Paranormal Beliefs

Approach	Point of View
1) AFFIRMATION	Paranormal phenomena exist.
a) violater	Scientific laws can be violated.
b) subsumer	Science is valid, but more general forces exist and operate than those yet studied by scientists.
c) deducer	Science is valid, but scientists interpret the evidence incorrectly.
d) dimensionalist	Science looks at the material dimension; on the spiritual dimension, material forces and scientific laws can be overruled.
2) RADICAL SKEPTICISM	Each paranormal assertion should be tested separately, on a case-by-case basis, for empirical validity.
3) DISBELIEF	Paranormal assertions are invalid.
a) ignorer	Since they are invalid, paranormal assertions should be ignored.
b) debunker	Since they are invalid, paranormal assertions should be disproved.
4) CONSTRUCTIONISM	Who believes in paranormal claims, and why, are more important than their empirical validity.
a) radical	Empirical validity is irrelevant; "everything is relative."
b) moderate	Empirical validity is secondary.

The moderate constructionist. Sociologists can go about gathering evidence about the truth or falsity of beliefs, the moderate constructionist would argue, in much the same way they go about collecting information about the existence of the beliefs themselves and their role in the lives of believers: they observe, listen, ask questions, examine the relevant evidence. In principle, determining whether faith healing works is no different from determining the role that faith healing plays in the lives of its believers. It is true that whether faith healing works is secondary, but it is not completely irrelevant.

In principle, it is not a very difficult task to separate the various views of paranormalism into distinct approaches. However, *in practice*, some of these approaches blend into one another. Someone may be a "believer" of one type of paranormalism but a "disbeliever" of another; someone may adopt a "subsumer's" approach to one aspect of a given paranormal but a "violator's" approach to another. For instance, practitioners of "alternative" medicine claim that traditional medical scientists are biased against their claims and refuse to evaluate the data supporting them properly or objectively. That makes them "deducers." However, they also claim that there are forces that operate in their practice (such as "energy fields") that can be felt but not measured by any known medical equipment; this makes them "dimensionalists." So, let's keep in mind that these categories are not distinct, clearly separable compartments. Instead, they overlap, combine, and merge into one another.

WHY STUDY PARARANORMALISM? THE CULTURALIST'S ANSWER

I see my position as consistent with moderate constructionism. I'm going to divide my answer to the question, "why study paranormalism?" into two parts. The easy part is explaining why I view paranormalism primarily as a departure from science. The hard part is explaining why the issue of facticity, or whether a given claim is factually true, matters.

Adopting and holding a belief that has little or no credence in the dominant circles in a society has very different dynamics from adopting beliefs that are dominant or hegemonic. It is said that Sigmund Freud (1865–1939) had a patient who believed that the center of the earth was filled with jam. None of us has ever been inside the center of the earth, but scientists have perfectly good reasons for believing that the center of the earth is made up of molten metal or rock. The important question is, *what kind of a person* believes that the center of the earth is filled with jam? In contrast, nobody cares why the rest of us believe that the center of the earth is molten metal because that's what we've all learned in school.

The fact is, accepting the dominant belief system is not very interesting or intellectually problematic. Because the belief of Freud's patient departs so radically from the norm, we want to know *how* and *why* he came to hold such a belief. It hardly requires an explanation to account for dominant beliefs, but to the extent that beliefs *depart* from them, our interest is aroused, and we want to understand the derivation. Put another way, if belief in the scientific way of reasoning is hegemonic in a given society, then paranormal thinking is anomalous and in need of an explanation. On the other hand, if belief in paranormal modes of reasoning is hegemonic, then scientific thinking is anomalous and in need of an explanation.

Adherence to paranormal beliefs is non-normative in much of conventional, mainstream American society (although it may be normative within certain subcultural social circles, or even among most Americans). It violates accumulated wisdom concerning how the world works and what is generally accepted in Western society. For the most part, a paranormal approach to reality isn't taught in most universities as truth. It isn't confirmed in the most prestigious media. While the media generally tend not to discourage or refute paranormal thinking—in fact, they tend to encourage it—the higher up one goes on the media prestige hierarchy, the lower the likelihood that the media support paranormal claims. For example, *The New York Times* (America's most prestigious newspaper) has no horoscope; the New York *Daily News* (a tabloid with far less respect in the world of journalism) does, as do the six major supermarket tabloids. When a widely respected figure voices approval of one or more paranormal beliefs, this creates something of an uproar. One example occurred when former First Lady Nancy Reagan consulted an astrologer before making up then-President Ronald Reagan's White House schedule.

In other words, paranormal beliefs are not fully institutionalized, firmly established, or completely legitimate in this society. We rarely question how someone comes to believe that the earth revolves around the sun. We do wonder how someone learned to believe that the sun, the moon, the planets, and the stars rule our destiny. It is the departure from the norm that makes paranormalists interesting to sociologists in the first place. Another way to describe a departure from conventional beliefs is to label them deviant. By "deviant" I do not mean mentally ill, sick, or pathological. I mean that persons who hold such beliefs are regarded in specific social circles or quarters as unconventional, odd, peculiar, socially unacceptable.

If a fundamentalist Christian were to enroll in a biology course at a mainstream university and answer questions on an exam consistent with creationism, negative consequences would follow, such as an "F" for the exam or advice from the instructor to drop the course. If a reader were to advise the powers that be at *The New York Times* to include an astrology column in the paper, the advice would be dismissed. When the Harvard psychiatrist John Mack published a book endorsing the view that many of his patients really were abducted by aliens, a committee was formed to strip him of his position. (The effort failed.) When rumors that Immanuel Velikovsky had submitted to Macmillan, a book publisher, a manuscript that made certain claims astronomers regarded as false, steps were taken to block the book's publication. (Again, the effort failed; the book was put out by Doubleday.) In many instances, views that do not conform with mainstream thinking meet a negative, punishing, or condemnatory reaction, or the assertion that the claimant is a fraud, or self-deluded. What makes paranormalism deviant is the fact that its believers are rejected or censured by the more conventional members of the society.

For these and other reasons, the social constructionist's interest in paranormalism is aroused. Belief systems that depart from science lie outside the standard boundaries. They elicit interesting responses from much of the society and the intersection is worth studying from a sociological perspective. Once again, the constructionists are primarily interested in the issues of who holds such unconventional beliefs, why, and with what consequences, and how do adherents of each perspective organize and promulgate their views. In our society, paranormalism demands more explanation than a belief in science does. In many dominant social circles it also produces punishing reactions by persons who adhere to the mainstream position.

However, I do *not* believe that the issue of facticity or scientific truth or falsity is completely irrelevant or can be ignored altogether. I do not believe that dominance or hegemony versus deviance and marginality is the *only* interesting dimension in the paranormal equation. (In fact, how do we assess the issue of dominance versus marginality? Empirically, of course.) While I do not see science as infallible, I do believe that, empirically, the scientific version of reality is more likely to be factually correct than the paranormal version. Frankly, most of us do; in fact, most of us stake our lives on that belief. (We fly in airplanes, not on magic carpets; we consult physicians, not faith healers; we are more likely to rely on phones and E-mail than on telepathy or astral communication.) The question is not, however, what we believe is going to happen most of the time, but what *can* happen, what is *possible*. And here is where scientists and paranormalists part company. I do not believe that, as a general rule, scientists and paranormalists reason in quite the same way. Treating the claim that one has been kidnapped by aliens solely as a "text"—that is, regarding the question of facticity as completely irrelevant—will make certain kinds of investigations possible and others impossible. While versions of reality are constructed they are not constructed out of whole cloth; some versions of reality require entirely different construction processes than others.

Allow me to say this in another way. For many issues, the objective truth or falsity of paranormal assertions is not relevant because most of us do not come into direct confrontation with hard, concrete facts. For most of us, the question of whether the earth revolves around the sun or the other way around is not factually relevant; either way, as far as we are concerned, our lives don't change. However, for us to accept certain assertions as true, we have to engage in a variety of mental processes that manifest a certain typical pattern. This pattern represents something of a departure from the way scientists reason.

Many paranormal lines of thinking make use of commonsensical "heuristics" or rules of thumb that are not necessary for (and are even alien to) scientific reasoning. What these rules of thumb are will become apparent in later chapters. I'd like to emphasize that not all forms of paranormalism display them, nor are scientific formulations immune from them. I do believe that some ways of thinking about how the world, including the social world, works are more empirically adequate than others are, just as some ways of thinking about the world are more emotionally adequate, a different proposition altogether. The only way of assessing these two assertions is through—and let's be clear about this—an empirical investigation. Even constructions about the world have to be investigated from a scientific or, at least, a social-scientific fashion.

To put the matter in another way altogether: if UFOs are *not* real, then aren't the reasons why some people say they have been kidnapped by aliens psychologically and sociologically interesting? Aren't the reasons why so much of the public embraces such assertions likewise interesting? If these accounts were literally and concretely true, from a social and social-psychological perspective, doesn't this make them *less* interesting? (They may be more interesting for entirely different reasons.) If these events literally and concretely happened, persons who observed them are simply reporting what they have seen. But if they didn't happen, *what caused them to believe they did?*

Likewise, if events take place in people's lives that bear little or no correspondence to what psychics and astrologers say is true or will happen, then isn't belief in these assessments and predictions a lot more interesting than if they had been verified by material events? What causes people to accept something that evidence suggests doesn't happen? Isn't belief in the special, spiritual, or mystical significance of coincidence even more interesting *after* statisticians give a perfectly ordinary account of why they should occur than if no such account can be worked out? Isn't the public's rejection of non-ordinary explanations of coincidence worth much more sociological study than a scientist's acceptance of them? I believe so, and this is one of the reasons why I wrote this book.

VIEWS FROM THE INSIDE, VIEWS FROM THE OUTSIDE

These assertions have to be qualified slightly, however. I'd like to follow up on the point I made earlier, which distinguished between what scientists believe to be true versus what is "really" true, by introducing two closely related conceptual distinctions: *emic* versus *etic*; and *epistemology* versus *ontology*. The "emic" versus "etic" distinction comes from anthropology, and the "epistemology" versus "ontology" duality is philosophical in nature. These distinctions do not grow directly out of concerns about paranormalism, but they are relevant to any investigation of extraordinary claims.

Emic and Etic

The *emic* perspective is the insider's view of things: beliefs and practices take on meaning only *within* a given cultural system. To Hindus, the slaughtering of cattle is taboo; for an orthodox Jew, eating pork is forbidden. For biologists, evolution is a fact. Among fundamentalist Christians, the creation of the universe by God in six days a bit more than 6,000 years ago is an accepted fact. Taken emically, it is a *fact* that each belief is held by the members of a society or a particular social circle. The emic perspective says nothing about the ultimate validity of claims or views, only that they are accepted as valid *in* a given society, tribe, group, or social circle. The emic perspective does not go beyond the assertion that a given belief is held within a given social collectivity. Looking at beliefs as emic realities passes no judgment about their facticity or factual truth. They are believed in a certain cultural context and, from an emic perspective, that's the whole story. Proving or disproving them empirically and scientifically is a totally irrelevant, external—and etic—exercise.

The *etic* perspective comes from *outside* a given social grouping. In this approach, outsiders apply *their* beliefs, distinctions, and ways of looking at things to another group or culture. For example, Western views of reality may have no meaning in a non-Western culture, but the etic perspective might apply Western standards to Chinese society. Another example would be telling an orthodox Jew that pork is a good source of protein. In the orthodox Jewish religion, ham, bacon, and ribs are *forbidden* by God; this overrides their protein content and renders them off-limits to human consumption. The outsider's or etic definition of pork as good food violates the rules of Jewish orthodoxy; it is an external imposition and, hence, irrelevant. Likewise, Westerners are outraged by the Chinese practice of eating dogs. The etic or outsider's view of dogs exclusively as pets and companions (and therefore off limits to any cuisine) is meaningless within the scope of Chinese society. Thus, from an etic perspective, such as orthodox Jewish eyes, the Western practice of eating pork violates Jewish law, just as through the outsider Western eyes the Chinese practice of eating dogs is wrong. The etic approach evaluates the beliefs and practices of a given collectivity according to criteria that come from outside that grouping. This emic-etic distinction becomes absolutely crucial when we look at paranormal beliefs.

An image that appears on a series of window panels on a building in Florida seems to resemble the head of Mary, the mother of Jesus. To the faithful, the appearance of this image is a miracle. The fact that it can be explained by physical and material forces is irrelevant. From the point of view of the believer, the materialistic explanation of Mary's image is etic in origin. The emic view shouts, "miracle"; the etic view emphatically insists, "material forces." (It must be said that the Catholic Church adopts a very skeptical position toward the proliferation of miracles.) The two views are incongruent, incompatible, mutually impenetrable—ships passing in the night. They operate on the basis of entirely different assumptions about how the universe works. Of course, what is emic to one belief system is etic to another. Judging claims of a miracle according to scientific evidence makes about as much emic sense as finding the absence of God in the scientific framework a fatal flaw of science. Both adopt criteria that are outside of or alien to each belief system.

The emic approach argues that we cannot reduce paranormal claims to formulations that can be tested with scientific evidence. In fact, many such claims, because they are based on definitions that have no meaning within the scientific framework, are impervious to scientific tests. (Likewise, many scientific claims cannot be tested with the use of many paranormal criteria, since, again, those criteria emanate from outside the scientific framework.) In other words, much of our understanding of paranormal beliefs entails adopting the emic approach (though

not all of it, as I explained in the previous section). To understand paranormalism we must investigate the "insider's" perspective. In order to
do so, we must temporarily set aside our judgments about whether
assertions are empirically true or false and examine their origin, their
dynamics, what role they play in the lives of believers, and what impact
they have on the society as a whole. This is one feature of the social scientist, culturalist, symbolic interactionist, or constructionist perspective
I spelled out earlier.

Epistemology versus Ontology

Epistemology is a branch of philosophy that deals with how we go
about establishing what we know. In contrast, *ontology* is the study of
the inner essence or nature of reality. Many philosophers do not believe
that we can ever get at the "essence" of phenomena; they argue that ontology is a fruitless, metaphysical, "holy grail" kind of enterprise. Nonetheless, some philosophers persist in the quest.

When a theologian attempts to prove (or a skeptic to disprove) the
existence of God, that is an *ontological* enterprise; it represents the effort
to demonstrate that there is (or is not) an entity "out there," a deity all
of us would acknowledge as God. An ontologist is like the courtroom
observer who asks, "Did the defendant *really* commit the crime?" The
ontologist wants to know what is really, really true.

In contrast, an epistemologist would investigate what sorts of arguments satisfy observers that God does, or does not, exist. The epistemologist wants to know how rules for knowing are established and followed. The epistemologist does not look at the existence of God as a
relevant question, but is concerned with the *idea* of God, the arguments
for and against God, the evidence marshaled to demonstrate or refute
the existence of God. In the courtroom, the epistemologist is like the
observer who asks, "What sort of evidence will *convince* the jury that the
defendant is or is not guilty?"

All societies on earth accept "heuristics," or rules of thumb, what
might be referred to as a kind of folk epistemology. Heuristics, rules of
thumb, or folk epistemologies might be defined as *ways of knowing*.
How do we know something is true? The rules differ from one society to
another. In some, portents of events to come may be found in dreams,
a pile of bones, or chicken entrails. In others, we can predict the future
only by consulting experts who interpret elaborate statistical formulas.
All of us follow certain rules that allow us to know what we know; all of
us interpret evidence of the world in somewhat different ways. That is,
we all have our own epistemology, our own ways of knowing.

Epistemology is absolutely central to any investigation of paranormal claims. Far too many commentators assume that everyone holds (or should hold) the same rules of evidence and accepts (or should accept) the same ways of knowing. In contrast, the social scientist knows that people in different societies, and people variously located in the same society, apply very different rules for knowing things—different folk epistemologies.

A wife prays to God for the recovery of her seriously ill husband. When he survives, she "knows" that God intervened to save his life, that his survival is evidence of God's divine mercy. The evidence a medical scientist accepts as valid is very different. It is not based on personal experience but on the data of decidedly impersonal statistics, epidemiology, pharmacology, physiology, and etiology. The evidence a medical researcher accepts as valid has far less meaning for the spiritually inclined wife whose husband survived a life-threatening illness. Likewise, the evidence the spiritually inclined wife accepts is not valid to the medical researcher. Each has a different epistemology or "way of knowing."

In the hypnagogic twilight zone before being fully asleep, a man dreams of being captured by aliens. When he wakes up, he does not recall the dream. A week later, he watches an episode of *The X-Files* that deals with extraterrestrials and suddenly has a vivid recollection of his dream. For the rest of his life, he narrates the dream to anyone who will listen as an event that literally and concretely happened to him. To a psychologist familiar with processes of hypnagogic hallucinations, the man's tale reveals the manifestation of a fantasy-prone mind (Baker, 1987–88).

A couple purchases a lottery ticket with numbers based on a combination of their birthdays. They win ten million dollars and are convinced that their special formula of selecting the numbers led to their good fortune. To a statistician, that claim is true only in the very narrow sense that any number has a very limited—and the same—possibility of being selected. The couple's success demonstrates little more than the operation of the laws of chance (Paulos, 1988).

The people in these three examples look at the evidence and draw a conclusion. Each, in other words, has a "way of knowing," an epistemology that leads to a specific conclusion. Each works within what may be referred to as "plausibility structures"—a framework that renders certain conclusions reasonable and others unreasonable. Each *knows* what he or she believes because each follows a different set of assumptions or rules for interpreting the evidence of the material world. The folk epistemology of each is different from the way of knowing that a scientist follows. But all of them—the scientist included—are similar because they have rules for knowing in which they place unshakable faith.

To the social scientist, the fact that the nonscientists are wrong *from a strictly scientific point of view* is not the only or even the main point (just as the fact that the scientific approach is wrong according to the rules followed by the nonscientists is *also* not the only issue of interest to us). What counts is that ways of knowing have a logic and consistency all their own; they are culturally derived and have social and cultural consequences. The facts of the material world, as interpreted by scientists, are not the central issue to us; how the many perceptions and experiences that people have are *interpreted* as facts is far more important. Faced with the same apparent evidence (for instance, the configuration on a panel on the side of a building that resembles the head of the Virgin Mary), two people will draw entirely different conclusions about what it means. It is not a sufficient explanation to say that people hold a given belief "because it is true." Different people in the same society, and people in different societies, "see" different things when they examine the evidence of the world.

This applies no less to scientific than to paranormal beliefs. Very few of us have conducted scientific experiments ourselves to verify the principles we've read in a textbook. Even if we were to do so, we have to accept the *kind* of evidence that scientists use to draw conclusions. Likewise, the kind of evidence a religionist uses to verify the existence of a miracle (for instance, moisture on a statue's cheeks) is not likely to be acceptable to a more scientifically minded observer. The way that people "read" evidence of the world is the central issue in the sociological study of paranormalism. The central issue for our understanding of paranormalism is folk epistemology, or "ways of knowing" how the world works or establishing what is true.

Scientists are permitted to have hunches or guesses about many of the things they investigate. In fact, a hunch is a hypothesis, and it is a necessary building block of scientific research. But scientists are permitted to "know" something only after the evidence has been accumulated. (Do they sometimes violate this principle? Of course they do! Are they less likely to do so than the man and woman on the street? Probably.) This is the most fundamental difference distinguishing the way that scientists "know" something from the way that everyone else "knows" a thing to be true. In principle (although not always in fact), scientists rely on the impersonal evidence of the laboratory far more than they do on intuition, hunches, feelings, anecdotes, or personal experience. We will revisit this crucial point in a later chapter.

Part Two

Science and Paranormalism

Both scientists and paranormalists have notions or ideas about the assertions of the opposing side. The proponents of each system of beliefs have devised a complex and detailed rationale or justification for why their opponents are wrong. What are the flaws in paranormal thinking? If asked, nearly every working scientist will explain what they are. What's wrong with a scientific explanation of reality? Paranormalists have a fairly clear idea, and can usually supply a ready-made critique that is convincing to them. At the same time, each side is likely to be aware of the criticisms of the other, does not find them convincing, and has handy refutations of them.

Both science and paranormalism are the product of a certain way of looking at the world. Each system of thinking and reasoning is based on assumptions that are extremely fundamental, insulated from criticism. Science works only if certain unprovable assumptions are accepted; paranormalism is plausible only if one agrees that certain things are possible and that evidence to verify them can be interpreted broadly. Each version of reality is based on a particular model or paradigm of how the world works. Once we can agree on the basics, certain kinds of observations make sense. Without that basic common ground, the observations of the other side make no sense whatsoever. The observations that proponents of each side make, the rationale for why each system of thinking is valid and true, and the critiques both sides launch against the other, are all cultural products, not much different from folk tales and legends from distant lands.

How do paranormalists look at science? What arguments do they use to attack its assertions? How does the scientist launch a counteroffensive? What makes science distinctive and unique among all the possible systems of thought the human mind has created? How is it different from common sense, from the everyday reasoning processes we all use in thinking about mundane events of our lives? What parallels exist between paranormal thinking and our everyday mentality? Does science stand apart from both of them? This section is devoted to an exploration of issues such as these.

Over the past two decades or so, modern physics has become vastly more theoretical and speculative than it was in the past. It discusses and researches a number of theories and phenomena that would have seemed outlandish, almost paranormal in nature to a previous generation. Quarks, mesons, cosmic strings, anti-matter, black holes, and so on, are the stuff of modern physics, but it's possible that some of them may not even exist. (Although assuming that they do may be heuristically beneficial, that is, theoretically or empirically fruitful in the long run.) In view of such seemingly wild speculations, it might seem that my educated guesses about what scientists regard as paranormal are old-fashioned, but I'm going to stick to my guns for two reasons.

First, I maintain that a nose-count of current, practicing natural scientists, as well as the discussions that appear in college science textbooks, would give us a reading that is very close to my characterization. Cutting-edge science is conducted by a tiny percentage of any field; I'm interested in the weight of opinion in a field as a whole.

Second, most natural scientists would say that their *reason* for designating, say, string theory as science and astrology as paranormal is because the former fits into currently accepted physics and generates falsifiable predictions, whereas the latter does not. It is these criteria, they would say, that make a science a science. When these principles are violated, a field does not have the right to be designated as a science. I suggest that the majority of scientists would agree that all the endeavors and belief systems discussed as paranormal in this book deserve to be so designated. I'm willing to be proven wrong; I just need strong evidence and a plausible argument to the contrary to convince me.

In the past 25 years or so, a system of thought called "postmodernism" has emerged in Western philosophical discourse. There are many different versions of this perspective, some more radical than others, and several contradicting one another on major points. One issue on which nearly all versions of postmodernism agree, however, is their position on science. Postmodernists argue that science is simply one system of discourse among many, that science has lost its dominance or hegemony as the voice of authority, that value-free science does not exist, and scientific research is inevitably implicated in questions of ideology, morality, and social "embeddedness." Thus, postmodernists and paranormalists share a common ground in that both launch attacks on traditional science.

It is easy to see why paranormalists have not adopted the postmodernist perspective in their critique of science, however. Most paranormalists believe that *their* claims are correct, and the claims scientists make are wrong. In contrast, postmodernists argue that discourse (any discussion about a given topic) has become so fragmented, disintegrated, and lacking in authority that no single voice is sufficiently legitimate to establish the veracity of "factedness." In short, there is no universally agreed-upon system whereby we can establish whether claims are true or false; all such claims entail attempts to dominate, control, and suppress.

Paranormalists argue that they alone have a grasp on an essential reality that scientists fail to understand; postmodernists argue that all reality narratives are questionable. Paranormalists argue that essential dimensions of reality really exist, if only we have the eyes to see and the heart to understand; postmodernists argue that all versions of reality are socially constructed—promulgated within a specific social structure to further specific social aims. Perhaps most important, postmodernists are intellectuals, the vast majority of whom are affiliated with the academic world, while paranormalism is a grassroots phenomenon with little prestige and practically no currency in the academy. In short, while there are striking parallels between postmodernists and paranormalists, the differences are far more significant.

Chapter Four

PARANORMAL (AND EVERYDAY) VERSUS SCIENTIFIC THINKING

To understand the fundamental differences between paranormal and scientific thinking, it is necessary to grasp two main points, which I intend to argue in this chapter. One is that most strains of paranormal reasoning are very similar to the way the ordinary man and woman in the street think, commonly referred to as "common sense." The second is that scientific reasoning is quite different from all other ways of thinking. As I'll argue, paranormal and commonsensical thinking share much more in common than either does with the way scientists think. The main goal of our discussion is not to support either the paranormal or the scientific way of reasoning, but to show how different they are. Their respective practitioners use different epistemologies or "ways of knowing" and different strategies for obtaining information and drawing conclusions.

Four points of departure distinguish these modes of reasoning from one another: *uncommon versus common sense, uniformitarianism, falsifiability*, and *teleology*. These points of departure do not distinguish all forms of paranormal and commonsensical thinking from all modes of scientific reasoning, but they do distinguish paranormalism and common sense in general from science.

UNCOMMON VERSUS COMMON SENSE

Most of us have a great deal of faith in what we call "common sense." When we endorse something as true, we say it's common sense; when we criticize something as untrue, we say it's just not common sense. To most of us, "common sense" means *that which, to any reasonable person, is obviously and self-evidently true*. Most of us rely on conventional cultural wisdom to tell us what's true.

Scientists see things differently. What is referred to as common sense usually turns out to be what *seems* to be true. From a scientific perspective, what seems to be true to most of us is based on cultural convention and may be very different from what *is* true. In fact, a great many things that are scientifically true don't make any sense at all.

Black holes—dead stars so small, heavy, and condensed in mass that no light can escape from their gravitational field—cannot be understood by means of conventional wisdom. (What could be lighter than, well, *light*? How can light possibly be subject to gravitation?) According to atomic physics, most of the volume in seemingly solid objects, such as a table or a chair, is made up of empty space. Does that make sense? And does it really make any "common" sense that the earth is a globe weighing quadrillions upon quadrillions of tons, suspended in space, whirling around the universe at an almost unimaginably rapid speed? Scientific thought is not only very different from paranormal thinking, it is also very different from "commonsensical" thought. Far from being common sense, the scientific way of looking at the world is *uncommon* sense (Cromer, 1993; Wolpert, 1993).

What is considered common sense or conventional wisdom is often false. Practically every basketball player in the world will tell you that the "hot hand" phenomenon is true; that is, when a player makes two or more shots in a row, the likelihood of making the next one is greater than if he or she had missed the earlier ones. It makes a great deal of "common" sense that making a few shots will give a player confidence to make the next one; missing several shots will lower that confidence and lower the likelihood of making the next one.

It turns out that the "hot hand" phenomenon is just so much "hot air"; it isn't true. A careful tabulation of actual shots taken in real-life basketball games shows that the likelihood of making a shot, given a player's overall shooting accuracy, is no greater after making than after missing two or more shots in a row. (Is the same thing true for hitting in baseball? I suspect not—"streaks" and "slumps" are too consistent to be mere random variation—but it's an empirical question, and if baseball is different, there are likely to be social-psychological reasons for it.) But no amount of evidence can undermine a believer's faith in the hot hand. When the authors of the hot hand study approached basketball coaches with their findings, they were ridiculed and disparaged (Gilovich, 1991, p.17). After all, the hot hand phenomenon is just plain common sense! Whatever evidence they gathered was deemed irrelevant.

To a scientist, common sense is too often wrong to serve as a guide for making correct or accurate conclusions. Just as the empirical evidence often falls on the side of *uncommon* sense, common sense is often contradicted by the evidence. To the scientist, the fact that the man and woman on the street believe or disbelieve something is not the issue; what counts is what the systematic evidence of the senses says. People have observed the material world for thousands of years and noted how that world operates. It makes good "common" sense that their observations would lead them to draw reasonably valid conclusions. Scientists say this is not necessarily the case. Many commonsensical notions that work perfectly well under everyday conditions fail miserably when those conditions change more than just a bit.

Which strikes the ground first: a stone that is dropped or one that is thrown horizontally from the same height? Presumably, humans have observed dropped and thrown stones since, well, the Stone Age. Most of us would say it makes common sense that the dropped stone hits the ground first, because it travels a much shorter distance. The fact is, it wasn't until 1632 that Galileo published his findings reporting on a series of systematic experiments he conducted on the topic. What he found was completely contrary to common sense: an object that is dropped and one that is hurled will hit the ground at the same time. In other words, our everyday experience has not been sufficiently accurate to guide us to make the correct conclusion. Since Galileo's time, the same generalization has held up in experiment after experiment. Objects obey the physical laws of motion, not human notions of what makes sense (Cromer, 1993, pp.23–24).

This is not to say that common sense is always wrong. For hundreds of years, grocers have known that the most efficient way of stacking oranges has been in the form of a pyramid. But it was not until 1998 this that commonsensical belief was demonstrated mathematically (Singh, 1998). To the mathematician, such proofs are important. In contrast, the grocer simply continues to stack oranges the best way because, well, because it's common sense. Common sense often works, but its wisdom is highly fallible. Not always wrong, but wrong often enough for scientists to demand more, and more systematic, evidence.

Most scientists would argue that commonsensical and paranormal thinking have a great deal in common. Belief in fate or destiny, for instance, is deeply ingrained in the conventional wisdom of most, perhaps all, cultures. It is even possible that it serves a positive function for human and social survival. Fate or destiny is also a major feature of paranormal thinking. But it is completely alien to the way the scientist reasons; it is a magical, mystical concept that has no place in science. Belief in lucky numbers is a widespread, commonsensical notion, just as it is a fixture in paranormalism. The scientist, however, rejects the idea entirely. Both common sense and paranormalism tell us that since earthly human existence is significant, it must lead to an afterlife, opening the door for the existence of spirits, angels, reincarnation, and other nonmaterial entities.

But science argues that, in the absence of concrete evidence, there is no need to resort to belief in such insubstantial beings. (These beliefs are not necessarily wrong, the scientist would say, just unconfirmed, as well as unnecessary to the workings of scientific principles.) It is clear that common sense and paranormalism overlap heavily, while scientific thinking represents a sharp break with both.

UNIFORMITARIANISM VERSUS THE EXCEPTIONAL CASE

Here, two basic facts are central. In a way, they sound contradictory; in fact, they are two pieces of the same puzzle. One is the *nature of the contrast* between the way scientists and paranormalists reason, how they make use of evidence (uniformitarianism versus the exceptional case). The second is the *implications of the logic* of each mode of reasoning. Science *cannot* disprove each and every paranormal assertion; this means that the paranormalists are right in arguing that *if only a single paranormal assertion were to be validated, paranormalism will have been validated in general.*

One basic feature of scientific reasoning, scientists argue, is universalism, uniformity, or *uniformitarianism*. This means that principles or processes that operate in one time and place also operate elsewhere—in fact, everywhere in the universe. There are no special, distinctive, or unique times or places that suspend the laws of nature. What appear to be exceptions represent the operation of *other* laws of nature exerting a simultaneous effect.

Thus, a principle that is valid *here* is also valid *there;* a force that held sway in the *past* also holds sway *now* and will also do so in the *future*—in fact, as long as the universe exists. The principles of gravity work on earth, on the moon, on Mars, and in distant galaxies. Objects are suspended in space only where there is no larger body near enough to attract them to its surface. No exceptions exist to the law of gravity. Whenever we think we have found an exception (such as objects that are lighter than air), it conforms to the same principle, except in slightly more complex ways. Thus, as mentioned previously, any claim that persons or heavier-than-air objects levitate or float in mid-air through the force of the human mind is *always* and *necessarily* fraudulent or due to misperception, scientists argue.

Accepting the principle of uniformitarianism leads scientists to reject the reasoning of ufologists. Most scientists would say that such occurrences as traveling faster than the speed of light, moving through solid objects, and "beaming up" humans, cars, or entire cities onto spaceships violates the laws of nature and hence are impossible. Ufologists argue that extraterrestrials can do these things, which *seem* to violate the laws of physics, because they have discovered principles of which terrestrial scientists are ignorant. As we saw, many ufologists are "subsumers"; they believe aliens have made use of scientific principles we haven't yet discovered.

Most scientists are firm about this: principles that hold true for earthlings are also valid for aliens. The speed of light is *inviolate*, the one constant in the universe. It will *always* be physically impossible for one solid object to "move through" another. There is no known or *knowable* force that can generate the necessary energy to "beam up" large, physical objects. These powers are impossible because they violate laws that apply everywhere and at all times—or so most scientists would claim.

The assumption of uniformitarianism leads to one of the most basic requirements of scientific research: replication or *replicability*. If natural forces are distributed throughout the universe, and a scientist conducts research and discovers how a given force operates, then another scientist should be able to repeat, duplicate, or replicate the first scientist's findings. In fact, if a given study cannot be replicated by other scientists, it is unlikely to enter into the scientific mainstream. Scientists do not trust a study whose findings are not confirmed by later studies. What was wrong with the original study? Did a flaw exist in the experiment? Did the researchers reach too far beyond their data? Replication is a social control device; it protects a field against fraud. If scientists know their experiments will be repeated or checked, they are motivated to be honest and accurate (Zuckerman, 1977; Cole, 1992, p.13). To the extent that the practitioners in a given field do not routinely replicate scientific findings, that field will rank low in scientific prestige.

In any experiment, however carefully devised, anomalous, odd, or "outlying" findings pop up, observations that don't quite fit into the paradigm or general scheme of things, that don't conform to the rule. Most of these anomalous findings turn out to be experimental artifacts, mistakes of measurement, statistical flukes, misdiagnoses, errors of observation, random variation, numerical miscalculations. Since these oddities occur even when the observer or researcher is a trained scientist, they are likely to be *much* more common when the untrained layperson is the observer. Hence, scientists reason, their attitude of skepticism is a healthy antidote to the vagaries and quirks to which all investigation falls victim. As a result, to quote physicist Paul Grannis in a personal communication: "It takes something of an earthquake to topple the [already established] edifice. Little tremors won't do it." And that is as it should be, scientists insist.

For the most part, paranormal thinking rejects uniformitarianism. Paranormalism argues that certain forces need not operate everywhere or all the time. Paranormalists are sympathetic to the idea that "anything is possible," a principle that science emphatically rejects. (Scientists would say that anything is technically *possible*, but all things are not equally *likely*.) The logic of the two systems of thought is entirely different: for the paranormal position to be correct, it takes only a *single exception* to disprove a rule. Scientists are looking for general principles that are valid *everywhere*, while paranormalists are looking for one or more examples or instances where a general principle does *not* hold.

These two different approaches to reality have enormous implications for how practitioners of these two perspectives think and reason. The vast majority of paranormal claims are based on *anecdotes*, that is, personal experiences narrated by specific individuals. To most of us, personal, first-hand accounts are extremely persuasive.

Advertising, the arguments presented by courtroom lawyers, debates between intimates, propaganda, political discussions—in fact, non-scientific or lay arguments of all kinds—are based on personal testimony, not on dry, abstract, impersonal, quantitative data. Systematic evidence—the evidence that scientists use to persuade—is *not* persuasive to the majority of the population. (In contrast, anecdotal evidence is not persuasive to scientists.) First-hand, personal, anecdotal evidence persuades in the world of the paranormal. But notice: in a way, the paranormalists are right. It is completely true that if a *single* aircraft were unambiguously identified as extraterrestrial in origin, that would be sufficient for paranormal thinking to be correct. *Everyone*—scientists and paranormalists alike—would be persuaded by the exceptional case, again, if it were incontestable. If the proverbial extraterrestrial craft landed on the White House lawn for all to see, the debate is over: aliens are real, and they are here. This would be true *even if every other UFO sighting and report were mistaken or bogus*. Again, it *really does* take just one case to prove the paranormalist's position.

In contrast, for the skeptic, debunker, or mainstream scientific UFO position to be right, *every sighting* would have to be shown to be routine or non-extraterrestrial. The same holds for ghosts, angels, ESP, levitation, vampires, psychokinesis, spontaneous combustion, miracles—and just about every paranormal phenomena ever dreamed up by the human mind. If even a single instance of any one of these phenomena exists or works, the paranormal principle is valid. In contrast, to be correct, scientists would have to refute *every single case* where a paranormal force was reported or claimed to be operating—an obvious impossibility.

Skeptics who argue against the existence of extraterrestrial craft flying around the earth use the phrase, the "irreducible minimum." This means that after all the UFO frauds, hoaxes, misperceptions, flights of fancy, and so on, are eliminated and identified as such (that is, "unidentified" flying objects or UFOs have turned into "identified" flying objects, or IFOs), there remains a residue that cannot be explained away. This is the "irreducible minimum."

Even the most dyed-in-the-wool skeptic or debunker admits that such cases exist. Still, someone with this position would say, the residue of the "irreducible minimum" probably does *not* include extraterrestrial craft. Even if these cases can't be identified, the skeptic or debunker would say, they aren't genuine because the evidence supporting them isn't iron-clad. They look a bit too much like the cases of flying objects that *have* been identified as routine. In other words, an anomalous *observation* or *claim* is not the same thing as an anomalous *phenomenon*.

Whether or not this is a valid means of reasoning, the point is, the conventional scientist has an entirely different task or mandate from that of the paranormalist. Conventional scientists argue that the validity of a scientific law demonstrates that *particular* claims that seem to support paranormalism *cannot* be true. It is impossible, the conventional scientist argues, to run around producing evidence demonstrating that each and every paranormal assertion is false. Every time one claim is beaten down, another pops up, and on and on and on—into infinity. "There, science—disprove *that!*" the paranormalist challenges (Hines, 1988, p.3). The fact is, it quite literally cannot be done.

Moreover, the traditional scientist would say, disproving one assertion does not lead to the paranormalist abandoning similar claims. If we disprove an example of levitation in Australia, another one pops up in France; if that one is successfully refuted, someone in India claims to have levitated; and so on. Once again, the two lines of reasoning—the paranormal and the scientific—*cannot* be reconciled. Nor can either be refuted or challenged to the satisfaction of adherents of the other, because the entire logic of each—the way practitioners on each side of the controversy reason, and the nature of the evidence each accepts to verify their claims—are incompatible. In effect, conventional science and paranormalism exist in separate epistemological universes. Their respective practitioners "know" something to be true in very different ways.

Not all paranormal claims rest on a case-by-case basis. Some paranormalists do argue that certain occult or mysterious forces operate pretty much all the time, under most conditions, or under clearly specified conditions. For instance, some people believe that crystals have the capacity to heal the body and mind and generally to impart special powers to someone who fondles them. (One qualification: you have to have faith that this will work.) Astrologers believe that the destiny of every single person on earth is governed or at least influenced by their "birth sign," that is, the location of the sun and moon, the planets and stars, at the time of birth. Psychics claim to have special powers that permit them to predict the future. These and several other supposed paranormal forces should operate not only in particular, in once-in-a-while instances, but in general.

Conventional scientists attempt to overcome this problem of proof by setting forth more stringent criteria for the paranormalist than for routine or traditional science. The *burden of proof* rests on the paranormalist, not on the conventional scientist, they say (Hines, 1988, pp.3–4). This means: extraordinary claims require extraordinary evidence. The fact is, scientists insist, any claim, regardless of how absurd it is, can be falsely protected from challenge if the burden of proof were to rest on the conventional hypothesis. If you wish to overturn conventional wisdom, you'd better have very good evidence, they insist. Some critics have questioned this principle, arguing that it "stacks the cards against the maverick claimant" (Truzzi, 1998, p.150). Still, it is the standard which is accepted by the scientific community, and so the "maverick claimant" (for instance, the paranormalist) is not likely to convince scientists in any other way except by presenting extraordinarily convincing evidence.

The burden of proof assumption is closely related to science's uniformitarian stance. As we saw, thousands upon thousands of claims have been made to the effect that UFOs are extraterrestrial craft. As we saw, it is literally impossible to refute each and every one. To some believers, this means that the extraterrestrial hypothesis must be true. "There must be something to it," the believer says, meaning that, even if 90 or 95—or 99, or 99.9—percent of reports of UFOs are found to be of objects that have a quite ordinary origin, at least some of the remainder *must* be sighting of aliens. The paranormalist believes that the sheer *weight* of the huge number of the cases of UFO reports should be persuasive. In contrast, the scientist is more inclined to ignore their substantial numbers and be more persuaded by the quality of the cases. (Moreover, a scientist is likely to reason, if there really *were* as many cases as ufologists claim, why don't we have one single irrefutable case, such as a landing in the White House Rose Garden, a clear photograph, or the hull of a crashed ship?) Given the burden of proof, most scientists would say, the evidence for the existence of extraterrestrials on earth is unpersuasive.

FALSIFIABILITY

Karl Popper, a philosopher of science, argued that *falsifiability* is the one defining feature of science (1959, pp.40–43). In order to be scientific, he argued, a claim must be capable of being disproven with the appropriate empirical evidence. No claim that cannot be falsified, Popper argued, can be regarded as scientific. This means that if your hypothesis is always right no matter what the facts say, it is not a true scientific hypothesis. Oddly enough, Popper argued, a hypothesis that could, in principle, be demonstrated to be *wrong* is a *true* scientific hypothesis, while that which can *never* be demonstrated to be wrong is a *fake* or *false* scientific hypothesis. Later, after encountering substantial criticism, he modified his views somewhat by distinguishing between "experimental" sciences (such as physics and chemistry), whose statements are always falsifiable, and "historical" sciences (such as geology, evolutionary biology, and archaeology), some of whose claims may not be falsifiable.

Suppose you claim that a high-level government conspiracy is involved in covering up the presence of extraterrestrials on earth. Let's say I have investigated the question very carefully and found no evidence of such a conspiracy. You counter with the claim that the conspiracy is so well organized, evidence of it cannot be located. In fact, you say, it's even possible that my assertion proves that I am actually a *part* of that conspiracy! Then I say that many books making the claim of a conspiracy have been published; if such an elaborate cover-up exists, why would the government allow the arguments and the evidence contained in these books to be publicized? You say, that only gives the *appearance* of no cover-up; such books are allowed to be published because they are no threat to the government. In fact, their very publication proves that this conspiracy exists. And so it goes, back and forth. There is no possible evidence I could ever present that will convince you that you are wrong. You see the point: if you are incapable of telling me what evidence would disprove your argument, then that argument is unscientific, according to Popper. He argues that nonfalsifiable claims are by their very nature unscientific.

Popper's argument has been discussed among philosophers of science for decades, and his criterion of falsifiability has both adherents and opponents, as we might expect. In real life, scientists conduct their research in ways that approximate but do not correspond precisely to falsifiability. They are far more likely to refer to "testing" a theory rather than falsifying it. Scientists work with the methods of research they learned in graduate school. Most do not spend a great deal of time worrying about satisfying the criteria set up by philosophers of science. To most scientists, falsifiability is a vague abstraction, a pie-in-the-sky ideal rather than a reality. Scientists may pay lip service to it instead of explicitly using it in their research (Wolpert, 1993, p.95). Most of the time, most practicing scientists formulate their hypotheses in such a way that they can be disproven. If their hypothesis is challenged, scientists are able to spell out the nature of the evidence that would demonstrate their thesis to be wrong.

The problem is, however, falsifiability is not always the best policy; it does not always produce the most valid or powerful scientific conclusions. For instance, if an experiment disproves a hypothesis, does that mean the hypothesis is wrong or the experiment is faulty? If evidence shows a theory to be wrong, is the theory wrong or is the evidence flawed? Many famous scientists, from Copernicus, the astronomer (1473–1543), to physicist and chemist Robert Boyle (1627–1691) to physicist Robert Millikan (1781–1855), rejected or ignored the findings they gathered in their initial observations or experiments because they were convinced their *theory* was right and their *findings* were wrong. In these cases, it was the scientists who turned out to be correct, not the results of their experiments (Wolpert, 1993, 94–100). So crucial is theory to scientists that researchers often disbelieve findings that seem to falsify a well-established theory. In fact, one scientist, Michael Polanyi (1958) has openly argued in favor of dismissing evidence that violates or contradicts current scientific notions of how the universe works. Most such disconfirming findings, he argues, are almost inevitably due to experimental error.

In 1781, soon after Uranus was discovered, astronomers realized its orbit was somewhat irregular; it did not conform precisely to Newton's laws of motion. Should Newton's theory have been abandoned because it did not predict this new planet's orbit? Was Newton's theory wrong? Or were the observations wrong? Some astronomers speculated that there could be a third possibility: *another* planet, as yet undiscovered, tugged Uranus out of its predictable orbit. As it turns out, Neptune was observed in 1846, and the inconsistency between Newton's theory and the observed orbit of Uranus was solved. Note, however, that in

1781, it would have been extremely foolish to have argued that the path of Uranus, an empirical fact, disconfirmed Newton's laws of motion.

Some scientists argue that Popper's perspective is negative rather than positive. We can never know for sure that something is right, only that it is wrong, Popper argued. At no point can we relax and have confidence that a given assertion is true. What if a new finding comes along and falsifies a given claim? We can never discount that possibility because we have not subjected our proposition to every conceivable test. While the principle of falsifiability can weed out fraudulent or empty claims, it does not offer anything positive to the practicing researcher who is convinced by the evidence that something is true. Most practicing scientists do not agree. They are satisfied that a proposition that has stood the test of time and works after it has been independently tested in a variety of different ways by dozens of researchers and also accurately predicts observations over and over again is, for all practical purposes, *true*. Most are not overly concerned that their conception of what's true does not quite meet Popper's technical criteria.

The point is, there are parallels between paranormal statements, which are very *rarely* falsifiable, and scientific thinking, which is *usually* falsifiable. But it's likely that their differences are even greater than their similarities.

Perform the following experiment. Locate a dozen natural scientists and a dozen people who hold one or more paranormal beliefs. (Astrology, crystal power, ESP, psychokinesis, and numerology would be good examples, but, as we've seen, there are many others.) Interview each group. Ask them to spell out their belief in a specific or concrete force or phenomenon. Then ask each the following question: "What kind of evidence would disprove or falsify this belief?" The chances are, the scientists would be very specific about the evidence that could falsify their claim. In contrast, the paranormalists are more likely to respond by saying, "Disprove my claim? What's wrong with you? I'm right, and that's the end of it!" Mind you, this informal (and decidedly nonscientific) experiment is extremely unlikely to yield results that all point in the same direction. In fact, it makes use of "ideal types," not real scientists or paranormalists. It's possible that some scientists will *not* have a clear notion of falsifiability and some paranormalists *will*. But if I am right in my guess, the scientists will be much more *likely* to think in terms of falsifiability than the paranormalists will.

Once again, this difference does *not* mean that the scientists are correct in the way they think, reason, or draw conclusions from the evidence and that the paranormalists are wrong. But it does point to the gulf or chasm that separates scientific from paranormalist thinking. The very fact that paranormalists are *more likely* to think that cases, instances, or exceptions will prove their position, rather than being concerned with generalizations that apply across the board, means that *in fact* there is no manner of evidence that can disprove their claim. Once again, all it takes is a single instance. If every single test of paranormal forces is falsified and a single one seems to be verified, the paranormal claim is correct. Again, this informal experiment points to a difference in the way that these two categories reason. Their "ways of knowing" are different. Hence, in communicating with one another, scientists and paranormalists simply talk past one another. They hardly even use the same language.

TELEOLOGY

It is possible that no single axiom of belief separates both paranormalism and common sense from scientific reasoning more sharply or profoundly than their respective views toward *teleology*. The issue of teleology produces a chasm of separation between these perspectives, an unbridgeable gulf; it is the Great Divide.

What is teleology? Nowadays, its principal dictionary meaning is "the belief or theory that certain phenomena are to be explained in terms of purpose or intention." Teleology is a commonly-held assumption about how the world works. Nearly all paranormalists and most of the general public accept some version of teleology. Most of theology is concerned with the search for signs of God's cosmic design or purpose. Paranormalists search for teleological purpose in UFOs, astrology, ESP, psychic visions, and ghosts and spirits. In my own survey of the students at one state-supported East coast university, over three-quarters of the respondents (78 percent) agreed with the statement: "Everything has a purpose." Only a small minority (13 percent) disagreed, while the remainder (9 percent) weren't sure. In contrast, the vast majority of scientists reject the very idea of teleology, arguing that it is a fallacious way of thinking.

Of course, humanly-manufactured items were made for a purpose. A hammer was made to drive nails into wood; a saw was made to cut wood. But these purposes do not indicate teleology, because it was humans who manufactured these things for a purpose. The mind of humans conceived of their purpose in the first place and created them to achieve that purpose. The locus of the purpose is not "in" the hammer or the saw, since they are inanimate objects; it is in the minds of the humans who created them. Likewise, a human can use a rock for a specific purpose—for instance, as a projectile, or a hammer—but, again, it is not the rock that "has" the purpose, it is the human who uses it to achieve a specific goal. Purposes do not dwell within inanimate objects. The same object can be used for a variety of purposes. For instance, the owner of a hardware store might conceive of a hammer or a saw strictly for the purpose of earning a profit; an archaeologist might look at ancient tools solely as a means of understanding the past; and so on.

Jean Piaget, a Swiss psychologist (1896–1980), found that teleo-logical thinking is characteristic of children's thinking. For instance, children below a certain age say that the purpose of clouds is to bring rain, the purpose of rain is to water plants, the purpose of plants is to feed humans and animals. One child Piaget interviewed said that, of the two mountains that loomed over Geneva, the higher one was for adults to climb and the lower one was for children to climb. Small children believe that inanimate objects and natural phenomena think and act as humans do—that they reason, have goals, and act to achieve those goals.

Teleology is both universal and has ancient roots. Aristotle held that natural phenomena had a "destiny." In fact, the natural world was saturated or permeated by mind. It was the destiny of an acorn to become an oak; the acorn works at becoming an oak because it wants to. Living things "strive" toward their natural end; they have a goal that is prescribed by nature; their goal is the achievement of their *true form of being*. Those living entities that do not achieve their natural destiny have come to an unnatural or abnormal end. For instance, if acorns do not become oaks and instead are used as fertilizer, food for animals, or toys for children to play with, their true destiny has been subverted or perverted.

Scientists argue that children, Aristotle, most of the population, and paranormalists all need more than mere assertions to demonstrate their belief in teleology; it has no place in scientific reasoning. Belief in purposiveness or a grand design is comforting. It reassures us that things—even terrible things—happen for a reason. A baby dies as a result of a rare disease. The religious teleologist says, "God took her because she was so pure and innocent," or words to that effect. In contrast, the scientist says the baby's death was tragic but was the result of a genetic or environmental roll of the dice. Belief in the randomness of fate is terrifying. To imagine that we or our loved ones can be wiped off the face of the earth for no reason at all means that we simply can't protect ourselves or others from the cold, cruel, capricious hand of fate. Contrarily, it is immensely gratifying to know that a transcendental entity is looking out for us and has some sort of grand plan for our future. It is no mystery why most people believe in purposiveness. In contrast, given that rejecting it breeds such insecurity, even terror, it is mysterious as to why anyone would not embrace it. Sociologically and psychologically, the commonsensical and paranormal position makes a great deal of sense; the scientific orientation does not. Why would people subject themselves to insecurity and terror?

Most scientists would argue that purposiveness does not exist in the abstract or in the cosmos. Only conscious, intelligent beings have a purpose in mind when engaging in certain actions. In contrast, inanimate or non-conscious entities cannot be shown to have a purpose. Only conscious minds have intentions or purposes, only conscious minds seek to achieve a goal or end. We cannot assume a transcendental purpose in phenomena or events, scientists would argue, unless we have the evidence to back up this assertion. No such evidence exists, at least evidence that is convincing to most scientists.

George Paskesz, 50, a bachelor and a watch salesman, was something of a legend in his community. He often walked into Goldberg's Grocery and paid the bills of poor families who had accounts there. One day in July, George went to a synagogue to say a prayer for his father, who had died 19 years earlier. After saying Kaddish, the traditional prayer for the dead, Paskesz walked toward a nearby subway station. As George passed the storefront of 18th Avenue Plumbing and Supplies, a propane tank dropped off a delivery truck, exploded, and killed him and three other people in the vicinity, injuring 11, and leveling the plumbing store to the ground.

Paskesz's friends and neighbors struggled to understand his senseless death. Although he was saying Kaddish for his father, he was doing it a day earlier than the actual date of his father's death. Said a rabbi, Paskesz committed a fatal mistake: "The anniversary date," he said, "was really the next day. . . . At the last moment of his life, he was given the opportunity to pay respects to his father. . . . It was like being told by God, 'your days are over, so we will allow this mistake to happen so that you can fulfill your obligation.' That's the mystical significance." Added Hershel Goldberg, "Why would he make that kind of mistake after all these years? Kaddish is usually said by children for their parents, but since he had no children it was sort of like an act of God. He was saying Kaddish for himself" (James, 1987).

Humans are significance-seeking creatures. We search for meaning in acts that have major—and even minor—consequences. We fear senselessness, absurdity, and meaninglessness in the universe. We attribute meaning to acts that by themselves have no meaning. Scientists would say that *we read meaning into* events to satisfy our hunger for it. We want to believe that there was some purpose for or significance in George Paskesz's death, that it was not senseless or random in nature; there must have been a reason for it. Why did he die? No one wants to hear that he died because his body was, quite by accident, in physical juxtaposition with an exploding propane tank. No, his death has to have some meaning for us. He died because he said a prayer for his dead father *a day early*. And why did he say his prayer a day early? Well, *because he was about to die!* Having "explained" away his tragic death, we can now feel a little better about it. The world, somehow, doesn't seem quite so senseless. To repeat: this logic is acceptable to much of the public, acceptable to most paranormalists, but *unacceptable* to most scientists. Immanent or transcendental purposiveness does not exist, although humans *manufacture* or *construct* purposive explanations for phenomena or events of this world. And they do so not because these explanations are true in some empirical or factual sense, but because they are emotionally comforting.

THE PARANORMALIST'S REPLY

Paranoramalists would argue that parallels between commonsensical thinking and paranormalism make sense. Of course their way of thinking is rooted in ancient and popular modes of reasoning; why should that be regarded as a fatal flaw? They also argue that scientists have to demonstrate, not simply assume, uniformitarianism. Given the case-by-case approach adopted by paranormalists, their practitioners are unlikely to be persuaded by the scientist's more general stance. And let's face it: for most paranormal claims, even one clear-cut paranormal example *would* certainly clinch their case.

Falsifiability, the paranormalist would say, is not even stringently followed in science. Why should paranormal claims, but not claims made by scientists, have to follow this rigid and outmoded criterion? Why should paranormalists concern themselves with the fact that their reasoning does not conform to the criteria of science, anyway? We tap dimensions scientists can't even envision, they would argue. Hence, we need more flexible and less confining methods of determining what's true.

And teleology: why is it a "fallacy" in the first place? Transcendental, higher, or immanent purpose is plain for all to see; it seems ornery and perverse to reject such a time-honored, universally embraced principle. In one form or another, teleology is the foundation-stone of practically every society, religion, or spiritual system on earth. Doesn't it seem arrogant of the scientist to be so dismissive of this eternal truth? Isn't it *obscene* to argue that our death has no meaning beyond the termination of our earthly consciousness and the decay of our fleshly body?

Once again, let's not fall into the trap of imagining that, because paranormalism fails to measure up *according to the criteria of science*, it is therefore invalid. (Of course, if we are interested in the criteria of science, that is another matter altogether.) Such an argument, as I said before, is equivalent to demanding that an orthodox Jew appreciate a cuisine built around pork. In a like manner, scientific reasoning does not measure up to the criteria the paranormalist might impose on the proper way to think about how the universe works. My job here is not to debunk or to demonstrate to the reader that paranormalism is wrong (or that science is wrong). The fact is, most forms of paranormal thinking *do* depart from traditional science. In fact, that is how we *defined* paranormalism in the first place. In this chapter, I attempted to specify some of those differences in a bit of detail. The fact that paranormalism departs from science gives us leverage in understanding it and predicting some other beliefs held by its believers. To use criteria that are alien or "etic" to paranormalism to challenge or undermine it is not the culturalist's job. In this book, my effort is *mainly* (although not exclusively) emic: understanding what makes the paranormalist tick.

Chapter Five

PARANORMALISM CRITIQUES SCIENCE, SCIENCE REPLIES

Paranormalists argue that science should not be accepted as a measure of all things. Science is highly fallible, based on unprovable assumptions, and extremely limited in scope. Supporters of paranormal belief systems argue that scientists are conservative, traditional, and highly resistant to considering any assertion that challenges their theories or claims. If the ordinary man or woman on the street could make a discovery that undermines the basic assumptions on which scientific reasoning rests, where would that leave the authority of the scientific establishment? In addition, a great deal of contemporary science is not that different from paranormal thinking, with speculation, unprovable assumptions, and investigation into unobservable phenomena often being the rule. Moreover, paranormalists would say, science is not an especially benign force in contemporary society; it is possible that scientists have done more harm than good. After all, they gave us the atomic bomb, environmental contamination, the greenhouse effect, and global warming.

Much of paranormalist thinking challenges conventional science. In a way, the two systems of thought compete for the hearts and minds of society's citizenry. Both perspectives marshall arguments to appeal to that citizenry and to question the arguments of the other side. The arguments and rhetoric both sides use are worth investigating.

THE FALLIBILITY AND LIMITATIONS OF SCIENCE

Science is far from infallible. Some postmodernist critiques of science are so devastating as to suggest that science should not exist at all. Jean-Francois Lyotard, one of the most prominent proponents of post-modernism, defines it as a perspective that argues for the "incommensurability" and "heterogeneity" of different approaches to reality, the fact that there is an "absence of a supreme tribunal," such as science, to determine what is real, what is true. In effect, and with some slight exaggeration, postmodernism is the view that all views are equally valid, that there is no definitive means of determining the validity of one assertion over another. Here are just a few problems with the institution and practice of science, as well as with the way that scientists reason, that pose difficulties with anointing scientists as the arbiters of reality.

First, the reward system in science is so fierce and competitive that scientists occasionally fake data and plagiarize the work of other scientists. To receive grants to conduct research, as well as professional recognition and rewards, some scientists have been know to cut corners, "cook," "fudge," or fabricate data, and publish findings that are probably false. Other scientists have stolen the work of legitimate researchers and passed it off as their own. In short, some scientists are *deviant* in the way they conduct research; they do not play by the rules of legitimate science (Ben-Yehuda, 1985, pp.168–207).

Because of such incidents of dishonesty, paranormalists argue that scientists are in no position to decide for the rest of us what's real and true. Of course, dishonesty and all manner of wrongdoing exist in every profession, indeed, in all human endeavors. Some clergy seduce children; some physicians fake billing records; some business executives pad expense accounts. What makes the sins of scientists seem especially heinous is that we expect these seekers of truth to be above such dishonesty. Somehow, it seems reasonable to most of us to hold the scientific fraternity to a higher standard. Both the public and believers in the paranormal have a view of science as the accumulation of factual knowledge. When a particular finding or assumption is later revealed to be false, what does that say about its prior status as knowledge? And how many other scientific assertions now accepted as true will be later revealed to be false?

Second, not infrequently an important scientific discovery is made that is not recognized for many years. Science possesses two contradictory qualities: it is both innovative and conservative. Its innovative side permits scientific discovery, but its conservative side resists such discoveries. On some questions, evidence is later uncovered revealing scientists' earlier views to be incorrect. If theories thought to be wrong at the time they were proposed are later proven correct it was actually the majority of scientists who were wrong.

For instance, the theory that continents "drift" on a fluid layer below the earth's surface, put forth by Alfred Wegener in 1912, was rejected by most geologists until the 1950s. Later research demonstrated its validity beyond a shadow of a doubt, and all geologists today accept the thesis of continental drift (Ben-Yehuda, 1985, p.124). Thus, the fact that in 1930 most scientists rejected this thesis turned out to be irrelevant to its validity. In fact, the thesis was valid in 1930 and most scientists were wrong. True, the theory did not challenge what was then regarded as scientific principles or laws, but it was nonetheless a fact that was rejected by the majority of scientific opinion.

In the 1930s and 1940s Karl Jansky, a radio engineer, discovered that stars emit radio waves and that heavenly bodies can be studied by means of these signals. Conventional astronomers failed to accept the validity of this momentous discovery for nearly 20 years, roughly a generation, which is a very long time in science (Ben-Yehuda, 1985, pp.124–130). Today, radio astronomy is a crucial part of the field, a valuable tool in understanding stellar phenomena.

There is, in other words, a certain amount of *resistance* by scientists to some discoveries (Barber, 1961), or "delayed recognition" in granting deserved respect to some scientists and their work (Cole and Cole, 1973, pp.209–213). In short, when they are made, certain discoveries suffer from *prematurity*. At the time of their discovery, their implications cannot be linked up with generally accepted scientific knowledge. Hence, they are rejected as false, scientifically irrelevant, unimportant, or at the very least, not yet proven. Critics of science ask: why does it take so much time for valid findings to be verified and accepted by a field?

This is an important point because it enables paranormalists to say, "The scientific establishment ignores or ridicules our theories. Well, it treated Galileo, Mendel, Semmelweis, and Einstein the same way! It shows that our theories are just as valid and true as theirs were! One day, our theories will be accepted just as theirs were."

The point is well-taken. Scientists are sometimes mistaken about the validity and value of some scientific work that is later recognized to be important and true. Although such resistance is less likely to take place today than in past generations (Cole and Cole, 1973, pp.211–213) paranormalists can point to examples such as those above and say, "My theory is not recognized by conventional science because it is ahead of its time!"

Third, occasionally, an amateur comes up with a theory that later turns out to be valid, a theory the established scientists of the day simply fail to recognize. Jonathan Swift (1667–1745), the Irish-British novelist who wrote *Gulliver's Travels* (1726), made a lucky guess about the moons of Mars, even though the relevant astronomical observations were not made until 150 years later (Gardner, 1957, pp.10, 30). Samuel Johnson (1709–1784), an English intellectual, writer, and wit, happened to be right about microbes causing dysentery 80 years before research demonstrated that this was in fact the case (p.10).

As we've seen, for generations before the 1700s, peasants told astronomers that "stones fell out of the sky," and yet these good men of science rejected such tales as superstitious nonsense. No less a personage than Thomas Jefferson, after hearing of a report of these "stones," stated, "I would rather believe that two Yankee professors would lie than believe that stones fall from heaven." In 1803 a French scientist, Jean-Baptiste Biot, conducted a thorough and systematic study of the matter and wrote a research report that was so convincing that henceforth, nearly all scientists acknowledged these "stones" to be meteorites (Westrum, 1977, p.272).

So, it sometimes happens that a layperson or non-scientist has a more accurate notion of how some aspect of the material world works than some, or even most, conventional scientists (Gardner, 1957, pp.10, 30–31). Because scientific issues and scientific research today are so abstract and removed from our sensory, visceral experience, these sorts of valid laypersons' hunches and lucky guesses are extremely unlikely. Still, they are not impossible. And such examples do tell paranormalists that, even without traditional scientific training, their observations, speculations, theories, intuitions, or hunches may become the basis of scientifically valid theories.

Fourth, all science rests on or takes for granted certain assumptions about the nature of the universe, and all findings should be regarded as provisional. At the cutting edge or "frontier" of science there are always controversies, unsettled issues, and imaginative speculations. In fact, some of these explorations involve so much speculation and so little evidence that it is difficult to know just what the scientific community will conclude about them a generation into the future. To the scientist trained a half-century ago, contemporary writing on black holes, quarks, mesons, antimatter, cosmic strings, virtual particles, ten-dimensional space, and the nature of chaos must resemble science fiction (and paranormal thinking) more than it does traditional science. To paranormalists, these speculations demonstrate that their theories are not so bizarre after all.

Fifth, as we've seen, scientists claim that, in order to be scientific, propositions must be *empirical*, that is, based on information derived from one or more of the five senses. No proposition or hypothesis that is incapable of being observed can be regarded as scientific. At the same time, the very enterprise of science rests on assumptions that must be taken on faith, assumptions that cannot themselves be tested empirically. The first is, "The world is materially real." The second is, "We can know the material world through our senses." How can we test these statements? Only by assuming that they are true in the first place! It is literally impossible simultaneously and independently both to *test* them and *assume* that they are true. We can't go outside these assumptions and determine whether they are true. They have to be taken on faith! So much for the empirical foundation of science! In that sense, how different is paranormal thinking? Or so some supporters of paranormal powers claim.

Sixth, science cannot account for ultimate causes. As for the origin of the universe, astrophysicists either shrug or provide conflicting or fanciful explanations. (Most scientists do not even regard this matter as a deficiency in their reasoning.) Even if we were to admit that the "big bang" began everything 10 to 15 billion years ago, what was the universe like *before* the "big bang"? In fact, scientists cannot provide an adequate account of many of their most basic explanatory factors.

For instance, when Isaac Newton first proposed his theory of gravity—that bodies are attracted to one another in direct proportion to their mass and in inverse proportion to their distance from one another—he was charged by his contemporaries as making use of occult, mysterious, and mystical forces. What causes gravity itself? Newton admitted he had no answer.

When Charles Darwin (1809–1882) first proposed his theory of evolution in 1859, he had no notion whatsoever of its genetic basis. He saw that evolution worked, and he argued that its basis was natural selection, but he had notion of the source of genetic variation. (Since then, biology has supplied an answer.)

What causes the theory of quantum mechanics to work? Physicists have no idea; they just know it works, that's all (Wolpert, 1993, pp.143–144).

Scientists can calculate the speed of light (in a vacuum, a constant 186,300 miles per second) but have no idea why it travels at precisely that particular speed, not significantly slower or faster.

Given the fact that science relies on what can only be described as mysterious, almost mystical and occult (but, scientists would say, *replicable*) forces, how different is its reasoning processes from paranormal thinking? While scientists usually shrug their shoulders at the issue, some paranormalists argue that the inability of scientists to explain final causes indicates the affinity of the two modes of reasoning.

Seventh, science is immoral. To be more precise about it, science is *amoral*. Science does not offer a blueprint for living the good life. It does not have an answer to society's problems. It does not teach us how to be decent to our fellow human beings. It is not a fountain of ethical wisdom. What kind of guidance on how to live does science offer? Indeed, on such matters, science is silent. In fact, it offers itself to any agent who comes along and wishes to use its powers, much like a gun that can fall just as easily into the hand of a villain as into the hand of a hero. How can anyone with a moral view of life possibly adopt a scientific perspective?

Indeed, science is as much a part of the *problem* as its solution, say its critics. During much of human history, many of the most innovative ideas from technologically creative minds have been used for the purpose of developing military hardware—tools to destroy, not enhance, human life. Perhaps the watchword of science should be: "From the people who brought you the atomic bomb"! What other social institution has developed the capacity for complete and total global annihilation? Today, environmental degradation has destroyed untold species of wildlife and millions of acres of woodlands. Is humanity next? Western science, hand in hand with industrialization, has accelerated human ecological destruction to a degree that is unprecedented in human history. Does this represent enlightenment? Do we really want to collude in this destruction? Given its track record, argue its critics, should science be held up as a model for us all?

Eighth, science is part of the establishment. Its research methods are expensive (and difficult to learn) and hence available only to a small institutional elite. Science can be conducted only by representatives of powerful, mainstream institutions who obtain huge government or private grants. Science is hierarchical, with the general public at the bottom of the pyramid, a very large number of undergraduates one rung up, a smaller number of graduate students at the next highest rung, postdocs a rung higher, junior colleagues above them, and a very tiny number of successful, powerful, mostly middle-aged, mainly white, predominantly male senior scientists at its pinnacle. Whatever the personages at the top assert is taken as authoritative; whatever contrary claims are made by those at the bottom are ignored or ridiculed. Moreover, much of what scientists say is so obscure, difficult, esoteric, and arcane that only a tiny band of specialists understands the statements.

In contrast, paranormalism is democratic. Everybody has the floor; everyone has a voice; and credence doesn't depend on relative position in a hierarchy but on how the argument resonates with the audience. While science is a "closed" communication system, paranormalism is "open," with free and unfiltered communication between the people with ideas and those who wish to listen. Someone with a new way of looking at things can set up a web site or publish a newsletter and be taken seriously by like-minded thinkers everywhere. Which, then, is the superior model for communicating ideas? Should the rest of society really emulate the hierarchical or elitist way that science works? Why shouldn't all of us learn from the free and open exchange of ideas that exists among paranormalists? Or so the advocates of paranormal thinking assert.

THE SCIENTIST'S REPLY

Scientists agree that there is resistance to scientific innovation—as there should be. It is true that there is both an innovative and a conservative aspect to science. If scientists accepted every interesting, imaginative idea that someone dreams up, science would be in a chaotic state. Even the most expert archer can't hit the bull's eye with every shot. Yes, it is true that scientists have rejected a few theories that later turned out to be true. But out of a thousand new ideas, at most, one proves to be true and worthwhile; most are quietly forgotten. And whether acceptance takes place immediately or over a period of a decade or more, scientists eventually incorporate true and important ideas into the structure of scientific thinking. There are several reasons why some scientific innovations initially meet with resistance, but this is not necessarily a bad thing. To understand this process, we need to distinguish the "core" knowledge and the research "frontier" of science.

Scientific core versus frontier. In science, there are two types of beliefs or assertions. First, there is a "core" set of beliefs that almost all scientists accept as true. Second, there is a research "frontier"—a cutting edge in which there is far less consensus and far more speculation about issues. Core knowledge is seen by scientists as reflecting the laws of nature. At the frontier, there is *dissensus*; different scientists often reach very different conclusions about how the world works (Cole, 1992, p.16). Hence, agreement or consensus is extremely high about core beliefs and much lower about theories or hypotheses in the frontier. In a field's textbooks, core knowledge will be referred to as "facts," while frontier assertions will be highlighted as speculation or theory.

This distinction between core facts and the frontier of knowledge allows the scientist to assert that some of the most basic assumptions of paranormalism are false. When they are told that their assertions cannot possibly be true, many paranormalists will say, "Anything is possible," "Nothing is known for sure," or "Whatever scientists believe now will be overturned in the future" (Rothman, 1989). Scientists argue that this is complete rubbish. The foundations for certain scientific truths have *already* been laid; they are secure, not subject to debate, and will never be overturned. It is only in the field's frontier that disagreement is widespread; even here, only certain issues are disputed, not everything.

The earth is round, not flat; no new discoveries will ever turn up anything different. The periodic table of chemicals cannot be overturned; it spells out invariant physical properties of the elements of nature. The earth revolves around the sun, not the other way around; in all likelihood, it is impossible to travel faster than the speed of light; the universe is billions of years old; and so on. Scientists believe these statements to be true and not "relative" to time or place. There is no disagreement about them among the vast majority of scientists. Members of different cultures may have different *beliefs* about nature, but the characteristics of nature do not change according to what people believe. Or so scientists say.

In contrast, it is true, scientists will add, that some issues are on the frontier and therefore are debated in the scientific community. For instance, how dinosaurs died out 65 million years ago, or whether the universe began with a "big bang" 10 to 15 billion years ago, or what existed before the "big bang," or what lies beyond the borders of the known universe, are questions that are on the frontier of science and hence, about which consensus is far from universal. However, once a new theory has been verified to the satisfaction of the scientific community, it enters into a field's "core" and becomes accepted knowledge (Cole, 1992, p.16). All too often, laypeople take scientific disagreement as the norm, when, in fact, vigorous debate characterizes assertions on the frontier but not in the core.

Thus, most practicing scientists would reject the implications of Thomas Kuhn's theory (1962), which argues that new science is not accepted until it fits into current frameworks or paradigms. When new findings are accepted, Kuhn argues, science makes a break with the past, rejects the old paradigm, and veers off in an altogether different direction. This theory, most scientists argue, is weak because it fails to take into account the difference between the core and the frontier of science and to recognize the *cumulative* nature of the scientific enterprise (Cromer, 1993, pp.4–5, 19).

Core assumptions are referred to as facts because they have been *verified* as true and are *assumed* to be true. Questioning and then reaffirming their validity over and over again, scientists believe, serves no purpose (Cole, 1992, pp.15–17). If someone were to come along and question such facts, scientists would roll their eyes and mutter, "Here we go again!"

Science as self-correcting. Scientists would say that it is misleading, even wrong, to assert that they reject many true ideas. The fact is, all new ideas are controversial, and have to compete with tradition in all spheres. (And again, keep in mind the fact that most new ideas turn out to be wrong.) As we saw, in science, there is a core or foundation of knowledge that remains unquestioned. At the cutting edge or frontier, innovations have to struggle to get accepted, as they do in all spheres of life. But read an astronomy, physics, or biology textbook published in 1950, then compare it with one published in 2000. They look very different, don't they? And the differences in the later texts lie not merely in their glossy pages and color format, but in their content. Contemporary textbooks not only contain thousands of recent discoveries, they cast a new light on older, core facts, qualifying and reformulating them in ways that was not possible half a century earlier.

Scientists argue that science is *self-correcting*, while this is not true of many other approaches to reality. After making the comparison of science texts published a half-century apart, compare two books on astrology written at different times. Astrology doesn't change nearly as much; scientists would say that it is because it is hardened dogma, not science. Practitioners argue that in science what is true eventually wins out over what is false, whereas in paranormal claims, since evidence is irrelevant, what is said in 1950 isn't radically different from what's said in 2000.

The scientist points out that Galileo's observations were rejected by religious, not scientific, authorities; Einstein's discoveries were recognized by scientists almost immediately; and Mendel and Semmelweis's contributions were eventually recognized, albeit after several decades of neglect or rejection.

The case of Ignaz Philipp Semmelweis (1818–1865) is especially poignant. A Hungarian physician, he designed an experiment to determine why so many women died in childbirth. The experiment demonstrated conclusively that the deaths of these women were due to the fact that their attendant physicians had dirty hands. The women whose doctors washed their hands did not die in childbirth. But the medical profession ridiculed Semmelweis and his experiments, and he was hounded from one hospital position to another. Ultimately, Semmelweis was driven insane, and he committed suicide. His findings on the need for childbirth asepsis, or the absence of germs, were not accepted until about 1890, a full generation after his death. Medical scientists would agree that the recognition of this pioneering medical researcher's work was tragically delayed, but the fact is, it was finally accepted as valid. If anything, the case of Ignaz Philipp Semmelweis demonstrates that valid findings are eventually accepted as true, even if that recognition is delayed. Where can we find a comparable case in the world of the paranormal?

Scientists may fail to recognize good work or accept bad work occasionally, but eventually, the good work triumphs and the bad work dies. Thus, when critics attack scientists because they "keep changing their minds" about things, they are really pointing to a positive, not a negative, quality. Scientists do not so much "change their minds" as propose a theory, test it, and if it fails the test, reject it. Isn't that approach vastly superior, scientists insist, to issuing doctrinal assertions, then dogmatically insisting that they are right regardless of what the evidence says? Sticking to a position that is wrong is a fatal flaw, not a virtue.

Science: Ideal versus reality. Scientists assert that there is a major difference between science as an idea, a concept, an *ideal* and science as a concrete *institution*—that is, the real-life behavior of real-life scientists. Scientists have been known to do incredibly stupid things, even in the name of science, but that does not mean that science itself is stupid, invalid, wrong, or that it is identical in significant ways to paranormal thinking. Science *as it is practiced* is a thoroughly human and therefore fallible institution; science as an *ideal* is an altogether different matter.

Scientists admit they make mistakes. The behavior of scientists is sometimes contaminated by nonscientific considerations, such as nationalism, professional jealousy, egoism, or complicity with the powers that be. However, these are *deviations from* science, not science itself; this is how some scientists *behave*, not how science should be practiced.

Science is limited. Scientists acknowledge this criticism: there are issues of great importance to many of us that the scientific approach is not allowed to investigate. Certain issues cannot be addressed with material or empirical data. Does God exist? Is a given action good, ethical, morally correct? Why do loved ones die? Is there life after death? Why does evil exist in the world? Why is there so much suffering in the world? How can I lead a good and decent life? The answers to certain questions surpass what can be determined with the data of the senses. Science is not equipped to know about spiritual issues, issues that can be known only with the heart or the soul, that are based on faith and intuition. In fact, science is impotent to grapple with, let alone answer, many of our most troubling, important, and interesting questions.

The fact is, science cannot be a complete blueprint for living. Science is only a tool, much like a hammer, which has limited uses. Scientists see these limitations as a strength not a weakness. Just as science cannot tell us how to live our lives (although it may provide information about the relative risks of certain choices), in a like fashion, theology or philosophy cannot provide explanations for physical or biological processes. Any intellectual tool kit contains a variety of instruments for a variety of purposes; scientists today do not claim that their framework provides the answer for every question. Paranormalists, ideologues, moralists, critics, and philosophers expect too much from science. They proclaim its failure in reaching goals that even scientists do not set for themselves. Most scientists do not see science's inability to deliver on goods not promised as a relevant criticism. Science must be supplemented with other perspectives, and what those perspectives are is up to the individual. The only restriction, the scientist would say, is that, *from a strictly scientific point of view*, the individual cannot hold a belief that is contradicted by the evidence of science or that would undermine science. Otherwise, just about "anything goes."

Is science destructive? Most scientists do not blame themselves for the harm that results from their ideas. Most of the innovations that have been used to destroy human life or to harm the environment have been produced by technology, not science. That is, scientific principles have been *applied* by non-scientists, often engineers, to the problems of the world. While technology is driven by money—that is, the economic marketplace—science is driven by the marketplace of *ideas*, the fame and esteem that intellectual innovation brings to its creator (Wolpert, 1993, p.31). Scientists would argue that they are not responsible for the social structure within which they live, and they are not responsible for the uses to which their discoveries may be put. While it is true that scientists directly participated in developing the atomic bomb during World War II, at the time, their work seemed to be beneficial. In that specific case, it was aimed at the destruction of fascism.

Moreover, scientists would argue, do the critics of science really want to return to a technologically primitive age? There is an irony, they would say, in these critics stepping on planes to attend conferences, e-mailing messages to one another, writing articles and books on computers, all devoted to attacking science as being guilty of generating ideas that spawned technologies that have done more harm than good. The ultimate irony is that science has helped to create a class of intellectuals who are critical of science. If science hadn't existed, these critics wouldn't exist. It is not the flaws of science that have launched their critiques, but the fact that science—or at least the technological applications of scientific principles—has given them the leisure, intelligence, and critical capacity to *attack* science. Not one of them would suggest a return to the Stone Age, when neither science nor nattering intellectuals existed.

Is science elitist? Scientists would agree that, *in one sense*, science is an elitist enterprise. Yes, its research methods and language are difficult to learn and yes, the research projects that are necessary to generate new knowledge are very expensive. The likelihood that an ordinary lay-person, untrained and unaffiliated with a scientific organization, will produce and publish a paper whose conclusions are recognized by the scientific profession as a contribution is extremely small, almost nil. Although such a thing was possible in the past, today it is very nearly impossible.

However, in a very different sense, science is open, the defenders of science would say, while paranormalism is the closed system. Scientists are persuaded by the evidence that is presented, not by the authority of the author of a paper, article, or book. After all, Newton's science came to be accepted by all scientists, while his astrology was ultimately rejected. Aristotle's natural science writings are rejected by scientists because much of makes up a dogmatic, closed system; that which is capable of being empirically tested is nearly always empirically wrong. Einstein was a scientific unknown in 1905 when his first papers were published—he had no status or authority whatsoever in science at the time—but his ideas virtually swept the field of physics because they were powerful and persuasive.

What science does, its defenders would say, is engage in objective, empirical investigation by means of research methods that are spelled out and capable of being conducted by anyone with the training and the resources. Anyone with the requisite training and wherewithal can reproduce any experiment any scientist has conducted and determine whether the conclusions are valid. Moreover, the principles of science can be taught to any half-way intelligent and motivated student. The same things cannot be said, these scientists would argue, of paranormal claims or assertions. Some paranormalists claim that only certain of us possess the "gift" of predicting the future or viewing faraway events and objects. What is more elitist that this? On the other hand, others have claimed that everyone can learn to acquire paranormal powers. If this is true, why doesn't the evidence show that these powers can be taught so they can be harnessed and are predictable, as the forces of the natural world are? It is Newton's astrology, Aristotle's metaphysics, and paranormal thinking that are "closed" systems, scientists argue, while the methods and conclusions of science are exposed to the open air of the real world, for anyone who wishes to do so to scrutinize and evaluate. In other words, we have to distinguish, traditional scientists say, between the scientific *method*, which is sound and not likely to change any time soon, and the scientific *establishment*, which is highly fallible, often unsound, and frequently subject to error.

Part Three

Four Types of Paranormal Belief Systems

Sociologically, we look at paranormal beliefs by focusing on how they are generated and sustained. The routes through which this takes place are many and varied. Perhaps five are most likely to be interesting to the sociologist. For each, we should ask the basic question: "Who is the paranormalist's social constituency?" And for each, the answer is significantly different.

First, there are paranormal beliefs that originate from the mind of a social isolate, a single person with an unusual, highly implausible vision of how nature works. The isolate's message is presumably directed mainly at scientists, although any connection with the scientific community is tenuous or nonexistent. Scientists refer to these people as *cranks*. Here, the social constituency of the crank usually does not extend beyond himself (most cranks are men). It is deceptive to think that cranks address their message to the scientific community, since they do not engage in science-like activities or associate with other scientists; their goal is to *overturn* or *annihilate* conventional science, not contribute to it. Not enough attention has been paid to the crank for us to devote an entire chapter to the subject, but it is a subject worth mentioning.

Second, there are paranormal belief systems that begin within a religious tradition that existed long before there was such a thing as a scientist. Such beliefs sustain, and continue to be sustained by, an identifiable religious organization. Creationism is a prime example. The social constituency of the creationist is the like-minded religious community.

Third, there are beliefs that depend on a client-practitioner relationship. In other words, the key fact of certain belief systems is that they are validated by professionals who possess special expertise that is sought by laypersons in need of personal assistance, guidance, an occult interpretation of reality of their lives, or a demonstration of paranormal proficiency. Astrologers and other psychics exemplify this type of paranormalism. The social constituency of the astrologer and the psychic is made up primarily of the client and secondarily, of other astrologers and psychics.

Fourth, another form of paranormalism is kept alive by a core of researchers who practice what seems to be the *form* but not the *content* of science. Many adherents are trained as scientists, they conduct experiments, publish their findings in professional journals, and maintain something of a scientific community of believers, but most traditional scientists reject their conclusions. As we've seen, parapsychology offers the best example here. Unlike astrologers and psychics, parapsychologists do not have clients. They are researchers and theorists, not hired for a fee. While a substantial number of laypersons may share the beliefs parapsychologists claim to validate in the laboratory, these paranormal scientists or "protoscientists" form the sociological core of this system of thinking. For the *professional* parapsychologist, that is, the parapsychological *researcher*, the social constituency is that tiny band of other professional parapsychologists and, ultimately, the mainstream scientific community.

Fifth, there are paranormal belief systems that can be characterized as "grassroots" in nature. They are sustained less by individual theorists, a religious tradition or organization, a client-practitioner relationship, or a core of researchers than by a broad-based public. In spite of the fact that it is strongly influenced by media reports and the fact that there are numerous UFO organizations and journals, the belief that unidentified flying objects (UFOs) are "something real" has owed its existence primarily to a more-or-less spontaneous feeling among the population at large. The ufologist's social constituency is primarily other ufologists, secondarily the society as a whole.

The assertions of the scientific "crank" represent one of the more interesting of all paranormal belief systems. He is a self-styled scientist or (from most scientists' point of view) a *pseudoscientist* who persists in advancing views of how nature works that are regarded as either nonsensical or contradicted by the available evidence (Gardner, 1957, pp.7ff.). While many legitimate scientists have advanced theories that were later overturned, falsified, or refuted by evidence, most of their peers regarded their theories as plausible, even though they were ultimately proven false. Moreover, many of the legitimate scientists who propose erroneous theories are able to recognize the error of their ways once the evidence against their hypotheses begins piling up. (To the extent that a real scientist continues to advance an incorrect theory, even after it has been disproven, he or she is more likely to be called a *curmudgeon* than a crank.) In contrast, the crank usually advances theories that are completely implausible to most scientists, or irrelevant or contrary to the way the world operates, or simply impervious to empirical test.

Have proponents of novel theories that were eventually validated and accepted been regarded as cranks? Did any physicist in 1905 regard Albert Einstein as a crank for proposing his theory of relativity? One physicist says no, that Einstein's contemporaries did not and would not have branded him a crank (Bernstein, 1978). To begin with, Einstein published his ideas in a recognized journal of physics. Second, his theory of relativity passed the test of the "correspondence" principle, that is, it proposed exactly *how* it corresponded with, fit into, or extended, existing and established theory. In other words, Einstein's theory was very clear on just where Newton's principles ended and where his own theory began. In contrast, crank theories "usually start and end in midair. They do not connect in any way with things that are known" (p.12). Third, most crank theories "aren't even wrong." Says physicist Jeremy Berstein, "I have never yet seen a crank physics theory that offered a novel quantitative prediction that could be either verified or falsified." Instead, they are "awash in a garble of verbiage . . ., all festooned like Christmas decorations." Einstein's paper was very clear about its predictions; it virtually cried out to be tested empirically (p.13).

Cranks tend to have at least two basic characteristics. First, they usually work in almost total isolation from orthodox scientists. They have few, if any, fruitful contacts with genuine researchers, and are unaware of, or choose to ignore, the traditional canons of science, such as falsifiability and reproducibility. Cranks tend not to send their work to the recognized journals; if they do, it is rejected for what scientists regard as obvious, fundamental flaws. They tend not to be members of scientific academies, organizations, or societies. And they tend not to receive grants or fellowships or awards from scientific organizations. In short, they are not members of the scientific *community.*

Second, cranks have a tendency toward *paranoia*, usually accompanied by *delusions of grandeur* (Gardner, 1957, pp.12–14). I am not using these terms in the clinical or psychiatric sense, but descriptively. That is, they believe they are unjustly persecuted and discriminated against because they are geniuses, because their ideas are so important and revolutionary they would threaten the scientific establishment. Cranks argue that practitioners of entire fields are ignorant blockheads; they are wrong blinded by pig-headed stubbornness and stupidity. Only they themselves, the true visionaries, are able to see the light. Consequently, they have to continue to fight to expose the truth. If the scientific establishment ignores them, that only demonstrates their arguments are unanswerable. If scientists challenge their charges and attempt to answer their arguments, that only shows they are out to destroy them. It is all part of a plot. It never occurs to cranks that this opposition is, in all probability, generated by basic flaws to their work (Gardner, 1957, pp.8ff.). As a consequence, cranks are usually *driven*, compelled to spell out their theories and get them recognized as valid. Like many other paranormalists, they are seized with a messianic zeal (Kossey, 1994, p.56).

The central concept in the field of sociology is the group. In fact, it can be said that sociology is the *study* of group life. Sociologists are very interested in the social "glue" that binds the members of a society—the networks of relations and associations, both formal and informal, that make interaction an ongoing enterprise. It is the shared expectations people have of who we are and what we should be doing, as well as the sanctions we apply to transgressors, that bring most disruptive and destructive behavior under control. In the absence of such communal links, mutual obligations, and shared meanings, social life as we know it would be impossible. It is the sociologist's job to understand exactly how social life operates.

Social isolates choose to live apart—or have been driven—from the bosom of the conventional group and hence, from these social influences. (Although, even before their isolation, all of them have already been influenced by the groups that have shaped them, and will manifest that influence to their dying day.) As a result of this social isolation, sociologists have not paid much attention to cranks.

In my estimation, this is a mistake. Cranks and their theories are worth examining, even by sociologists. In fact, I'll state this even more strongly: sociologists ought to be *especially* interested in cranks. They seem to defy the sociologist's insistence that the group is the measure of all things. In a way, the crank offers an example of the limiting or negative case: someone who pursues a line of action that is not validated by any relevant social groupings. How did the crank come to generate ideas that practically everyone else considers crackpot? Where did these ideas come from in the first place? What motivates the crank? What keeps him (again, they are usually male) at the task of churning out missive after elaborate, detailed missive, spelling out theories or interpretations of reality that only he grasps? Where does the crank fit into the sociologist's relentless pursuit of understanding group dynamics?

All crank theories take scientists to task for the error of their ways, their inability to see what is clearly and plainly in front of their noses. Nearly all deride or demean the existing scientific hierarchy of power, prestige, and influence. All argue that the "crank" creators and proponents are vastly wiser and more intelligent than the scientific establishment. Nearly all assert the wisdom of good common sense and challenge the warping, distorting perspective of encrusted scientific dogma. Many challenge the narrow specialization of practicing scientists and respond with their own broad, sweeping view of things. Most offer a critique of the dehumanizing tendency of science, especially its emphasis on rationality (Kossey, 1994, p.58). It might be said that cranks possess much the same hubris, arrogance, and self-righteous audacity manifested by biblical prophets. They offer a kind of apocalyptic vision of how we ought to view reality and, hence, to re-order our lives, reform our behavior, and transform the society. Cranks are a cultural phenomenon; rather than debunking or dismissing them, we should attempt to understand them.

In a way, then, cranks want it both ways.

On the one hand, they want to *annihilate* the prevailing theories of established science. "Scientists are wrong, I am right; they are ignorant, I am well-informed" seems to be the prevailing position of the crank. The hubris or *arrogance* of the person possessed of superior wisdom and knowledge seems to suffuse the crank's self-presentation.

On the other hand, the crank also lusts to be *accepted* by the scientific fraternity. Otherwise, why do they send established scientists their writings? Cranks deeply and sincerely believe that, through the presentation of their evidence and the sheer power of their argument, they will convince the scientific powers that be that they are right.

What they want is contradictory, of course; it can be said that cranks have a *love-hate* relationship with established science. On the one hand, they do not play by the rules of conventional science. But on the other, they are sufficiently removed from social contact with those who set those rules that they are either unaware of what those rules are or are deluded into thinking that such rules are mere technicalities that can be swept away by the tidal wave of truth. And it is they alone who are possessed of that truth.

Chapter Six

ASTROLOGY AND PSYCHIC POWERS

One major type of paranormal belief system is sustained by the client-practitioner relationship. While a substantial proportion of the population accepts the validity of many occult beliefs, such as astrology, it is the occult professional or *practitioner* who constitutes the foundation of this belief system. The paranormal practitioner engages in occult rituals or activities, or exhibits occult wisdom, that is meant to be marveled at or intended to minister to the needs of his or her clientele.

Mainstream science and medicine reject these methods, just as they reject the theories of cranks. But occult practitioners differ from the crank in at least three ways. First, they do not develop their version of reality in isolation. Rather, they typically draw from an already established and ongoing tradition. Second, they belong to a network of like-minded practitioners, the "cultic milieu" or the "esoteric community" (Jorgensen and Jorgensen, 1982). This informal organization of occult practitioners and their audiences influence, validate, and exert control over one another. Third, the occult practitioner is not a theorist, spinning out ideas about what is happening "out there" in the material world. Rather, he or she is a kind of professional who offers a service to paying customers in a market context. Of course, the practitioner's procedures are *based on* theories of how the world works, but generating novel theories or ideas is not the practitioner's principal goal.

Faith healers, astrologers, psychics, occult performers who hold seances to communicate with the dead, "psychic surgeons," "New Age" consultants, healers who employ alternative medicine, tarot card readers, practitioners of "therapeutic touch," palm readers, advocates of "facilitated communication," "crystal power" and "pyramid power" consultants, and "previous lives" therapists are some examples of paranormal practitioners.

Some of these practitioners perpetrate a conscious fraud on the public in claiming to possess occult powers (Tierney, 1987). But most of them really do believe they have extraordinary psychic powers that are unavailable to the ordinary man and woman or that they are capable of awakening powers that their clients are unaware they possess.

Astrologers and psychics are the two most well-known of the many varieties of paranormal practitioners. Astrology is based on the assumption that the position of the sun, moon, planets, and stars (which are said to have personalities of their own) at the moment of our birth determines or influences our personalities and therefore our fate. There are many different varieties of astrology. The ancient Babylonians, Indians, and Chinese each had their own unique and distinct astrological system. In addition, one astrological tradition ("tropical" astrology) is based on the constellations formed by the stars (which are in an entirely different position from where they were thousands of years ago), while another ("sidereal" or "planetary" astrology) is based on the positions of the sun, the moon, and the planets in relation to the signs of the zodiac. Today the various schools "disagree violently" with one another in chart construction and interpretation (Carlson, 1988, p.293). Some take the effect of "esoteric" or imaginary planets into account, others do not; some ignore planets discovered in the past thousand years, others do not; and so on. Despite the differences, there are core beliefs shared by all astrologers and psychics. This core includes: science does not have all the answers; spiritual forces influence our lives; one can foretell the future with the assistance of occult wisdom; and the heavenly bodies have a great deal to do with our personality and fate.

As we've seen, a substantial proportion of the American public believes in astrology, horoscopes, psychics, and related occult powers. A 1996 survey sponsored by *Newsweek* found that four in ten Americans (41 percent) believe in astrology. A 1996 Gallup poll revealed that 17 percent have consulted a fortune-teller or psychic at least once. Clearly, when we refer to having the beliefs that make consulting an occult practitioner a credible enterprise, we are not discussing a small or marginal segment of the American public, but a substantial minority. The portion of this segment who have acted on those beliefs and paid money for advice or services is also sizable. Carl Sagan claimed there were more professional astrologers in the United States than astronomers.

What makes astrology and psychic predictions paranormal? The vast majority of credentialed scientists argue that the available evidence disconfirms the contentions of astrology (Culver and Ianna, 1984; Kelly, 1979, 1980; Carlson, 1985, 1988) as well as the capacity of psychics to foretell the future (Hines, 1988, pp.21–59; Hyman, 1981, pp.119–141;

Marks and Kammann, 1980). Moreover, as we've seen, a perusal of psychic predictions will demonstrate that most are often so vague as to be all but scientifically meaningless. In addition, when specific, concrete, and falsifiable predictions are made, they typically turn out to be wrong. We'll look at the predictions made by psychics in supermarket tabloids momentarily.

Even in the unlikely possibility that one or another study *were* to present evidence that seemed to confirm astrology or psychic predictions, scientists would *still* argue that these beliefs are invalid. This is because neither psychics nor astrologers are capable of presenting a plausible account of just *how* their principles operate. *Through what specific causal mechanism*, the scientist would ask, does astrology work? Exactly *how* does the psychic foresee the future? If the explanations that are offered do not satisfy a scientist's demand for a materialistic cause-and-effect account, the systems on which they are founded, scientists believe, are fatally flawed.

What *causes* the sun, the moon, the planets, and the stars to influence or determine someone's personality and destiny? they would ask. Is it gravity? The gravitational pull of these bodies on the newborn is negligible, barely measurable. Electromagnetism? No known relationship exists between this barely detectable force at the time of someone's birth and their subsequent human behavior. Is it the supposed correspondence between configurations in the sky that the ancients imagined to resemble animals or humans on the one hand and their presumed qualities and characteristics on the other? Both the qualities and the correspondences are entirely invented, most scientists would say, without a shred of real-world facticity. And what conceivable material force, power, or ability can possibly enable someone see into the future? None has been supplied, and none that can be imagined is scientifically plausible. It is their *theoretical* inadequacy, scientists would say, far more than their empirical failure, that convinces scientists that astrologers and psychics base their systems on paranormal, and therefore false, assumptions.

I've been stressing throughout this book the difference between the reasoning on which science is based and that which underpins the thinking of nearly all believers in astrology and psychic predictions. These two systems of thought make use of entirely different reasoning processes and accept different kinds of evidence as validating their approach. Each has its own epistemology. More specifically, science formulates hypotheses that can be tested systematically, across the board, for conditions that are generalizable. "If X, then Y," is the basis of scientific reasoning. If Y does not take place, there are only three possibilities: the experiment is flawed, there are unaccounted-for forces preventing Y from taking place, or the hypothesis is wrong and must be abandoned.

Scientists charge that paranormal belief systems do not operate in this way. To the paranormalist, what counts is not the number of times when Y does *not* take place, but the number of times when it *does*. For the most part, the advocates of the paranormal ignore or forget the negative cases. For instance, if someone tells us something will happen and it does, we remember it; if it does not happen, we forget about it. We fail to note the total number of times predictions are made, exactly and specifically what would have to happen for them to be verified, and the percentage of times they are validated versus the times when they are falsified. What counts to much of the public is that *sometimes* these predictions seem to be verified; what does *not* count to many of us is that often they are not.

While psychic and astrological readings and predictions are conducted for free, for instance among friends, consultation for pay introduces a qualitatively distinct dimension into the interaction. The paid professional "feels constantly on trial" (Jorgensen and Jorgensen, 1982, p.383). All clients expect expertise of the practitioner, who is more informed and knowledgeable than they are. Skeptics or nonbelievers pose a special problem; since they doubt the legitimacy of the whole enterprise, they must be won over by a display of esoteric wisdom. If the practitioner truly believes in the truth of occult knowledge, this implies an awesome responsibility. Said one tarot card reader: "When you're going into people's lives with the cards you have to be very careful because you can flub them up. . . . It is a powerful thing, and it's a responsibility" (p.383). In short, the reading-for-pay situation "provides the most severe test of expertise" (p.383).

The validation of the practitioner's expertise is extremely crucial in his or her relationship with clients. Any client is likely to ask: What am I getting for my money? What does this expert know that I don't? Will his or her advice be of some practical utility in my life? Why should I believe what he or she says?

PSYCHIC PREDICTIONS

Consider the difficulty of making accurate, specific predictions. The *National Enquirer* hired a team of ten psychics to foretell the events that were to take place during the decade of the 1990s (from the beginning of 1990 to the end of 1999). These psychics were paid to render accurate predictions of things to come during the ten years that lay ahead.

Seen from our contemporary vantage point, these predictions had very close to a zero percent rate of accuracy. In fact, of the nearly three dozen predictions, I could not find even one that turned out to be true.

Here are a few of the predictions made for the *National Enquirer.* During the decade of the 1990s: Oprah Winfrey will marry the next mayor of Washington, D.C., and she will become "queen of the nation's capital." (Actually, the mayor of Washington, D.C. who followed Marion Barry was a woman.) Cancer will be cured "by reprogramming DNA molecules." Turkish shepherds will discover the "wreckage" of Noah's Ark. Massive earthquakes will "devastate" the West Coast, turning San Diego and Los Angeles into islands. Mike Tyson will hold onto his heavyweight title until 1999, the longest in boxing history. (Actually, "Iron Mike" lost his boxing crown in 1990 and sat out a portion of the 1990s in prison for a rape conviction and for violating his parole.) Cuban president Fidel Castro "will be jailed after his cruel government is overthrown in a massive revolt," and he will die in prison five years later. Madonna will take fertility drugs, have quintuplets, and refuse to name the father. (A partial "hit"? She did have an out-of-wedlock child but did name the father.) Liz Taylor will marry millionaire Malcolm Forbes. (Actually, Forbes, a homosexual, died in 1990). Dan Quayle, vice president under George Bush in 1988–1992, will be dropped from Bush's second-term ticket after a "scandalous clinch with a female TV reporter." The "steamy event" will be videotaped (Plamann, 1990).

Professional psychics consistently strike out with such predictions. If their predictions are specific and involve events that either will or will not happen, they turn out to be wrong roughly 99 percent of the time (Wallechensky, Wallace, and Wallace, 1981, p.403; Hines, 1988, pp.44–45). Not only are psychics wrong about events that were *supposed* to have taken place, they also fail to predict the most important events that *do* take place. It can be agreed that predicting specific, concrete events is a very difficult proposition. (Astronomers can predict the movement of planets with mathematical certainty, but meteorologists have to be satisfied with only a 70 or 80 percent accuracy rate when predicting the weather.) Nonetheless, we should think about why the readers of the tabloids continue to take seriously the predictions of professional psychics after their extraordinarily high rate of failure. After all, defense attorneys who lost 99 percent of their cases would not have a successful practice; imagine the reputations of surgeons if 99 percent of their patients died.

It is entirely possible that these predictions are appealing to the readers of supermarket tabloids for reasons in addition to and other than offering an accurate glimpse into the future. (Of course, psychics do place a great deal of emphasis on the accuracy of their predictions, and if one turns out to be valid, they emphasize this fact.) I'd like to suggest two such reasons: the entertainment factor and the validation of a specific worldview.

Whatever else one might say about psychic predictions, the ones that are published in supermarket tabloids are *interesting*. They tell a dramatic story, capture our attention, and cause us to marvel at the wonder of it all. Moreover, an anthropologist would say that folklore, and that would include astrology, is not supposed to be true in the scientific sense. It's *supposed* to tell an interesting, engaging, and revealing story: who we are, why we're here, what's in our future, and so on. Clearly, the scientific and the astrological narratives exist on planes or dimensions that are to some degree independent of one another.

Consider the predictions made in 1998 for 1999 from "a blue-ribbon panel of ten of the world's most gifted psychics" for another tabloid, the *Sun* (published on December 1, 1998). A massive earthquake causes such extensive damage to Los Angeles the city is abandoned for two years. For 30 minutes, the Virgin Mary appears before the House of Representatives, tearfully begging the assemblage to work for world peace. In January, a 100-ton meteor strikes a Scottish nuclear power plant, spreading deadly radiation as far away as the United States. First Lady Hillary Clinton announces that she will run for the presidency in 2000, with Oprah Winfrey as her vice-presidential candidate. In May, a star appears in the sky over Bethlehem; this "will signal the rebirth of Christ and the salvation of all mankind."

It is easy to appreciate the excitement such events would stir up *if* they were to take place; to readers who anticipate or even contemplate them, reading that they might happen is *almost* as exciting as their actual occurrence. (And by the time they are revealed as invalid, nearly everyone who read them the previous year will have forgotten what they were, and a new round of predictions will be made for the *next* year.) The similarity of these predictions to the plots of popular films and made-for-TV movies is striking and obvious. Setting aside their confidence in visions that grip them, certainly the psychics who predict events such as these must know that they are extremely unlikely, if not outright impossible. At the very least, the editors and publishers who include such predictions in the pages of their tabloids know that they will probably not happen in the year or years to come. But no one can doubt that reading them is an entertaining endeavor.

Remarkably enough, while psychics and other paranormalists think of themselves as rebels struggling against the dominant secular trend in contemporary society, their predictions also display a thoroughgoing *conventionality*. The tabloids that publish these predictions overwhelmingly "support the status quo" (Hogshire, 1997, p.49).

These tabloids oppose leftwing regimes; hence we find the prediction of the overthrow of Fidel Castro and his death in prison. They support the sanctity of the nuclear family; hence the prediction of Quayle's embarrassing comeuppance resulting from his (predicted) infidelity with a reporter. Hillary Clinton became extremely popular with the public following her husband's infidelities; hence the prediction of her run for the presidency. In the tabloids, the line between religious and more conventional paranormalism is blurred; hence the predictions of the discovery of Noah's Ark, the second coming of Jesus, and the visitation by the Virgin Mary at the House of Representatives. Tabloids devote a great deal of attention to curing diseases and make little or no distinction between legitimate medical discoveries, quack or folk remedies, and outright miracles; hence the predictions of the cure for cancer and Madonna's use of a fertility drug to have children. (Perhaps having quintuplets symbolizes Madonna's multiple sexual partners or represents a punishment for her promiscuity.) Not naming the father indicates that, however unconventional she may seem, she's supposedly ashamed of the illegitimate birth of her child. The tabloids' fixation on celebrities in many of these predictions, likewise, shows that our conventional notions of fame and notoriety are legitimate.

All in all, the "subtext" (or hidden message) of these predictions is to affirm and uphold traditional, mainstream values and to avoid seriously challenging the existing hierarchies of power. While the scientist's view of reality and causality is often challenged, science is nonetheless accorded enormous respect and influence. Tabloid articles often note, for instance, that a certain event or phenomenon "amazed" or "baffled" experts, scientists, and physicians. The conventionality of psychic predictions makes them acceptable to much of the public, renders them plausible, makes it seem as if they are the sort of events that *could* take place in the future.

THE FORER EFFECT

Many psychic and astrological character assessments are so broad and vague that it is difficult to disprove or falsify them. Psychologist Bertram Forer became so incensed after witnessing a psychic's performance that he went home and devised an experiment based on the astrological charts he found in his daily newspaper. He summarized his findings as: people tend to regard broad, vague characteristics, those that fit practically everybody, as distinctive to themselves (Forer, 1949). Other psychologists have also devised experiments to determine the influence of the Forer effect. Here is a personality assessment that another psychologist, Richard Kammann, gave to his students:

> You have a need for other people to like and admire you, and yet you tend to be critical of yourself. While you have some personality weaknesses you are generally able to compensate for them. You have considerable unused capacity that you have not turned to your advantage. Disciplined and controlled on the outside, you tend to be worrisome and insecure on the inside. At times, you have serious doubts as to whether you have made the right decision or done the right thing. You prefer a certain amount of change and variety and become dissatisfied when hemmed in by restrictions and limitations. You also pride yourself as an independent thinker and do not accept others' statements without satisfactory proof. But you have found it unwise to be too frank in revealing yourself to others. At times you are extroverted, affable, and sociable, while at other times you are introverted, wary, and reserved. Some of your aspirations tend to be rather unrealistic.

Close to 90 percent of Kammann's students said this rating was either "excellent" or "good" in fitting their own personality (Marks and Kammann, 1980, p.188). Other psychologists around the world have found the same thing. One received some of the following statements from students reading the assessment and applying it to themselves: "agree with all your statements"; "all true without a doubt"; "I believe this interpretation applies to me individually, as there are too many facets which fit me too well to be a generalization"; "surprisingly accurate and specific in detail"; and so on (p.189). Does Kammann's personality assessment fit you? Of course it does. But is it distinctive and unique to yourself? No. Would you consider it remarkable if a psychic summed up your personality with it? You shouldn't, since this assessment is so vague that it fits practically everyone. The vaguer, broader, and "mushier" a statement is, the less capable it is of being falsified.

Horoscope predictions, likewise, are filled with vague, nonfalsifiable claims that have no meaning in science but often resonate with believers. "You could meet a stranger who will possibly turn your life in a new direction." In other words, maybe it will happen and maybe it won't. And how should we measure or specify a "new direction"? "Happiness is just around the corner." Well, all of us experience some happiness as well as some sadness during different moments in our lives. This statement would be false for very, very few people we're likely to know. "A stranger may pay you a compliment and give you some advice." Even if we ignore the "may," again, what do we take as disconfirming evidence of this prediction? How long should we wait for this to happen? And what constitutes a "compliment"? "Advice"? It's not clear. "A phone call about money is possible." Considering how often money figures in our conversations, this prediction is hardly startling. Notice, it is "possible," not certain. (These predictions are taken from the June 16, 1998 issue of the *Weekly World News*, p.43.)

This is not to say that psychics, astrologers, and horoscopes do not make specific, concrete predictions that can be falsified. They do, as we saw. While scientists would look for general patterns that apply across the board, believers search out one or two ways to validate a psychic or astrological prediction and forget about those that do not pan out. Although there are exceptions, for the most part the typical paranormal prediction is unlikely to be formulated in such a way that evidence can ever overturn it.

To the believer in astrology, the nonfalsifiability of these assessments and predictions is not a problem; to most believers, the very notion of falsifiability is not likely to be relevant. The stringent criteria of scientific predictability are outside the astrologer's scope of thinking. In fact, they are likely to be regarded as meddlesome, technical, rigid, and nit-picking—in a word, irrelevant. What counts is the "feel" of a prediction or an assessment. To a scientist, the fact that astrological assessments and predictions cannot be falsified is a fatal flaw, dooming it to scientific meaninglessness. Once again, these two ways of thinking about how the world works are mutually incomprehensible, incommensurable. They exist in separate and incompatible spheres.

ASTROLOGICAL READINGS

Like psychics, astrologers face a serious problem of legitimacy and credibility. In order to be believed, they must formulate their prognostications in such a way that they correspond with what their clients both want to hear and find remarkable. In other words, there is a "recipe" for a successful reading, and astrologers are successful to the extent that they follow that recipe. In a way, then, the scientific status of astrology is irrelevant to the faith clients place in its efficacy. When clients state that astrology "works," what they really mean is that it "feels right," and feeling right is based on personal meaning, not empirical validity (Hyman, 1977, p.19).

In principle, there are two sets of factors that make an astrological reading or interpretation "feel right." The first set is related to what the professional *does* and the second is related to what the client or audience *expects* or *believes*. In reality, these two dovetail with one another. The professional gives the client what he or she expects.

Psychologist Ray Hyman (1977) examined the techniques of "cold" readings conducted by astrologers and psychics. A cold reading is one in which the professional conducts a psychic assessment of someone he or she has never met before. There are four basic principles that guide the cold reading.

First is the use of the "stock spiel," a statement of the standard character assessment that fits nearly everyone, but which clients feel applies to them uniquely. After the practitioner presents the generic, boilerplate stock spiel, many clients are astounded at the accuracy with which their special and unique characteristics have been described. "How could she know that?" they ask. "He must have psychic powers to know so much about me." A client's willingness to accept a generic character sketch as a description of himself or herself specifically and uniquely is referred to as the fallacy of personal validation.

The second cold reading principle is the idea that most people are motivated by the same forces and factors to seek consultation. Birth, health and illness, death, love, marriage, loved ones, and money usually generate most of the problems for which we want an answer. In other words, there is a "common denominator" in all clients (p.21).

The third principle is that certain clues may be found in the client's appearance or remarks that provide evidence on which to base a psychic assessment. Some of these clues include age, inferred social class, weight, posture, manner of speech, eye contact, and so on. In other words, the client is sized up with respect to the statistical or actuarial likelihood that certain problems will be of concern to him or her.

The fourth principle is that through skillfully designed probing questions, "tentative hypotheses" may be formulated and tested, based on the client's answers. Reactions (eye movement, body language, tone of voice) will supply information to the professional that the client is unaware he or she is supplying. Clients walk away from a consultation without being aware that everything the reader told them was what they themselves said, in one way or another, to the reader (p.22).

Three concluding points are in order here. One, the practitioner need not be dishonest in making use of one or more of the reasoning processes outlined here. They may not even be aware that they are using standard gimmicks to convince the client of their powers. If they are aware of using generic devices, they usually think of them as setting the stage or putting the client in the right frame of mind so that they can use their occult powers appropriately.

Two, the success of these techniques does not mean that the client is gullible. It is not easy to convince paying customers that one has supernatural powers. One needs sensitivity and intelligence to pull it off. By being a functioning and sensitive member of the general society, one learns to make use of cultural understandings. The inferences we draw about statements others make form the basis of human communication. We learn to make sense out of what others say by "filling in the gaps" and drawing conclusions that are usually right (Hyman, 1977, pp.32–33). Assuming that someone knows a great deal about us because he or she makes statements that we feel are accurate is not gullible, it is commonsensical.

The fact that most of the statements made by paranormal professionals can be understood largely as a product of standard tricks of the trade does *not* demonstrate the falsity of paranormal powers. Even if some aspects of the practitioner's performance is gimmickry, it is possible that other aspects are based on genuine supernormal powers.

Sociologically, the validity of paranormal claims is secondary. Social scientists are interested in the *enterprise* of paranormalism and that enterprise makes extensive use of techniques and reasoning processes that resonate or correspond with what the client believes to be true. As such, they are sociological or cultural products. Their origin, validation, and dynamics can be understood through social forces such as socialization, interaction, stratification, hierarchy, deviance, conformity, and persuasion.

Chapter Seven

CREATIONISM

"In the beginning God created the heaven and the earth." So intones chapter 1 of the Book of Genesis of the Hebrew Bible. According to this account, God, the divine creator, brought forth, out of nothing, light, water, dry land, grass, fruit trees, seasons, years, aquatic life, birds, cattle, creeping creatures, and other beasts of the earth, and "man" ("in our image, after our likeness"), both male and female. This narrative states that these events took place over a period of six days; on the seventh day, God rested. Chapter 2, verse 7 of Genesis backtracks a bit and states that God formed man out of the "dust of the ground." In verses 21 and 22, God caused Adam, the first man, to fall into a "deep sleep"; He took a rib out of Adam's side, closed up his flesh, and out of it "made he a woman," presenting her to the first man. There is no mention in these verses of the fact that both "male and female" humans (generically, "man") had already been created in the previous chapter, before God took His rest.

By chapter 6 of Genesis, God began to see wickedness in the descendants of Adam. Hence, He resolved to destroy humans and all the animals living on dry land. Noah, an exceptional and virtuous man, was commanded by God to build a giant ship or ark so that he himself, his family, and two of every kind of being on earth could be saved. Noah built the ark and called all these creatures onto it, two by two. God caused it to rain for 40 days and 40 nights; water covered even "all the high hills." The earth was submerged for 150 days, and all other humans and fleshly creatures on the face of the earth perished. Only Noah, his small band consisting of his wife, three sons and their wives, as well as the creatures who were put on board, survived. After 150 days, God created a wind to pass over the earth, causing the waters to become "abated." The ark came to a rest on the "mountains of Ararat" and Noah and his brood descended onto dry land; they then repopulated the earth. Noah, who was 600 years old at the time, lived another 350 years and had countless descendants, in fact—in principle—every human being on earth.

Christian fundamentalism and Jewish orthodoxy maintain that every word of this account is literally and concretely true; this belief represents faith in the *inerrancy* of the Bible. *Biblical creationism* (or "strict" creationism) rests on the literal truth of the Genesis account of, first, the creation of the universe, the earth, and all living beings on earth by God out of nothing in six days, and second, the worldwide Noachian flood, the destruction of nearly all humans and land animals by this flood, and the survival of the passengers on the ark.

It should be emphasized that creationism is not made up of a completely homogeneous belief system. There are in fact several varieties of creationism.

To begin with, there is the matter of the passage of time. Biblical scholars have added up the life spans and the generational sequences of the characters mentioned in the Bible and have tabulated that the event of creation would have to have taken place roughly 6,000 to 10,000 years ago. Bishop James Ussher, Irish prelate (1581–1656), was even more precise; he calculated that the creation took place at precisely 4 P.M., Sunday, December 23, 4004 B.C. Hence, to take the Bible as literally and concretely true is to believe that the earth is less than 10,000 years old. "Young earth" creationists are literalists and believe that the Bible referred to actual, 24-hour earthly days, exactly as we know them today. In contrast, "old earth" creationists believe that the "days" mentioned in the Bible are figurative and refer to indefinite but very long periods of time, each "day" representing entire geological epochs. Old earth creationists merge into "gap" creationists, who believe that there was a huge period of time between Verse 1 and Verse 2 of Genesis. The line of thinking in old earth and gap creationists allows billions of years for geological formations, a rich fossil record, and the destruction of many forms of life long before Adam and Noah. What binds all varieties of strict creationism together is that their proponents reject evolution, especially human evolution. Strict creationists would not regard Christians (and Jews) who accept the scientific view that God created the universe 10 to 15 billion years ago, then, billions of years later, breathed life into primordial ooze, and "guided" the process of evolution to produce humans, as creationists at all.

In addition, there is a group of authors who refer to themselves as "scientific" creationists. They claim that their account of the origin of the universe is not based on religion at all but is derived exclusively from the scientific record, that is, data and observation. Evolutionist Philip

Kitcher argues that they "masquerade religious doctrines as scientific explanations" (1982, p.6). But its proponents claim that the fact that the account of scientific creationists is identical to the account that appears in Genesis should be regarded as incidental and of no consequence. It is possible that no one believes this claim, that it was made only to skirt the principle of the separation of church and state.

Recently, a small and possibly growing band of perhaps two dozen "neo-creationists" have begun conducting what they regard as empirical research on creationist assertions. For instance, John Woodmorappe's *Noah's Ark: A Feasibility Study*, calculates matters such as how all the animals were assembled in the necessary time, the "biomass" of all of the ark's animals ("kinds" rather than genuses or species), what food they would need to eat to survive, and how the ark was lighted—perhaps fireflies, the author suggests. Three chapters are devoted to the removal of the 12 tons of animal waste that would have to have accumulated each and every day (Hitt, 1996). Most evolutionists are not likely to regard this work as a major challenge to their position.

Conventional scientists do not regard the vast majority of "scientific" creationists as scientists at all. Creation scientists very, very rarely hold a Ph.D. in the relevant area—that is, in geology, biology, genetics, biochemistry, or astrophysics. (A number of them are engineers.) One major exception: Kurt Wise, director of the "Origins Research Department" at William Jennings Bryan College, a fundamentalist Christian institution of higher learning. Wise graduated from the University of Chicago with a degree in geology, attended graduate school, where he studied paleontology, was a research assistant of Stephen Jay Gould, the most famous of all evolutionists, and received a Ph.D. from Harvard. "Most creation science is garbage," says Wise (Hitt, 1996, p.57); his intention is to change that. As a general rule, however, most scientific creationists do not engage in science so much as poke holes in the research findings of evolutionists. But as with all other generalizations, there are exceptions, and they are made up of a small group of "neo-creationists," who, along with Wise, conduct investigations of "real-world" phenomena that pertain to creationist matters. Nonetheless, the theory that creationists offer explaining the origin of the universe (that is, divine creation) has nothing to do with science; indeed, it specifically denies most of science's central tenets.

In point of fact, scientific creationism is an oxymoron, a contradiction in terms. This is not because their critiques of evolution are not sufficiently scientific (they may or may not be; that is a separate issue). It is because the explanation scientific creationists put in place of evolution is distinctly non-scientific, in fact, *paranormal* in nature. (Or, if it does not rely on paranormal forces, it is of necessity nonfalsifiable.) If it is true that God created the universe out of nothing, this event corresponds to no known scientific law. It has no natural, material, or scientific basis; it is outside the boundary of known laws of physics, chemistry, and biology. Scientific creationists do not offer a mechanism or causal sequence of the creation that would satisfy any scientist, *given the laws of science*. Science is not merely observation, but the linkage of observation with theory, or explanation. There is no such linkage with scientific creationism (indeed, no observation of any kind). Hence, the discomfort most scientists feel when encountering the term.

In contrast to scientific creationists, most grass roots biblical creationists do not feel it necessary to resort to scientific or empirical data for them to know that the Genesis account is true; with them, it is a matter of faith, not scientific fact. If scientists were to present evidence that contradicts their belief, they would simply dismiss or ignore the evidence. In contrast, if scientific creationists were to be presented with such evidence, they would actively attempt to debunk or disprove it.

Another important issue that needs to be addressed is that the Catholic Church has come to terms with evolution. Over the years, a number of papal encyclicals have been issued by the Vatican that argue that Christian faith and belief in evolution can be reconciled; that is one can be a good Catholic and an evolutionist at the same time. In fact, along with Catholicism, the mainstream, ecumenical Protestant denominations have accepted or endorsed evolution as a factual account of the origin of species. The charge many creationists make that one cannot be a good Christian and an evolutionist simultaneously must be read in view of this fact. In addition, among the Jewish denominations, Reform and Conservative Judaism have accepted evolution; only orthodoxy rejects it.

Let's be clear on one major point: most Christians believe in deistic or godly creation, that is, that the universe and life itself were created or inspired by the hand of God. In that sense, most Christians are technically "creationists." But most secular, ecumenical, denominational Christians are not *strict*, *biblical*, or *literal* creationists. That is, they do *not* believe that the universe is less than 10,000 years old, and they *do* believe that humans evolved from earlier, less complex life forms. Biblical fundamentalists have coopted the term "creationists" for themselves, ignoring the fact that most secular Christians do not share all or even most of their views, but nonetheless do believe that God created the material world out of nothing. In other words, strict creationists reserve the term "creationist" for themselves alone.

SCIENTISTS TAKE ISSUE WITH GENESIS AS A FACTUAL ACCOUNT

Nearly all biologists, geologists, biochemists, and astrophysicists believe that the story of the creation, as narrated in the Bible, is factually incorrect. (There are a very few practicing scientists who are creationists, but their numbers are very small.) Advanced training in one of these fields is possible if their specialty does not directly confront issues of geological time. For instance, some creationists have advanced degrees in hydraulics. The vast majority of natural scientists believe that the biblical account of the origin of the universe, the earth, creatures on earth, and humanity, contradicts the available evidence and the laws of science; that is, given what we know about how nature works, it virtually *cannot* be true. Given our definition, creationism is a paranormal theory. The scientific version of the origin of the universe and its components differs from that of creationism in a number of particulars.

First, as to God creating the universe *ex nihilo*, or "out of nothing," a substantial proportion of scientists argue that the universe came into being with the "big bang" nearly 15 billion years ago. (What existed before and how the "big bang" occurred and generated matter—presumably, also out of nothing—is far from clear.) Clouds of hydrogen and helium, expanding outward, began to coalesce into galaxies; this process took billions of years. Solid structures such as planets formed billions of years later and, even in its simplest and most primitive form, life followed the appearance of planets by another several billion years. Therefore, scientists would argue that the *simultaneous* appearance of all constituents of the universe, created out of nothing, is so improbable as to be all but impossible. In reality, they say, these constituents appeared *in sequence* because the later ones grew out of the earlier ones. Thus, clouds of gasses underwent gravitational collapse and became stars and, eventually, planets; it is only on planets with a nearby star that life could develop; and so on. The "void," the earth, light, water, the heavens, life on earth, and so on, cannot have first appeared in the same six-day period, because some of these constituents had to develop out of others in order to come into being, and in the requisite sequence.

Second, as to age, most scientists accept the fact that the universe is extremely old. As we saw, they say the universe had its origin about 15 *billion* years ago. The earth itself is between four and five billion years old, and life began on earth as microscopic, single-celled creatures between three and four billion years ago. Hence, a literal reading of the biblical account, which places the creation of the universe at not much more than 6,000 years ago, is of necessity false. *Every* empirically plausible method of dating physical matter, from stratigraphy and radiocarbon to obsidian hydration and potassium argon, yields dates that are *a million times older* than the date at which we arrive by using the Bible as a literal historical record of the passage of time. There is *no* known plausible dating method, scientists argue, that gives us an age of the universe that is even remotely close to less than 10,000 years.

For instance, astronomers tell us that the light from stars far outside our solar system takes light years to reach us. They are so far away that we are seeing the light they cast millions, even billions, of years ago. Hence, the universe *cannot* be just a few thousand years old, since we are seeing the historical record of light from long, long ago. Of course, old earth and gap creationists accept the antiquity of the universe and for them, this is not a problem. In addition, many new earth creationists argue that God created events *in process* and, hence, it is not necessary to posit the universe as very old. For instance, He created light from distant stars *already on its way* to earth, geological formations that *appear* to be billions of years old, and so on. Most scientists regard this reasoning as fanciful.

Third, as to the process of evolution, the overwhelming majority of scientists believe that all species on earth cannot have appeared during the same six-day period. Instead, they say, every species evolved over extremely long periods of time, again, in sequence, from simple forms of life that emerged out of primordial ooze to vastly more complex creatures with skeletons, muscles, and a nervous system, including a brain. The more complex species on earth are all descendants of earlier, simpler forms of life, evolutionists say. All species, including humans, owe their very existence to genetic variation from one organism to another, to the selective adaptation of certain traits, and to the fact that creatures that are adapted to their environments produce more offspring than those that are not. Remarkably, the protein composition and the DNA sequences in all creatures on earth mirrors their anatomical and evolutionary relationships almost perfectly. Genetics demonstrates the relationships between and among organisms, scientists say, and provides an irrefutable independent validation of the evolutionary process; in other words, biochemistry verifies evolution; in fact, the two fit into one another like pieces of a jigsaw puzzle. Creationists cannot explain the extremely close correspondence between biochemistry and evolution.

The fourth feature of the Genesis account that scientists have a problem with is the Noachian flood. The first objection is that the biblical story is not even original. A very similar tale was narrated in the Babylonian *Gilgamesh* epic, which appeared a thousand years before the Hebrew version. If the Bible is "the word of God," then what were earlier versions? If the Bible validates the tenets of the Judeo-Christian tradition, then what do earlier, nearly identical tales from a religion that perished long ago validate?

Another aspect that strains credulity for evolutionists is to imagine that the million or so animal species, including the polar bear, the three-toed sloth, and the duck-billed platypus, could have been gathered together from the ends of the earth in the requisite period of time. (Some creationists argue that it was genuses or even, vaguely, "kinds," not species, that were called to the ark, but that contradicts their argument that new species cannot arise through the evolutionary process.) By what mechanism did they get to the Middle East? How long did it take? How did they survive for so long outside their natural habitat?

Even if that objection is overcome, how could a vessel have been built that was sufficiently commodious to hold all species of animals? It would have to have been vastly larger than any known vessel of ancient times. Thousands of years before the principles of navigation were devised and systematized, how could a sufficiently seaworthy vessel have been built to hold all these creatures?

Many biologists also wonder how these animals were kept alive for the necessary period of time. (And how did Noah know about the eating habits of exotic, unfamiliar, far-flung species?) In addition, once they were released, how was it possible for only two of each species to be sufficient in number to repopulate their kind? (Once the numbers of a given species fall below a few dozen, biologists consider extinction almost certain.) And how was it—unlike what actually happens in nature—that all pairs of animals turn out to be fertile? It simply isn't very likely, say biological ecologists.

Another fact to consider, scientists say, is that the fossil record does not remotely correspond to what supposedly happened in the Noachian flood. Fossils are arranged in strata in the ground in a way that corresponds with an evolutionary process that stretched over millions of years. The only exceptions can be explained as a result of unusual geological processes, for instance when earthquakes or other disturbances of the earth, such as the twisting and flopping of geological plates, jumble up the evolutionary fossil sequence.

Finally, scientists say, the claim about Noah's age has no other known equivalent; no human whose age has been reliably recorded has lived much beyond 120 years. Even setting aside this issue, there remains the question of Noah's descendants. For the biblical account to be literally true, all humans on earth would have to have been descended from Noah and his wife. What generated the substantial racial diversity among humans we now observe? This cannot have taken place in the short span of a few thousand years. How were the ends of the earth repopulated in such a brief span of time? And if Noah is the patriarch of all humans on earth, this should be reflected in our DNA chemistry. Why hasn't any creationist proposed a falsifiable, empirical test of this proposition?

In short, most scientists regard the account of the Noachian flood as extremely implausible—a parable or legend rather than literal fact. Once again, the opposition of scientists to the biblical narrative as a record of literally factual events does not mean that it is wrong. Whether the scientists or the creationists are right is a separate matter. But the rejection of Genesis as concrete reality by scientists *is* a fact. It can be verified by the writings of scientists, by inspecting polls and surveys, by interviewing the representatives of science departments in colleges and universities around the country, and so on. It would be self-defeating to attempt to cite a few scientists who disagree or to advance the claim that a majority of scientists really can be located who support the Genesis account. Among scientists, majority rule holds that the biblical account of the creation is wrong. Better to claim that the scientists are wrong than to argue that there are plenty of scientists who believe otherwise.

ARE ALL EVOLUTIONISTS ATHEISTS? WHAT DO THE POLLS SAY?

Most committed creationists believe that evolutionists are not only atheists but secular humanists who, supposedly, seek to replace society's religious foundation with relativism, socialism, communism, pornography, homosexuality, women's liberation, sex education, drugs, crime, abortion, and rock music (Toumey, 1994, p.96). However, the fact is, the vast majority of supporters of evolution are theists who believe that God actually played an active role in the evolutionary process. In 1997, the Gallup organization conducted a survey on the American public's beliefs on evolution. The question the Gallup poll asked read: "Which of the following statements comes closest to your views on the origin and development of human beings—human beings have developed over millions of years from less advanced forms of life, but God guided this process, or human beings have developed over millions of years from less advanced forms of life, but God had no part in this process, or God created human beings pretty much in their present form at one time within the last 10,000 years or so?"

In this survey, 44 percent of the respondents are strict creationists; that is, they agree with the statement that God created human beings in their present form in the past 10,000 years. (Old age and gap creationists would not have agreed with all the particulars of this statement, but their numbers are minuscule.) The respondents in this category hold beliefs that correspond very closely to the most important particulars of creationism.

Only 10 percent of the respondents are "secular" evolutionists; that is, not only do they believe in the fact of evolution and the fact that it stretched out over millions of years, but also that "God had no part in this process." These respondents believe that the process took place as a result of material, not spiritual processes. Not all the respondents in this category would declare that they are atheists, but many would.

Not quite four respondents in ten (39 percent) say that they believe in human evolution, but that "God guided this process." This could have happened, for instance, by God breathing life into the primordial ooze that became the first living entities on earth. Rather than evolution being a blind, random process it could have been influenced by God to ensure that humans would eventually emerge from it. The important point is that four out of five evolutionists (that is, 39 percent out of the total of 49 percent in this survey) are *theists*; they not only believe in God but also believe that God guided evolution. (In a sense, these respondents are evolutionists *and* creationists: they accept the validity of evolution, but believe that God "created" the universe, including human life. But they are not *strict* creationists.) Only one out of five who believe in evolution (10 percent out of the total) figure God had "nothing to do" with the process. Thus, the creationist's characterization of evolutionists as atheists is clearly wrong. In fact, among persons who believe in evolution, the vast majority also believe in the existence of God.

Do Scientists Believe in God?

Among scientists belief in God is substantially below that for the population as a whole. In the United States, believing in God is nearly universal in the general public. In poll after poll, year after year, between 90 and 95 of all Americans believe in a personal God. The same is not true of scientists. In 1916, James Leuba surveyed a randomly selected sample of 1,000 scientists and found that just over four in ten (42 percent) said that they believe in God. The remainder were either atheists (42 percent) or agnostics (17 percent). Leuba predicted that, as higher education became more widely available, disbelief would grow (1916).

Leuba's study was replicated seven decades later. The sample, as was Leuba's, was a random selection of 1,000 of the names listed in the

1995 edition of *American Men and Women of Science*. Half of the sample were biologists; almost certainly, nearly all of them are evolutionists. A quarter were mathematicians, and a quarter were either astronomers or physicists. The figures on belief and disbelief in God for 1996 were almost identical to those of 1916. Again, roughly four scientists in ten (39 percent) said that they had a personal belief in God, a slightly higher figure (45 percent) professed atheism, and about one in seven (15 percent) proclaimed themselves agnostics.

It is unlikely that the creationist will take much comfort in these figures. In fact, they are more likely to confirm the creationist's view that, although *all* evolutionists may not be atheists, evolutionists are *highly likely* to doubt or disbelieve in God. It is almost certain that *most*, although far from all, atheists are also evolutionists. There are exceptions, of course, as there are to any rule. In fact, some "scientist-theologians" believe that evolution "provides clues to the very nature of God" (Begley, 1998, p.48).

EPISTEMOLOGY

A central theme of this book is that each perspective or belief system holds to its own distinctive epistemology or "way of knowing." What is creationism's special way of knowing? How do creationists verify or validate their worldview? More specifically, how do they decide, contrary to the scientific consensus, that evolution is invalid, did not take place, and is a false way of reading the empirical record? Creationists and evolutionists differ on at least four points of epistemology.

Direct observation. Creationists adopt what scientists refer to as a naive, "one-eyed," or *Baconian* epistemology. Francis Bacon (1561–1626), an English philosopher of science, argued in favor of direct observation, neglecting the fact that many observations—as in geology, archaeology, psychology, and sociology—must be indirect or inferential. As it turns out, the way of thinking about the world shared by Bacon and the creationists also agrees with the commonsensical or "folk" epistemology of the man and woman on the street. This is the view that something is the total "reliance on sensory impressions" (Eve and Harrold, 1991, p.62). Science, this line of reasoning goes, deals with demonstrable, concrete facts, events that can be observed simply, directly, in a straightforward fashion, with one's five senses. Since the evolutionary process cannot be observed directly, it cannot be verified and hence, is not scientific. Therefore, evolutionary theory is little more than mere speculation. Or so the creationist (or "Baconian") line of reasoning goes. The fact that divine creation cannot be observed either is not a contradiction for the creationist, since the word of God, the *Bible*, can be observed. Or so the creationist's argument goes.

The creationist's demand for observable data might seem similar to the scientist's rule of empiricism, but this is not the case at all. As we saw, all scientists realize that many events cannot be observed directly and must be inferred with the use of indicators, measures, or other indirect evidence. In many ways, direct observation may be misleading. As we've seen, our senses tell us a rock is solid, but atomic physics has determined it is mostly empty space; the earth is more or less flat, but geology informs us it is more or less round; the earth is stationary and the sun moves across the sky, but astronomers have shown us it is the earth that moves around the sun. The fact is, science says direct sensory data alone "are not sufficient" (p.62). In fact, in these cases, sensory data yield observations that are completely incorrect.

The material versus the spiritual. Scientists argue there is a vast territory of questions that cannot be answered with any conceivable evidence. Certain issues or questions "surpass experience," that is, they are outside the realm of the material; they are non-empirical in nature.

For instance, no amount of scientific evidence, most scientists would argue, can answer the question of whether a fetus is a full-fledged human being or whether abortion is murder; these are spiritual or theological, not scientific, questions. The supernatural dimension, including questions of the existence or the will of God, is beyond the reach of any and all conceivable empirical verification. Science cannot verify (or refute) spiritual claims (Eve and Harrold, 1991 p.63) unless they manifest themselves directly and concretely in the material realm. It is improper to argue that "humanity originated as part of God's plan or that oxygen and hydrogen combine to make water because God wills it" (p.63). Scientists examine causes and effects in the material world. Hence, these conjectures about teleology or the will of God are neither right nor wrong, but completely outside the scope of science. Given the tools of science, they cannot even be addressed, let alone settled.

Fundamentalist Christians, creationists all, would disagree. They would argue that it is self-evident that the fetus is a full-fledged human being and that abortion is therefore murder. They would see the scientist's argument that such a question cannot be answered with the empirical tools of science as a cop-out, a justification for the slaughter of millions of innocent babies. They would argue that the *spiritual righteousness* of their position demands that fetuses be regarded as human beings. Randall Terry, leader of "Operation Rescue," an anti-abortion social movement, cites Proverbs in support of his position:

"Rescue those who are unjustly sentenced to death; don't stand back and let them die" (1988).

Fact versus method. The fundamentalist Christian claims to know things for certain. For the creationist, science is a search for "known truths," for "facts, demonstrated facts" (Morris, 1984, p.24).To the mainstream scientist, science is a *method*, not a collection of facts, a means of ascertaining that which has a high probability of being true, not asserting by edict that which is believed to be true. Scientists argue that the way to do science is to propose a hypothesis generated by a theory, suggest a means by which this hypothesis can be tested, and determine with the use of systematic, empirical evidence whether the hypothesis stands up to the test. Facts should grow out of the proper application of the scientific method. It is the scientific method that counts, not the emphatic assertion of a supposedly true "fact."

In principle, as we saw, all scientific hypotheses and theories must be falsifiable. If a hypothesis is not falsifiable, it is not scientific. If I am right, scientists say, this is how the data must fall; if I am wrong, they must fall in another way. For instance, evolution is a falsifiable theory, biologists argue. Micro-changes in organisms can be observed as adaptations to the environments in which they live; if these changes did not occur, evolutionary theory could be challenged. Genetic biochemistry mirrors the proposed evolutionary sequence; if it did not, evolution could be challenged. Every available method of dating yields ages of life on earth that are consistent with evolutionary theory; if they did not, evolution could be challenged. In contrast, the evolutionist argues, the creationist account is not falsifiable because every conceivable discrepancy between the empirical record and the biblical narrative is explained away by an appeal to the authority of literalism. Creationists do not propose a way of falsifying the validity of the Genesis account of creation because they assume it to be true in the first place. Hence, scientists say, evolutionary theory is scientific, while "creation science" is not.

In effect, creationists do away with the principle of falsifiability. Ask a creationist, "What manner of evidence would falsify the literal truth of the Biblical account of creation in Genesis?" The answer is likely to be that *no conceivable data* will falsify Genesis. It is the *Bible* that falsifies the geological record, they argue, instead of the other way around. Says Henry Morris, a leading scientific creationist: "No geological difficulties, real or imagined, can be allowed to take precedence over the clear statements and necessary inferences of Scripture" (1970, p.33). In other words, God has recorded it; hence, it is God's word. Therefore, it must be true, so anything that contradicts it, including empirical evidence, is false. To the traditional scientist, this statement demonstrates that the term scientific creationism is a contradiction in terms, since no principle (short of suspicion of flawed research or the intervention of as-yet unknown forces) takes precedence over the principle of falsifiability. If there is no possible way a claim about events of the material world can be demonstrated to be false, that claim *must* be scientifically meaningless.

One last point about scientific method versus the simple declaration of an assertion to be true: creation scientists often refer to the biblical account of creation as "special" creation. This means that the principles that operated at the moment of the creation of the universe were distinctive and unique. It is pointless to argue that they cannot be replicated today because God may not choose to act in that way today. Hence, any evidence brought to bear on whether the creation was scientifically all but impossible is meaningless. Says Duane Gish, a leading scientific creationist: "We do not know how the Creator created, what processes He used, *for He used processes which are not now operating anywhere in the natural universe.* . . . We cannot discover by scientific investigation anything about the creative processes used by the Creator" (1978, p.42). This argument violates *uniformitarianism*, the view that scientific principles apply to all places at all times. Mainstream scientists see the claim to "special" creation as a cop-out, a virtual admission that creationism cannot be a science; they find it impossible to support the view that certain principles operated at one time and then stopped. There is no way of disproving such a claim; hence it has no validity as science, or so scientists argue.

CREATIONISTS: A SOCIOLOGICAL PORTRAIT

As we've seen, many public opinion polls have been conducted on the beliefs of the general public. Many of these have included questions on creationism. The public is more or less evenly split between creationism and evolution: about 45 percent of the American population, give or take a few percentage points, are strict creationists; that is, they believe in the literal truth of the account in Genesis. About the same percentage is made up of evolutionists. Some evolutionists believe that the process of evolution was aided by God ("divine" evolutionists) while others feel that God had nothing to do with it ("non-theistic" evolutionists). But both agree that the origin of species is biological rather than divine intervention, and that this process took many millions, indeed, billions, of years rather than less than 10,000. To a sociologist, what is even more interesting than the simple magnitude of these two figures is their social composition. That is, there are important sociological differences between creationists and evolutionists.

As we will see in a bit more detail in chapter 10, perhaps the most striking difference between creationists and evolutionists is their educational level. Creationism is *negatively* correlated with education. That is, the *higher* the level of education, the *less* likely it is that someone believes in biblical creation; the *lower* the education, the *greater* that likelihood is. In contrast, belief in evolution is *positively* correlated with education. That is, the higher the education, the greater the likelihood that someone believes in evolution; the lower the education, the lower that likelihood is. The correlation between education and belief or disbelief in creationism is not iron-clad. There are many well-educated people who believe in divine creation, just as there are many poorly educated persons who believe in evolution. However, just about every study or poll that has ever been conducted on the subject has found the same basic relationship. It is not an artifact or accidental feature of a particular study conducted at a particular time. The relationship is extremely strong or "robust."

For instance, in the poll conducted in 1997 by the Gallup organization for Cable News Network/*USA Today*, a majority of high school dropouts (58 percent) and high school graduates (54 percent) believe in divine creation. In contrast, a minority of the respondents with some college (38 percent), the college graduates (37 percent), and those with a postgraduate education (24 percent) do so. There is a consistent, stepwise relationship between creationism and education, with this belief decreasing regularly as education increases. This gives us confidence that this correlation is real, significant, and strong.

At the other end of the spectrum, we have belief in evolution, which, as we saw, comes in two varieties: non-theistic, or evolution without God ("God had no part in this process"), and theistic, or evolution with God ("God guided this process"). Added together, the non-theistic and the theistic evolutionary positions were supported least by high school dropouts (31 percent), next least by high school graduates (40 percent), then respondents with some college (57 percent), then college graduates (58 percent), and most strongly, by far, by persons with a postgraduate education (72 percent). Clearly, the more well educated one is, the more likely one is to believe in evolution; the less well educated one is, the more likely one is to believe in creationism.

The second crucial factor that influences whether someone holds creationist or evolutionist views is the rural-urban dimension. Residents of rural and small-town areas are significantly more likely to believe in creationism than are residents of large cities and other urban areas. Turning the equation around, residents of cities and other urban areas are more likely to believe in evolution than is true of residents of small towns and rural areas. Some of this relationship is due to education, since urban residents are better educated than rural dwellers. But it is likely that, by itself, where one lives influences one's views of the origin of the species.

The General Social Survey conducted by the National Opinion Research Corporation in 1994, based on a nationally representative sample of over 2,500 residents, found that as the size of the community increased, belief that evolution is "definitely true" increased correspondingly. Only 5 percent of the respondents who lived in a rural area ("open country") said that evolution is definitely true; this figure was four times as high (21 percent) for residents of cities with a population larger than 250,000. On the other hand, the proportion saying that evolution is "definitely not true" decreased from 50 percent for rural dwellers to 31 percent for the residents of the largest cities.

Several other social factors or variables are *significantly*, though not strikingly, related to belief in creationism versus evolution. In the Gallup poll, men were slightly more likely to believe in evolution (54 percent) than women (45 percent), and slightly less likely to believe in divine creation (39 versus 49 percent). Whites were more likely to be evolutionists (51 percent) than African-Americans (34 percent), and less likely to be creationists (43 versus 54 percent). Residents of the East, West, and Midwest were more likely to support evolution (51, 54, and 52 percent, respectively) than were residents of the South (43 percent). On the flip side, easterners, westerners, and midwesterners were less likely to be supporters of creationism (39, 42, and 42 percent) than were southerners (50 percent). Of practitioners of the three major religious bodies, Jews were by far most likely to believe in evolution (70 percent) and least likely to believe in creationism (18 percent); Protestants were the least likely to believe in evolution (42 percent) and most likely to believe in creationism (52 percent); and Catholics were in between in both respects (54 and 40 percent). Lastly, the political spectrum paralleled religious beliefs. Self-designated liberals were highly likely to believe in evolution (61 percent), much less likely to believe creationism (34 percent); with self-designated conservatives, it was the reverse (38 versus 57 percent); moderates were in between in both respects (54 and 41 percent).

WHAT DOES CREATIONISM SYMBOLIZE?

It would be glib and superficial to claim that creationists are not concerned at all about evolution per se. In point of fact, for them, evolution stands for, represents, or symbolizes a larger, broader, more general moral and ideological stance. Creationists do not regard evolutionary theory as insignificant or symbolic. In their view, someone who questions Genesis questions the Word of God; someone who affirms evolution denies the very existence of the Divine Creator.

However, in another sense, belief in evolution is, if not symbolic, a cornerstone, a foundation for an entire worldview, a way of thinking, feeling, and acting. For the creationist, belief in evolutionary theory is an indicator, a sign, or a manifestation of a broader, all-encompassing way of looking at life, reality, and morality. It points to a vast, seething cauldron of ungodly beliefs. It tells the Christian that the holder of this one belief also holds a swarm of others, all of which are dedicated to the proposition that God must be wiped away from the human consciousness. (This creationist belief in the evolution-ungodliness equation is largely false, but that fact is secondary; the fact that it is believed is crucial here.) Belief in evolution *means* secular humanism; secular humanism, in turn, means everything and anything the observant, conservative Christian finds repugnant. Belief in evolution is, both by its very nature and by implication, the denial of Christianity, of Jesus, and of God Himself. Evolution equals humanism; humanism equals atheism; and atheism equals amorality. Evolutionary thinking is the chink in the armor, the crack in the wall, the hole in the dike, the foot in the door. Question strict creationism and you begin to question everything that fundamentalists regard as godly. Creationism is seen as a house of cards that can come tumbling down when one card is removed.

The alliterative words of Judge Braswell Dean of the Georgia Court of Appeals sum up this sentiment: "This monkey mythology of Darwin is the cause of permissiveness, promiscuity, pills, prophylactics, perversions, pregnancies, abortions, pornography, pollution, poisoning, and proliferation of crimes of all types" (Toumey, 1994, p.94).

Says Neil Segraves of the Creation-Science Research Center: "the results of evolutionary interpretations of science data results in a widespread breakdown of law and order," producing "moral decay . . ., divorce, abortion, and rampant veneral [sic.] disease" (1977, p.17; Toumey, 1994, p.94). In other words, opposing creationism is both important in and of itself as well as representing a foundation-stone of an entire way of thinking and behaving.

According to historian Christopher Toumey, the "most vehement" spokesperson for the view that evolution equals amorality is Henry Morris of the Institute for Creation Research (Toumey, 1994, p.94), who argues that "the deception of evolution" caused "Satan's rebellion against God, Eve's deception of Adam, and Satan's deception of the world" (Morris, 1963, p.93). Satan invented evolution at the Tower of Babel (Morris,

1974, pp.74–75). The foundation of "false teaching in every discipline of study, and therefore of all ungodly practice in all areas of life," claims Morris (1984, p.223), has been evolution. If evolutionary theory is true, he argues, "then the morals of the barnyard and the jungle" are more "natural," "healthy," and acceptable than those of chastity and fidelity. "Self-preservation is the first law of nature; only the fittest will survive. . . . Eat, drink, and be merry, for life is short, and that's the end. So says evolution!" (Morris and Gish, 1976, p.172). Morris even traces pagan religions, which existed countless centuries before the theory of evolution was developed, to evolutionary thinking.

Since most evolutionists do not support the majority of the beliefs fundamentalist Christians ascribe to them, it might be instructive to inquire as to how the fundamentalists came to hold this view. To understand the creationist's characterization of evolutionary theory, think of an assertion about evolution not merely as a claim about the nature of reality, but as a *morality tale*. It is not only a story about events of this world, the creationist claims, but about what these events *mean*.

What is evolution? the creationist asks. Just as important, accepting evolution means accepting the idea that life arose as a result of a random, essentially meaningless process. Evolution denies teleology, and to the Christian, teleology refers to God's design and purpose, with humans at its very pinnacle. The very essence of evolution is "random mutation"—a natural accident—rather than progress to a higher and more spiritual plane, guided by an intelligent mind (p.91). The molecules that supposedly created life had no purpose in doing so; according to the story of evolution, they combined irresponsibly, if you will, without any direction or guidance. If this is true, humans, likewise, would be permitted to behave "irresponsibly" and without direction or guidance. According to W. L. Wysong, a leading creationist theorist: "If life came into existence through purely natural, materialistic, chance processes, then, as a consequence, we must conclude [that] life is without moral direction and intelligent purpose. . . . Atoms have no morals, thus, if they are our progenitors, man is amoral" (1976, p.6; Toumey, 1994, p.92).

The fact that this is a gross misrepresentation, that, in fact, *most* evolutionists interpret the events of the past four billion years in an entirely different fashion, is not the point here. As we've seen, most rank-and-file evolutionists believe that God *did* guide the progress of the development of life. Even non-theistic evolutionists deny that this process is "random." All agree that natural selection forces direction on the process. But the fact that most creationists, and especially creationist theorists and thinkers, *believe* that evolution automatically implies purposelessness and meaninglessness is crucial here.

In short, creationism "is much more than a narrow doctrine extrapolated from a handful of biblical verses. It represents a broad cultural discontent, featuring fear of anarchy, revulsion for abortion, disdain for promiscuity, and endless other issues, with evolution integrated into those fears" (Toumey, 1994, pp.98–99). The causal linkage of evolution to morality addresses the genuine puzzlement of the conservative Christian over the disappearance of a traditional way of life, the subsequent spread of secularism, and the proliferation of all manner of undesirable developments. While the role that evolution plays in this change was constructed by fundamentalist Christian intellectuals, not the rank-and-file, belief in this assertion is widespread in the conservative Christian community.

The argument that secularization is the product of all-encompassing and irrevocable changes that cannot be stopped offers no comfort or hope whatsoever to the creationist. Demonizing evolution has become a satisfying explanation for the problems posed by godless secularization. Attack the target evolution, creationists say, and society's problems will be solved. The fact that this interpretation offers a palpable, visible symbol or target for the creationist, and hence offers its obliteration or defeat as a kind of salvation, means that the controversy will be with us for some time to come. In paranormal beliefs, as in so many areas of life, it is symbolism that counts.

To the sociologist, what is crucial about belief in strict or biblical creationism is that it is strongly correlated with a wide range of beliefs and behaviors. This is especially the case with those in the realm of sex—for instance, homosexuality, abortion, premarital intercourse, marital infidelity, pornography; male-female sex roles. In addition, creationism's hostility to evolutionary theory also undergirds its adherents' support of school prayer; the infusion of morality into politics; law, crime and justice; illicit drug use; and so on. The point is, one's stance on these basic, fundamental issues cannot be verified or refuted empirically or scientifically. They surpass evidence; they are strictly in the realm of morality and ideology. Hence, to apply to the issue of creationism the same standards of scientific verification that apply to laboratory experiments is naive. Creationism provides the foundation for what is seen by fundamentalists as a "Christian" stance toward morality. In this sense, the issue of the scientific validity of creationism is irrelevant; strict creationism is "true" because what is regarded as a Christian way of life is "true." To the right-thinking, God-fearing Christian, that's the beginning, middle, and end of the story.

Chapter Eight

PARAPSYCHOLOGY

We receive a phone call from a friend about whom we were just thinking; simultaneously, two people blurt out exactly the same sentence; someone predicts that an event will take place, and it does. "That must have been ESP!" we declare. Does such a power exist? Can two people communicate with one another without the use of words? Can we picture things miles away, in our mind, without devices of any kind? Is it possible to predict the future? Or "see" events that took place in the past that we did not witness and no one told us about?

Although different observers define parapsychology somewhat differently, common elements that are most often included in definitions are: *telepathy*—mind-to-mind communication; *remote viewing* (sometimes referred to as "clairvoyance")—the ability to "see" or perceive objects from a distance without the aid of technology or information; *precognition*—seeing the future; *retrocognition*—seeing the past without the requisite information; *psychokinesis* (PK)—the ability to move physical objects solely with one's mind. All or some aspects of these parapsychological powers are known as "psi." The terms other than psychokinesis are also referred to as *extrasensory perception* (ESP) or, less commonly (and a bit confusingly), *clairvoyance*. Psychokinesis is sometimes referred to as "telekinesis"; clairvoyance (again, confusingly) sometimes refers to seeing the future and the past. The essence of psi is mind-to-matter and mind-to-mind influence or communication.

A very high proportion of the public believes that ESP or other parapsychological powers exist. In 1996, *Newsweek* sponsored a poll that asked respondents whether they believe in "ESP or extra-sensory perception." Two-thirds of the sample (66 percent) said they believe that the power of ESP is real. The proportion saying they believe in "telepathy" or the ability of some people to "communicate with others through

117

means other than the five senses" represented a slight majority (56 percent). For "clairvoyance, or the power of the mind to know the past and predict the future," the figure was slightly above a quarter of the sample (27 percent), and for "telekinesis, or the ability of the mind to move or bend objects using just mental energy," it was 17 percent. (The figures for a similar Gallup poll taken about the same time were slightly lower.) Interestingly, except for the fact that residents of the West were considerably more likely to believe in these powers than residents of other geographic locations, correlations between social characteristics and these beliefs seem to be practically nonexistent. Worldwide, the proportion believing in some type of parapsychological power almost certainly adds up to roughly three or four billion souls. A belief this widespread demands attention.

For our purposes, even more interesting than the beliefs of the rank-and-file or grassroots is the small social grouping whose members are engaged in conducting systematic research on this belief. Internationally, there are a few hundred parapsychologists (professionals with Ph.Ds.) who use the techniques of conventional science—that is to say, controlled experiments—to conduct research designed to test or verify the existence of psi. This is not true of any other paranormal belief system. As we saw, very few scientific creationists are professional scientists with a Ph.D. in a relevant field; nearly all ufologists are self-taught in their chosen field; and there are no programs in higher education that offer an advanced degree in how to be a psychic or horoscope reader.

In contrast, parapsychology researchers conduct scientific investigation of the reality of psi, a particular type of paranormal power. While astrologers and psychics claim to possess psi themselves, parapsychologists study or examine psi in others. The research methods of parapsychologists are far more science-like than is true of the practitioners of any other area of paranormalism. As a result, mainstream scientists are less likely to reject the tenets of parapsychology out of hand. These facts make this belief system interesting for a variety of reasons.

As we've seen, the man and woman on the street rely much more on anecdotes and personal experience in drawing their conclusions than on the results of systematic research. In fact, they are likely to regard the controlled experiments that parapsychologists conduct as overly technical and restrictive. In contrast, the professional parapsychological researcher argues that the controlled experiment is one of the most essential tools in establishing the validity of psi. Note that the parapsychologist does not *necessarily* believe that psi exists (although the vast majority do), but practically all believe that systematic research is the only means of testing its reality (Truzzi, 1980, p.37). In this chapter, I'd like to look at the research-oriented parapsychologists as a sociological collectivity whose members study a set of ideas that contradict what more conventional scientists believe is possible or at least likely.

One of the most remarkable aspects of the research of parapsychologists is that it manifests the *form* but, according to most scientists, not the *content* of science. In other words, the research *methods* of parapsychologists are no less rigorous and "scientific" than those of conventional, mainstream psychologists. And, if the research were to deal with a conventional subject, the *findings* of these studies would be convincing to most scientists, at least to most social scientists. But scientists find two problems with the research of parapsychology.

One is that parapsychologists offer no convincing conventional explanation for *why* their findings turn out the way they do. Moving objects with the mind? *How?* the conventional scientist asks. What is the *mechanism* by which someone can bend a spoon without touching it? *How* do subjects view faraway objects without the aid of instruments? *In what way* do minds "communicate"? What *causes* psi or parapsychological powers? The problem is, parapsychologists give no answers that satisfy the conventional scientist. Since the latter consider only *material* forces or mechanisms within their explanatory scope, they find it difficult to accept the parapsychologist's arguments. (As we saw, the same objection can be raised about some features of conventional or cutting-edge science. For instance, why do superstrings exist? No physicist alive has any idea, but most believe in them.)

Physicists make use of material forces such as velocity, mass, friction, gravity, and heat; biologists invoke molecules, cells, genetics, biochemistry, and anatomy; social psychologists and sociologists speak of socialization, peer influence, prestige, power, and social sanctions. These concepts, forces, or factors can be readily understood in a straightforward, naturalistic, cause-and-effect fashion. (Or so scientists say. Poke too far into the structure of any natural and especially social science, and inexplicable forces begin to appear.)

What is the parapsychologist's cause-and-effect explanation for psi? Even if their studies of empirical regularities demonstrating that *something* is going on were accepted, what *material* explanation for such effects do parapsychologists offer? Some resort to theories of electromagnetic forces (Irwin, 1994, pp.167–169), "energy field" explanations (p.169), the action of "elementary particles" (p.170), or quantum mechanics (Radin, 1997, 277–278, 282–286). Still others "treat psi as a negative 'wastebasket' category . . ., atheoretic anomalies in need of an explanation" (Truzzi, 1987, p.6). But none has an explanation of how these forces generate or cause the effects their findings point to that is plausible to most scientific observers. In the words of Dean Radin (who holds a doctorate in educational psychology), "The only thing we can do is to demonstrate correlations. . . . *Something* is going on in the head that is affecting *something* in the world." To most scientists, this assertion is not sufficient; science needs a convincing explanation.

Traditional scientists have a second problem with granting a scientific status to parapsychology: its inability to *replicate* findings, or what Truzzi calls "psi on demand" (1982, p.180). As we saw earlier, scientists take replication seriously. When a scientist produces a finding in an experiment or study, if the principle on which that finding rests is valid, another scientist should be able to conduct the same research and come up with the same finding. Findings should be repeatable, experiment after experiment, study after study. (Replicability is taken more seriously in the natural sciences than the social, however, and more seriously in psychology than sociology.) If entirely different results are obtained in repeat experiments, something is wrong with either the experiment or the finding. Radin (1997, pp.33–50) argues that parapsychology does not display replication any less than traditional science. In addition, he claims that psi is elusive, subtle, and complex and that our understanding of it is incomplete. Hence, experiments demonstrating psi are difficult to replicate.

Conventional scientists are not likely to find his argument convincing because parapsychology is an experimental field and parapsychologists have been unable to replicate the findings of their experiments. In some experiments, psi "effects" appear, while in other almost identical experiments, they do not. Psi seems fragile and elusive. The assumption that forces are consistent throughout the universe is the bedrock of science itself.

To most scientists, the lack of a plausible explanation and the inability to replicate research findings are serious deficiencies in parapsychology, which "will probably prevent full acceptance" of the field by the general scientific community (Truzzi, 1982, p.180). Hence, many observers refer to the field as a "pseudoscience" (for instance, Hines, 1988, pp.77–108). In contrast, Truzzi prefers the term "protoscience" (1980, p.180).

When paranormalists say that the field is "scientific," they mean that the evidence demonstrating some sort of effect is strong, convincing, statistically significant. (While psi is not predictable in that it consistently appears across subjects and experimenters, in the aggregate of *many* experiments, psi "effects" *do* appear vastly more often than by chance.) Says Dean Radin, "the strength of the scientific evidence . . . stands on its own merits" (1997, p.5).

In contrast, when mainstream scientists say that the field is *not* scientific, they mean that no satisfying naturalistic cause-and-effect explanation for these supposed effects has yet been proposed and that the field's experiments cannot be consistently replicated. "Is there such a thing as mind over matter? Can energy or information be transferred across space and time by some mysterious process that on the face of it seems to confound the principles of biology and physics?" asks journalist Chip Brown. "Most scientists believe the answer is no—no, no, no, a thousands times no" (1996, p.41).

As we've so often seen, different ways of looking at a given phenomenon are often inconsistent. This principle is most emphatically the case with paranormalism. Without being overly repetitious, our job is to look at the sociological features of belief systems, not to establish or deny their validity. What is important about parapsychology is that it presents a case study of two social circles, its practitioners and traditional scientists, each of which makes very different assertions about the elusive phenomenon of psi.

IS PSI A PARANORMAL PHENOMENON?

It might seem obvious that psi or parapsychological powers are paranormal in nature. Physics says the mind cannot move physical objects by itself; anyone who says it can is affirming a spiritual, supernatural, occult—or paranormal—power.

This point of view does not sit well with many parapsychologists. Says one parapsychologist, "I . . . don't see these things [the effects of psi] as paranormal." Says another: "My worldview is actually rather materialistic. I feel certain that the phenomena studied by parapsychologists will eventually be integrated into physics. There's nothing inherently mystical about psi" (McClenon, 1984, p.187). H. J. Irwin argues that conventional scientists simply *conceive of* or *define* parapsychology as paranormal because the field invokes forces that are *supposed to be* outside the realm of human capabilities. "Within the theoretical framework of modern behavioral science, an extrasensory experience . . . simply could not have occurred as it is reported to have done" (1994, p.4). Irwin suggests that one day ESP will be "shown conclusively to be due to some presently recognized psychological processes" (p.4), at which point, it would have to be reclassified as psychological rather than paranormal. Better, Irwin argues, to refer to parapsychology as a field that invokes principles that *appear* to be paranormal in nature but that may very well have a satisfying naturalistic explanation. At the present time, he says, this is an empirical question that remains to be resolved with the relevant evidence; it cannot be assumed in the first place.

I believe this distinction is worth making, but it is not entirely relevant. Since I base my definition of paranormalism on what the majority of the scientific community *believes*, we need not be concerned with whether or not psi will one day "really" be demonstrated to have a naturalistic cause-and-effect basis. What is important here is that the scientific community *thinks* parapsychology has no scientific basis. Some observers claim that this is changing (Radin, 1997, p.3), but parapsychology's current non-scientific status *in the eyes of scientists* is the point here. If that status changes, and the field were to discover causal mechanisms that scientists consider plausible, then, according to my definition, the field would no longer be paranormal in its orientation. It is parapsychology's *socially constructed* nature I am interested in here, not its *essential* or "real" nature. The objective reality of parapsychology remains controversial; in contrast, its image is a fact.

As an aside, there may be a socially constructed, political reason for parapsychology's insistence that psi is not paranormal—that it does not belong in the same company with fairies, astrology, tarot cards, and the Bermuda Triangle. Parapsychologists may feel that these phenomena have a fanciful, even silly, public image. Hence, to include parapsychology among them taints, contaminates, or *discredits* a field that is grounded in empirical fact. Instead, these researchers argue, psi should be included among ideas that were later scientifically verified and explained, such as "stones falling from the sky" (which turned out to be meteors) or the proposition that germs cause disease. These phenomena are not and never were paranormal, so why should parapsychology be so regarded? Is parapsychology paranormal? No! say psi researchers. Most (but, again, not all) believe that psi effects are real, they have been established; it's just that we just don't quite understand why they appear. But one day, we will. Or so the parapsychologist's argument goes.

PRACTICAL APPLICATIONS OF PSI

Does psi exist? Most scientists say no, and the "effects" observed in the laboratory have been explained away as due to experimental error and bias (Gardner, 1957, pp.299–314). Departures from chance *have* been recorded by parapsychologists in their experiments. Do these departures represent the effects of psi? Whether they do or not, the "effects" described by parapsychologists are not massively greater in frequency than random occurrences. If psi exists, it is far from being infallible. It sometimes "produces" results that are a bit better than guessing and sometimes does not. Over the course of thousands of experiments, the cumulative likelihood of these differences becomes massively greater than chance. But in a single experiment, this is rarely the case. Consequently, it is unfair and premature of skeptics and debunkers to insist that psi achieve more than its advocates claim it is capable of achieving.

What if the powers of psi could be refined and harnessed? What if, through the discovery of *how* psi works, its powers could be magnified a thousand times? Thus, the curious observer is forced to ask, if these powers exist, why haven't they been fully exploited? Why haven't they been used to benefit all humankind? Let's look at the possible uses for the power of psi. They are immediately relevant to the field's practitioners because harnessing psi's powers would legitimate parapsychology both as a science and as a profession.

The practical applications of psi, if they exist, are almost unlimited. If parapsychological effects were shown to be real and they could be controlled, there would be almost no end to the uses to which they could be put. Indeed, some parapsychologists have worked for corporations and government agencies to harness the powers of psi. Dean Radin (1997) has conducted "cutting edge" parapsychological research for AT&T, Contel Technology, and the United States government. In addition, the Sony corporation and a number of U.S. government agencies, including the Central Intelligence Administration (CIA), the Federal Bureau of Investigation (FBI), the Drug Enforcement Agencies (DEA), the National Security Council, the Customs Service, the Defense Intelligence Agency, and the Secret Service, have spent millions of dollars in attempts to harness and make use of the powers of psi (Radin, 1997, pp.194, 195, 198).

Not all the evaluations of the results of these studies have been positive. One report, issued by the American Institutes for Research, concluded that remote viewing "has not been shown to have value in intelligence operations" and that continued support for psi projects "is not justified" (Mumford, Rose, and Goslin, 1995). But after reviewing the evidence, at least five government evaluation studies concluded that psi could exist, could have practical applications, and is worth "serious scientific study" (Radin, 1997, p.3). Consider only a few of its potential uses.

Detective work. Some police departments have worked with psychics to help solve crimes (Lyons and Truzzi, 1991). This is but a grain of sand compared with the potential assistance that psi could lend to police investigation. If some people really do have the power to view the past, they can "see" what happened at the scene of a crime. As a result, all police departments could make use of their powers on nearly all crimes. Injustice would become a thing of the past: all guilty parties would be arrested, charged, convicted, and punished accordingly, and no innocent parties would be convicted of crimes they did not commit.

Indeed, crime could even be prevented by means of remote viewing. Has a bomb been planted on an airplane? It can be found. Is an assassination attempt being planned? It can be prevented.

History, archaeology, paleontology, geology, biology. If the *distant* past can be seen by possessors of the power of psi we have a window to historical and prehistorical events. It opens the possibility of seeing Jesus on the cross, the sacking and burning of Jerusalem, the building of the pyramids, the arrival of Asians to the Western Hemisphere, the very first humans on earth, the age of dinosaurs, indeed, the origin of life itself. The controversy between creationists and evolutionists will be settled once and for all.

Government intelligence. Several U.S. government agencies have already hired remote viewers for the purpose of spying. During the Cold War, the National Security Council hired Joe McMoneagle who apparently saw the construction and launching of a previously-unknown Soviet *Typhoon* class submarine. Months later, his observations were confirmed by means of surveillance photographs (Radin, 1997, pp.194–195).

In addition to spying on other states, psi can help citizens spy on the doings of representatives of the state. There would be no secrets from possessors of psi. Consequently, corrupt, dishonest governments would fade into historical memory. Psi would reverse the slogan, "Big Brother is watching you," to citizens telling representatives of the state, "All of us are watching *you.*"

Averting disasters. If we can see the future, we can prevent events in advance. In the case of natural disasters, we will be able to minimize their impact. If we know for certain the exact hour a disaster will strike, we will be able to save perhaps a million lives a year worldwide by means of the appropriate intervention. Indeed, given PK, we should be able to remove the conditions that *cause* a disaster. Perhaps we will even be able to calm the fury of hurricanes, floods, tsunami, volcanos, earthquakes, and tornados.

The stock market. According to Dean Radin (1997, p.201), in 1982, the *St. Louis Business Journal* hired a psychic to predict the movement of the stock market. Over a six-month period, the psychic outperformed eighteen out of nineteen professional stock-brokers. Why not make use of this power on a vast scale? The ups and downs of the stock market could be anticipated and controlled. Indeed, the market's customary and harmful wild swings would become obsolete.

Medicine. "Intuitive" diagnosis and "distant" healing can be done with psi, some claim. No need for blood tests or X-rays, CAT scans or mammograms, drugs, scalpels, or laser beams. If PK really does work, that cancerous tumor or those pathological microbes can be removed from the body with the power of the mind. All disease will become a historical footnote. Millions of lives and billions of dollars could be saved by harnessing our mental powers.

Psi applications: some questions. This list could be expanded at great length. It is only somewhat facetious, since the likelihood that these applications will be realized on the scale I suggest is so remote. As we saw, limited aspects of psi have already been tried: psychic detectives have been hired by police departments, the CIA has investigated the possibility of remote viewing, and the Sony corporation has sponsored research into alternative medicine, X-ray vision, and telepathy. Indeed, in his book on "the scientific truth of psychic phenomena," Dean Radin (1997, pp. 191–202) devotes a chapter to the practical applications of psi in medicine, military and intelligence, detective work, technology, and business. "In other applications," Radin claims, "psi has been used to guide archaeological digs and treasure-hunting expeditions, enhance gambling profits, and provide insight into historical events." Why have mainstream scientists been so reluctant "merely to admit the existence of psi"? he asks. They just don't understand, Radin argues.

If psi has been shown unambiguously to work in the practical areas in which it has been employed, why hasn't it become vastly more widespread and adopted everywhere? The business world, for instance, is extremely hard-headed and practical about the bottom line. If psi has been shown to produce results, it would seem that every corporation on earth would have hired and made extensive use of parapsychological consultants. Why hasn't this happened? As Radin says, most practical people of the world are not interested in *why* psi works, only *that* it works. And if it does, why has it been adopted so tentatively by so few decision makers? There is a possibility that the practical applications of psi are limited by *who* (that is, some people may have this power, while others don't) *what* (psi may produce certain kinds of effects but not others), and, possibly, even *where* (certain settings may be more conducive to it than others).

REMOTE VIEWING: 1998

What about predicting future events? How good are contemporary possessors of psi at "remote viewing" events of the coming year? In chapter 6, we saw that ordinary astrologers and psychics do not have a very good track record of predicting future events. Are people who possess psi (meaning they are able to make use of normal powers that science hasn't yet discovered) any better at their predictions? On several broadcasts of a radio show, "Coast to Coast AM," Ed Dames made 13 predictions for 1998. These are "not psychic predictions," Dames said, but "technical remote-viewed future events." How accurate was he in "viewing" these events?

Determining a "hit" is not always a simple matter. Conditions or outcomes are not always exact. In addition, if an event does not take place within one year, how long do we wait before declaring the prediction is accurate? In any case, most observers would feel that almost none of Dames' 13 "remote-viewed future events" came to pass. During 1998:

- The globe was not "totally ravaged" by "microbes and so on" which became "so virulent so rapidly" that the Centers for Disease Control (CDC) in Atlanta was "unable to keep up" with the tabulation of these diseases.

- There was no major volcanic eruption at Mammoth Mountain, or anywhere else in North America.

- As far as we know, no "cylindrical object" from outer space landed near Lake Victoria or anywhere else in Africa, creating an impact crater and spreading a "pathogen" that killed plants for miles around.

- The North Koreans did not attack the South Koreans with a missile. (Though they did launch one into the sea, perhaps as a warning.)

- There was no nuclear accident in Spain.

- The global economy did not "collapse." (Yes, the economy in Asia and Russia did worsen.)

- Said Dames about President Clinton, "I don't think he's going to make it to the end of the year." Clinton remained in office after surviving an impeachment by the Senate.

- There was no significant or out-of-the-ordinary increase in deaths of young children or infants.

- There was no tornado in the Midwest "so big it rips people apart."

- There was some crop damage from natural causes, as there is every year. The major crop-damage story was the freeze in California and Florida, causing the price of citrus products (mainly oranges and lemons) to rise. Dames gets a half a "hit" for this prediction.

- There were no reports of "cannibalism" in Eastern Europe.

- The PLO and Israel did not give up on the peace process and announce "we're going to war."

- And a "solar flare" did not hit the earth, causing people to see it and feel its heat and those who looked directly at it to go blind.

It's difficult to imagine anyone being impressed by half a "hit" out of what would seem to be 13 mostly incorrect guesses. The record of other "remote viewers" in being able to "see" events of the coming year is equally dismal. On January 1, 1998, for the coming year, Peter Petrisko "saw" the New York Knicks winning the 1998 NBA championship (actually, the Chicago Bulls repeated) and the appearance of a UFO over a major East Coast city. If remote viewing really is possible, why aren't persons who say they possess this power more accurate in "seeing" future events? What gives them the confidence that they are actually "remote viewing" future events? What maintains that confidence after years of failure? These questions are not aimed at debunking the existence of psi. Instead, they raise the questions: What is the basis for the remote viewer's images? And how does the remote viewer reinterpret failure so that it does not challenge the veracity of his or her ability to predict the future?

Did Nostradamus possess the power of psi? Was he capable of precognition? Was he truly "the man who could see tomorrow," as many of his supporters have claimed? This is another issue on which scientists and the paranormalists would disagree. Why the difference?

Many skeptical observers argue that it's not even clear that Nostradamus' statements are supposed to be prophecies. But if they are, they are not precise enough to be plausible to scientists as predictions. Their meaning is so vague that it becomes clear only *after the fact*. No one saw the quatrains in the first chapter of the book as predictions of the coming of Hitler, World War II, the assassinations of the Kennedy brothers, Saddam Hussein, and the Gulf War *before* they took place. In fact, statements as vague as Nostradamus' verses could be interpreted in many ways. When an event takes place that seems to fit one of them, an interpretation is fabricated to make it seem *as if* it had been a genuine prediction. Only if a prediction comes before an event, and clearly and unambiguously points to the occurrence of that event, can it be regarded as scientifically meaningful (Hines, 1988, pp.39–42; Randi, 1993). Scientists apply the same reasoning to biblical prophecies (Callahan, 1997).

RESEARCH ON PSI

What do parapsychologists claim are the powers of psi? What are its dimensions, and what are its limitations? Who possesses these powers and why? According to Irwin (1994, pp.9ff.), three issues have preoccupied the field of parapsychology: *authenticity* (Does psi exist in the first place?), *mechanisms* (How does it work?), and *phenomenology* (What is the experience like?). The vast majority of the studies conducted by parapsychologists have centered around the issue of authenticity. These controlled experiments have been guided by the question: Do the effects that are observed occur more often than chance?

Although mediums and spiritualists have existed for thousands of years, the modern age of parapsychology is said to have been born with the research of Joseph Banks Rhine and Louisa Rhine. The Rhines both received Ph.Ds. in botany and plant physiology. In 1928, J. B. Rhine was appointed instructor of psychology at Duke University; his chair, William McDougall, encouraged his interest in parapsychology.

Experiments had been conducted on ESP previously, but they were heavily flawed. For instance, an ordinary pack of playing cards was often used; subjects were asked to guess a given card, face down, that had been drawn from the pack. Since subjects tend to display a preference for certain cards (the ace, for instance), their guesses were not randomly distributed. (This is referred to as the "stacking" effect.) In addition, playing cards convey two pieces of information, not one: face value and suit. Consequently, how does a researcher score a correct guess? On only one of these pieces of information—and if so, which one—or both?

To test departures from a random guessing model, a colleague of the Rhines, Karl Zener, suggested using cards with five geometric symbols: a rectangle (later, a square); a circle; a cross or plus sign; a star; and wavy lines. A pack consists of 25 cards, five bearing each symbol. The task of the subject was to guess the identity of each card in a shuffled deck. Correct guesses were referred to as a "hit," incorrect guesses, a "miss." ESP was indicated when a subject obtained significantly more hits than misses in a given trial run, given the laws of chance. Thus, if the 25 cards in the deck were dealt out, one by one, and subjects obtained significantly more than five hits, the Rhines felt that this suggested an ESP "effect." Whether this effect was due to clairvoyance (the subject somehow perceiving the symbols) or telepathy (the experimenter mentally conveying the symbols to the subjects) was secondary; both were measures of ESP. J. B. Rhine's first book summarizing the results of these experiments, *Extra-Sensory Perception*, was published in 1934. A volume aimed at the general public appeared three years later (1937); it became a best seller.

The Rhines were interested in two issues: the psychic ability of subjects as a whole and the extraordinary psychic ability of specific individual subjects. As for the first, if subjects guessed at random, hits would occur 20 percent of the time. Rhine's experiments demonstrated that, more or less consistently, subjects intuit the identity of cards more frequently than chance. For instance, in one set of 800 trials conducted between 1931 and 1932, subjects got 207 hits, or slightly better than 25 percent (Irwin, 1994, p.72). While this effect occurred only slightly more often than chance, the departure from randomness was statistically significant, and it was fairly consistent over a large number of trials.

Even more remarkable, a number of experimental subjects displayed a *strikingly* higher than average ability to select the correct card. For instance, Hubert Pearce, a graduate student in theology, participated in a series of four runs. He averaged a mean number of 8.3 hits per run (Irwin, 1994, pp.81–82), substantially above the average of five. Moreover, Pearce's ability to select the cards did not diminish over time.

What should we make of this finding? Between 1934 and 1940, the Rhines' research met with "vehement criticism" from conventional psychologists (Irwin, 1994, p.73). Some of the critiques were strictly rhetorical; these critics refused to accept that anything significant was happening, and reduced the Rhines' work to "superstition and mysticism" (p.73). But some of it was substantial, usually of a methodological nature. For instance, what if the backs of the cards became marked or scuffed and their identity could be discerned by subjects? What if subjects counted the cards and developed the ability to determine which ones had a higher than chance likelihood of appearing next? Was there any "sensory leakage," cues from researchers concerning upcoming cards, in the experiment? That is, did researchers emit information to subjects about the identity of the cards? Was shuffling adequate? Was fraud possible? Was the erroneous but unconscious recording of wrong answers as right likely to take place by researchers who wanted to demonstrate the power of psi (Gardner, 1957, pp.199ff.)?

One particularly controversial methodological aspect of the study was the "suppression of null results." Many subjects consistently guessed at the random or 20 percent level; they were classified as "not sensitive," and their trials were discontinued. At the .05 level of statistical significance, simply as a result of random variation, positive results can be obtained one out of 20 times. If the researcher saves the results of the one trial that produced positive results and throws away the 19 that produced no differences, significance can be fabricated out of simple random variation. Were the Rhines' findings a product of saving what seemed significant, and throwing away what did not? It is true that discontinuing trial runs of "not sensitive" subjects was common practice in experiments by the Rhines. But since the results of all their experiments were saved, a check reveals that this practice does not account for most of their results. Moreover, it does not account for the extraordinary success of those especially "sensitive" subjects such as Hubert Pearce (Irwin,

1994, p.75). It is clear that *something* was happening. Exactly what that "something" was, no one knows for sure.

Since the Rhines conducted their card-intuiting experiments, numerous parapsychologists have engaged in systematic investigations into the validity of psi in a variety of ways.

Remote viewing. Between 1978 and 1987, a series of studies was conducted at PEAR, the Princeton Engineering Anomalies Research Laboratory. A "percipient" (remote viewer) was asked to describe the physical or geographical site or setting in which an "agent" (an individual known to the viewer) was located. Some possible descriptions included whether the agent was inside or outside, whether the setting was light or dark, whether animals were present or not, what nearby structures, if any, looked like, whether there were sounds at the site, and so on. The agent filled out a thirty-item form and, in most cases, took a photograph of the scene. Experimental conditions included agent-selected sites ("volitional") and sites the experimenter instructed agents to go to ("instructed"). Of the 334 trials, the odds against the matches between such a close correspondence between what the remote viewer described and what the agent saw directly at the site were 100 billion to one. Interestingly, correspondences were greater for the instructed than for the volitional sites (Radin, 1997, pp.103–105).

Perception through time. Honorton and Ferrari (1989) summarized over 300 studies reported in over 100 articles published between 1935 and 1987 that were concerned with the phenomenon of "future-telling" or "forced-choice precognition." More than 50,000 subjects participated in almost two million trials. They were asked to tell the experimenters what they thought would happen in the future. These "targets" included average daily low temperatures in cities around the world, the value of the numbers on dice about to be tossed, ESP card symbols, and the appearance of randomly-generated numbers. Twenty-three of the 62 investigators produced successful results; the odds against successful results being obtained by all of the studies, taken as a whole, were "ten million billion to one" (Radin, 1997, p.114).

Telepathy. Between the late 1960s and the early 1970s, a series of 25 "dream" studies were conducted, which reported on 450 sessions. In these studies, one subject selected a picture from an envelope while a second slept in another room. When sleeping subjects manifested REM (rapid eye movement) sleep, they were awakened by a researcher and asked to describe the content of their dreams. In 19 out of the 25 experiments, the outcome was positive; that is, there was a better-than-random chance that the subject of the picture corresponded in crucial ways to the content of the sleeper's dreams. With the 450 sessions added together, the odds against the number of hits obtained was, Radin claims, seventy-five million to one (1997, pp.72–73), ruling out any like-lihood of chance.

Ganzfeld. Ganzfeld (in German, "whole field") experiments entail placing subjects in a low-stimulus environment, taping a halved ping-pong ball over their eyes and, after a period of relaxation, asking them to think about the target imagery. This may be a picture placed in an envelope in another room (which could entail remote viewing) or the thoughts of the experimenter or another subject who is located, again, in another room (which could entail telepathy). Researchers claim a remarkably high correspondence or hit rate and hence, impressive evi-dence for psi (Irwin, 1994, pp.103–105). According to Radin (1997, p.84), Honorton's summary of 25 Ganzfeld studies (1985) which ran 762 trials demonstrates a hit rate of 37 percent, corresponding to odds of a trillion to one.

Mind-matter interaction. In 1991, parapsychologists Dean Radin and Diane Ferrari summarized all the systematic studies, published in English, that were conducted over the previous half-century on the out-come of tossed dice (1991). The outcome of experimental conditions (solely with the power of the mind, attempting to control the value of the die face) versus control conditions (not attempting mentally to control the value on the die face) were compared. Seventy-three relevant publi-cations were located; over 2,500 subjects took part in these experi-ments, and they threw the dice 2.6 million times when they applied "mental influence" and 150,000 tosses without mental influence. For the outcomes stipulated, the hit rate for the control conditions was 50 per-cent and for the experimental condition, it was 51.2 percent. While the percentage difference between them is small, the odds against it occur-ring in this many trials is one billion to one (Radin, 1997, p.134).

Psi in the casino. If psi truly exists, one would imagine that gam-bling would provide an adequate test of its existence, since the casino setting is very similar to that of the experiments parapsychologists devise (Radin, 1997, p.175). Indeed, many observers might be extremely interested in controlling psi so that they could earn a fortune at games of chance. Radin (Brown, 1996, p.44) argues that "the state of mind most people attain in a casino isn't conducive to psi," and hence the secrets of parapsychology are unlikely to unlock vast fortunes to gam-blers. Still, Radin did test the relationship between the lunar cycle and the payout rate at a particular gaming house. It turns out that the casino payout rate "peaked at about 78.5 percent of the day of the full moon, and they dropped to a low of about 76.5 about a week before and after the new moon" (p.184). Again, the difference is small, but the odds against it occurring are roughly 25 to one.

Research by Parapsychologists: Summary and Conclusions. By now, the number of published studies conducted by scientifically oriented parapsychologists runs into the thousands. Several professional, peer-reviewed journals are devoted more or less exclusively to parapsychology—for instance, the *European Journal of Parapsychology,* the *Journal of the American Society for Psychical Research,* the *Journal of Parapsychology,* the *Journal of the Society for Psychical Research,* and *Research in Parapsychology.* A substantial proportion of the researchers who have conducted these studies are competent, honest, and dedicated to convincing the scientific community that their results are real. Many, although not all, of these studies meet adequate scientific standards; that is, controls are applied and efforts are made to rule out contaminating influences. The "effects" observed tend to be small, but taken cumulatively they are hugely above and beyond what could be obtained by chance or random variation. In other words, *something* is undoubtedly happening. What is it? Is it the elusive psi? And how does psi work? Answers to these questions await a later generation of researchers.

Skeptics and Debunkers. Skeptics and debunkers of parapsychology abound. The pages of the journal, *Skeptical Inquirer,* the organ for The Committee for the Scientific Investigation of Claims of the Paranormal (or CSICOP), are filled with critiques of parapsychology. In one of its articles, Paul Kurtz (1978) delivered something of a standard critique of parapsychology, arguing that the field is a pseudoscience; it is lacking in experimental rigor, a coherent testable framework, and a scheme that is replicable; it is subject to experimenter bias; its central concepts are unexplained, inexplicable, and deny a fundamental law of science, namely, the conservation of energy principle; it has been a handmaiden to fraudulent psychics, magicians, and mediums, who have been uncritically endorsed by professional parapsychologists; its proponents hold a mystical, spiritual, and metaphysical worldview that they are motivated to vindicate; they deny the basic principle that extraordinary claims need to be verified by extraordinary evidence, and this is what they are unable to supply. "Is parapsychology a science?" Kurtz asks. Unless its proponents manage to convince its skeptics, "their claims will continue to be held suspect by a large body of scientists" (Kurtz, 1978, p.31; see also Truzzi, 1980).

One of the most well-known and prolific skeptics of parapsychology is Susan Blackmore. What is interesting about her case is that she used to be a parapsychologist herself. In 1970, while she was a first-year psychology undergraduate at Oxford, her tutors disapproved of her interests, and her school work remained rather traditional. Three personal experiences had a "lasting impact" on her outlook: an out-of-body experience, using psychoactive drugs, and a trip to India (1986, p.10). As a result, in Blackmore's words, "the fish" was "hooked." She "hatched the desire to show all the psychologists that they had been missing out on the most important clue to understanding mind and memory—the paranormal" (p.11).

After completing her undergraduate work and obtaining a master's degree, Blackmore wrote to the Oxford and Cambridge departments of psychology inquiring about programs in parapsychology; both advised her to look elsewhere. Blackmore wrote to John Beloff, a parapsychology researcher at the University of Edinburgh, who sent her a warning stressing the "gamble" such a career path would entail. Said Beloff, "the prospects of a full-time career in parapsychology . . . is virtually nil" (Blackmore, 1986, p.23). Unfortunately, there were no funds at Edinburgh, so Blackmore worked out an arrangement with a supervisor who taught where she had received her master's, the University of Surrey. She even taught the university's first course on parapsychology, during the academic year 1976–1977. The results of her first set of experiments showed no sign whatsoever of the presence of ESP. Blackmore was enormously disappointed. As she wrote in her diary: "Pretty pathetic! I concluded that parapsychology is a lot of rubbish and I should do something else!!" (p.35).

In experiment after experiment, Blackmore simply could not find any ESP effects. Many parapsychologists believe that an experimenter's faith in psi can influence a study's outcome. If the researcher is a skeptic (or a "goat"), this could dampen psi effects; if he or she is a believer (a "sheep"), this could bring out psi effects. Parapsychologists refer to this phenomenon as "psi-mediated experimenter effects." Because of the negative results of her experiments, one parapsychology researcher claimed Blackmore needed psychotherapy; another suggested she didn't have "sufficient rapport" with her subjects (Blackmore, 1986, p.121).

The logic behind this line of thinking is completely contrary to the scientific ideal. In fact, most scientists would see it as a justification for failure, a formula for non-falsifiability. They would say parapsychologists want it both ways. Psi researchers want their field to be regarded as a science. But they also want to be allowed to use unscientific methods. If the possession of psi is a special talent, then its study is not science; if parapsychology is a science, psi can be detected, in varying degrees, in everyone. After all, science can be taught to everyone (again, in varying degrees); why not psi? The physical world is either there or not there, it can be detected or it can't; why isn't this true of psi? scientists ask. Blackmore was surprised that the supporters of parapsychology did not regard her negative results as a challenge to the existence of psi.

To them, these negative findings merely demonstrated that she had been a skeptic all along.

In the concluding thoughts of her Ph.D. thesis, *Extrasensory Perception as a Cognitive Process* (1980), Blackmore ruminated on her failure to find psi. She concluded she simply did not know whether this was due to inadequate experimentation or the fact that, perhaps, we live "in a world without ESP." And in her autobiography, *The Adventures of a Parapsychologist* (1986), she asks herself: "So could psi be just a red herring, a very elusive and very alluring red herring, one that had everyone chasing after it for a hundred years? In the future, when we are closer to understanding man's spiritual nature, will we look back at parapsychology as a pointless detour?" (p.241). Her answer, the last words of her autobiography, was: "I don't know, I don't know, *I don't know!*" (p.242).

PARAPSYCHOLOGY AS A DEVIANT SCIENCE

From a sociological perspective, perhaps the most interesting feature of parapsychology is that it is an excellent example of a deviant science. This does not mean that it is wrong, invalid, pathological, or a "pseudoscience," only that it tends to be condemned or ignored by mainstream scientists. Dean Radin's question, "Why has mainstream science been so reluctant merely to admit the existence of psi?" (1997, p.202) says it all. While he argues that this is changing, the fact remains that among the conventional sciences parapsychology remains an outsider. Science rejects "extraordinary anomalies," and, given the laws of physics, chemistry, and biology, the findings of parapsychology represent anomalies; they cannot be incorporated into the existing theoretical framework. Hence, they must be debunked or neglected.

McClenon (1984, pp.128–163) conducted a survey among the council members and selected section committee representatives of the American Association for the Advancement of Science (AAAS). His sample was made up of elite scientists in that they are in positions of leadership and hence can influence whether parapsychology is granted full scientific legitimacy. His final sample (N=339) includes social as well as natural scientists. Overall, a minority, only 29 percent, consider ESP "an established fact or a likely possibility" (p.138). Moreover, disbelief in ESP is strongly correlated with denying legitimacy to the very subject of its investigation. Thus, "parapsychologists are labeled as deviant because scientists do not believe in the anomaly that they investigate" (p.145). Being a skeptic versus a believer is also related to reporting one or more personal paranormal experiences (p.150). Still, half as many of these scientists report having had an ESP experience (26 percent) as is true of the American population as a whole (58 percent).

McClenon (pp.164–196) also conducted interviews with parapsychologists, attended their meetings, and read their journals. Before conducting his study, he hypothesized that the field of parapsychology was a kind of science-like cult that righteously defended its belief in psi and actively proselytized outsiders to their position. Contrary to his expectations, parapsychologists did not believe that proselytizing was necessary and felt that, eventually, because of the rigor of their research methods and the robustness of their findings, the "truth will be revealed" (p.165). In this respect, parapsychologists are traditional or positivistic scientists. They accept the scientific ideal.

The vast majority of parapsychological research is excluded from the mainstream natural science and psychology journals. In fact, says one of McClenon's interviewees, the *best* work in the field "can't get published there. The editors reject it because it was conducted by people within the field of parapsychology. . . . The editors of most [mainstream] journals aren't that knowledgeable about parapsychology. They don't know what to look for in a piece of research" (p.167). According to the field's proponents, the best work is published in the specialty or parapsychology journals, thereby contributing "to the oblivion to which this body of information has been committed" (pp.167–168).

The few exceptions prove the rule. Beloff, the Edinburgh psychologist with whom Blackmore wished to study, selected his seven best examples demonstrating the existence of psi (Beloff, 1980); only one of them received even brief mention in a mainstream journal. When Harold Targ and Russell Puthoff (1974) published the results of a remote viewing experiment in the prestigious journal *Nature*, they were accused of fraud and incompetence. The vehemence of their critics was characteristic of the heat generated by assertions of psi. Neither a recalculation of a minor methodological flaw nor a more tightly controlled subsequent study attracted any commentary from scientists. Critics continued to pick apart the earlier, slightly flawed, study (McClenon, 1984, p.168). Later replications by other researchers, published in parapsychology journals (Dunne and Bisaha, 1979; Schlitz and Gruber, 1980), are likewise ignored.

In addition to being virtually frozen out of the mainstream science journals, and in spite of the scientific rigor of its experiments, parapsychology "has no professor/graduate-student training like that which exists for the rest of science" (p.171). Parapsychologists "are often discriminated against in academic circles and find it difficult to gain legitimate teaching positions, promotion, and tenure." As a result, few are in academic positions that are necessary to train graduate students (p.171). The prospective parapsychologist "is advised to become something else" (p.172): "Conceal your interest in parapsychology," they are told. "Get a doctorate in whatever subject interests you. Then you can be of value to the field" (p.173).

Common sense would tell us that parapsychologists would react to their outsider status, as many deviant groups do, by becoming even more deviant and far-out and by enlarging their ranks as much as possible. In this case, common sense is wrong; neither is the case. Parapsychologists have stuck to a rigorous scientific methodology and rationale. And the membership policy of the Parapsychological Association (PA) is highly restrictive. Full members generally hold the Ph.D. degree, and to be admitted prospective members must demonstrate evidence of having conducted scientific research in the relevant area (p.174). Said one parapsychologist who talked to McClenon: "The PA is one of those organizations that was founded with the intention of keeping people out rather than letting them in" (p.174).

The socialization process apprentice parapsychologists go through makes them more rather than less cautious and conservative (McClenon, p.176), more skeptical, more attuned to fraud and unfounded enthusiasm. Many parapsychologists argue that valid research can be conducted only under tightly controlled laboratory conditions, thereby cutting the field off from the very real-life conditions which, presumably, the field wishes to investigate (p.177). Interestingly, parapsychologists reject the validity of the personal and anecdotal experiences that lead much of the general public to believe in psi. McClenon says that this suspicion often extends even to the work of other parapsychologists, an effect he refers to as "paranoia in defense of science" (pp.178, 181). Said one researcher: "I can only be sure of the people I have worked with in the past" (p.181). The "symbolic hardware" (that is, exceptionally rigorous methodological strategies) used by parapsychologists "often goes beyond that of normal scientists" (p.182), extending, for example, in some journals, to submitting the design of a planned study "before it is carried out" (p.182) and the publication of nonsignificant results (p.183).

Two Last Points

The science-parapsychology debate is precisely the same sort of debate that prevails for all paranormal claims. Most scientists would insist that psi does not exist, that *all* departures from random results, *all* claims to anomalous or psychic effects are false and due to routine causes such as experimental error or fraud. Imagine a scale from zero to 100, with zero being "no effect" and 100 being "psi on demand," for any person, at any time Perhaps *no* parapsychologist stands at the 100 point on the scale. In fact, most would stand much closer to the zero than the 100. Many would claim a score of "1" for psi: that *some* effect exists, and it can be detected. For the believer in psi to establish the view that *something*—anything, even the slightest departure from chance—exists represents a triumph.

And the last point: the public image of psi bears almost no resemblance whatsoever to what parapsychologists actually do. The public pictures psychic powers vastly beyond what any parapsychological researcher will claim. The experiments these researchers conduct do not, for the most part, lend themselves to dramatic imagery or representation. Most people imagine levitating gurus, infallible, mind-reading clairvoyants, spiritualists who can melt cancer away with a touch of the hand, minds that can bend a laser beam. The parapsychologist's assertion of obtaining experimental results that depart from statistical chance are not what the public has in mind when psychic powers are discussed or depicted. The field of parapsychology occupies a territory somewhere between the public stereotype and the scientific ideal.

Chapter Nine

UFOs ARE REAL

Why is the belief in UFOs as real considered paranormal? The belief that aliens or intelligent extraterrestrials exist is not a paranormal belief. In fact, many, possibly most, scientists believe it is *almost certain* that intelligent life exists on planets outside our solar system. There are billions of stars in each galaxy and billions of galaxies. The laws of chance almost dictate that the universe must be *swarming* with life.

Instead, the paranormal belief is that aliens are *here*, on earth or in its atmosphere. The fact that the distances from other stars to our own solar system are so vast means that there simply isn't enough time for extraterrestrials to get here within the time span of any conceivable lifetime. Scientists, basing their argument on Einstein's theory of relativity, claim that nothing can travel faster than, at, or even remotely near, the speed of light. Fast as it is, light takes *four years* to get here from our nearest star. The speed of light through a vacuum is a constant, and it cannot be violated. (Light can be slowed down, but not sped up.) How did aliens get here? How did they traverse such immense distances to arrive at our doorstep? Most ufologists are unconcerned with this problem, but it vexes scientists so much they feel it is insurmountable. Hence, the belief that UFOs are real is regarded by scientists as paranormal.

Most people use the term "UFO" or "unidentified flying object" as a catch-all phrase for "extraterrestrial craft." Actually, the term means what it says it means—a flying object that hasn't yet been identified. Some UFOs are eventually identified and turn out to be nothing more than the planet Venus, swamp gas, weather balloons, northern lights, or a hoax. In other words, UFOs become IFOs—"identified flying objects." However, some UFOs remain unidentified. A substantial number of observers claim that they *have* identified objects they saw in the sky specifically as alien craft. Herein lies the source of the controversy: are UFOs "something real"? Are they alien aircraft? Why should sociologists be interested in the controversy?

A VERY BRIEF HISTORY OF UFOs

Reports of strange flying objects seen in the sky have been made for centuries. In 1896 and 1897, following the publication of an article in the *Sacramento Evening Bee* that reported an inventor would pilot his airship from New York to California, roughly 100,000 sightings were made of a cigar-shaped aircraft in the sky (Bartholomew, 1990; Bartholomew and Howard, 1998, 21ff.). At about the same time, another rash of tens of thousands of sightings erupted as a result of announcements that Thomas Edison was sending balloons aloft in a series of experiments. Most of these sightings took place nowhere near Edison's laboratory (p.80). Likewise, thousands of sightings of balloons were reported over Canada following the report that a Swedish scientist was to attempt a flight to the North Pole; the balloon perished hundreds of miles from Canada. In 1909, following announcements that the Germans had developed a navigable dirigible, tens of thousands of New Zealanders reported seeing "Zeppelin-like dirigibles" in the sky (p.92). In 1909–1910, following an announcement by a New England businessman that he had invented a heavier-than-air flying machine, tens of thousands of New Englanders reported seeing an airship flying about (pp.109–121). During a five-month period between 1912 and 1913, following announcements of a German arms buildup, waves of claims that Zepplins were flying over Britain broke out (pp.125–133). In 1946, a "panic swept like wildfire across Sweden as tens of thousands of people reported seeing missiles" (p.163). These reports followed rumors that the Soviets, assisted by technology invented by captured German scientists, were poised to invade Sweden. No physical evidence of missiles or rockets of any kind was ever turned up (pp.163–178).

Prior to 1947, reports of strange things seen in the sky came in isolated waves. In between, there were distinct, discontinuous periods during which no, or very few, sightings occurred. In addition, in the overwhelming majority of the pre-1947 sightings, these flying "things" were attributed with an earthly origin. Very few were said to originate from another planet. Moreover, before 1947, very few individuals reported seeing saucer-shaped objects, and none of these reports came on a mass or collective basis. It was not until 1947 that sightings of and interest in UFOs became more or less continuous and uninterrupted and that saucer-shaped craft were observed on a mass basis. (Interestingly, according to the *Denison* [Texas] *Daily News* of January 25, 1878, farmer John Denison claimed to have seen something in the sky that, he said, was "about the size of a large saucer." He did not say it *looked like* a saucer.) It was not until after 1950 that most sightings, and most beliefs about UFOs, attributed them to an extraterrestrial origin.

On June 24, 1947, Kenneth Arnold, owner of a "fire control company,"was flying his private plane near Mt. Ranier, Washington. He saw what he later described as nine crescent-shaped objects flying at high speed, much like geese in formation. They flew, he said, "like a saucer would if you skipped it across the water" (Gardner, 1957, pp.55–56). Notice that Arnold did not say they *looked* like saucers, but rather that they *moved* like saucers. No matter; the phrase, "flying saucers" stuck in the public's mind (p.56). Significantly, Arnold's observation was not said to be of extraterrestrial craft. A Gallup poll taken less than two months later revealed that 90 percent of the respondents had heard of the sighting of "flying saucers," but most believed that they were secret American or foreign military craft, hoaxes, or balloons. Not even a measurable one percent in this survey entertained the idea of aliens as the source. Arnold himself believed that the saucers may have been some kind of "guided missiles" (Bartholomew and Howard, 1998, pp.191–192).

In 1948, an article appeared in the *Aztec Independent-Review* claiming that a flying saucer had crashed near Aztec, New Mexico. Over a hundred newspapers carried this "little men from Venus" report. Later, it was revealed the story was written by the paper's editor as a tongue-in-cheek joke (Peebles, 1994, p.47). In May 1950, the results of a survey appeared in the *Public Opinion Quarterly*. Nine out of ten of the respondents questioned (94 percent) said that they had heard of "flying saucers" and of those, a quarter believed them to be "secret military devices." Only 5 percent said that they were comets, shooting stars, or "something from another planet" (p.193).

A few months later, three books appeared that were focused on the flying saucer theme: Donald Keyhoe, *The Flying Saucers Are Real*, Frank Scully, *Behind the Flying Saucers*, and Gerald Heard, *The Riddle of the Flying Saucers*. Scully's book claimed that aliens from a crashed saucer were being held secretly at a military base; a bestseller, it was later revealed to have been based on a hoax (Peebles, 1994, pp.47–50). Heard's book hypothesized that flying saucers were actually alien "bees." As a result of the publication of these books, numerous articles were published in newspapers and popular magazines, including *Life, Look, Time*, and *Newsweek*. By the early 1950s, the extraterrestrial hypothesis had become firmly entrenched in the public's mind.

SCIENTISTS AND THE PUBLIC LOOK AT UFOS

The belief that unidentified flying objects are of extraterrestrial origin is unquestionably influenced by media presentations, along with UFO organizations and journals. As noted above, this notion was first disseminated by the media. A variety of explanations of the origins of UFOs have been presented in the media and floated by the public, but it is only the extraterrestrial hypothesis that has stood the test of time. Clearly, there is something about this belief that is widely appealing. It is my contention that the belief in the presence of aliens on earth owes its primary existence and sustenance to a more-or-less spontaneous feeling among the population. In other words, a substantial segment of today's public (roughly 45 percent) believes at least some UFO sightings are of alien craft. In all likelihood, most people would continue to feel this way regardless of what experts, commentators, or the media say on the matter. In fact, belief in the reality of UFOs is one of the most grassroots or populist of the forms of paranormalism we might examine. It challenges the existing scientific and educational establishments and its affirmation fits neatly into the theory that the government is involved in a conspiracy to hide the truth from the public.

The belief that UFOs are real and aliens are out there in our skies, even living among us, has become an essential ingredient of American culture (Dean, 1998). However, it is not universal. Our culture has become so fragmented, so lacking in coherence that agreement about what is real and true—what constitutes convincing evidence one way or the other—does not exist. As with so many other paranormal beliefs, scientists on the one hand and certain social circles in the general public on the other have become distinct and separate subcultural groups. They are exposed to the same evidence yet draw entirely different conclusions.

It would seem that some scientists, especially astronomers and astrophysicists, would *most* welcome the idea, if empirically supportable, that UFOs are visitors from another planet. Indeed, the late Carl Sagan spent much of his life thinking and speculating about and searching for extraterrestrial intelligence. Yet he did not believe that UFOs were "something real." (He did, however, believe it possible that aliens could travel to earth through extraordinary, unconventional means.) Why not? With the use of radio waves, NASA's SETI project (the Search for Extra-Terrestrial Intelligence) has devoted millions of dollars to the search for life on planets *outside* the solar system (Broad, 1998). Ufologists question the search in another solar system. They ask, "isn't there plenty of evidence demonstrating that alien life is *right here*, circling the earth at this very moment?" If extraterrestrial craft really are circling the earth, the discovery would be very possibly the most important fact ever disclosed in the history of humanity. If true, why would anyone deny it? Why are so many scientists skeptical about the validity of UFOs?

Let's elaborate a bit on what it is that makes the majority of scientists, especially astrophysicists, uncomfortable about the extraterrestrial hypothesis. Since Einstein's discoveries on relativity just after the turn of the nineteenth century, physicists have revolutionized our conception of the universe and how it works. Specifically, during the course of the twentieth century, much of what we thought of as absolute or constant has turned out to be relative to time and place. For instance, the speed of light, is a constant: light travels at 186,000 miles per second— through a vacuum—everywhere in the universe and, according to scientists, has done so since the "big bang" 10 to 15 billion years ago. (Light can be made to slow down, but not to speed up.) Hence, the equation, E (energy) equals M (mass) C (the constant—the speed of light) squared.

According to Einstein's theory of relativity, as I explained, objects *cannot* travel faster than the speed of light; nature prohibits it. As an object approaches the speed of light, it becomes infinitely heavy. In the other planets of our own solar system, to which human technology can travel, there seems to be no life of any kind, let alone intelligent life. All other planets, that is, those that revolve around stars more distant than our sun, are *extremely* far away. Hence, to get here from any distant planet—barring bizarre and improbable modes of transportation ("worm holes," black holes, parallel dimensions, a time warp, and so on)—would require almost unimaginably long periods of time.

Most laypeople do not realize just how far away stars (hence, planets) other than those in our solar system are. The star nearest our sun is Alpha Centauri; it is four light years away from us. That means that light, traveling 186,000 miles *per second*, takes four years to get here. If a space ship were to travel a million miles an hour, a feat that is theoretically possible but vastly beyond current human technology, it would have had to have left the vicinity of Alpha Centauri at the time of Moses, roughly 3,300 years ago, to arrive here today. All the other stars are much farther away than this. Most scientists regard the technology of traversing extremely vast distances as a major, even fatal, obstacle to interstellar flight. In contrast, most laypeople regard this problem as a mere technicality to be brushed aside or an obstacle to be overcome by being smart enough. This is the reason that scientists consider the belief in UFOs to be paranormal in nature. The evidence contradicting the belief that UFOs are alien space ships or "something real" is a separate although related issue. Scientists tend to be more concerned with the theoretical implications of the violation of a law of nature than with the many reports of UFO sightings.

Ufologists believe that alien science is simply more advanced than earthly science. In the seventeenth century, scientists would have said that heavier-than-air flight is impossible. (True, scientists then had not worked out a *theoretical* rationale for why this was supposedly not possible, only an intuitive sense that this was so.) The achievement of flight in the twentieth century was not a violation of the laws of physics but an affirmation of them. Humans simply have not yet discovered principles that are scientifically valid, many scientific lay observers believe, which scientists of the future will eventually verify. Just as today we have achieved powers thought impossible by scientists centuries ago, the science devised by beings from planets outside our solar system, so much more advanced than ours, can achieve powers we imagine today are impossible.

Traditional scientists consider this line of reasoning invalid. They regard advances in science not so much as a violation of previously devised laws and principles but rather as an extension of them. No matter how smart extraterrestrials are, they say, nature *prohibits* chemicals that contradict Mendeleyev's table of periodic elements, speeds faster than light travels, and the nullification of Newton's laws of gravitation. Once again, scientists and a sizeable segment of the public greet one another's claims with mutual bafflement and incomprehension.

ARE UFOS REAL? SOCIOLOGICALLY, DOES IT MATTER?

Most people who think, talk, and write about UFOs are interested in one issue and one issue only: *Are they real?* Have extraterrestrial craft visited the earth? Are they observing us at this very moment? Is it really true that "we are not alone"? Are persons who say they have been abducted by aliens telling the truth? Do extraterrestrials really grab humans, take them to their mother ship, strip them naked, and examine them from head to toe? Are aliens using humans to *breed* hybrid beings in a vast and bizarre intergalactic genetic experiment? These questions are not uninteresting. Indeed, as I said, even if the answer to only the first one or two of these questions were yes, this would very possibly be the most momentous discovery in human history.

But is the question of the physical reality of alien craft the only interesting issue we might investigate? Sociologically, don't more interesting questions exist aside from the matter of whether or not UFOs are something real?

Imagine two scenarios. In the first, all UFO sightings are disconfirmed; not a single one is of "something real." In the second scenario, all are false except one, which turns out to be an actual alien vessel, complete with extraterrestrials on board. In the first scenario, the one in which all UFO reports are something other than alien craft, we can look at the patterns of the reports and attempt to understand how and why they are generated, what social and social-psychological forces are at work to generate these patterns of misperception, how these reports are sustained by cultural beliefs and, in turn, how they contribute to these beliefs. In other words, UFO reports can be *accounted for* by social and behavioral science explanations and not by the factual or concrete reality of alien beings. In the second scenario, *exactly the same* forces are at work to produce the *very same patterns* in all cases except one. In only that one, an alien aircraft was sighted and verified to exist.

In these two scenarios, identical sociological forces and factors are at work. Reports of various craft, the reception the reports receive, and the generalizations we use to account for them would be identical. A single genuine case, or even several genuine cases, would not change the picture one bit because exactly the same collective behavior dynamics are at work in both scenarios. In other words, our sociological interest in the UFO phenomenon is not confined or restricted to whether or not UFOs are alien spaceships. In fact, our concern is uninfluenced by the fact that some or at least one of these reports are valid or factually true. The sociological generalizations we make about UFO reports do not depend on whether or not a tiny minority of the sightings turn out to be authentic. They *do* depend on the falseness of *most* of them, which is why I argued that facticity is secondary but not irrelevant.

Literally thousands of UFO sightings are made in the United States each year. Roughly 10 percent of adults living in the United States say that they have personally seen a UFO, that is, something in the sky for which they have no routine explanation (Gallup, 1988, p.52). This computes out to roughly 20 million people, and that does not count sightings in other countries. Supporters of the UFO hypothesis argue that the very *volume* of such reports provides strong evidence that at least *some* of them are valid. How could *all* of them be false? they ask. They insist, "something must be out there! Indeed, if 90 percent, or even 99 percent—or even all except one—of these reports turn out to be hoaxes or misperceptions, then the extraterrestrial hypothesis would still be correct. After one eliminates many, most, or nearly all false reports, there remains an *irreducible minimum* that can't be dismissed or explained away. For the anti-UFO position to be correct, *every single report* of a UFO would have to be disproven, which is an obvious impossibility.

To put the matter another way, in principle, the fact that there are *no* valid UFO sightings is readily falsifiable. All that would be necessary is for a single extraterrestrial craft to park itself in a location for everyone to see (as I said before, a classic flying saucer landing in the Rose Garden of the White House during a press conference with two hundred reporters in attendance), complete with tiny green creatures emerging from the craft and uttering the classic line, "Take me to your leader."

On the other hand, the view that UFO sightings are interplanetary craft is *not* falsifiable. There is no conceivable evidence that could be presented or even imagined that will satisfy all or even most committed pro-UFO adherents that space creatures have *not* visited earth. If one sighting is shown to be a hoax or a case of misperception, another will be offered. If a hundred are refuted, ufologists will come up with a hundred more. There is no conceivable possibility of refuting all of them. This is not a matter of the bias of UFO believers, it is a matter of the bias in both positions. One needs a single piece of evidence to be verified; the other needs all the evidence in the world. Hence, all reports of UFO sightings do not *have* to be refuted for the position to be false, according to the scientist. The fact that most follow a pattern is important.

The social scientist is also interested in the general patterning of sightings, but not for the purpose of falsification of the pro-UFO position. To the sociologist, culturalist, or constructionist, the patterning is important because it reveals what is crucial to the various parties in this controversy and how they think, reason, and use evidence. In other words, the UFO controversy is interesting because it is a sociological and cultural phenomenon; it says something about the role that thinking about aliens plays in our society. Let's see what I mean by this assertion.

WHY ALIEN CRAFT?

While misperception makes it possible to "see" something in the sky that appears to be strange or anomalous, it does not explain why it is alien craft specifically that is seen. Why not cigar-shaped airships, as was the case in the United States in the 1890s, or balloons, which is what was seen in Canada at the same time, or Zeppelins, which were seen in New Zealand and Britain just before World War II, or rockets, which Swedes saw just after the war? Why not flying monsters, witches, goblins, demons, the devil, or ghosts of long-dead ancestors, which members of traditional cultures have seen for thousands of years—or gigantic, glowing insects? Why were the pre-1950 UFO sightings in the United States *almost always* thought to be of earthly origin, while those after 1950 were usually ascribed to interstellar craft? Why were UFO sightings and interest in UFOs sporadic before and continuous after 1947? Misperception supplies only a mechanism by which a variety of phenomena or interpretations are read into ambiguous stimuli. What supplies the *content* of what is seen? *Cultural* and *individual* factors must be considered in answering this question.

People see an unusual, luminous formation in the sky and "attempt to interpret it in terms of whatever ideas may be in vogue at the time" (Menzel, 1972, p.124). The "ideas" that were "in vogue" in folk cultures dictated that strange things seen in the sky were monsters, ghosts, and demons. In these cultures, their members were told, that's what these things are. In Catholic countries or communities, what is seen is the manifestation of God's wondrous powers: miraculous manifestations of Mary, Jesus, or a favored saint.

At the turn of the nineteenth century, the guiding idea that was in vogue was technology, wondrous machines that could do things humans only previously dreamed about, especially flying. Just before the First World War, fear of the German "Huns" raining death from the sky gripped many residents of the British Empire. Just after World War II, once again, military images were in vogue, and many of the objects seen in the sky (including Arnold's famous "flying saucers") were rockets, weapons, and military aircraft. By the early 1950s, the "time was ripe" for the concept of the extraterrestrial UFO. The idea that flying saucers were alien visitors emerged because the public was culturally prepared for the notion that intelligent creatures from another planet, with a technology vastly more advanced than our own, could devise sophisticated aircraft and traverse the vast expanses of space (Menzel, 1972, p.125).

Members of contemporary society see interplanetary aircraft in the sky because that is a component of our culture's "plausibility structures," because the belief that such phenomena are possible has become entrenched and widely accepted. Space exploration was contemplated, although considered fanciful, late in the nineteenth and early in the twentieth centuries, in part as a result of fiction such as Jules Verne's *From the Earth to the Moon* (1865) and Georges Melies' film, *Voyage to the Moon* (1902). It was H. G. Wells who, in his novel *War of the Worlds* (1898), added the touch that, instead of humans visiting the moon or other planets, the inhabitants of those other worlds would visit earth. And in 1938, Wells' novel was dramatized in an extremely realistic and infamous radio play, produced by Orson Welles.

Still, before the close of World War II, no technological basis existed for the belief that space travel was possible. During that war, we learned that hundreds of bombers could rain death from the skies, unmanned rockets could be launched from one country and explode in another, and a single bomb of immense, almost unimaginable power could flatten an entire city and annihilate nearly 100,000 people in one awesome thermonuclear blast. Of course, the launching of the Soviet satellite *Sputnik* in 1958 and the landing of U.S. astronauts on the moon in 1969 accelerated the credibility of space travel.

The technological advances that took place on earth provided us with the mind set to imagine that civilizations on other planets could send spaceships here and observe us. People began to realize the scope of what the intelligent mind is capable of devising, what science and technology can accomplish. In most early science fiction, extraterrestrials were destructive, bent on obliterating earthlings so that they could inhabit the planet themselves (H. G. Wells' *War of the Worlds* provides a good example). More recently they are depicted in more varied terms—sometimes destructive (the *Alien* series, *Independence Day*) but at least as often benevolent (*E. T.*, *Close Encounters of the Third Kind*). More contemporary versions have to contend with the question: If aliens are here and possess the capability of wiping us out, why haven't they done so by now?

In addition to looking at social and cultural factors to understand the UFO phenomenon, we also have to focus on the role of individual or personal factors. It must be emphasized that persons who believe in the reality of, or who are convinced that they have observed, alien aircraft are not mentally disturbed, distressed, clinically depressed, suffering from hysteria, or dissatisfied with their lives or the society in which they live. For the most part, they are not kooks, weirdos, socially marginal or maladjusted, nor do they reject reality wholesale. As we've seen, nearly half of the U.S. public believes that UFOs are real, only a very slightly lower percentage believes that UFOs are spaceships from another planet, and roughly one in ten say that they have personally seen a UFO. These figures represent a substantial proportion of the population, far too great a percentage to be explained by psychopathological explanations. Some studies show that UFO believers are slightly better educated than UFO doubters (D. Miller, 1985, pp.134–135); others (such as the public opinion poll data I cite in chapter 10) show the reverse. The point is, ignorance and superstition (J. Miller, 1987) does not and cannot account for the belief that aliens are among us. The fact that the education of UFO believers is equivalent to that of doubters suggests that the "mass hysteria" explanation is likely to be invalid (D. Miller, 1985, pp.134–135). How, then, do we account for belief in the reality of UFOs from an individualistic perspective? How do believers differ from doubters?

The major dimension along which believers and doubters differ is the likelihood of accepting alternate realities. Some people have a mind set that regards anomalous stimuli as a verification of paranormal phenomena. Others encounter the same stimuli and assume that it must be conventional or routine in origin. Just as devout Catholics see a miracle in a form or shape that resembles Mary or Jesus (Goode, 1992, pp.160–163), ufologists see an alien space ship in lights or unexplained objects in the sky. Seeing UFOs as real is correlated with reading science fiction, believing that astrology is accurate, and believing in the occult. Believers do not so much reject mainstream culture as they adapt it to their own version of reality. They are entranced with the mysteries of life, the anomalous, the unusual, the hidden, the fantastic. They believe that there is a dimension beyond the mundane plane of existence that is every bit as real as that which we see in our everyday lives. In addition, it is far more interesting, entrancing, and captivating. Moreover, they are more likely to believe that what they see in their everyday lives provides a clue to that alternate reality; the clues are there if only we have the sensitivity, intelligence, and insight to look for them.

In my study of undergraduates' paranormal beliefs (Goode, 1999), there was an extraordinarily strong relationship between belief in the reality of UFOs and acceptance of a wide range of paranormal assertions. I asked my respondents to tell me if they agreed or disagreed with the question: "Many of the unidentified flying objects (UFOs) that have been reported are really space vehicles flown by intelligent beings from another planet." Just under one respondent in five (19 percent) agreed; four in ten disagreed (40 percent); and the rest weren't sure. Respondents who agreed with the UFO question were also significantly, and in some cases strikingly, more likely to agree that: the Loch Ness Monster is real; King Tut's curse is real; astrology is scientific, valid, and true; some people have ESP; ghosts are real; angels exist; the devil is real; and God created the earth in six days, as recounted in the Bible.

In short, belief that UFOs are something real rests on a more general paranormal outlook. Indeed, believers tend to hold to a view of reality that is compatible with the idea that: traditional empirical science is incomplete; scientists are often wrong, and what they regard as scientific laws can be skirted or violated; there are dimensions or manifestations of reality not noticed or explained by conventional natural scientists; strange things happen that require unconventional explanations; the ordinary man or woman may notice phenomena that are missed by scientists; it is plausible that occult, supernatural, or spiritual events take place in the material world; and the line between the material, spiritual, and paranormal is often unclear. Theirs is a world-view that finds it perfectly understandable that anomalous, ambiguous stimuli in the night sky are alien craft.

THE ROSWELL INCIDENT

The facts of the matter, at least as they appear to most scientists and reputable journalists, can be related fairly briefly. On June 14, 1947, ranch foreman W. W. ("Mac") Brazel, found the remains of what appeared to be an aircraft of some kind in the desert 80 miles from Roswell, New Mexico. Material was strewn along a 200-yard path. In an interview conducted on the 8th of July, Brazel described it as consisting of tinfoil, wooden sticks or struts, strips of rubber, tough paper, and tape, some of it with a floral design. He said he initially "did not pay much attention to it" and continued on his rounds around the ranch.

Eleven days later, pilot Kenneth Arnold's report of seeing "flying saucers" was broadcast across the nation. The news touched off hundreds of similar sightings nationwide. However, Brazel, living in a shack in the desert with no radio, was unaware of the furor the Arnold sighting had touched off. He did not consider his discovery important enough to report until several weeks later. On July 4, he collected the debris, rolled it up and tossed it underneath a bush. On July 5, Brazel drove to Corona, where he may have heard a rumor floating around that there was a reward for anyone who located the remains of a crashed saucer. He returned to the desert and, with his wife and two children, gathered up the debris, which weighed about five pounds, and brought it home.

On July 7, Brazel drove back to Corona for the purpose of selling some wool. He brought along the material he found in the desert, taking it to Sheriff George Wilcox, telling him that he "might have found a flying disk" (Jaroff, 1997, p.68). Wilcox then called nearby Roswell Army Air Field and got in touch with a Major Jesse Marcel, the base's intelligence officer. Marcel, thinking the material could be the remains of a flying craft, drove to Corona with another officer, Captain Sheridan Cavitt, picked up Brazel, followed him to the ranch, collected the debris, put it into the trunk of his car, and brought it to the base. Cavitt stated on public record that there was nothing out of the ordinary about the material. In addition, Marcel stated that there were no crash or scoop marks on the ground where the material was found. Back at the base, Marcel and Brigadier General Roger Ramey were photographed with the debris. Officials at the Roswell base then shipped the wreckage to a regional command center, Carswell Army Air Force base in Fort Worth, Texas. From there, it was shipped to what is now the Wright-Patterson Air Force base in Ohio. It is crucial to emphasize that, at the time, very few observers thought of flying "disks" or "saucers" in terms of extraterrestrial craft. Nearly everyone assumed that they were secret military aircraft, possibly Soviet in origin.

On July 8, authorities at the airfield issued a press release which stated that the debris from a "flying disk" had been recovered. This prompted an article in *The Roswell Daily Record* entitled "RAAF Captures Flying Saucer." The news created a sensation, and inquiries flooded in from around the world asking about the craft. The night of July 8, General Ramey called the media, issuing a statement that the remains were from a high-altitude weather balloon, not a flying saucer. We now know that the general's statement was false, a story to cover up Project Mogul, an airborne system of spying on Soviet atomic explosions. The next day, the *Daily Record* ran the headline: "General Ramey Empties Roswell Saucer." The disclaimer quieted things down, and for over 30 years, the matter was largely forgotten.

In 1978, Stanton Friedman, a former nuclear physicist, interviewed Major Marcel, who remained convinced that what Brazel gave him was the wreckage of an unusual craft of some kind. Unfortunately, Marcel's accounts reveal the decay of memory over time. For instance, he could not recall the year when the incident took place, the fact that he had appeared in two press photos and not just one, that a total of seven photographs were taken, and that the material in all of these photographs is identical. These details assume enormous importance later on. Friedman ignored these problems and interviewed several other witnesses; he coauthored a book with Charles Berlitz and William Moore (coauthors of the infamous and now-discredited *The Bermuda Triangle Mystery*), entitled *The Roswell Incident*, which was published in 1980.

Two features of the Friedman/Berlitz/Moore book were remarkable. The first is that it put forth the contention that the debris discovered in the desert near Roswell was the wreckage from an alien craft. Note that the first three published claims of crashed alien ships (in 1948 and 1950) were either a hoax or a joke (Peebles, 1994, pp.47–50; Ziegler, 1997, pp.13–14), indicating the rarity with which this belief was held at the time of the collection of the Roswell material.

The second remarkable feature of the claims made in this book was a story, told secondhand, of a man who died in 1969. The man claimed he had seen another crash site on the plains of Saint Agustin, 150 miles from where Brazel had found the debris. The story is that this other site was littered with tiny humanoid bodies. At the time, no one, Friedman included, placed much credence in the secondhand story from a deceased man, since it seemed to have no relation to the Roswell crash. But eight years later, the second tale assumed prominence in a book written by two science fiction writers, Kevin Randell and Don Schmidt, *UFO Crash at Roswell*, who claimed that the government had found and "spirited away" the extraterrestrial bodies. New alleged Roswell eyewitnesses emerged, including a mortician, who had been asked for "child-sized coffins," and a nurse, who claimed to have seen an autopsy performed on "strange-looking, small bodies" (Jaroff, 1997, p.69).

Since that time, dozens of books claiming that alien space ships crashed in the desert near Roswell have been published; in all likelihood, dozens more are in the works. With each succeeding book, new witnesses turn up, claiming to have seen extraterrestrial bodies. It has become a full-time job to track down each and every claim. According to a poll conducted by *Time* magazine, among the segment of the public accepting the idea that UFOs are alien airships, two-thirds believe that a UFO "crash-landed near Roswell"; four-fifths believe that the U.S. government "knows more about extraterrestrials than it chooses to let on" (Handy, 1997, p.63).

The fact is, contrary to the conspiracy theorists, the U. S. military was actively seeking to locate physical evidence of an alien crash long after the Roswell incident. Secret documents that the government was forced to release under the Freedom of Information Act contain statements by top Air Force officials to that effect. For instance, in a document dated March 17, 1948, Colonel Howard McCoy, chief intelligence officer at the air force base where the remains of the Roswell crash were supposedly shipped, stated: "We are running down every [UFO] report. I can't tell you how much we would give to have one of those [mysterious craft] so we could recover whatever they are" (Handy, 1997, p.70). Moreover, if the material from Roswell were extraterrestrial and were vastly superior to earthly materials, it makes sense that the military would have conducted a huge research project to unlock its secrets. (Remember, the "Cold War" with the Soviet Union began just a year before the Roswell incident.) Yet, engineers who worked on military contracts at that time were not aware of the existence of any such research (Klass, 1997, pp.226–231). Clearly, the military was aware of the fact that the material collected in the desert was not of extraterrestrial origin.

In 1994 and 1997, the Air Force released two reports on the Roswell incident. (They are summarized in Broad, 1994, 1997; Weaver and MacAndrew, 1995; MacAndrew, 1997.) Both admitted that the weather balloon story had been a cover-up for top-secret Project Mogul, which was designed to monitor Soviet atomic tests.

The materials used to assemble Mogul's balloons match perfectly Brazel's 1947 description of what he found in the desert, as well as the seven photographs taken of the debris before they were shipped from the Roswell base. The balloons were fitted with "corner reflectors" which were held together with beams made of balsa wood and coated with glue; the seams were reinforced with the same tape (with "pinkish-purple . . . flower-like designs") which Major Marcel interpreted as bearing "hieroglyphics" (Ziegler, 1997, pp.8–9). Records show that one train of balloons was released in the first week of June (p.4), about a week before Brazel found the debris. The train disappeared off the radar screen that was monitoring its movement just 20 miles from the ranch where Brazel found the debris. Moreover, military records show that there were no unusual operations, movements, or maneuvers during the period in question, nor did pilots assigned to the Roswell base at the time report any rumor or hubbub occurring just after the discovery of the debris.

According to the Air Force reports, the small bodies some witnesses claimed to have seen may have been test dummies, 67 of which were released in projects High Dive and Excelsior, which took place in the area between 1954 and 1959. Some critics charge that these projects took place *after* the Roswell incident. But remember, in 1947 *no one* reported having seen alien bodies. In all cases, the recollection of supposed eyewitnesses of extraterrestrials took place well after the Roswell incident; the passage of time collapsed their recollection to 1947. For instance, the autopsy that the nurse-eyewitness reports could not have taken place until 1956, when she was first assigned to the Roswell base (Gildenberg and Thomas, 1998). In 1978, a man told author Friedman that another man, who died in 1969, had told him about dead bodies that he claimed to have seen in 1947, but clearly this story cannot be verified. In other words, we have no evidence that is unassailably contemporaneous to 1947 that says anything about alien bodies. This part of the tale was tacked on much later, after the notion of extraterrestrials had become believable to the American public.

Thus, the interesting questions about the Roswell incident are not physical and forensic, but sociological and anthropological. In other words, what is important about Roswell is not what happened, because we already know what happened. (At least, we know the version that is most credible to scientists, historians, and journalists.) I am not attempting to verify the scientific, historical, or journalistic account, but to show how different it is from that believed in by the ufologists. What is important from the perspective of a social scientist is how and why the tale that aliens crashed in the desert arose and what role it plays in contemporary culture. The official version of the crash is questionable only if one buys into the notion of a vast government conspiracy. But if one believes that the government released false information to cover up the real story, that there was an alien craft, one is free to construct any story one might choose. After the 1970s, alien crash stories became essentially unfalsifiable; that is, no amount of discrediting information could possibly falsify any assertion because that information is inevitably part of a government cover-up of the truth (Ziegler, 1997, p.15). This mythical story needs close examination.

According to anthropologist Charles Ziegler, there are at least six separate, distinct, and partly contradictory although overlapping Roswell tales (1997, pp.17–29). All have tidied up their assertions so that they are consistent with the alien angle. For instance, in several versions of the tale, Dan Wilmot and his wife saw a flying saucer in the air on July 2. In these versions, Brazel is supposed to have discovered the wreckage in the desert after July 2, not on June 14, when he said he found it. But all contain the same core elements. Our intellectual puzzle is this: What makes one or another version of the Roswell story plausible to some observers but not to others? Why do close to 75 million Americans believe that the debris Brazel collected in the desert near Roswell was extraterrestrial in origin?

Ziegler classifies the six versions of the Roswell incident that assert the alien origin of the crash as myths. By this he does not mean they are necessarily false, only that they follow a stereotypical or folkloric structure, much like the tales told in tribal and folk societies. The Roswell myth contains themes that have been embedded in stories for thousands of years. The central motif of the Roswell tale is that "a malevolent monster (the government) has sequestered an item essential to humankind (wisdom of a transcendental nature, i.e., evidence-based knowledge that we are not alone in the universe)." The tale has a hero as well as a villain: "The cultural hero (the ufologist) circumvents the monster and by investigative prowess, releases the essential item (wisdom) for humankind" (1997, p.51). Hoarded-object folk narratives in which the hero, through intelligence, bravery, and zeal, releases or liberates the hoarded object "are truly ubiquitous and geographically widespread" (p.52). Once again, the folkloric quality of the Roswell story does not automatically invalidate its validity, but it does shed light on its appeal. According to Ziegler, the Roswell incident "is a folk narrative masquerading as an exposé" (p.155).

In addition, the Roswell UFO story is appealing to many believers because:

- It represents a "vehicle for social protest" against the government; it is an expression of "antigovernment sentiment," dramatic testimony to ongoing government conspiracies (p.68).

- It is unfalsifiable; it cannot be disproven. Any fact that is presented to counter its validity is interpreted as a government cover-up.

- It contains a strong religious element. For many observers, aliens are contemporary angels possessing wisdom humans need but lack (pp.70–74).

- It is an ingredient in affirming group solidarity and distinguishing believers (who are wise and virtuous) from nonbelievers (who are fools, knaves, and narrow-minded dogmatists) and stressing the superiority of the former over the latter (p.66).

• It is a means by which the "we are not alone" notion is made manifest and, simultaneously, an assertion that our earthly imperfections could be rectified by the wisdom of infinitely superior, superhuman, almost supernatural beings.

Ziegler argues that the image scholars and scientists hold on the Roswell incident is based on a "way of knowing" that is radically different from that which believers use (p.154). Scholars and scientists tend to have different, and usually stricter, standards regarding acceptable and decisive evidence. Issues that concern them tend to assume less importance to advocates, believers, and ufologists.

For instance, scientists and scholars place far more emphasis on physical and forensic evidence, while believers have more faith in eyewitnesses (if they agree with their own version of the truth). Discrepancies in different versions of the Roswell tale (indeed, as I said, some of them are contradictory) are more distressing to the expert and less so to the believer. The fact that the tale follows well-worn traditional and stereotypical folk idioms that have existed for thousands of years arouses more suspicion in the scientist and the scholar, less so in the believer. The fact that some supposed eyewitnesses have come forward decades after the event, or have been shown to have been dishonest in other matters, or changed their stories over time, is far more discrediting to the scientist and the scholar than to the believer.

In contrast, believers more readily discount evidence that issues from the government, assuming that it is "tainted" by a conspiracy; scientists and scholars are less likely to do so, arguing that conspiracy theories are an excuse for protecting a theory that cannot be falsified.

Once again, as we have so often seen, the ways that scientists "know" something to be true are very different from the ways that believers or laypersons "know" their version of the truth. Each is based on an epistemology that *cancels the other out*. Given their incompatibility, it is almost unimaginable that the mystery of Roswell can be solved to the satisfaction of all parties any time soon.

It must be emphasized that the account I render here does not represent a validation of the skeptic's version of Roswell and a critique of the ufologist's. It does, however, represent an effort to emphasize that *different sorts of evidence* are accepted by the two sides. Believers feel that the fact that the government has covered up in the past is crucial evidence in the Roswell mystery; given the fact of a cover-up, it *must have been* about aliens. In contrast, skeptics argue that, in principle, the cover-up could have been about anything; in fact, it was about a secret anti-Soviet surveillance program. The fact that six *entirely different* and in large measure, contradictory, extraterrestrial Roswell stories circulate is crucial for the scientist, almost irrelevant for the believer. (After all, *at least one* has to be true, they reason.) The fact that these tales resonate with and address cultural and societal concerns is important for the scientist, a mere distraction for the believer. Once again, a narration of the events of Roswell underlines the fundamental differences in epistemology between ufologist and scientist, it does not prove that one version is right and the other is wrong. At this point, neither side could possibly be successful in convincing the other of the validity of its position.

ALIEN CONTACT

When we enter the world of alien abductions, we enter the world of extraterrestrial contact of the closest kind, or "close encounters of the fourth kind." Abductees (who prefer the term "contactees") describe all manner of contact, a great deal of it sexual in nature. (The parallel with satanic ritual abuse is extremely strong; see Goode, 1992, pp.337–342, for a brief summary of this extremely large literature.) With contactee tales, the gap between evidence that is convincing to believers and that which convinces scientists is vastly greater than with the Roswell incident. With abductions, all we have are stories by supposed eyewitnesses or victims. No physical or forensic evidence of alien origin has been turned up that would convince the scientific fraternity. Female contactees report having been impregnated and bred for alien-human hybrid offspring, yet gynecologists detect no such physical changes in their bodies. Contactees report having been cut open, yet no scars, or only conventional scars, can be found. Electronic devices are reported to have been implanted in their brains, yet none, again, that are indisputably extraplanetary have been located. (For a contrary view, see Leir, 1998.) As an explanation, contactees claim that the technology of the extraterrestrials is so powerful, advanced, and sophisticated that aliens can make evidence of such interventions disappear or blend in with human tissue.

Moreover, contactees claim, aliens display powers that scientists say are all but impossible. They move through solid objects, beam up humans onto the mother ship, appear before entire cities and remain undetected. It is not surprising that most scientists remain extremely skeptical of the claims of contactees. Ufologists invoke forces that are contrary to the laws of science, and they offer no plausible evidence to back up their claims.

Stories of alien contact have been narrated for centuries. Francis Godwin's *The Man in the Moone* (1638) and Ralph Morris' *A Narrative and the Life and Astonishing Adventures of John Daniel* (1751), are taken today as intended fiction. However, in 1758, in *Concerning Earths in Our Solar World*, Emanuel Swedenborg appeared to make the claim that he had actually visited all the then-known planets, which he described in great detail as being inhabited by creatures who had devised ideal societies. We now know of the existence of planets that were not described by Swedenborg (Uranus, Neptune, and Pluto), and we know the ones then known about are very different from his description and are, in all likelihood, uninhabited.

The pre-1950s literature on alien contact usually has the contactee visiting another planet. These narratives include an account given in 1890 by Helen Smith of Martians speaking a language that sounds very much like French; in 1906 by Sarah Weis, who described nonexistent Martian canals in great detail; in 1918 by Aleister Crowley, who describes contact with "Lam," an inhabitant of a distant constellation who has a bulbous head and tiny, beady eyes; in 1930 by Willard Magoon, who described Mars as a "beautiful, lush planet of forests, parks, and gardens" (Melton, 1995, p.1; Adams, 1997); and in 1935 by Guy Ballard King, who describes contact with a dozen Venusians, who played the harp and the violin inside a vast cavern inside the Royal Teton Mountain (Melton, 1995, p.2). Today's contactees rarely tell stories of being transported to the extraterrestrial's home planet; instead, they are nearly always abducted and taken onto an alien space ship.

Remember John Mack (1994, 1995; Rae, 1994) the Harvard psychiatrist who endorsed the idea that the stories his patients told him about having been abducted by aliens were literally and factually true? Mack's evidence? He was convinced because of the intense, heartfelt emotion that accompanied their stories, and because of their narrative consistency. They had to be telling the truth, Mack reasoned, because they had no reason to lie, they told their stories reluctantly, their stories were similar to one another, and their therapeutic sessions with him were filled with genuine terror. They aren't faking or seeking attention, Mack reasoned, nor are they insane. They sincerely *believe* that they are telling the truth. For Dr. Mack, this was sufficient.

The fact that members of folk and tribal societies have told consistent stories of being attacked, seduced, apprehended, abducted, threatened, or terrorized by ghosts, goblins, elves, demons, fairies, "old hags," and assorted incubi and succubi with great emotional intensity for thousands of years (Hufford, 1982) did not seem relevant to Dr. Mack.

Mack's evidence for the fact that his patients were telling the truth was their sincerity and emotional intensity. For him, the way tales were told was the empirical observation that convinced him of the reality of aliens on earth. For the great majority of scientists, these criteria are not sufficient. Once again, whether or not we take these stories as literally true or not is not our main goal. For us, what is central is the fact that different observers have different ways of knowing an assertion to be true.

There are several issues that force scientists to be skeptical about contactee reports. The fact that contactees can almost never point to witnesses who can confirm their stories, even if they have been abducted in an urban environment such as New York City, seems to be of little concern to believers. To the scientist, this consideration makes the assertion highly suspicious. The fact that a remarkably high proportion of abductions take place during hypnogogic (in the twilight state when falling asleep) and hypnopompic (when waking up) states, forces the scientist to wonder whether these are hallucinations or genuine, real-world events. To the ufologist or UFO believer, this fact is of little concern or interest. The fact that abductees return, claiming to have had experiences that leave physical traces when in fact, there are none or leave those that are unremarkable, causes the scientist to be extremely skeptical that such experiences actually took place.

Mack claims implants have been recovered from the bodies of contactees (1995, p.27), but when retrieved, they turn out to be unremarkable and not uncontestably of extraterrestrial origin. Mack argues that, since aliens are capable of altering the genetic or chemical structure of material left in contactees' bodies that conform to earthly specifications (p.28), this fact proves nothing. In other words, the contactees' claims cannot be falsified by the lack of physical evidence, again a detail that is extremely troubling to the traditional scientist but of little or no concern to the believer. Once again, these evidentiary issues do not disprove the contactees' claims, but they do explain why many scientists are skeptical about claims that attract many fervent, committed adherents.

Part Four

Institutional Connections

Sociologists are very interested in a number of extremely important social factors, variables, or dimensions. Where a person stands on one or all of them is related to or correlated with a broad range of beliefs and behaviors. For example, sex or gender is such a factor or variable. Being a man or a woman influences one's political views, religious beliefs and practices, sexual behavior, and drug use, to name a few. Age, likewise, is crucial in determining what one does, believes, and feels. Some other basic factors or variables that have a significant impact on behavior, style of life, way of doing things, practices, and beliefs include: race, religious background, rural-urban residence, geographical residence, education, and social class or socioeconomic status (which is often shortened by sociologists to SES). Researchers refer to such factors as "independent variables" because they influence or cause many other things in life.

Sociologists are also interested in what they refer to as *social institutions*. A social institution is defined as a cluster of values, norms, statuses, and roles that emerges around a given social need, theme, or activity. Institutions are *webs* or *networks* of associations that bind the occupants of specific statuses or positions together in certain ways, reg-

159

ulating the manner in which these persons interact with or relate to one
another. All of us are expected to act a certain way toward family members, our teachers, store clerks, and the clergy, occupants of social statuses that are located within specific institutional realms. We may be
punished with sanctions if we fail to live up to these expectations.

Sociologists identify or focus on five basic or *major* institutions: the
family, religion, the economy, politics and government, and education.
Each of these institutions is universal. In one manifestation or another,
each is found in all societies, everywhere around the world, and throughout recorded history. Every person in every society has a position, location, or *status* in each of these institutions. Major institutions are linked
to each other and to the society as a whole in crucial ways that influence
the lives of all of us. In addition to these major institutions, there are
countless other, perhaps not quite so major, institutions: for instance,
medicine, sport, entertainment, fashion, and the media.

We can look at the linkages of institutions on the "macro," or the
large, structural level. On the *macro* level, we can examine how, in a given
society, for example, the economy influences its art, or how the content
of its educational curriculum reflects its religious teachings. On the
micro or individual level, we can examine how a person's statuses in one
institutional realm influence belief or behavior in other areas of life—for
instance, how being a Catholic influences voting patterns, or how being
a parent influences one's consumption of illegal drugs.

On the micro or individual level, each one of us is a "bundle" of statuses, each status corresponding to a specific position in a given institutional realm. In other words, we all have a "person set," which is this
collection or roster of statuses. Person A is a middle-aged man, a devout
Catholic, a husband, father, brother, son, an active Republican and a
conservative, an affluent corporation lawyer, a college graduate with a
post-graduate education, living near a medium-sized city in the Midwest.
Person B, a 30-year-old lesbian, unmarried with a young daughter, has
a long-standing relationship with another woman, is an atheist, a political radical who rarely votes, a successful writer, a college graduate, and
a resident of a large city in California. Each of these persons is influenced
by his or her statuses in each of these major institutions. Each is influenced, pulled, and tugged by each of these identities and by the expectations that the other people in their status "sets" have of what he or she
should do. All of the statuses together—this "bundle" or "set" of statuses—will exert an influence on what someone who holds them will do
or believe.

In short, all of us can come up with specific answers to the basic
question, "Who am I?" We can think of our most basic statuses or characteristics—male or female, rich or poor, Black or white, liberal or con-

servative, religious or irreligious—as answers to that question. For instance, women are more likely than men to be involved in childcare; African-Americans are more likely than whites to vote Democratic; the middle-aged are more likely than the young to be involved in institutionalized religion.

Sociologists are fascinated with how these various characteristics, and how statuses in key institutions, link up with one another, and how arrays of beliefs and behaviors link up with them as well. Every imaginable belief or behavior is statistically related to or *correlated* with almost any social characteristic we can think of. *Beliefs* include accepting the reality of God, heaven, angels, extraterrestrials, that abortion is murder, that sex outside of marriage is wrong, or that animals have the same basic rights as humans. *Behavior* might include the use of marijuana, voting in the last presidential election, purchasing a new car during the past year, drinking more than three cups of coffee per day, or attending more than three religious services during the past month.

Paranormal beliefs interlock on the individual or "micro" level with numerous social characteristics or statuses, such as sex, education, and geographical location. That is, women are more likely than men to hold certain kinds of paranormal beliefs, while with other beliefs, it is the reverse; the same holds for the less versus the more well-educated; persons living in certain areas of the country as opposed to others; African-Americans versus whites; and so on.

In addition, paranormalism as a belief system is linked up in crucial ways on the "macro" or structural level with a number of major and less-than-major institutions. Three whose linkages seem the strongest are religion, the media, and politics and social movements. There are strong parallels between paranormal thinking and the belief system of many traditional religious bodies. Paranormal thinking is presented in the media in certain ways, and this is likely to have certain consequences. And many paranormal assertions have clear-cut political implications. It is the task of this section to explore how paranormal beliefs are linked up with the social structure, on both the micro and macro levels.

Chapter Ten

CORRELATES OF PARANORMALISM

With which social characteristics might beliefs and behavior correlate? When pollsters conduct a survey of public opinion, they select the most basic social characteristics: sex, age, race and ethnicity, education, socioeconomic status and/or income, geographical residence, and political orientation. Pollsters and sociologists consider social characteristics to be *factors* or *variables*. That is, they are attributes that cause or influence other things, such as beliefs and behavior. If we think of events that happen in the world as being influenced by certain conditions in a cause-and-effect fashion, we can distinguish between *independent* and *dependent* variables. Independent variables are those that influence other things in the world, while dependent variables are those that are themselves influenced *by* other things.

For instance, *age* can be thought of as an independent or causal variable with respect to drug use: teenagers and young adults are more likely to use drugs than is true of the middle-aged or the elderly. In this case, age is the *independent* or "causal" variable, while drug use is the *dependent* or "caused" variable. Clearly, using drugs cannot cause someone to be younger or older, but being younger or older can and does cause or influence whether one uses drugs. The relationship between certain other variables or factors is not quite so clear-cut. Does drug use cause poverty or does poverty cause drug use? Here, the cause-and-effect sequence is less straightforward, far more complicated than it is with age and drug use.

PARANORMALISM IN THE POLLS: AN INTRODUCTION

Occasionally, pollsters include questions about paranormal beliefs in the surveys they conduct. One basic issue very much worth exploring

163

is whether and to what extent such beliefs are related to or correlated with any of our basic sociological characteristics or positions or statuses in major social institutions. It is possible, for instance, that *certain* paranormal beliefs are related to specific statuses in one way, but others are related in a somewhat *different* fashion. Contrarily, it could be that paranormal beliefs are related to specific sociological characteristics wholesale, across the board, in a more or less consistent fashion.

For instance, are men or women more likely to believe that UFOs are "something real"? Are less well-educated or highly educated persons more likely to believe in creationism? Who is more receptive to belief in the powers of astrology—the young or the old? Are African-Americans or whites more likely to accept the view that ESP exists? These are the sorts of questions likely to be asked by researchers and pollsters who are interested in the links between paranormal beliefs and social characteristics or statuses in specific institutions. We'll explore these and related questions in this chapter. (I make use of survey data supplied by the Roper organization.)

Before we embark on our exploration, however, one qualification is in order. In seeking the correlates of paranormalism, it should be emphasized that this endeavor is not meant in any way to be derogatory toward either paranormal beliefs or the members of the categories in the population who are more likely to hold them. My position contrasts with a number of other researchers in this field. Some sociologists, pollsters, and survey researchers argue that holding "unscientific" and "pseudoscientific" beliefs is correlated with specific social attributes because respondents who possess them are uneducated and hence, ignorant of the truth of scientific findings.

In an article entitled "The Scientifically Illiterate," Jon Miller has stated: "For the 25 million Americans who do not have a high school diploma, the world is a strange, hostile, and somewhat dangerous place" (1987, p.30). Since, in the survey he summarizes, each paranormal belief discussed is negatively correlated with education—the lower the respondent's level of education, the higher the level of acceptance of each of them—Miller blames the educational system for not stamping out belief in such "superstition and pseudoscience" (p.30) as astrology, lucky numbers, and creationism.

Here, it is *not* my intention to identify belief in paranormalism (or in traditional Bible teaching) as a form of superstition or pseudoscience, or to dub any categories of the population as superstitious or pseudoscientific if they are highly likely to hold such beliefs. I am interested solely in how paranormalism is linked with sociological characteristics and membership in one or another social institution. The correlates in no way suggest conclusions about the validity of beliefs. Rather, they help us understand how the society hangs together and functions.

TRADITIONAL RELIGIOUS PARANORMAL BELIEFS

Many of the earliest and, for some believers, the most fundamental religious beliefs are paranormal in nature. Such beliefs make claims that scientists would argue transcend or violate the laws of nature. For instance, belief in most miracles, in heaven and hell as actual places, in angels and the devil as actual, physical beings, and in creationism, violate what scientists know about how the universe works. Hence, they would dub them paranormal.

Let's look at the relationship of the following beliefs with key sociological factors and variables: belief in angels, the devil, heaven and hell, and divine creation. Who believes in these assertions? Since a given specific poll does not necessarily include all the questions in which we are interested, I'll be examining the results of several polls that were conducted recently of nationally representative samples of Americans. However, a drawback of using several polls is that the wording of their questions and the categories they use vary somewhat. For instance, all polls include Blacks and whites, but some include Asians but not Hispanics; for others, it is the reverse. For some surveys, the oldest age category includes respondents age 65 and older, while for others, that category is age 70 and older. Despite these inconsistencies, a consideration of poll data on paranormal beliefs, especially with respect to their relationship with key sociological variables and factors, is absolutely crucial.

In a survey conducted by the Gallup organization in 1996, interviewers asked the following question: "For each of the following items I am going to read you, please tell me whether it is something you believe in, something you're not sure about, or something you don't believe in." One item asked about was angels. Not quite three-quarters of the sample (72 percent) said that they believe in angels.

Belief in angels is correlated with several important sociological variables. Women are significantly more likely to believe (79 percent) than men (64 percent). African-Americans are slightly although significantly more likely to believe (81 percent) than whites (72 percent) and Hispanics (76 percent). And the less well-educated are more likely to do so (76 and 79 percent for high school dropouts and graduates, respectively) than the well-educated (college graduates and respondents with a postgraduate education, 65 and 56 percent, respectively). Southerners believe in angels a bit more (80 percent) than do residents of the East

(67 percent) and the Midwest (70 percent), while westerners believe least of all (65 percent). Protestants (77 percent) and Catholics (76 percent) differ in this respect hardly at all, while Jews, whose theology does not include angels, are very unlikely to believe (21 percent); remarkably, Jews accept angels even less than persons who declare no religious affiliation at all (34 percent). Interestingly, age is only weakly correlated with belief in angels, with the very young (18 to 29) and the very old (70 and over) believing only slightly more than the in-between categories.

When it comes to belief in the devil, some of the figures are similar to belief in angels while others are somewhat different. In a 1998 survey conducted for CBS News, the following question was raised to interviewees: "Do you personally believe in the existence of the Devil or not?" Just under two-thirds of the total sample (64 percent) said that they did.

Women are only very slightly more likely to believe in the devil (65 percent) than men (62 percent); African-Americans a bit more (74 percent) than whites (63 percent), and considerably more than Hispanics (55 percent); the less well-educated a bit more (for both high school dropouts and graduates, 63 percent) than the better-educated (61 percent for college grads and 52 percent for postgrads). Again, southerners most strongly support the idea of the devil (73 percent); easterners (51 percent) and westerners (55 percent) the least; and midwesterners are in-between (68 percent). Unlike the notion of angels, Protestants are significantly more likely to support the devil idea (72 percent) than Catholics (60 percent); but here again, to Jews, the concept is even more alien (23 percent) than it is for the "no religions" category (35 percent). Once again, age provides no clear-cut pattern here, with the two youngest categories, 18-to-29-year-olds and 30-to-39 year-olds, supporting belief in the devil a bit more strongly (64 and 66 percent, respectively) than the two oldest categories (60-to-69-year-olds and respondents 70 years old and older, both of which stood at 56 percent).

A slightly different but related question elicits a much lower level of agreement than simple belief in the devil. In a survey conducted by the Princeton Survey Research Associates in 1995, respondents were asked, "Do you think the Devil can make people do evil things they would not do otherwise?"; overall, roughly four out of ten, or 42 percent, answer that they do believe this.

Several of the patterns or correlations that exist with the simple belief in the devil become much more pronounced when respondents are asked about people being possessed by the devil. This more active version of belief in the devil reveals that southerners are almost three times as likely to believe (47 percent) than westerners (17 percent); Blacks nearly twice as likely (59 percent) as whites (30 percent) and Asians (31 percent); and less-than-high-school-educated respondents over three times as likely (44 percent) as those with a postgraduate education (13 percent). Here, the two factors of age and political affiliation do not seem to be very strongly related at all to belief in the evil doings of the devil. Clearly, even though *some* well-educated respondents believe that a devil exists, a substantial proportion believe that, if he does, we should be able to resist his temptations.

Belief in heaven and hell as actual physical places, likewise, are linked with social characteristics and statuses in ways similar to those that characterize belief in angels and the devil. (Remember, only some believers picture heaven and hell as an actual physical location; many see it as having a reality in a dimension separate from the physical.) A survey conducted by Yankelovich Partners in 1997 for *Time* magazine and Cable News Network posed a number of questions to its respondents, among them the following. First: "Do you yourself believe in the existence of Heaven, where people live forever with God after they die, or don't you believe in that?" and second: "Do you believe in Hell, where people are punished forever after they die, or don't you believe in that?" Roughly eight respondents out of ten (81 percent) believe in heaven, and six out of ten (63 percent) believe in hell.

High school dropouts are significantly more likely to believe in heaven (85 percent) and hell (66 percent) than was true of respondents with a postgraduate education (68 percent for heaven, 48 percent for hell); the in-between educational categories are also somewhere in-between with respect to their belief in heaven and hell. Women are slightly more likely to believe in heaven (85 percent) and hell (64 percent) than men (76 and 63 percent, respectively), and African Americans (86 and 77 percent) somewhat, but significantly, more than whites (63 and 81 percent). Southerners (87 percent) and midwesterners (87 percent) are more likely to accept heaven as real than easterners (75 percent) and westerners (67 percent); much the same pattern is revealed for belief in hell (75 and 66 percent, 52 and 53 percent). Age is related to belief in heaven and hell only among the elderly. After the age of 65, interestingly, acceptance of the reality of them dropped off moderately sharply. And once again, Protestants (87 percent heaven, 69 percent hell) and Catholics (89 percent heaven, 65 percent hell) are quite close together, while Jews are strikingly less likely to accept the reality of these domains (34 percent heaven, 19 percent hell)—again, even less than was true of respondents who said that they have no religion (39 and 27 percent, respectively).

And last, we might consider belief in divine creation, that is, that God created heaven and earth and all living creatures on earth in six earthly days 6,000 to 10,000 years ago, as described in the Book of Genesis. A Gallup poll conducted for the Cable News Network and *U.S.A.*

Today asked respondents the following question: "Which of the follow-ing statements comes closest to your views on the origin and develop-ment of human beings—human beings have developed over millions of years from less advanced forms of life, but God had no part in this pro-cess, or God created human beings pretty much in their present form at one time within the last 10,000 years or so?"

Not quite four respondents in ten (39 percent) agree with the strict creationist position, that God created humans within the past ten mil-lennia, as the Bible says; only one in seven (14 percent) say that evolution with no God is an accurate description; and four in ten (40 percent) believe in evolution, but feel God guided the process. The last of these might be referred to as a "divine" evolutionary position, in that it *rejects* the supposed event of divine creation of the universe at a recent point in time and *accepts* the process of the evolution of species, including human beings, over a very long period of time.

Let's look at who believes in creationism versus who believes in evolution, whether the latter is guided or unguided by God. That is, I am combining the "divine" evolutionist and the "secular" or "non-divine" evolutionist positions into one category, and comparing it with the strict biblical creationist position.

In this poll, women are more likely than men to believe in divine creation (49 versus 39 percent), and less likely to believe in evolution (54 versus 45 percent). African-Americans are more likely to be creation-ists than whites (54 versus 43 percent).

As we've already seen, belief in creationism is strongest among the least well educated, weakest among the most well-educated. High school dropouts are slightly more likely to believe in divine creation (58 per-cent) than high school graduates (54 percent), who, in turn, are much more likely to do so than respondents with some college (38 percent) and college graduates (37 percent), who, likewise, are more likely to do so than interviewees with a postgraduate education (24 percent). Clearly, belief in creationism is *negatively* correlated with education, while belief in evolution is *positively* related: the lower the education, the higher the likelihood of a belief in divine creation; the higher the education, the higher the likelihood of a belief in evolution.

The South had the highest proportion of creationists (50 percent), while the East and the West had the highest percentage of evolutionists (51 and 54 percent, respectively). Protestants (52 percent) were more likely to accept divine creation than Catholics (40 percent), who, in turn, were more likely to do so than Jews (18 percent) and persons who des-ignated no religion (17 percent). People over the age of 60 believed in cre-ationism considerably more than any other age category.

Special attention should be paid to the correlation between self-designated ideological labels, "liberal," "conservative," and "moderate," and these religious beliefs. *In nearly every case*, respondents who labeled themselves conservatives were more likely to hold religious beliefs than liberals did. In a CBS poll, seven in ten of the conservatives said that they believed in the devil (72 percent), while this was true of only half the liberals (50 percent); a Gallup poll found these figures to be 50 and 37 percent. A Gallup poll found that three-quarters of the conservatives (77 percent) believed in angels, while two-thirds of the liberals (66 percent) did so. In the Princeton Survey Research Associates poll, nine in ten conservatives said that they believed in heaven (90 percent), while slightly fewer, eight in ten, of the liberals did (82 percent). The comparable figures for hell were eight in ten (78 percent) and six in ten (61 percent). The Gallup poll showed that a majority of conservatives were creationists (57 percent), while this was true of only a minority of liberals (34 percent), most of whom believe in some version of evolution (61 percent). For just about all answers to these question tapping traditional religious belief, "moderates" fell somewhere between these two extremes.

These ideological designations may not have a straightforward relationship with politics. Instead, for most respondents, "conservative" may simply mean "traditional" or "conventional" in a very broad or general sense, while on the opposite side of the coin, the self-designation of "liberal" may refer to their more unconventional, non-traditional lifestyles or attitudes toward life. Clearly, accepting religious beliefs (specifically those with a paranormal component) measures, taps, or indicates a broader conservative, traditional, or orthodox set of beliefs or way of life.

Let us summarize. What sociological picture do we draw of religious, mainly traditional Christian, paranormalism? Women, African-Americans, southerners, the least well-educated, and the politically conservative, are significantly more likely than men, whites, northerners, the well educated, and the politically liberal to believe in angels, the devil, heaven and hell, and divine creation. Age is a weak factor in each of these beliefs with the exception of a belief in heaven, which the elderly are *less* likely to accept, and divine creation, which the elderly are *more* likely to accept. Jews are *strikingly* less likely to accept these largely Christian tenets of belief, as are respondents who answer "none" when asked about their religious affiliation. Differences between Protestants and Catholics are small, except for belief in creationism, which Protestants are significantly more likely to accept; contrarily, Catholics are more likely to accept the validity of evolution. And lastly, ideological conservatives are more likely to embrace the tenets of these religious beliefs, liberals are less likely to do so, and moderates fall somewhere in between.

NON-RELIGIOUS PARANORMAL BELIEFS

Taken as a whole, paranormal beliefs which do not have an origin in the Christian religious tradition do not display as clear or consistent a relationship with our key sociological variables as religious paranormalism seems to. Let's look at the relationships of paranormal beliefs with five variables: sex, race and ethnicity, education, geographical residence, and ideological or political stance. Once again, I make use of the results of a half-dozen public opinion polls supplied to me by the Roper organization.

Sex. Fairly consistently in these polls, women are more likely to believe in a broad range of quasi-religious, supernatural, or spiritual claims than men, while, contrarily, men are somewhat more likely to believe most claims about the reality of extraterrestrials. A Gallup poll showed that a higher proportion of women (23 percent) than men (10 percent) say that they had ever "consulted a fortune-teller or psychic"; believe in "ghosts, or that spirits of dead people can come back in certain places or situations" (34 versus 25 percent); that people "can hear from or communicate mentally with someone who has died" (24 versus 16 percent); that "houses can be haunted" (35 versus 31 percent); in "telepathy, or communication between minds without using the traditional five senses" (37 versus 32 percent); in ESP (52 versus 43 percent); and in "astrology, or that the position of the stars and planets can affect people's lives" (27 versus 22 percent). These differences are not huge, certainly not overwhelming or striking, but they are significant, and they are consistent. We are on firm ground when we assert that women are more likely to hold a fairly wide range of spiritual, supernatural, occult, and paranormal beliefs. This generalization is consistent with their higher level of acceptance of religious belief generally, and more specifically those religious beliefs that harbor a paranormal dimension.

In contrast, men are somewhat more likely to believe that UFOs are of extraterrestrial origin. Again, the differences are not enormous, but the various surveys, as well as the different measures or indicators of this belief, seem to point in the same direction. The Gallup poll asked: "In your opinion, are UFOs . . . something real, or just people's imaginations?" Slightly more men (51 percent) than women (46 percent) answered "something real" to this question. In this same survey, respondents were also asked, "Do you think that UFOs . . . have ever visited earth in some form, or not?" Again, men (51 percent) are more likely than women (40 percent) to assent. More men (15 percent) than women (10 percent) say that they had seen something they thought was a UFO. In the Princeton Survey Research Associates poll conducted for *Newsweek*, again, men are more likely to agree with the UFO questions than women. When asked, "Do you believe that UFOs . . . are probably alien ships or alien life forms, or that they have some natural scientific explanation," 22 percent of the men and 18 percent of the women give the "alien" answer. When this survey asked if "the government is keeping information from the public that shows UFOs . . . are real or that aliens have visited the Earth," again, men are slightly more likely to agree (53 percent) than women (46 percent). It seems clear that men support a somewhat, although not strikingly, stronger belief than women in the reality of UFOs.

Race and Ethnicity. Hispanics are somewhat more likely to accept the tenets of a variety of paranormal belief systems than is true of African-Americans, who, in turn, are more likely to do so than whites. It is possible that the number of Asians interviewed in these polls is too small to yield a consistent pattern.

The Gallup poll asked respondents whether they believe in astrology; 22 percent of whites, 39 percent of Blacks, and 43 percent of Hispanics say that they do. In the Princeton Survey Research Associates poll, the same ranking of racial/ethnic categories prevails, although the figures are somewhat different (whites, 40 percent; Blacks, 44 percent; Hispanics, 68 percent). Over twice as many Hispanics (44 percent) than whites or Blacks (16 percent each) say they had ever consulted a "fortune-teller or psychic". To return to the Gallup poll, acceptance of belief in clairvoyance, or "the power of the mind to know the past and predict the future," is highest among Hispanics (56 percent), lowest among whites (26 percent), and in-between, but far closer to whites, for African-Americans (29 percent). A similar pattern turned up for belief in ghosts (19 percent Hispanics; 8 percent, whites; 12 percent Blacks); experience with being in a haunted house (31, 15, and 21 percent, respectively); communication with the dead (30, 21, and 19 percent); reincarnation (34, 21, and 24 percent); and channeling, or allowing a spirit being "to temporarily assume control of a human body during a trance" (30, 11, and 15 percent). Not all paranormal beliefs assumed this pattern, but most did.

Belief in the reality of UFOs does not follow this same tendency. In the Yankelovich survey, whites are more likely to believe in the reality of UFOs (41 percent) than Blacks (24 percent) and Hispanics (37 percent). In the Princeton Survey Research Associates poll, whites (21 percent) and Blacks (20 percent) are equally as likely to say that UFOs "are probably alien ships," while Hispanics are less likely (13 percent) to do so. The Gallup poll found that whites (49 percent) are barely more likely to believe that UFOs are "something real" than Blacks (45 percent), while Hispanics are much more likely (64 percent) to do so. But when the same poll asked whether UFOs "have ever visited earth in some form," these numbers change to 45, 49, and 51 percent agreement, respectively. In short, the polls we have at our disposal do not reveal a consistent pattern by race or ethnicity in belief in the reality of UFOs.

   Education. The Gallup poll reveals that the respondent's belief that he or she had ever been in a haunted house was *negatively* correlated with education: persons who had not graduated from high school are much more likely to say they had been in a house they felt was haunted (24 percent) than was true of college graduates (10 percent) and postgraduates (7 percent). The same pattern holds for the experience of having "seen or been in the presence of a ghost" (14 versus 8 and 4 percent). Likewise, belief in astrology, "or that the position of the stars and planets can affect people's lives" is correlated negatively by education: 28 percent for less than high school graduates; 26 percent for high school graduates; 21 percent for college graduates; and 12 percent for post-graduates. Belief in reincarnation, too, shows a slight tendency to rise as education declines: 26 percent of high school dropouts believe in it, 15 percent of postgraduate respondents do so. Thus far, it seems that belief in paranormal assertions that do not originate from a Christian tradition, like those that do, rise as education declines, and decline as education rises.

   In the survey sponsored by *Newsweek*, the Princeton Survey Research Associates asked a sample of respondents the following question: "In general, do you consider yourself a believer in the paranormal and supernatural, or not?" The lowest-educated category (not a high school graduate) is barely more likely to agree (43 percent) than the highest-educated category, interviewees with a postgraduate education (39 percent). No apparent pattern emerges for the in-between educational categories. The survey conducted by the Gallup organization asked a question about reincarnation that read as follows: "Have you ever felt that you were here on earth in a previous life or existence in another body?" The percentages saying yes are almost completely flat for the five categories: less than high school graduates, 9 percent; high school graduates, 8 percent; some college, 10 percent; college graduates, 9 percent; postgraduates, 9 percent. In other words, no relationship at all exists— a *random* relationship.

   When the Gallup poll questioned a sample of respondents concerning their belief in "telepathy, or communication between minds without using the traditional five senses," a slightly *higher* proportion of respondents with a postgraduate education say that they believed (38 percent) than is true of respondents who are not high school graduates (30 percent). In this survey, the same relationship prevails for belief in ESP or extrasensory perception (48 versus 41 percent).

When these surveys asked questions about whether UFOs "are something real" or "just people's imagination," no clear correlation with educational level is established. While most find a very slightly higher level of belief in the reality of UFOs among the least well educated categories, the differences are small, and the in-between educational categories often have lower—or higher—levels of belief than the highest or lowest educational categories. In fact, practically no correlation whatsoever seems to exist between a respondent's educational level and his or her belief in the reality of unidentified flying objects. Even if we grant the *very* slightly greater tendency of least well educated respondents to believe in the reality of UFOs than the respondents with the highest level of education, once again, the in-between categories are all over the map.

Geographical Residence. Californians have a reputation for "kookiness," for embracing the latest fad or trend in "far out" claims, for accepting all manner of paranormal beliefs. This reputation is not entirely undeserved. In most respects, the residents of California do tend to be less traditional and less conventional than are residents of other regions of the country, especially those living in the South and the Midwest.

Bainbridge and Stark (1980) found the Pacific region of the United States (made up mainly of Californians) to rank *lowest* in organized church membership among all areas of the country. But the Pacific region ranked highest with respect to letters published in *Fate*, a prominent paranormal publication, describing their own "true mystic experiences" and their "proof of survival" (apparitions, near-death experiences, and messages from the dead). In addition, the Pacific region ranked highest in the number of cults per million residents (pp.26–29). With respect to the "geography of the supernatural," say Bainbridge and Stark, Californians rank at the top on the paranormal dimension.

The surveys we have at our disposal divide the country into four geographical areas—East, Midwest, South, and West. A majority, or near-majority, of westerners live in California. When asked by the Princeton Survey Research Associates poll, "In general, do you consider yourself a believer in the paranormal and supernatural, or not?", westerners are most likely to say yes (49 percent), easterners next most likely (42 percent), and southerners (36 percent) and midwesterners (35 percent) the least. In comparison with residents of other regions of the country, the Gallup poll revealed, westerners are most likely to say that they: had ever been "in touch with someone who has already died" (26 percent, versus 13 percent for residents of the East, 18 percent for midwesterners, and 15 percent for southerners); "seen or been in the presence of a ghost (17 versus 8, 5, and 7 percent, respectively); been in a house they "felt was haunted" (20 versus 11, 17, and 14 percent); feel that they "were here on earth in a previous life or existence in another body" (16 versus 6, 8, and 6 percent); believe in telepathy, "or communication between minds without using the traditional five senses" (55 versus 29, 28, and 31 percent); and believe in ESP (59 versus 51, 38, and 47 percent). Curiously enough, belief in astrology does not follow this same pattern.

Westerners tend to be slightly but not strikingly more likely to believe that UFOs are "something real" than is true of residents of other areas of the country. When the Yankelovich survey asked, "Do you personally believe in the existence of UFOs?", 45 percent of westerners say yes, 38 percent of easterners agree, as do 42 percent of midwesterners, and 32 percent of southerners. The Princeton Survey Research Associates survey found that just under a quarter of westerners (27 percent) believe that UFOs are alien ships, while a lower proportion of easterners (20 percent), midwesterners (20 percent), and southerners (17 percent) do so. According to a Gallup poll, a fifth of the western residents (19 percent) say that they had seen something they thought was a UFO, more than was true of residents of the East (10 percent), Midwest (14 percent), or South (8 percent). While the regional differences in the figures on UFOs are not strong, they are at least moderately consistent.

Ideological Orientation. Almost without exception, respondents who designated themselves as "liberal" are more likely to agree with paranormal beliefs than is true of those who said that they were "conservative," with "moderates" in between. Interestingly enough, as we saw, this relationship is almost exactly the opposite of the one we find for our paranormal religious beliefs (the existence of angels, the devil, heaven and hell, and divine creation), where conservatives are considerably *more* likely to agree. In addition, while these broad *ideological* designations correlate strongly with the Democratic-Republican-Independent *political* designation, the latter demonstrates practically no relationship at all with the paranormal dimension. As every researcher knows, variables that correlate with one another do not necessarily correlate with a third variable.

Self-designated liberals are more likely to say that they believe in astrology (34 percent) than conservatives (23 percent); that the spirits of the dead can come back (37 versus 24 percent); that houses can be haunted (41 versus 28 percent); in reincarnation (28 versus 17 percent); in ESP (52 versus 44 percent); in previous lives (13 versus 5 percent); in witches (24 versus 17 percent); in UFOs (54 versus 48 percent); that

UFOs have visited the earth (56 versus 39 percent); and that the government knows more about UFOs than they are telling us (83 versus 68 percent). In nearly every question, "moderates" fall somewhere in between these two figures.

It seems clear that liberals are consistently more likely than conservatives to embrace paranormal beliefs. We need not read a specifically political message into this correlation, however, since, as we've seen, "liberal" may very well be a code word for "receptive to new or unconventional ideas," while "conservative" might mean "I prefer the traditional, conventional view of things."

Chapter Eleven

RELIGION AND PARANORMALISM

While religion and paranormalism cover vast and heterogeneous territories, they do overlap. There is something of a common core, and it is this core that I shall discuss in this chapter. Before we look at the commonalities, however, it is necessary to introduce a historical dimension. In Europe, between the Middle Ages and the nineteenth century, both science and religion underwent drastic transformations. In the earlier era, both shared a great deal in common with paranormal thinking. By the latter period, however, there is a sense that both science and religion became domesticated, civilized, tamed—institutionalized practically beyond recognition.

While no contemporary scientist would refer to what medieval magicians, alchemists, necromancers, sorcerers, and astrologers did as legitimate science, nonetheless, it is out of such efforts that later scientific inquiry grew. What was distinctive about these early figures is that they promised to transcend material reality—to turn lead into gold or to attain immortality by discovering a magic elixir. They had "a thirst, a hunger, a taste for hidden and forbidden powers" (Nietzsche, 1974, p.240). We have only to picture William Harvey (1578–1657), discoverer of the circulation of the blood, violating the edicts of the Church by digging up corpses at night; Johannes Kepler (1571–1630), discoverer of several laws of planetary movement, with his fanciful"harmony of the spheres" theory; and Isaac Newton (1642–1727), co-discoverer of the calculus and sole discoverer of the three most fundamental laws of physics—and a strong believer in astrology—to realize the extraordinary, almost otherworldly character of early science.

Over the centuries that stretched after the Renaissance, science lost this fantastic, demonic, otherworldly quality; it became rationalized, routinized, harnessed to more mundane, more secular concerns and subject to their influences. Science entered the establishment, the main-stream, the educational curriculum. In a sense, it became bought and paid for by the political hierarchy and the economic elite.

Likewise, religion—while very much an aspect of established power during the Middle Ages—came to lose its emphasis on the occult, the charismatic, the supernatural, the divine. The emotional passion that had characterized the Inquisition, the Crusades, the Renaissance witch craze, all manner of religious persecution and holy wars (not to mention uncountable believers who hurled themselves into a religious frenzy through self-flagellation, martyrdom, starvation, castration, and the slaughter of infidels) all but disappeared from Western religious expression. Today, when such religious expression does break out into open conflict, as in the Kosovo crisis (1999), it is taken as exceptional; in the past, it was the rule.

By the nineteenth century, manifestations of mainstream religious sentiment took on a staid, demure, far less passionate, and altogether composed quality. Like science, the institution of religion had become domesticated, tamed, stripped of its wilder, passionate side. Of course, many specific religious sects and cults retained that intensely emotional, somewhat irrational quality—not on the scale that existed when religion was dominant, to be sure—and managed to fulfill their flocks' hunger for a charismatic feverish religious expression. But they remained marginal and relatively powerless. In contrast, the dominant, middle-class, mainstream religious expression became denominational, distinctly tame, distinctively ecumenical, and distinctly secular.

As a result, the religious expression which I shall compare with paranormalism will not be that which prevails in the pews of the more tame, ecumenical, secularized, and middle-class denominations across the country, but the more emotional, charismatic sects and cults that remain at the margins of the culture and the society. The religious expression of the latter is far more similar to that of paranormalism than it is to the secular mainstream.

Perhaps just as important as the early, wilder character of both science and religion in past centuries as compared with that which prevails today is the fact that the initial empirical inquiry into the workings of the universe—the beginnings of science, if you will—and religion were viewed as entirely compatible. For centuries, it was believed that God was the creator of the natural world and, hence, any scientific discovery was likely to be a revelation of God's mind. St. Thomas Aquinas (1225–1274) spent much of his illustrious but brief career attempting to synthesize science and religion. He influenced a long, scientific tradition which consisted of attempting to decipher God's divine plan. Even Galileo (1564–1642), who was subject by the Catholic Church to house arrest after his announcement that the earth revolved around the sun, said: "Mathematics is the alphabet with which God has written the universe."

But the roots of conflict between science and religion had been laid long before Galileo. The illustrious Islamic philosopher and theologian Averroes (1126–1198) argued that faith and reason existed in separate domains. Giordano Bruno (1548–1600) was burned at the stake by the Catholic Church for his heretical, relativistic, philosophical views. The French Enlightenment philosophers were explicitly rationalistic, humanistic, and very often anti-clerical. When asked by Napoleon if he believed in God, astronomer Pierre Laplace (1749–1827) replied: "I have no need of that hypothesis."

With the publication of Charles Darwin's *On the Origin of Species* (1859), which spelled out the mechanism by which biological evolution worked, the rift between science and traditional religion was complete. In the words of the late astronomer Carl Sagan, after the creation of the universe, the laws of physics entirely explain nature; hence, "there was nothing for a Creator to do." Every thinking person, he concluded, is forced to admit "the absence of God" (Begley, 1998, p.48).

Of course, today, many theologians are extremely sympathetic to science, and many scientists are religionists. Still, at least since Darwin, the reasoning processes of science and those of theology have been regarded by the practitioners of each side as separate. Systematic efforts to reverse this rift and reconcile science and religion have been under way for a decade or more (Begley, 1998), but the way most scientists and most religionists think about the universe are likely to remain irreconcilable for the foreseeable future.

PARALLELS BETWEEN PARANORMALISM AND RELIGION

What are the parallels between paranormalism and religion? To begin with, entire areas of fundamentalist religious belief are distinctly and specifically paranormal in nature. Each time an article of traditional religious dogma that scientists argue is contrary to the laws of nature— angels and the devil as physically real, miracles, holy visions, divine creation, and the like—is enunciated or accepted, we are in the realm of the paranormal. As I mentioned earlier, most religious dogma emerged at a time when science either did not exist or was not culturally or institutionally dominant. Hence, at that earlier time, the two realms did not compete with one another. It makes less sense to refer to religious belief as paranormal if science is nonexistent, incipient, or weak than if it is hegemonic. These articles of faith continue to be believed today by a strong minority of religionists; hence, they must be regarded as paranormal in nature.

There are paranormal beliefs that are specifically *rejected* by organized religions. For instance, the validity of astrology, Tarot cards, non-Christian prophecy, pyramid power, crystal power, and so on, is specifically and emphatically contrary to the teachings of Christianity. However, the religious foundation of many paranormal beliefs is clear-cut and obvious. To begin with, there are the paranormal beliefs that are *themselves* religious in origin and nature, many of which are rejected by the more secular, more mainstream, less traditional and less fundamentalist religions.

Belief in miracles; holy visions; the material intervention of angels; the devil as an actual, concrete being; and the creation of heaven and earth in six days less than 10,000 years ago, while rejected by ecumenical denominations in America (such as the Episcopalians, Presbyterians, Congregationalists, and Methodists) are embraced by the majority of the adherents of the more charismatic, fundamentalist, evangelical sects. Hence, a sizeable segment of the array of beliefs that scientists would argue violate the laws of nature (which are, by definition, paranormal in nature) are distinctly religious in character. In specific articles of faith, the overlap between the two approaches to reality, religion and paranormalism, is enormous.

Independent of these *specifically* religious beliefs, that is, those paranormal beliefs that have their very *origin* in organized religion, there are at least two *general* dimensions that are shared by both religion and paranormalism that distinctly mark them off from other, nonreligious, nonparanormal orientations to reality. They are, first, a rejection of strict materialism and a corresponding emphasis on the crucial importance of spiritualism; and second, related to the first dimension, both religion and paranormalism are based on what anthropologists refer to as *non-hypothetical truths*, that is, beliefs which are incapable of being refuted with empirical evidence.

Let's sum up our argument in the following three points.

First, it is true that many specific paranormal claims are contrary to certain specific religious teachings. For instance, traditional Christian dogma rejects astrology. Whether real-life Christians accept or reject these claims is a separate and even more interesting issue.

Second, however, many articles of certain expressions of fundamentalist and/or charismatic Western religions, as well as those in some Eastern religions, are paranormal *by their very nature*. Examples include faith-healing, the occurrence of miracles, miraculous visions, reincarnation, creationism, and religious prophecy.

Third, a paranormal and a religious orientation to reality share much more in common with one another than either does with the contemporary scientific orientation. What paranormalism and traditional religion share is a *spiritual* orientation to the world. It is true, as sociologist Max Weber emphasized early in the century (1922/1963), that religions vary along a dimension of innerworldliness and otherworldliness. That is, the spirituality of believers may manifest itself in action *in* the material world, or in actions that achieve a withdrawal *from* the material world. The seventeenth-century Puritan banker believed he worked hard at his job to please God; his spiritual actions manifested themselves in *innerworldly* or material behavior. In contrast, the actions of the ascetic monk who prays twelve hours a day and never strays from the walls of his monastery are *otherworldly:* they are focused not on the material but the next, the spiritual or other world. Still, the guiding force of both is a voice from the beyond which cannot be apprehended by material tests.

Spiritualism vs. Materialism. The materialist-spiritualist dimension is crucial here. For the materialist, the world as the senses know it is all there is. This is commonly referred to as *positivism* or *empiricism.* What you see is what you get; what your five senses tell you exists is the sum total of all existence. The material world is the be-all and end-all of reality. In materialism, there isn't any sphere or dimension worth knowing about outside of what the senses tell us exist.

In addition, with materialism, there is no "higher" level of existence than this one, no more "advanced" entity or being beyond humans. When we die, we cannot assume that there is a soul that will "go" anywhere, a spirit or consciousness that exists beyond the death of the body; when the body dies, the consciousness dies. Communicating with the dead is a contradiction in terms, since death is the end of life, the termination of the mind. Or so strict materialists say.

To the pure materialist, God is a concept invented by humans to solve perplexing and troubling problems of existence. Religion claims to hold out the hope of understanding that which is actually inexplicable. When a materialist asks the question "Why?", the answer that is offered is a mechanical or materialistic one. John died because he had cancer; Joan died because she was hit by a car. There is always a measure of randomness in human existence that defies ready, pat answers; purposiveness does not exist in nature, only in the minds of humans. Imagining that there is some purpose for life, some divine or cosmic plan, is a fallacy—the teleological fallacy. Science supplies no handy formulas for making life easier, the materialist claims.

In comparison with the materialist, the spiritualist holds very different things to be true and seeks very different sorts of explanations for why things happen. Spiritualists see a plane of existence above and beyond the material dimension, which cannot be measured, tested, or discerned by the crude physical tools of science. Simply because a given assertion cannot be tested empirically does not mean that it is not true. Most spiritualists would accept the truth of the statement: "Some things you see with your eyes; others, you see with your heart."

When our physical existence ends, our soul or spirit—or con-sciousness—continues to exist on some separate plane of existence. We are not snuffed out like a candle flame, but we continue to exist on that other plane. The material world is a "lower" form or plane of existence, while the spiritual is the "higher" one. Our human form is higher than that of animals, it is true, but lower than that of angels. When we die, we enter that higher plane. The "Why?" questions that a spiritualist asks do not seek mechanical answers. The questions "Why did John die?" and "Why did Joan die?" are moral in nature; they demand a specifically spiritual answer. John was in the prime of his life, with three children and a good marriage; Joan was a good and decent person who always helped others. To the spiritualist, the "Why?" question probes the mirror issues of justice and injustice. Divine plan permits no random out-comes. Everything happens for a reason; everything has a purpose. Says Jane Howard, who "communicates" with angels, "God has a divine plan for everything" (1992, p.17).

I suggest that paranormal thinking is a great deal more similar to the spiritualist than to the materialist perspective, and I intend to explore some of the parallels. This is not to say that all adherents of every paranormal belief are basically spiritual in their orientation to life. There are some paranormal belief systems that are resolutely materialistic, while some represent a mix of both dimensions. Certainly many para-psychology researchers are as materialistic as any scientist, at least externally. But for the most part, paranormal thinking shares the spiri-tual foundation of all religions.

Believers in paranormalism, taken as a whole, are more accepting of a spiritual orientation to life than are persons who reject paranormal-ism wholesale. Likewise, this is not to say that all scientists are materi-alists in all aspects of their approach to life. Some, in fact, have attempted to blend the two approaches. What I mean to say is that the scientific approach to reality, taken as a whole, is materialistic, and that it is *experienced* by its advocates *as* materialistic. In general, *when sci-entists practice science*, they tend to be more materialistic than spiritual in the way that they view reality, and more materialistic than paranor-malists, taken as a whole, and religionists. Certainly the scientist's extremely low level of belief in God offers a major piece of evidence in support of this contention.

Nonhypothetical truths. Anthropologist Clifford Geertz, distinguishes four different perspectives toward the world: the everyday, the scientific, the religious, and the aesthetic (1973, pp.110ff.). What makes the religious perspective different from the first two is its adherence to "nonhypothetical truths" (p.112). A nonhypothetical truth is a commitment to that which cannot be demonstrated empirically, which is beyond experimental test, which must be taken on faith. The basis of the religious perspective is that he or she "who would know must first believe" (p.110). In the New Testament, John 20:29 says it well, "Blessed are they that have not seen, and yet have believed." This statement encapsulates the stark contrast between the empirical and materialist epistemology of the scientist and the spiritual epistemology of most paranormalists and many religionists.

In the words of science, many religious propositions are *nonfalsifiable*, they must be accepted as true independent of what the evidence of the senses say. Likewise, paranormal propositions, taken as a whole, are more likely to be nonfalisifiable than scientific propositions, again, taken as a whole. There are exceptions, of course. Parapsychologists claim that they have hard, concrete data that extrasensory perception and precognition exist. But adherents of paranormal beliefs, in general, share with religionists this faith in nonhypothetical truths. There is no way that their belief in a given hypothesis can be shaken with data of the senses. Most paranormal beliefs are nonfalsifiable. Relatively few statements made by scientists *as* science are of this type.

CORRELATIONS

Numerous researchers of paranormal beliefs emphasize the distinctly different nature and origins of traditionally religious beliefs and what most of us regard as paranormalism. For instance, Eve and Harrold (Harrold and Eve, 1986; Taylor, Eve and Harrold, 1995) distinguish two basic "pseudoscientific" belief systems, *fantastic science* (belief in the reality of UFOs, psychic powers, and scientifically unverified creatures, such as Bigfoot) and *creationism*. They argue that the two realms of belief constitute mutually exclusive empirical domains, with different sources and different rules of evidence.

Bainbridge and Stark (1980) hypothesize that New Age or paranormal beliefs tend to be strong in geographical areas in which traditional Christianity tends to be weak, and vice versa. When traditional religion declines in importance, belief in science does not automatically become strong. In fact, paranormalism is a *substitute* for traditional religion and emerges where persons with a religious background lose faith in religion and seek an alternative. Far from finding acceptance among the most strongly and traditionally religious, paranormal beliefs tend to be most strongly accepted among persons who proclaim to hold "no" religion.

In one study the "no religion" respondents were much more likely than born again Christians to agree that UFOs are spaceships from another planet; that Eastern religious practices probably have "great value"; that occult practices, such as Tarot cards, are probably of "great value"; that ESP "definitely exists"; and to have personally experienced ESP themselves. On the other side of the coin, the "no religions" were less likely to say that they strongly dislike "occult literature" and their local paper's horoscope column (Bainbridge and Stark, 1980, p.24). Clearly, in this study paranormalism and traditional religion are separate and distinct. Pseudoscience serves as a kind of "functional alternative" to traditional religious beliefs, substituting for them and serving much the same emotional and intellectual needs (Harrold and Eve, 1986, p.65).

The survey of students I conducted examined the relationship between these dimensions. On the paranormal side: roughly seven in ten of the respondents believed that "some people have special psychic powers (ESP)" (71 percent), and four in ten believed that some numbers are specially lucky for some people (43 percent). Between one in eight and one in five believed that astrology is "very scientific" (12 percent); King Tut's curse actually killed people (17 percent); astrology is "valid and true" (18 percent); reincarnation "is a fact" (19 percent); and that many UFOs are extraterrestrial space vehicles (19 percent).

Support of strongly religious beliefs was at least moderately high among these respondents. About half agreed with the statement, "There is a heaven where people who live good lives are eternally rewarded" (54 percent); a third agreed with "God created heaven, Earth, and all creatures on Earth, in six days roughly 10,000 years ago, as described in the Bible" (35 percent); and between one in ten and one in five agreed with "The Bible is the word of God; it is infallibly true, word for word" (19 percent); "The devil exists as an actual physical being" (15 percent); "Dinosaurs and humans lived at the same time" (15 percent); and "Atheists should not be allowed to teach in public schools" (10 percent).

I did not find that paranormalism and fundamentalist religious beliefs were either independent of or inversely or negatively related to one another. In fact, I found precisely the reverse. Students who held strongly positive feelings about paranormal beliefs tended to be the same students who strongly believed in tenets of Christian dogma, and vice versa. As a general rule, students who agreed with the paranormal statements also agreed with the religious fundamentalist statements, and vice versa (Goode, 1999). Notice that, though I define creationism as a type of paranormalism, in this particular study I examined creationism and other indicators of religiosity and measures of paranormalism as separate and independent dimensions.

Students who believed that UFOs are spacecraft from another planet tended also to believe that the devil is a real, physical being; those who disbelieved the first also disbelieved the second. While 22 percent of those who said UFOs are real also said the devil is real, only 12 percent who said that UFOs were not real believed the devil to be real. On the opposite side of the coin, while 53 percent of the respondents who said that UFOs are real said the devil is not real, 68 percent of those who said that UFOs are not real said that the devil is also not real. In a like manner, believing in the scientific validity of astrology is correlated with believing that the devil is real, that heaven is real, and that creationism is valid; believing in lucky numbers correlated with believing that the devil is real and that heaven is real; and so on.

To sum up, in spite of organized Christianity's opposition to a number of items of paranormal belief, the fact is that the two belief systems overlap heavily. Both affirm the validity of spiritualism, of life of the soul or spirit after physical death; both oppose the belief that science can explain everything with rational, mechanistic accounts; both argue that things can happen that science can't explain; both take evidence other than that which is acceptable in science as persuasive. The folk epistemology for paranormalism and traditional religious thinking are similar—that the data of the five senses cannot explain all phenomena or events. Thus, in spite of the content of specific items of paranormal belief, some of which may run counter to traditional Christianity, the general thinking process of the two dimensions are similar. Paranormalism is a *religion-like* approach to reality.

As a concluding general observation, consider the fact that both perspectives toward the connection between religion and paranormalism may be correct. That is, the divergent findings exist for a reason, and that reason may be that, among substantial segments of religionists, there is a strong and emphatic rejection of most tenets of paranormalism, whereas among other segments, the embrace of certain articles of paranormal belief is strong. Hence, it is not so much that some sociologists are right and others wrong on this issue, but that both are right *about specific sets of believers*. In my sample of university students, the correlation between holding religious and holding paranormal beliefs was positive and extremely strong. In other samples, that correlation turned out to be negative. Each dimension is made up of many strands, each one of which is endorsed or rejected by differing sectors of the population. Clearly, more research is needed to tease out of this complex relationship more precise and subtle interconnections.

A CASE STUDY: HEAVEN'S GATE

In 1997, a religious sect or "cult," Heaven's Gate, burst into the media spotlight when 39 of its adherents committed collective suicide. Heaven's Gate's theology took bits and pieces of belief from Christianity; from gnosticism, an early Christian sect that promulgated the belief that physical matter is evil and only the spirit is good; and from theosophy, a late-nineteenth, early-twentieth century group that sought a mystical understanding of and union with the divine. What was distinctive about Heaven's Gate is that its belief system was intertwined with a belief in UFOs. Heaven's Gate held that extraterrestrial craft are a kind of "heavenly taxi service" (Balch and Taylor, 1976, p.62) that will ferry true believers to what its members referred to as the "Next Level" of existence. They were convinced that behind the Hale-Bopp comet, which made a close pass to the earth in 1997, was an extraterrestrial craft that would take them to another planet so that there, they could lead a perfect existence. To do so, they had to "shed" their earthly "containers" (that is, their bodies). Hence, the collective suicide.

When the San Diego County sheriff's deputy arrived on the scene, the 39 bodies lay on "neatly made bunks." Near each body was "a neatly packed suitcase." Next to some of the bodies were "folded eyeglasses. All were dressed in comfortable black garb, including pleated, collarless tunics and spanking new, waffle-soled black-and-white Nike running shoes. They wore black plastic wristwatches and wide gold bands on their left ring fingers." In the shirt pocket of each member was a $5 bill and some quarters; in some, there was the recipe for the concoction they took to kill themselves, a mixture of barbiturates and vodka. "Each had closely shorn hair. Purple death shrouds were draped over the upper torsos of all but two." All wore triangular arm patches that read "Heaven's Gate" on the top and "Away Team" on the bottom (Hedges, 1997, p.28). Since the cult preached celibacy, six of the men, including the leader, had been castrated earlier.

In 1972, Marshall Applewhite, the son of a Presbyterian minister, while hospitalized with a heart problem, had a "near death" experience. Revived, he became involved with a nurse, Bonnie Lu Trousdale Nettles. Both were infatuated with reincarnation, astrology, and prophecy. They came to view themselves as "witnesses" from the New Testament's Book of Revelation. They imagined that they would be "assassinated by angry disbelievers," then rise from the dead and ascend "to heaven on a cloud." That cloud, they taught, "was a spacecraft that would imminently arrive to transport a select group of people to a new life" (p.28). Calling themselves "Bo" and "Peep" (later, "Ti" and "Do"), they then traveled across the country, preaching their doctrine, promising a ride in a spaceship as an inducement to join their cult. By the 1990s, they included references to *Star Trek* and *The X-Files* jargon in their pitch. In 1994, they purchased an expensive full-page ad in *USA Today* and launched a 22-state tour. Their central idea: the path to "the only real heaven" was aboard a spaceship (p.29).

Heaven's Gate left behind numerous documents in the form of messages on its website, videotapes in the house where some of its members committed suicide, and suicide notes. These documents assert that the cult's members were themselves extraterrestrials who "arrived in staged spacecraft (UFO) crashes." Many of their "discarded bodies (genderless, not belonging to the human species)," they proclaimed, "were retrieved by human authorities" (Hedges, 1997, p.30).

In short, the members of the cult believed that they were "aliens who had been planted here years ago by a UFO." Their mother planet was at "the level above human in distant space." A UFO was now using Hale-Bopp as a shield. In this spaceship, they would be transported to "their world" (p.30). All committed suicide of their own free will. However, none of the members believed it was a suicide. Instead, they were merely shedding their human "containers" in order to join their mother ship. "We are all choosing of our own free will to go to the next level," said one note. Proclaimed another, "We just wish you could all be here and doing what we are doing" (p.30). Explained a third, the cult "had a formula of how to get out of the human kingdom to a level above humans. . . . And I said to myself, 'That's what I want. That's what I've been looking for'. . . I've been on this planet for 31 years, and there's nothing here for me" (Goode, 1997, p.32).

The conjunction between religious belief and belief in UFOs is not limited to Heaven's Gate. Steven Stark, author of a book on television culture, appeared on a segment of *Primetime Live* (March 29, 1998) devoted to the TV program, *The X-Files*. He said the quest to discover aliens on earth is "ultimately a religious quest. It's kind of like our Crusades." *The X-Files*, he declared, is "the most religious show on television." Stark argued that when people are searching for the other side they are engaged in a spiritual, even heavenly quest. When they ask, "Do aliens exist?," what they're really asking, is, "Does God exist?"

Evangelist Billy Graham captured that spiritual quality of the yearning for extraterrestrials when he stated publicly, "UFOs are astonishingly angel-like in some of their reported appearances." Douglas Curran, photographer and author, spent several years traveling through the United States and Canada looking for, writing about, and taking pictures of UFO believers. "Every single flying-saucer group I encountered in my travels incorporated Jesus Christ into the hierarchy of its belief system" (1985, p.23). The most outstanding feature of the search for aliens is its religious quality.

A number of authors have traced the parallels between religion and the belief in the reality of UFOs. As might be expected, they are extremely strong. The occupants of extraterrestrial craft are seen as "godlike beings capable of transcending natural laws and thus potentially elevating humans to their immortal realm" (Bartholomew and Howard, 1998, p.220–221)—or, it might be added, destroying them, blasting them into the next world. Aliens are superhuman; "they have powers that far exceed human powers" (Saler, 1997, p.131). At the very least, aliens have supernatural powers; they are "not bound by nature in the ways that we are bound" (Saler, 1997, p.132). They have figured a way of traveling faster than the speed of light, which contemporary physics argues is impossible. They often "beam up" into their spacecraft humans, large animals, cars, in some cases, even entire cities, which is currently, on earth, a technological impossibility. They are described as moving through walls and closed doors (many of Mack's cases, 1995, report this phenomenon), again, a feat vastly beyond the capacity of human science and technology. The desire to transcend the limitations of our earthly material existence by attaining magical or supernatural powers represents a major theme of many religions, as well as many of our fondest wish-fulfillments (Bartholomew and Howard, 1998, p.221). If the knowledge of aliens is unimaginably beyond human attainment, perhaps their wisdom is equally vast. Perhaps they have perfected a means of living together in peace, harmony, and justice. What better means of learning their secrets than to organize one's life around learning from and welcoming these creatures?

Second, consider the orientation adopted by persons who take the UFO phenomenon seriously, believing them to represent alien craft. It is reverential, a feeling that is very close to religious and spiritual awe, rapture, joy, the kind of feeling that gripped Jesus' disciples when they beheld his transfiguration on the Mount of Olives, that seized the warrior chief Arjuna when he beheld Krishna's divine form (Saler, 1997, p.142). When even the supposedly hard-headed, unsentimental scientists in *Close Encounters of the Third Kind* witness the alien mother ship, they are portrayed as feeling precisely these emotions—reverence, rapture, awe, and joy. Of course, terror is also an ingredient in many believers' feelings toward aliens (as it is toward a wrathful God, bent on punishing the wicked). A corollary of awesome power is that the entities that possess it can use it in ways we may not fully comprehend.

Third, both charismatic, fundamentalist religion and paranormalism represent something of a repudiation of organized, institutionalized science. Since the majority of credentialed scientists reject the notion of extraterrestrial craft circling the earth, the UFO phenomenon represents a rejection of science and an affirmation of an alternative way of looking at reality. Science represents hegemony, institutionalized power. Science colludes with the dominant political power structure in denying the reality of alien craft "out there." To accept UFOs as real means to reject "Big Brother" who is both watching us and telling us what to do. Accepting the belief in UFOs means being a rebel.

In the same vein, the more emotional or charismatic and fundamentalistic religions walk the same path. They deny legitimacy to the more staid, mainstream, institutionalized religions—those that are perceived to have colluded with the corrupt political hierarchy, and they simultaneously deny legitimacy to institutionalized science, with its acceptance of rationality, amorality, secularism, materialism, and evolution. The parallels between the two modes of thinking in their rejection of science and glorification of anti-scientific lines of thinking are strong and undeniable.

Chapter Twelve

PARANORMALISM IN THE MEDIA

Perhaps the sharpest contrast between the position of the scientific debunker of paranormal thinking and that of the culturalist or social scientist may be found in their respective analyses of the media.

The debunker or critic of paranormalism argues that the representatives of the mass media are being perverse and ornery in their positive presentation of paranormal phenomena. If only their programmers hired a scientific consultant, they would not make the stupid and ignorant factual mistakes they commit and delude the public into thinking things could exist or events could take place that are scientifically impossible.

In contrast, the social scientist says that the media's presentation of the paranormal has to be understood on its own grounds, in its own realm. Paranormal phenomena are presented in the news, on television programs, and in film, for specific, concrete reasons. Not only do those reasons have to be understood, they are also likely to point to factors in the society, in the general public, and in the very nature of the media that make substantial change nearly impossible.

Critics of paranormalism are almost unanimous in their disapproval of the role of the media in reporting paranormal phenomena and promoting belief in their validity. Their criticism can be broken down into two issues. First, the *way* that paranormalism is presented—that is, positively, uncritically, without reservation or skepticism. Second, the extent to which this has an *impact* on audiences, more specifically, whether viewers or readers are more likely to accept the validity of pseudoscience after viewing or reading positively-oriented materials on paranormalism than before such exposure.

From a skeptic's perspective, the media tend to be uncritical in their presentation of paranormalism. "The media . . . have often acted with extreme irresponsibility in covering pseudoscience and the paranormal," says psychologist Terence Hines, author of a major critique of extra-scientific modes of thinking. According to Singer and Benassi, two psychologists who have studied paranormal beliefs, "The public is chronically exposed to films, newspaper reports, 'documentaries,' and books extolling occult or pseudoscientific topics, with critical coverage largely lacking" (1981, p.50).

Both fictional and documentary depictions endorsing paranormal phenomena are popular media fare. In fact, some of the most widely watched shows on the broadcast media have paranormal themes. As we saw earlier, programs such as *Touched by an Angel*, *The X-Files*, *Unsolved Mysteries*, *The Psychic Connection*, *In Search of . . .*, *The Unexplained*, and *Sightings* have drawn weekly audiences in numbers that, added together, approach half the U.S. population. Documentaries on paranormal phenomena are typically reported without commentary, as if an assertion that something occurred is the same as the actual occurrence of the event in question. In contrast, exposures of paranormal frauds receive far less attention. The fact is, the supposed occurrence of paranormal phenomena is news, while their nonoccurrence is not. From the point of view of media representatives, this bias makes perfect sense. From the point of view of the debunker, critic, or skeptic of paranormal forces, this bias represents nothing less than an assault on the truth. From the point of view of the culturalist or constructionist, the reasons for this orientation have to be understood.

In his book, *The Demon-Haunted World* (1995) published shortly before his death, Carl Sagan commented on the media presentation of science and pseudoscience. His point was that very little effort would produce much less fakery and much more validity. In a broadcast of *In Search of . . .*, an author appears who claims that there must be a planet in the solar system beyond Pluto. Why? one might ask. Well, because a message in a cylinder from ancient Sumer implies as much. No matter that the Sumerians had no telescopes, or that contemporary astronomers, with infinitely more sophisticated technology at their disposal, have been unable to locate this alleged planet. *The X-Files*, Sagan says, nearly always selects a paranormal rather than a mundane or scientific explanation for the events that unfold. What about depicting the occasional hoax? Or a psychological aberration? Why does it always have to be mysterious, bizarre, or inexplicable forces at work? Why do the media offer so little science and so much pseudoscience? Sagan asks.

Another good example of the media bias in favor of the paranormal is offered by the case of reports of a supposed poltergeist in the Resch home in Columbus, Ohio. While the print and broadcast media were dispatched to investigate the claims of the haunting, a team of well-known debunkers, headed by James Randi, a professional magician, were denied access to the house. When reporters looked directly at 14-year-old Tina Resch, nothing remarkable occurred. When they looked away, a variety of household items, including a phone and a lamp, began flying across the room. An enterprising photographer snapped several pictures when he caught some movement out of the corner of his eye, revealing that Tina had caused the objects to "fly" herself.

As a videocamera crew was packing up to leave, a camera, accidentally left running, recorded Tina physically pulling a lamp toward herself, then jumping away and issuing startled cries. Yet, far from exposing the entire episode as a hoax, the media underplayed Tina's fraudulent agency in the haunting, insisting that the teenager "only sometimes" cheated. The editor of the *Columbus Dispatch*, so embarrassed by the revelation that he and his paper had been duped, refused to grant permission to Randi to print the pictures that demonstrated Tina's trickery (Meyer, 1986; Hines, 1988, pp.66–67).[1]

As I said, while belief in the existence of creatures unknown to science (the field of "exobiology") is not itself an example of paranormalism, it has strong parallels with many paranormal beliefs (unless these creatures are biologically impossible, e.g., humans turning into vampires or werewolves.) Imagine the media attention to the discovery of hard, scientific evidence that such a creature exists. During "Operation Deepscan," a team of scientists in 20 vessels, laden with advanced and sophisticated scientific equipment, conducted a comprehensive sonar sweep of every cubic meter of Loch Ness. While the research project was concerned with a variety of scientific questions, some 300 journalists who came to the site to write a story on the expedition were interested in the answer to one question and one only: *Where's the Loch Ness Monster?*

In fact, the soundings produced no Nessie-sized readings. One recorded contact was, in all probability, a large, "shark-sized" fish, and another turned out to be a submerged tree stump. The event generated only a modest amount of news in the media. After the scientists announced their negative results to the media, "Disgruntled newsmen left the lake in droves. No sizzling centerspreads about prehistoric pleisosaurs. . . . No close-ups of huge, nightmarish leviathans rising from the very bowels of the Earth. No story" (Belfield, 1987). But imagine the volume of news the expedition would have generated had the Loch Ness Monster actually been sighted! It would have been one of the biggest stories of the year. Clearly, the public hunger to confront and verify paranormal claims is huge, while the desire to refute their validity is precisely the opposite. In other words, paranormalism is news; no paranormalism is not.

IS BELIEF IN PARANORMALISM INFLUENCED BY THE MEDIA?

It could be argued that, while the media tend to be sympathetic to paranormal claims, it is possible that their stories *reflect* but do not *influence* the public's belief in their validity. (Or perhaps these stories *both* reflect *and* influence the public's belief in paranormalism.) Sparks, Hansen, and Shah (1994) argue that it is ironic that skeptics, who condemn believers in paranormalism for their lack of evidence, are guilty of the same crime. They simply assume, with no data to back up their assertions, that the media's presentation of paranormal phenomena is an independent cause of the public's pseudoscientific beliefs. Is it true? While the media often endorse paranormal forces, is this endorsement a major reason why the public holds beliefs in the reality of forces outside the scope of science? A team of researchers, headed by communications expert Glen Sparks, designed and conducted a series of experiments to determine whether, to what extent, and under what conditions, the media's depictions of paranormal phenomena influence the paranormal beliefs of audiences.

In one set of experiments, all audience groups were exposed to a television program with a paranormal theme. Some were given no verbal introduction to the program; others were given the same introduction as appeared on its original broadcast; others were warned that the show was fictitious and for the purpose of entertainment only; and still others were told that the events depicted in the program were impossible and "violated the known laws of nature" (Sparks, 1998, p.36). Both immediately after viewing and three weeks later, audiences who had been exposed to the show along with warning tags tended to be more skeptical about the reality of paranormal phenomena than those who were shown the program without the disclaimers. Even "a relatively small difference in a media presentation can potentially affect viewer beliefs," the author concludes (p.36).

In a second set of experiments, two audiences were shown two different versions of a program about UFOs and space aliens, while the third, the control group, was shown one unrelated to the topic. In one of the versions on UFOs, special effects images of alien spacecraft were left in and shown to the experimental audience; in the other, the images were edited out but the original soundtrack remained. The audiences who watched the two UFO program were significantly more likely to believe in the reality of UFO reports than the control group, which watched a program unrelated to UFOs (p.37). Interestingly, the visual content of the program (whether UFOs were presented on screen) did not influence the subjects' beliefs. One wrinkle appeared in the findings: subjects "high on vivid mental imagery" expressed a stronger belief in the reality of UFOs after watching a UFO-related program, but only the version in which UFO images were edited out (p.37).

In a third set of experiments, subjects were asked to read three news stories, one of which was a report taken from a national magazine of alien abductions; the other two articles were to disguise the purpose of the experiment. For each experimental group, the researchers varied the content of the news story on aliens so that, in one, the validity of the report was affirmed, but no scientific authority was cited; in a second, this affirmation was attributed to a scientist; in a third, the reality of alien abductions was discredited, but no scientific authority was cited; and in a fourth, the validity of the report was discredited by a scientific authority. The highest level of belief in the existence of UFOs and alien abductions was attained by the group who read the news story in which a scientific authority affirmed their validity (p.38).

In a fourth set of experiments, the broadcast of a news program, *48 Hours*, on the alleged crash of an extraterrestrial craft in the desert near Roswell, New Mexico, was shown in two different forms to two groups. One group was shown only the footage from the show that reported testimony from eyewitnesses who claimed to have seen aliens and the crashed ship. A government "cover-up" of the event was alleged, and no contrary information was presented. This was labeled the "one-sided" version. In the "two-sided" version, a report of a team of experts who went into the desert in Arizona to record alleged UFOs was also shown. A video image of an alleged extraterrestrial craft turned out, as a result of computer enhancement, to be a conventional jet aircraft. Compared with their beliefs prior to the experiment, the audience who watched the "one-sided" version were more likely to believe in extraterrestrial craft, whereas the one who watched the "two-sided" version were less likely to do so (p.38).

The fifth study was a survey designed to determine the relationship between media exposure and paranormal beliefs. Belief in the reality of a range of paranormal phenomena was widespread, but was composed of two separate but overlapping dimensions: belief in supernatural beings (for instance, ghosts, devils, space aliens), and belief in psychic energy (ESP, astrology, levitation). The correlation between exposure to paranormal programs and belief in supernatural beings and belief in psychic energy for respondents with no prior experience with a paranormal event was strong and significant (p.39). For persons who claimed to have had paranormal experiences, the relationship did not hold up, presumably because the influence of such an experience outweighs the influence of the media.

In short, it appears that, under certain conditions, exposure to the media is related to paranormal beliefs of audiences. Programs presenting a one-sided view of paranormalism are likely to increase belief in its validity, while those presenting a more complex, skeptical view decrease it. The influence of the media is determined both by the form and the content of a program's introduction as well as by the scientific authority of commentators on a news item. Clearly, the media do play a role in influencing the public's views of paranormal phenomena. Even fictional depictions of supernatural events can have an impact on viewers' notions of their reality; they should not be regarded as "mere entertainment."

PARANORMALISM IN FILM

The depiction of paranormal themes has been a major feature of movies since their inception over a century ago. Characterizing the many film genres that depict paranormal events is not an easy task. At the very least, they would include many documentary, horror, science fiction, fantasy, and family comedy films, such as *Ghostbusters* (1984) and *Flubber* (1997). What applies to one genre may not apply to another. Still, a few limited generalizations seem to be in order.

Science fiction proved to be an extremely popular film genre right from the beginning. In 1902, as I've already said, Georges Melies released his classic, *A Trip to the Moon*, in which a variety of innovative cinematic techniques produced visual effects that were astounding to turn-of-the-century audiences. In one sequence, a crazy professor makes his opponents literally disappear; in another, moon creatures disappear in a puff of smoke; in a third, telescopes turn into stools. The Man in the Moon is hit square in the eye by a rocket ship shot from earth.

Early films such as these were more amusing than serious, but later productions took on an aura of surface plausibility that transcended their lack of scientific credibility. Young audiences in 1939 did not question that Buck Rogers could have been preserved by a mysterious gas for 500 years, revived, then encouraged to lead the fight against the evil he encountered when he woke up. Horror films, too, were produced early and often; they formed a major paranormal genre. The earliest version of *Frankenstein* was made in 1908, but it is the 1931 version that we remember. Today, the medical and scientific basis of the tale is regarded as so much mumbo-jumbo, as is true of *The Golem* (1913, 1920), *Nosferatu* (1921), *Dracula* (1931), *Dr. Jekyll and Mr. Hyde* (1921, 1931), and *Island of Lost Souls* (1933). The audiences of these early films typically were provided with a detailed scientific-sounding explanation for the unusual events that transpired. As a result, they were led to believe the depicted events were possible.

Over the decades, a major issue in films with a paranormal theme has been whether the paranormal "other" has been evil or benign. The early "mad scientist" movies (the previously-mentioned *Frankenstein, Dr. Jekyll and Mr. Hyde, Island of Lost Souls,* as well as *The Invisible Man*), stressed the fact that "playing God" by unleashing the forces of nature, supposedly beyond the capacity of human comprehension, would inevitably have evil and catastrophic consequences. The creatures these mad scientists produced—Frankenstein's monster, Moreau's half-human half-animal beings, Jekyll's Mr. Hyde, and the unnamed Invisible Man himself—were regarded as evil, despicable products of a decidedly demented, meglomaniacal act. They are most decidedly entities that are other than good and other than human. In the ultimate act of crossing the line between good and evil, as a result of his unholy experiments, Dr. Jekyll and the Invisible Man become products of their own evil.

In science fiction, the picture is a bit more complex. In the early and middle twentieth century, creatures from outer space were transformed from comical characters (*A Trip to the Moon*) to terrifying, destructive, subhuman entities, bent on wiping humanity off the face of the earth (*The Thing,* 1951; *War of the Worlds,* 1953; *It Came from Outer Space,* 1953; *Invasion of the Body Snatchers,* 1956; *The Blob,* 1958). In the midst of the "Cold War" between the Soviet Union and the United States, an invasion from outer space symbolized American fears of a Russian military attack.

With the easing of international tensions, extraterrestrials became vastly more intelligent, less uniformly belligerent, and, in some depictions, even altogether benevolent. *The Day the Earth Stood Still* (1951) represents a major exception to the generalization that, during the Cold War, extraterrestrials were depicted as bent on attacking the earth; it was the first post-World War II film in which the alien was good, in fact, a savior of humankind. The creatures in *Close Encounters of the Third Kind* (1977), *E.T. The Extra-Terrestrial* (1982), and *Cocoon* (1985) are not only benign but possess powers vastly beyond the scientific and technical capacity of humans. In the later films, far from fleeing in terror from extraterrestrials, we are attracted to them, seeking their company and wisdom with enthusiasm. Of course, the "alien creatures as evil and destructive" theme also remains with us, as *Alien* (1979), *Aliens* (1986), *Alien 3* (1992), *Independence Day* (1997), and *The X-Files* (1998) demonstrate.

Perhaps the most interesting theme in movies that deal with paranormalism is the conflict between the scientific skeptic and the supporter of otherworldly powers. In a way, this theme breaks sharply with the earlier films mentioned above, where the scientist, whether Dr. Frankenstein, Dr. Moreau, Dr. Jekyll, or the Invisible Man was the rebel who defied the authorities and unleashed the terror of paranormal forces. These films arose in the early part of the twentieth century, when science and technology were seen as having incomprehensible, demonic, almost supernatural, and potentially destructive powers. Authority figures, if they played a role at all, were depicted as benign and entirely reasonable in their·rejection of the scientist's mad experiments.

Today, scientists are still often the "bad guys," but for an altogether different reason. In contemporary films, scientists are jealous that paranormal forces will undermine the scientific worldview. The scientist is now evil because he (most of the evil scientists in these films are men) tries to deny or cover up the fact that paranormal powers exist. Far from being a rebel against authority, the scientists portrayed on film today often forge a corrupt alliance with the government to suppress knowledge about paranormalism. This is a theme that is central to movies from *Close Encounters of the Third Kind* and *E.T.* to *Independence Day* and *The X-Files*.

Many films with a paranormal slant begin with what might be referred to as a "skeptical baseline" (Hess, 1993, p.123). That is, the movie opens with a materialistic, secular point of view. In the opening sequences, the film's characters are engaged in mundane activities, such as doing household chores, eating breakfast or dinner, working at a job, going to school, and so on. This materialistic foundation is shaken by an event that is initially explained as naturalistic forces by a physician, psychiatrist, scientist, or other secular skeptic. Eventually, paranormal occurrences become overwhelming and impossible to explain away by secular accounts, and the debunker is discredited, often even killed.

The skeptic and debunker tends to be an authority figure, usually a male. The New Age paranormalist is often a woman or a girl; if a male, the paranormalist is an outsider, distanced from the existing, usually corrupt power structure. Carl Sagan's *Contact* supplies an excellent example. Ellie, the scientist searching for extraterrestrial life, finds her research project defunded by incompetent, unimaginative bureaucrats who, when she is successful, attempt to take all the credit for her discovery. And when she travels to another planet (by means of a mode of transportation about which most scientists would be extremely skeptical) and makes first-hand contact—as it turns out, with the spirit of her deceased father—she is unable to bring back to earth concrete evidence of her discovery and her claim is, once again, debunked by the authorities and the powers that be.

Paranormal films attempt to overturn, undermine, critique, or criticize the existing hierarchies of power and authority. They tend to glorify the maverick, the outsider, the unconventional figure rather than members of the establishment. Persons who are powerful in the secular hierarchy are shown to be completely powerless in the face of spiritual, paranormal forces. Paranormalism is associated with the people, the public, the non-elitist, even anti-elitist, populist forces in the society—in short, the common man and woman.

The viewer finds it easy to identify with the paranormal hero who represents the victimized underdog (p.139). The audience feels that justice is served when the skeptic is demonstrated to be wrong and is sacrificed to the paranormal forces he cannot control. The audience sides with "the underdog paranormal hero, who while socially disempowered is able to muster the power . . . to overcome the double (and doubly wrong) mights of skepticism and . . . evil." There is, indeed, an almost biblical flavor to the drama of the righteous individual who stands alone against the overwhelming forces of mammon and the devil in the land of milk and honey" (p.140).

Why are there no successful or popular films in which the *skeptic* is the underdog, exposing "a paranormal conspiracy of cranks and charlatans" who threaten the well-being of the society? The fact is, populism is based on a mistrust of the dominant, hegemonic, official worldview. Much of the public feels a sense of alienation toward skepticism. They feel that scientists are part of the elite who are hiding something from us, engaged in a kind of unholy alliance with the government in keeping the truth from the populace (p.141). This distrust of the official hierarchy cuts across political lines; it is characteristic of both liberals and conservatives. There is a suspicion of an "intrigue of invisible, shadowy layers of official power. . . . Disbelief and distrust—especially of centralized government—are part of the national psyche." United States culture has "spawned a left and right version of populism, as well as a left and right paranoid style in politics" (Rosen, 1997, p.B6). The popularity of programs and films such as *The X-Files* is based on the fact that they confirm what the viewer expects from government: "sinister cabals, shadowy conspiracies, convenient lies, and pandemic corruption" (p.B6). In short, "nothing is as it seems."

Given this basic belief structure in the general public, the criticisms and admonitions issued by skeptics and scientists against the paranormal bias found in the media, including film, is futile and a bit silly. There is no way of insinuating a less paranormal, more debunking stance into films without harming their popularity. Paranormalism *is* the populist— and popular—position. Scientists are mistrusted; the official view is suspect *by that fact alone*; the existing power hierarchy is resented; and belief is strong that paranormalism is valid. No amount of admonition by the likes of Carl Sagan, James Randi, Paul Kurtz, and representatives of The Committee for the Scientific Investigation of Claims of the Paranormal (CSICOP), a major paranormal debunker organization, will alter that basic fact. It is the role of CSICOP and its supporters to act as a kind of interest or pressure group to influence media executives and producers to insinuate more science and less paranormalism into their programs and films. My feeling is that this is a vain and wasted effort, since the paranormal is appealing to the public and hence, sells, while in comparison, science is not intrinsically appealing and does not sell. As a consequence, the media, movies included, will continue to have a bias favoring the paranormal for some time to come.

SUPERMARKET TABLOIDS, FOLKLORE, AND URBAN LEGENDS

Today there are six major supermarket tabloids (or "tabs" as they are known in the trade) in circulation in the United States. Tabs specialize in celebrity gossip, sensational news, and reports of a variety of paranormal doings. It is here that we will find lurid stories of headless people walking around for days, meetings with the dead, and women mating with extraterrestrials. The weekly circulations of these periodicals is immense (although declining), eclipsing those of nearly all mainstream magazines and newspapers when taken together. At its peak in the late 1970s, the *National Enquirer* sold five million copies a week; its circulation has declined to a shade over two million today. The *Star*, which sold just under four million copies weekly in the early 1980s, currently sells just under two million. The *Globe*, in the early 1980s, a two million per week seller, now has a circulation of under a million (Turner, 1998). The *Weekly World News* sells under one million; the *National Examiner*, one million; and the *Sun*, just over half a million. In spite of their decline, the tabs retain a huge readership. Combined, as a result of both purchases and "passalongs" (the purchaser giving a copy to a friend), the supermarket tabloids reach an estimated total weekly audience of 50 million, or about one U.S. adult in five.

While the tabs are often regarded in the public mind as more or less interchangeable, there are important differences between them. Although the *National Enquirer*, the most popular of the tabloids, is most frequently credited with paranormal stories, the fact is, except for articles on astrology, psychic predictions, and miracle medical cures, the *Enquirer* has largely given up on the theme of paranormalism. For the most part, only the *Sun* and the *Weekly World News* present paranormal stories as a major feature. The other four stick mainly, although not exclusively, to celebrity gossip.

It is not clear whether the readership of tabloids believes all or most of the stories published in their pages. Jim Hogshire, a former writer for the tabs, claims that many or most of these paranormal stories are taken as gospel by their readers (1997). Certainly many of their assertions defy credibility even to observers who are sympathetic with the view that scientific laws can be bent or broken. Consider only a few such stories: "Cat Eats Parrot—Now it Talks"; "Man Electrocuted by Static Cling"; "Human Head Transplant"; "Town Beamed up by UFO"; "Robot Gives Birth to a Human Baby"; "Baby Born with Mom's Tattoo"; "UFOs Found Hiding in Circus Freak Show"; and so on.

Extraterrestrial or UFO stories top the list of the most popular paranormal subjects printed in the two tabs that still cover such topics. Many supporters of the extraterrestrial hypothesis claim that the tabloid stories are so unbelievable, even outlandish, that they must have been planted in the pages of the tabs to discredit the viability that UFOs are "something real" (Hogshire, 1997, p.45). The *Weekly World News* story of December 17, 1996, whose headline read, "Family Claims 500-lb Space Alien Raided Their Refrigerator!" might lend credence to this suspicion.

Tabloids rely extremely heavily on what their reporters and editors refer to as the "Hey, Mabel!" principle. This is the catchy, attention-grabbing quality of a story. If a husband is reading a story and it is dramatic enough to grab his attention, he'll turn to his wife and exclaim, "Hey, Mabel! Listen to this!" This quality is what all tabloid writers and editors seek. Stories that have that quality resonate with the emotions of their readers; they have intrinsic dramatic appeal. To the tabs, a story that does not grab the reader's attention is not a good story. A story about a "Man Electrocuted by Lightning Bugs!" is a "Hey, Mabel!" story. A story about a scientist explaining why such an event is impossible is *not* a "Hey, Mabel!" story. (A non-sexist term for this principle, one which takes account of the fact that a woman is as likely to call attention to a noteworthy story as a man, might be the"Hey, Mabel! Hey, Fred!" principle.)

Many folklorists, who study stories, rumors, jokes, and tales that circulate orally, argue that there are strong parallels between the material printed in supermarket tabloids and what are referred to as "urban legends" (Bird, 1992, pp.162–200). The urban (or contemporary) legend is a story, usually told and listened to as true, that circulates without documentation on the basis of hearsay about local or national events, which are extremely unlikely to have happened. Urban legends tend to have an abstract, cartoon-like quality. Although they refer to actual people, almost anyone else could be substituted and the story would be the same (Brunvand, 1981, 1993; Goode, 1992, pp.303ff.).

Folklore generally, and the urban or contemporary legend specifically, are transmitted orally, between and among tellers and listeners of similar social and cultural circumstances. In contrast, the stories in tabloids are transmitted via the print medium, mainly by left-leaning writers who share neither their readers' conservative political views nor their naivete concerning the improbability of the events about which they write. There exists, in other words, a measure of cynicism in the fairly sophisticated and knowledgeable writers who concoct stories they do not believe for a relatively uninformed audience. At the same time, the parallels between folklore and the stories in the tabloids are strong.

Stories in the tabloids, like legends and folk tales, have a similar *form*. Both are simple, streamlined, clichéd, exaggerated, standardized, formulaic, and stereotypical. The characters are black-and-white with very little moral nuance or shades of gray. The dramatic form of tabloids, like that of folklore, is familiar, well-worn, and popularly understood (Bird, 1992, p.191).

Tabloid stories are a form of folklore in that both have similar *themes*. They typically have a dreamlike, mythical, nightmarish, or fantastic quality (Schechter, 1988). They repeat tales that have been told for thousands of years: humans mating with animals; women giving birth to strange creatures; people swallowing serpent eggs that hatch inside the body; creatures bursting out of the stomach; loved ones dying or disappearing under mysterious circumstances, and then returning as ghosts, communicating important messages; miracle cures of sick or injured relatives; weeping statues, visions of Mary or Jesus; mystical prophecies that come true; newborns who talk or have other astounding qualities; strange creatures that kidnap or help children; and so on.

The tabloids often run stories that *originated* as legends. For instance, the tale that president John F. Kennedy was not killed in the November 3, 1963 assassination attempt against him but was injured and paralyzed, a fact that is supposedly being kept from the public, *began* as legend and was retold by a number of tabloids a number of times, recently by the *Weekly World News* in its August 21 and November 6, 1990 issues (Bird, 1992, pp.175–178). Says Slater, "It does no good to write about a child who was born with two heads if there is not already a rumor to the effect, if people are not already talking about it in the streets" (1982, p.53).

The tabloid press, vastly more than the mainstream media, rely on "open-ended dialogue" with their readers (p.189). Readers are invited to contribute stories, and many of those that are contributed are run. For instance, the belief that Elvis Presley is alive remains an active legend to this day, firmly believed by many tabloid readers, who send in reports of sightings, that are then printed, further contributing to the legend. Far more than for the mainstream press, "tabloids rely on reader response and involvement. Reader letters and weekly circulations are tracked, and . . . reader preferences can be seen and acted upon quickly. Pleasing the customer (and thus selling more newspapers) is the only major consideration for tabloids, unencumbered as they are with a sense of needing to inform" (p.190). The tabloids do not so much *create* beliefs in reincarnation, prophecies, conspiracies, miracles, or contact with fantastic creatures—rather, they *articulate* and *rearticulate* them (p.190).

Both legends and tabloid stories are composed of "migratory anecdotes" (Barrick, 1976). A basic story core, with varying accompanying detail that changes over time, "migrates" from one context to another. Stories are told about celebrities, for example, in which the exact subject of the story is irrelevant, the same story "migrating" from one celebrity to another. For instance, in the late 1970s and early 1980s, a story circulated about a Black man stepping into an elevator with a dog; when he commands the dog to "sit," three elderly women standing next to him obey, slumping to the floor of the elevator. Exactly the same story was told about more than a half-dozen Black celebrities, "migrating" from one to another over time and locale. Of course, the event never took place, but that did not prevent it from being told, retold, and believed. Contemporary legends have that "migratory" quality, as do stories printed in the tabs. Many tabloid stories are recycled over and over again, precisely because they have such intrinsic appeal to wide audiences.

PARANORMALISM IN THE MEDIA: A SUMMARY

Skeptics and debunkers imagine that media executives and producers can tinker with the content of film, television programs, and newspapers and magazines to present stories that are more critical of paranormal assertions and claims so that the public will become less gullible. A sociologist with a culturalist or constructionist orientation regards this expectation as naive. It is true that the public's beliefs about paranormal claims are influenced by the media, as research has shown. But that influence is far from straightforward. Moreover, experimental subjects are a "captive audience"; they do not choose to watch the programs they view. In contrast, the public selects programs that interest them, and programs that support paranormal beliefs are immensely popular. Moreover, the public finds certain themes in paranormalism immensely appealing. One is populism—the triumph of the underdog over the evil doings of the powerful. Today, science is viewed as being in cahoots with the powers that be; its refusal to recognize occult, demonic forces is presented as part of the problem. The paranormal hero both acknowledges those forces and triumphs over them. These themes are fundamental elements in folklore and resonate with cultural beliefs that are strongly held by a substantial segment of the public.

In short, paranormalism corresponds with some of our most deeply-felt values and convictions. It comforts us to be reminded that the world works in this fashion. Contrary messages would feel jarring, dissonant, out of tune with our assumptions. Consequently, media presentations adopting a scientific or skeptical slant, specifically those debunking paranormalism, cannot attract the audiences now enjoyed by programs with a pro-paranormal orientation. Since media executives are in the business mainly for profit, they are unlikely to be persuaded by the skeptic's insistence that their programming be more scientific and realistic. Hence, paranormalism is likely to remain a fixture of the media for some time to come.

The argument that the media tend to affirm paranormal claims may seem to contradict my argument that scientific skepticism is the dominant narrative. It does not, and for two reasons. One is that a strong correlation exists between education, income, and occupational prestige on the one hand and consumption of media material espousing paranormal themes on the other. That is, audiences affirming paranormalism are more likely to be politically marginal and lower-ranking on society's ladder of success than audiences for more scientifically-oriented media material. The second reason is that presentations that adopt a skeptical or debunking stance tend to rank higher *in the media social structure*. As we've seen, *The New York Times*, a highly prestigious, influential newspaper, adopts a skeptical stance toward paranormal claims; the *Sun* and *The Weekly World News*, tabloids with very little prestige and influence, affirm paranormal claims. Even within the same media source, prestige and influence follow the same lines. In the hierarchy of a television network, straight or "hard" news reporters have more prestige and influence than journalists who make documentaries that affirm paranormal claims. The popularity of paranormal material does not contradict its relative lack of prestige and influence; interestingly, it emphasizes them.

Endnote

[1] Sadly, in 1994, ten years after this incident, Tina, a troubled young woman, was convicted of murdering her three-year-old daughter and sentenced to life in prison.

Chapter Thirteen

PARANORMALISM:
POLITICS AND SOCIAL MOVEMENTS

Politics is about power, and power is the capacity to get your way, in spite of the resistance of your opponents. It might seem that the worlds of the spiritual, the supernatural, and the paranormal have nothing to do with the dirty, gritty, and very earthly world of politics, but this is most certainly not the case. In fact, over the centuries, paranormalism and politics have been very closely intertwined, and in a variety of ways.

Paranormal beliefs have sometimes been dominant while science was the heretical, upstart system of beliefs. In other periods of history, it was science that was hegemonic, and paranormalism was the subversive challenger. Occasionally governments have coopted and used certain deviant or "aberrant" scientists and their unscientific, bizarre, paranormal views to further political goals. More often, regimes have expressed and implemented these views on their own. At other times or in other locales, regimes have persecuted scientists because the latter refused to validate the former's pseudoscientific programs. And in still other cases, social movements have developed beliefs of an occult, extrascientific nature in an effort to win converts and disseminate their views. In addition, many paranormal beliefs have clear-cut political implications that play themselves out on the battlefield of politics.

During the era of Freudian dominance, which ended by the 1970s, practically everything was interpreted as having sexual significance. Today, nearly everything is interpreted as having political implications. Even the very *designation* of a theory or view as "paranormal" will be interpreted as masking a hidden political agenda. Some observers will

205

argue that such a designation is intended to critique, denigrate, or de-legitimate a perspective or the persons holding it in an effort to glorify the status quo.

I would like to propose a somewhat different view. Let's keep our eyes on our central concept, paranormalism. Originally, I defined it as an assertion or claim that contradicts the way scientists say nature works; it violates a scientific principle or law. To repeat the central point, we are interested in how assertions come to be believed, made, how they are regarded and reacted to, and how they link up with other aspects of the society. The agreement or contradiction of these assertions with mainstream science is a *fact;* their objective truth or falseness is not a central issue here.

In a given country or society, some of the paranormal assertions that we'll examine are dominant or hegemonic; others are counter-hegemonic, struggling—typically unsuccessfully—to attain legitimacy and power. The process of challenging and struggling against a dominant discourse is a universal feature of all societies. It is a fascinating subject worthy of study—indeed, in this area, very possibly the most important sociological issue we could lay our hands on. In this chapter, we'll explore this extremely worthwhile issue.

*Pseudo*science is a fixture—probably a permanent fixture—of all political regimes. Listen to a dozen campaign speeches and you'll be rewarded with enough material for a lifetime study of bad science. One has only to recall then-President Ronald Reagan's statement that trees cause more pollution than cars and factories (Green and MacColl, 1983, p.99) to realize that politicians make statements that cause scientists to wince. But is bad science paranormalism? As I said much earlier, the answer is no, not necessarily. Making assertions that are contrary to what scientists believe are the facts does not constitute paranormalism. Once again, a paranormal belief is one that violates a scientific principle or law.

For instance, the view promulgated by Russian agronomist Trofim Lysenko that plants could acquire characteristics that could be passed on to their descendants was bad science, but not paranormalism. At the time that these ideas were in vogue in the Soviet Union in the 1930s and 1940s, it was not scientifically inconceivable that environmental experiences could be encoded into genetic material. The racist theories of the German Nazi regime (1933–1945), likewise, are atrocious as science, but at that time many anthropologists and human biologists held views that argued that some racial categories were inferior to others. Ernest Hooten (1887–1954), who taught at Harvard from 1913 until his death, wielded what many of his contemporaries believed were sound scientific reasons why persons of African descent are inferior to Caucasians— again, terribly bad science, but not paranormalism.

CONSPIRACY THEORIES

Before we look at paranormalism and politics, it is necessary to discuss a related but independent topic: belief in conspiracies. A substantial proportion of the public of many societies and nations on earth believe that there is an evil, shadowy group of persons operating in league against the rest of the society. Many of these conspiracies entail government operations. For instance, in a survey conducted by *George* magazine (published in its November 1996 issue), nearly three-quarters of the sample (74 percent) expressed a belief that the American government regularly engages in "conspiratorial and clandestine" operations. (As we'll see shortly, it is demonstrable and documentable that it does. The only questions are about the *scale* of the operations, as well as which of the many *different* assertions of secret government operations are actually true.)

Conspiracy theories have the following elements:

First, they involve treachery. Perpetrators are up to no good; they intend to do harm. Indeed, their actions are criminal, or at the very least, extremely unethical.

Second, their plot is designed to harm good, decent people.

Third, their actions are secret, surreptitious, hidden, clandestine. They cover their tracks so well, the rest of us have a hard time figuring out what they are up to.

Fourth, they are organized, in fact, so well organized that even some persons in very high places are in on the plot, pulling strings.

And fifth, it is necessary for decent people to expose the nefarious doings of these schemers to protect that which is true, virtuous, and good.

Perhaps the most important feature of conspiracy theories is their reliance on *demonology*. Demonology is a theory of evil, a doctrine that portrays certain figures as devils, demons, or evil spirits. Demonology has been used for thousands of years to identify the enemy, whether oth-erworldly (for instance, the devil himself), or earthly (such as members of another tribe or nation, opponents in war, political plotters, rival sor-cerers or shamans, competitors for a lover's affection, and so on). Con-spiracy theories *almost always* contain a demonological feature. A truly evil enemy is identified, analyzed, and denounced. Crimes of awesome wickedness and almost supernatural deviousness are attributed to him, her, or them. Conspiracy theories leave no room for subtlety, complexity, ambiguity, ambivalence, or doubt. They are morality plays in miniature; the conspirators are the very embodiment of evil. Conspiracy theories nearly always contain assertions about the cruel deeds of putative con-spirators, which are called "atrocity tales."

I'd like to make two qualifications about conspiracy theories, one of which pertains to their validity and the other to their connection with paranormalism. Then I'll put these qualifications into context.

Do conspiracies ever exist? First, claims of conspiracies are not necessarily false. As I suggested, conspiracies do take place. One often hears or reads that conspiracy theories are a product of "paranoid" thinking. In fact, the term "paranoid conspiracy theory" is often used, as if these words naturally belonged together. They don't. A popular saying that began in the contentious 1960s spelled the matter out: "Just because I'm paranoid doesn't mean that people aren't plotting against me." To some observers and critics of contemporary society, paranoia is a healthy, not a delusional, perspective.

In April 1961, a military force consisting of Cuban exiles landed at the Bay of Pigs in Cuba with the intention of fomenting rebellion in the Cuban populace and overthrowing the regime of Fidel Castro. It was crushed, and most of the rebels were either killed or captured. The oper-ation had been planned by the Central Intelligence Agency (CIA) since May of 1960. The CIA funded the training of the rebels and financed the invasion itself. The operation was secret and, for a time after its failure, the American government denied complicity. Without question, the Bay of Pigs operation was an organized conspiracy.

During the War in Vietnam, in the early 1970s U.S. forces began secretly bombing Cambodia. The action was illegal; it obviously harmed the Cambodians; and government officials lied about it and covered it up. This was clearly a conspiracy.

During the presidential campaign of 1972, President Richard Nixon authorized a series of "dirty tricks" against his Democratic rivals.

These tricks entailed, among other illegal tactics, releasing false and defamatory memos on Democrats' stationery; hiring prostitutes to seduce and spy on Democratic candidates; breaking into the office of the psychiatrist of a critic of the Vietnam War to steal confidential files; and bugging the headquarters of the Democratic National Committee. Finally, in June 1972, several employees of CREEP (Committee to Re-Elect the President) were apprehended while burglarizing the Democratic National Committee headquarters, and the plot was revealed. President Nixon denied knowing anything about the operation but was forced to resign the presidency anyway. Audiotapes located much later revealed Nixon's involvement and intimate knowledge of the illegal project. Unquestionably, CREEP's "dirty tricks" campaign against Democratic candidates in 1972 was a conspiracy.

For nearly a century after the Civil War, Blacks in the South (and even in parts of the North) were intimidated, threatened, and attacked by a conspiracy of white-sheeted hatemongers called the Ku Klux Klan. During the 1950s and the 1960s, the Federal Bureau of Investigation (FBI) spied on and conducted a clandestine operation against Martin Luther King, Jr. For decades, the United States Public Health Service conducted a secret experiment on Black men who were suffering from syphilis. Physicians observed the progress of the disease but did not inform their subjects of their condition, and permitted the latter to infect their wives and through them, their children. Even today, many real estate agents, banks, and insurers "redline" Black applicants, that is, conspire to treat them differently, charge them more, refuse to offer them coverage, or refuse to sell them houses in certain neighborhoods (Turner, 1993; Brackman, 1996).

In each of these cases the evidence supporting the existence of the conspiracy is convincing and overwhelming. Some of the participants later have admitted they took part in a conspiracy. These examples represent only the tip of the iceberg. In the history of the world, many conspiracies have been planned and executed. It is foolish to deny that conspiracies exist. It is possible some conspiracies are currently in operation that remain unknown to us. Indeed, it is even possible some will never be revealed. As a conceptual category, conspiracies are real-world phenomena.

Are all conspiracy theories paranormal? My second point is related to the first: conspiracy theories are not *in and of themselves* instances of paranormalism. Even belief in a conspiracy that doesn't exist is not necessarily a paranormal belief. Simply because someone argues that an imaginary conspiracy is afoot does not mean that he or she is using paranormal reasoning. Many, probably most, conspiracies—even those that have no basis in reality whatsoever—are not the product of *scientifically* unlikely or implausible forces. Within the scope of known scientific laws, many plots and schemes are *possible*. Even given what we know about sociological dynamics and processes, certain unlawful, treacherous cabals can *conceivably* be in operation, because even valid generalizations about social behavior do not and cannot be valid in each and every case. Of course, some conspiracies are far less likely and plausible than others, but most do not entail the action of supernatural forces; some do, most don't.

Conspiracy theories: comments and observations. Both qualifications made, I'd like to emphasize that *very few* of the conspiracy theories that have been proposed over the years provide enough convincing supporting evidence for us to say they are true. Evidence suggests the vast majority of conspiracies are demonstrably false. Consider the fact that Jews have been a common target of conspiracy theories for thousands of years. *The Protocols of the Elders of Zion*—perhaps the most famous conspiracy artifact of all time—was a document forged by the Russian secret police in 1905 purporting to lay out a plot for the Jews to rule the world. Taken as a whole, a large number of conspiracy theories are contradictory. One will say, "X did it," a second, "No, Y did," and a third will argue, "No, no, you're both wrong—Z did it!"

When it comes to evidence, conspiracy buffs are often extremely self-serving in their arguments. They frequently allege that "the powers that be" hide and contaminate evidence of conspiracies. When challenged with evidence that contradicts a given conspiracy, they say, "That's the evidence they have *allowed* you to see, because that's what they *want* you to believe. But *I'm* not fooled by their deceptive schemes."

As Robert Anton Wilson says, "nobody can refute any truly crazy conspiracy theory, because all such theories have a Strange Loop in their construction. Any evidence against them also functions to support them, if you want to look at it that way" (1998, p.9). When there is an investigation and no conspiracy is found, the agency engaged in it is part of the cover-up. (If something is found, that evidence is *not* part of the cover-up!) According to that logic, it's possible to verify any argument under the sun. If we were to believe the advocates of the most fanciful conspiracy theories, no evidence of any conspiracy would ever see the light of day, which is clearly false.

Consider only President Bill Clinton's "zipper problem." If the "powers that be," and that certainly includes the most powerful person in the world, the President of the United States, really were so successful at hiding inconvenient facts, this particular scandal would never have erupted. As it turns out, even he did not have enough power to prevent an extremely embarrassing and potentially harmful investigation and trial.

People believe in conspiracy theories because they are narratively interesting and dramatic, and for political and/or emotional reasons (Wilson, 1998, p.9). Belief in conspiracies validates a certain political or epistemological worldview and affirms solidarity with a specific social group or category. This is not the place to debate the empirical validity of one or another conspiracy theory, but the vast majority of conspiracy theories that have been thought up by the human mind are demonstrably false. They are invented *because* they are pleasing to persons who hold a certain world-view.

Conspiracy theories: the paranormal element. Many—not most, but a substantial minority—conspiracy theories *do* contain a paranormal element, which is why the topic is of interest to us here. An essential element of many paranormal theories is that the government is involved in an elaborate cover-up of the truth of supernatural or occult powers. In turn, the proponents of these theories are righteous crusaders struggling against ignorance, wickedness, corruption, and injustice. Here are just a few such conspiracies, each with political and paranormal implications.

- In 1996, Texe Marrs claimed that Lucent Technologies (formerly Bell Laboratories, AT&T's research subsidiary) is in reality a satanic conspiracy. His evidence? The name, "Lucent," is strikingly similar to the devil's name, "Lucifer"; Lucent's network operating system is called "Inferno"; and the company has an office at 666 (a numerical sequence believed by some to be the "mark of the beast," that is to say, the devil) Fifth Avenue, in New York (Wilson, 1998, p.288).

- William Cooper, a former naval intelligence officer, claims that "he personally" has seen documents that spell out the conditions of a treaty between extraterrestrial invaders and the United States government. These aliens have been behind countless abductions, cattle mutilations, and the CIA/cocaine connection. The government is powerless to stop these actions because of the superior weapons of the aliens (Wilson, 1998, p.123).

- Throughout much of the United States since the late 1960s, farmers and ranchers began finding their cattle and horses on the ground, dead, and mutilated "with surgical precision." Often, it is believed, their bodies were moved from one locale and "dumped" in another. The "cattle mutilation mystery" became the basis for a number of extremely elaborate conspiracy theories, one involving the government, usually the CIA; one involving a cabal of satanists, and a third, closer to our interests here, involving extraterrestrials.

- According to many right-wing white supremacist "patriots," the United States government, otherwise known as ZOG (Zionist Occupational Government), in league with the forces of Satan, is involved in a conspiracy of horrendous proportions. Its intention, with the assistance of the United Nations, is to herd all white Christians into concentration camps, kill them off, and rule the world. Not all "patriot" groups combine this scenario with paranormal elements, but many do. Some take their cue from the Book of Revelations of St. John the Divine, which predicts a coming apocalyptic Armageddon or armed struggle between the forces of good and the forces of evil. In addition, a number of these racist "militias," "patriots," or "survivalist" groups are based on the notion that white Anglo-Saxons are the true Israelites and that the Jews, an ethnic group from central Asia, stole their heritage.

- We are now quite familiar with the conspiracy to cover up the crash of an alien space ship in the desert near Roswell, New Mexico, in June, 1947. The "Roswell Incident," as it is referred to by UFO buffs, is the clearest example yet of alleged government cover-ups of extraterrestrial craft circling and landing on earth. Ziegler (1997) asserts flatly that "the Roswell myth has become a vehicle for the expression of antigovernment sentiment" (p.2). As we saw in chapter 9, the claim of an extraterrestrial origin for the wreckage is, according to scientific experts, extremely flimsy.

- *The face on Mars.* The famous "face" on Mars provides yet another example of supposed conspiracies afoot. In 1976, a picture of a formation on Mars was taken by a Viking spacecraft and released to the public by NASA. The formation seemed to resemble a face. Hence, some observers speculated it was deliberately built by an ancient Martian civilization. In 1998, the formation was rephotographed by NASA, this time by its Mars Global Surveyor. Unfortunately for the "face" theorists, the new pictures did not resemble a face at all, but a natural formation of some kind (Anonymous, 1998). The "face" theorists responded by accusing NASA of engaging in a conspiracy to cover up the truth for fear of unleashing panic and social disorganization in society (Foster, 1998).

Let's look at the last of these theories in a bit of detail. Picture the image of NASA, scientists, and the government that this charge of conspiracy implies. To begin with, the charge is based on the assumption that the relevant powers believe the public will experience panic or undergo social disorganization or demoralization as a result of learning of an ancient civilization on Mars. (This very theory was enunciated in the film, *2001*, in which news of the discovery of a "deliberately buried" black monolith on the Moon was withheld from the public for fear of precisely these consequences.) Such an outcome does not and will not take place, as any official can determine by reading the social and psychological literature on disasters (Goode, 1992, chapters 5 and 6). Humans are frequently exposed to conditions that are vastly more terrifying and life-threatening—real-life natural disasters, for instance—than learning that civilizations once existed elsewhere in the solar system. The fact is, they almost never panic.

This conspiracy theory also assumes that astronomers report their discoveries to officials in the government who must "clear" them before release to the public and that if government officials do not clear them the findings cannot be released. Indeed, this theory further assumes astronomers will collude in the conspiracy by doctoring or "retouching" their own photographs to conform to the official line. The fact is, there is no official "clearinghouse" for censoring astronomical findings. If any astronomer photographed any structure left behind by an intelligent civilization on Mars or anywhere else in the universe, they would report that finding to the public as soon as possible, whether or not they first reported it to NASA or other government officials. If images that were obtained previously were doctored or retouched to remove evidence of the hypothesized structures, every astronomer who had access to the relevant equipment would analyze and reanalyze those images and demand that the original, genuine images be released. Retouching past images would become the most serious scandal in NASA's history.

In science, the coin of the realm is scientific prestige. It is usually achieved only as a result of making a discovery so major that one's colleagues are profoundly impressed. There is very little that is even remotely as important as that in science. An astronomer's reputation would be secure for life if he or she were to discover undisputed evidence of an ancient civilization on Mars. The notion that an astronomer would pass up such an opportunity in order to conform to NASA's, or the government's, mistaken theory about panic or social disorganization strains one's gullibility almost beyond our capacity to express.

The structure of social control in astronomy is far too loose and too autonomous for the government to exert such influence. (And remember, there are astronomers sitting at the keyboards of extremely sophisticated computer equipment in dozens of countries around the world.) The entire theory simply runs counter to everything we know to be true, but it is an excellent example of the kinds of conspiracies that are devised in some quarters to account for a wide range of paranormal or paranormal-like events.

AMERICAN INDIAN PREHISTORY

Imagine that, through trickery and criminal conspiracy, someone were to purchase a cemetery in which your ancestors were buried. Imagine further that this party hired a group of historians, biologists, and archaeologists to dig up those ancestors' remains, study them, and write reports on them, exposing details that you and your relatives may feel are unacceptable, scandalous, or demeaning. Our guess is, you'd be outraged. You'd want to do whatever you could to put a halt to this atrocity. Many Native American or Indian spokespersons believe this is precisely what archaeologists have done, and are currently doing, to their sacred lands.

Once again, we are not addressing whether the Native American position or that of archaeologists has more validity. The hypothetical situation I presented may permit the reader to empathize with the feelings generated by many Indians when they confront archaeological research.

Let it be said that not all American Indians agree on the matter of the illegitimacy of archaeology. Some feel archaeology is the only way their ancestors can speak to those of us who are living in the present (Lippert, 1997). Others argue that a distinction should be made between burial and non-burial sites, and feel the latter can be dug up and studied, while the former are sacred and should not be touched (Kluth and Munnell, 1997). The Pequot Indians of Connecticut validated their tribal status by hiring archaeologists to study their past. The Pequots have set up an archaeological museum, which features the research they sponsored (Feder, 1997, p.80).

Still other Indian spokespersons believe that North American archaeology as practiced by persons of European ancestry is an illegitimate enterprise that has no right to exist. They feel the goal of archaeology is to denigrate their heritage, invalidate their interpretations of reality, deny them their rights to ancestral lands, and to justify white dominion over the New World. Hence, archaeology should be denounced at every turn, its racist goals exposed, and the voice of its practitioners squelched. The only truth of the Indian past, they believe, is the version told in ancient tribal tales thousands of years old; all other versions are false and defamatory.

Perhaps the most prominent, impassioned, and vociferous proponent of the point of view that traditional Native American accounts of the past are always true, while those offered by white archaeologists are by their very nature false, is spelled out in *Red Earth, White Lies* (1995) by Vine Deloria, Jr., a Standing Rock Sioux and author of the influential, widely respected *Custer Died for Your Sins* (1969). The basis on which Deloria's argument rests can only be referred to as paranormal in nature.

Deloria claims that archaeological estimates of Indian habitation in North America of 12,000 years (some estimates run as high as 30,000 years or more) are false. "We were always here," Deloria asserts, arguing for a Native American creationism. To argue that Indians have lived in the New World for only 12,000 to 30,000 years is to argue (he claims) that they can be legitimately cheated out of their land. In contrast, to argue that Indians "have always been here" is to assert the sacred right of Indians to this land and to proclaim that all other peoples living here are usurpers, interlopers, and thieves. Hence, any scientific method of dating archaeological artifacts are invalid, false, and subversive to Indian interests. More specifically, the claim goes, if chemical analysis can demonstrate ancient bones to be from peoples with no lineal relationship to tribal peoples living in a specific locale, it weakens the case that the latter have exclusive right over the land ceded.

Deloria takes Indian myth and legend as fact, with some embellishment of his own. Hence, references to ancient peoples as "giants" and "tall peoples" (p.167) must be literally true, he claims. He hypothesizes that a white-skinned race of people who drove some Indians out of their traditional homelands, drove eastward, "invaded Western Europe,

routed the Neanderthals, and are known as Cro-Magnon peoples"
(p.167). Pleistocene or ice age people and humans were huge because
back then, there were higher CO_2 concentrations in the air, until a "dump
of cometary water" changed all that and shrank everybody down to size
(pp.93, 172–173).

Deloria argues that Indian creation myths are literally true. These
creation accounts were devised long before a recognizable science
existed, of course, but, in contrast, Deloria's justification of them takes
place in an age in which science is dominant or hegemonic. There are
hundreds of these creation myths, and they are contradictory. Most, it
must be admitted given today's scientific orientation, are paranormal in
nature. In one, humans fall to earth from a land above the sky. In
another, they climb up from a world several levels below our own. In a
third, a sky-spirit builds a lodge on top of a mountain, and his daughter,
carried away by the wind, alights on land and mates with grizzly-bear-
men; their children were Indian ancestors. In a fourth, an elk plunged
to earth, at that time completely covered with water, and commanded
the winds to dry the land; overjoyed when it came true, the elk rolled
around on the new land, and the loose hairs that shed from his fur
became all the plants that grow on earth.

Each and every one of these creation stories is a historical truth,
Deloria claims. Since Deloria wishes to express ideological solidarity
with all Native American peoples, he sees no contradiction between or
among them. Hence, he does not specify which ones he endorses. Only
one account of the origin of Indians in the New World is false: the scientific version. All others are true (Feder, 1997). In fact, what Deloria
means by "white lies" in the title of his book is what archaeologists and
other scientists take to be the truth. What he means by "red earth" is the
political truth that North America belongs to the Indian, and any narrative that questions the veracity of that truth is a lie.

Deloria's critique of archaeology goes even further than this: "the
very concept of scientific fact *itself* is a myth" (Feder, 1997, p.79). In contrast, every cultural belief of all Indian tribes is valid and correct. The
fact that they entail events that science would argue cannot have taken
place—that, in fact, violate laws of the known universe and hence, make
use of principles that are paranormal in nature—is no barrier to his
assertions. In fact, quite the contrary is the case. They are true *because*
they violate the laws of science. They are true because they affirm the
rights of Indian peoples to New World land. They are true because they
subvert the myth of white dominion over the Western Hemisphere. They

are true because they serve a political and ideological agenda. Once again, we encounter the principle that the scientific and the paranormal versions of reality are at cross-purposes. The epistemologies on which they are built are incompatible; they inhabit different universes of meaning, valorize different dimensions of observation, take different sorts of data as valid. There is no conceivable manner in which they can be reconciled.

CREATIONISM

There are two absolutely crucial facts about the debate between evolution and creationism we should keep in mind. The first fact is that each version of reality is believed by just under half of the American public. The second fact is that evolution is the dominant discourse; it is creationism that is struggling to achieve legitimacy. As we saw earlier, the higher the level of education, the greater the likelihood that someone will accept the fact of evolution and reject the literal biblical version of creation as a valid account of how we got here. The mainstream media typically promulgate evolution, not creationism. Evolution, not creationism, is taught in nearly all institutions of higher learning, and the more prestigious and powerful the institution, the more firmly entrenched this view of reality is. As we'll see, most of the time, their efforts are rebuffed by the dominant institutions, such as the Supreme Court, the Smithsonian Institution, and state legislatures. And the more dominant the institution, the more that creationists' efforts are rebuffed. For instance, while local school boards may be influenced by creationists, the Supreme Court cannot be.

Most scientists are puzzled as to why there should be a debate over the issue of evolution in the first place. To them, there is no issue; the matter was settled over a century ago. It makes no more sense to debate this question, they would say, than to argue about whether the earth revolves around the sun or the other way around.

As I've defined the term, creationism is a paranormal theory. By that I mean that its assertions are not only contrary to what mainstream science teaches, but it asserts the operation of a mechanism which scientists say can be falsified and that contradicts the way nature works. Creationists have to struggle to achieve acceptance, legitimacy, and dominance. What is most interesting to us is not who's right here, but the very nature of the debate, the conflict, the controversy—the attempt to define for the society at large what the nature of reality is. This struggle may be referred to as "the politics of reality," that is, the political and ideological struggle to define what's true. It extends into a wide range of political venues and contexts. Both creationists and evolutionists use arguments that attempt to persuade others that their position is correct.

But as we saw, power is not balanced here; it is the evolutionists who have the upper hand. Supporters of creationism see themselves under siege, as righteous warriors fighting against an evil enemy for a virtuous cause. They feel that they have to destroy or at least nullify the corrupting monster of evolution because, as we've seen, it represents everything they find repugnant. Hence, they struggle to define reality to their liking and attempt to achieve that goal through the political process.

Strongly committed creationists believe that evolution is the foundation of secular humanism, which is attempting to corrupt American society. Secular humanism encourages a flood of social ills, including materialism, atheism, communism and socialism, feminism, sex education, fornication, illegitimacy, abortion, homosexuality, prostitution, pornography, incest, violence, crime, rape, drug abuse, alcoholism, and Satanism.

Historian Christopher Toumey interviewed North Carolina state senator Jack Cavanagh, opponent of evolution and staunch supporter of creationism. He argued that if secular humanists "don't have" evolution, then their entire premise "falls apart, because they believe that no deity can save us, we must save ourselves, that there is no God, that man is the beginning and end of all things. . . . So when you take away evolution, then you destroy it [secular humanism], because they have to account for something coming from nothing" (1994, p.174).

Not only is evolution the cornerstone of secular humanism, creationists claim, but the insinuation of evolution into American culture corrupts and destroys a decent, moral, Christian approach to life. "I've noticed," Cavanagh elaborated, "that men are losing a little bit of their self-esteem, their manhood . . ., their desire to achieve, to grow, to develop." It's "truly frightening," he added. "But where I really see it is in the church. The church is losing its backbone. It's losing its commitment. . . . If man needs to be brought back up to a position of good," Cavanagh argues, "and the only way he can do that, in the Christian religion, is to be redeemed, then he needs a redeemer. And that's Jesus" (p.174). In the creationist's scheme of things, evolution equals secular humanism equals corruption, ungodliness, and damnation; in contrast, creationism equals Christianity equals godliness equals salvation. The equation is seamless, impregnable, and unassailable. It should not be surprising, therefore, that creationists attempt to destroy the demon of evolution!

On their side, evolutionists are equally committed and unshakably certain. Evolution is referred to as a "theory," but scientists say this is a fallacy. Evolution was proposed long before Charles Darwin came along. Darwin had a theory of *why* and *how* evolution worked, not a theory of the *fact* of evolution. Natural selection is Darwin's "theory" of evolution, and as Darwin proposed it, it is not universally accepted among biologists. But *almost every* biological scientist regards the process of evolution *itself* as a fact, a fact that has been proved, says Richard Dawkins, "utterly beyond reasonable doubt." To claim equal time for creationism, he says, is similar to claiming equal time for the flat earth theory, the view that the sun revolves around the earth, or the claim that the stork brings babies. "It is absolutely safe to say," argues Dawkins, "that if you meet somebody who claims not to believe in evolution, that person is ignorant, stupid or insane (or wicked, but I'd rather not consider that)." The struggle for evolution, Dawkins states, and against fundamentalism is a struggle for "reason and the gentle virtues of civilization. This is so because the more you read, quietly and soberly, the evidence for evolution, the more powerful will you discover that evidence to be."

It is the most vociferous and singleminded of proponents on both sides who are most likely to state their position publicly and to receive the most attention. At the rank-and-file or grassroots level (the so-called man and woman on the street), for both creationists and evolutionists, there is a multiplicity of views. Very few hold these views as tenaciously or express them as dogmatically as the more vocal proponents of these two positions do. While the extremists force an either-or polarity on the issue, the beliefs and opinions of most people can be represented as a spectrum, far more complex and ambivalent than a simple dichotomy (Eve and Harrold, 1991, pp.3–4). But it is most often the either-or positions that break out into ideological and political struggles.

How does the creationist movement "do" politics? In what way is it a social movement? How does it champion creationism and neutralize the influence of evolutionist theory and thus, in their eyes, the influence of secular humanism? Through two vehicles: *rhetoric* and *organization*.

The creationist argument or discourse is constructed by means of a number of well-known and easily-identified rhetorical or persuasive devices. Sociologists Eve and Harrold (1991, pp.68–93) have located some of the most clear-cut of them. Here are a few.

The false dichotomy. One of the most prominent creationists lays out the argument in this fashion. "Since there are only two possible models, and they are diametrically opposed, it is clear that evidence against evolution constitutes evidence for [biblical] creation, and evidence against creation is evidence for evolution" (Morris, 1977). This is a false dichotomy, of course, since there are many other possibilities. For instance, both could be wrong, and a third theory correct. Demolishing evolution does not automatically mean that creationism is true. Any of the Native American narratives of creation could be true, or that of Hinduism, Buddhism, the ancient Egyptian religion, or any one of the many African tribal accounts. Morris' statement is a declaration, not an argument. But, since 90 to 95 percent of the American population believes in God, equating evolution with atheism is a clever debater's trick. The fact is, as we've seen, many evolutionists also believe in God (Eve and Harrold, 1991, pp.79–81).

Exegesis. Although many of the institutes that sponsor creationist studies refer to themselves as "research" enterprises, in fact, they do no scientific research at all. Following up on their use of the false dichotomy, as I've explained, what creationists do is attack evolution, not document creation. They do not, that is, set forth a hypothesis, gather facts in the field or the laboratory, test their hypothesis, and draw conclusions from the patterns they observe, as nearly all working scientists do. "Rather, they simply spray the edifice of evolutionary science with numerous volleys in an effort to hit a vital supporting element and bring it down. The structure they would raise in its place is biblical, not scientific" (p.85).

As I explained earlier, "neo-creationists" aim to provide factual documentation of the biblical account of the birth of the universe (Hitt, 1996). But a close reading of their research, scientists would say, shows that their minds are unlikely to be changed by contrary findings. Most of their arguments collapse "into a series of could-haves," for instance, Noah *could have* had a zoo at the ready for God's command to build the ark. Scientists do not find such reasoning satisfying.

Selective and dishonest use of evidence. The most persuasive biochemical evidence supporting evolution is the relationship between an organism's genetically determined sequence of amino acids constituting its proteins and its evolutionary relationship with other organisms. The fit is close to perfect: organisms that evolved from a common ancestor have very similar proteins, while those that didn't do not. On the PBS science program, *Nova,* Duane Gish claimed that studies showed no such general pattern. When scientists looked through the literature for studies to support Gish's claim, they could not find any. He said he'd provide documentation, but he didn't. After two years, he refused to address the question (pp.82–83).

When Gish attempted to demolish the relevance of Java Man as a humanoid ancestor, he cited sources decades old and ignored recent research that disproved his point. When he addressed the question of Peking Man, he found it suspicious that the original fossils had disappeared (during World War II) and claimed their plaster casts had been altered to look more humanlike, all the while ignoring photographs of the originals that were "faithful reproductions" (p.76–77). Chinese scientists have since found humanlike fossils near the original site, but Gish fails to mention this fact. When authors express reservations about the human ancestry of a given find, he quotes their reservations but ignores the fact that they nonetheless support the fact of evolution. The more generous interpretation of Gish's and other creationists' use of the available evidence is that they are extremely selective in their reading of it.

Persuading the relevant audiences. The creationists' arguments are not directed at the scientific community at all. As we saw, creationists do not conduct traditional scientific research, and they do not publish in the scientific journals. Their claim is that they submit papers to journals, which are rejected by biased editors. A scrutiny of 68 science journals shows that of 135,000 papers submitted to them during a period of time, only 18 creationist papers were submitted. During a nearly four-year period, of 28 prominent creationists, only six had published anything in the science literature, and all were on very technical matters having nothing to do with the creation-evolution question (Scott and Cole, 1985; Cole and Scott, 1982).

Creationists direct their message not to scientists but to the lay public. Within this public, there are two main audiences: first, evangelical and fundamentalist Christians who "desire solace in the face of perceived threats to their faith" (Eve and Harrold, 1991, p.86) and two, the "bystander public," that is, persons who are uninvolved in the debate but are ordinary citizens who might be counted on to support "equal time" for creationism in public education (p.87). Creationists have largely given up on the mainstream media, which do not support their arguments. Instead, they rely mainly on Christian and creationist channels of communication.

The fact that the creationist argument is directed to committed conservative Christians primarily and the lay public secondarily has important consequences. By doing this, creationists do not have to adhere to the much stricter scientific canons of evidence and argumentation. In fact, by using a variety of age-old debater's tricks, their arguments are far more persuasive than they would be if they were to stick to scientifically acceptable arguments, which are often baffling and confusing to the general public.

Creationists know their audience and know what arguments work, what is appealing and persuasive. Using rhetorical devices such as "card stacking" (a highly selective argument), personal testimonial, the glittering generality, adopting a populist, anti-intellectual, anti-science stance, and appealing to fairness in demanding equal time (p.89), creationists manage to persuade audiences that they are right. The fact is, most Americans "are ill-equipped to evaluate the claims of scientific creationism." Most of us have a "little understanding" of the rules of critical thinking and the rules of evidence (p.91); moreover, many of us are unconcerned about them. As we've seen, the so-called "average" American's folk epistemology or "way of knowing" is vastly different from the scientist's but very similar to that of the creationist.

The use of these clever rhetorical devices does not necessarily mean that the creationist position is wrong. It is possible to wield an argument that experts regard as fatally flawed in support of an empirically true proposition. Still, the incompatibility between what scientists and what much of the public—and the creationists—take as valid and persuasive should remind us of our much earlier point: paranormalism thrives because believers and the general public believe in very different kinds of evidence than that which scientists accept.

Organizational efforts. In addition to how the creationists put together their rhetorical arguments to persuade audiences that they are correct, we might wish to consider the *organizational* basis of the creationist movement. The creationist movement has attacked evolution—and, by extension, secular humanism—on four fronts: the courts, legislation, state educational bodies, and the grassroots level (Eve and Harrold, 1991, pp.143–167).

The courts. Ever since 1968, when the Supreme Court ruled that banning the teaching of evolution in the public school classroom was "out of the question" (p.144), creationists have used the courts to argue that keeping creationism out of the classroom violated their First

Amendment right of the exercise of free speech and the free exercise of their religion. Moreover, they have argued, evolution is the foundation of the "religion" of secular humanism. In addition to targeting the schools, one lawsuit was lodged against the National Science Foundation for funding a Smithsonian Institution exhibit, "The Emergence of Man," which adopted an evolutionary approach. The exhibit promoted secular humanism, not science, the plaintiff claimed. On this issue, the courts have been consistent. Evolutionary science, they have ruled, "is not a religion, and it cannot be excluded from education or museums because it offends some people's religious beliefs" (p.145).

Legislation. Since the 1970s, creationists have introduced dozens of bills into state legislatures calling for equal time for biblical creation in educational curricula. Once again, their argument has been based on the claim that creationism is a scientific theory and that its similarity with the Genesis account of the creation of the universe is coincidental. Moreover, once again, they claim that evolution fosters the "religion" of secular humanism.

Most of these state laws were not enacted. In fact, in all but two, they died in committees. But in 1981 in Arkansas and Louisiana, they became law. Immediately, a coalition made up of the American Civil Liberties Union, liberal Protestant, Catholic, and Jewish clergy, and national educational and religions organizations challenged the law in court. The Arkansas law was struck down in federal district court in 1981. The case involving the Louisiana law reached the Supreme Court in 1987, where it was found unconstitutional. Federal courts have not been persuaded that creationism does not represent yet another attempt to establish religion in the public schools. Discouraged, the creationists' legislative efforts have diminished since then.

State educational boards. Another front used by creationists to advance their cause is lobbying state educational boards to refuse to adopt textbooks favorable to the evolutionist position. Several of the larger states (for instance, California and Texas) are "adoption" states, which means local school boards must adopt among a list of texts approved by the state educational boards. Moreover, many nonadoption states go along with the choices made by the adoption states. Since it costs in the neighborhood of a million dollars or more to produce a high school biology text, and a successful adoption could result in sales of many millions of dollars, it would be disastrous to lose a major adoption, and alternatively, hugely profitable to obtain one. As a result, publishers began to cave in to pressure from school boards who, in turn, have been influenced by creationist lobbying to remove the evolutionary content of their biology textbooks.

While in the 1970s and early 1980s, the creationists' efforts were successful in watering down the evolutionary content of textbooks, by the mid-1980s, a counter-response by supporters of evolution produced a reversal of this trend. Still, many current texts are still dominated by "weasel" and "fudge" words and phrases such as "some scientists believe," "evolution is a theory," and "if the evolutionists are correct." Hence, the creationist effort to transform the content of biology textbooks taught in public schools was only a partial defeat (pp.155–161).

The grassroots level. It is at the grassroots level that creationists have had their strongest successes. At the same time, it is at the grassroots level that detailed information about what has happened is hardest to come by. What we have is a series of anecdotes or descriptions of local events. In addition, we have surveys of the beliefs of local high school teachers. In a number of local school boards, fundamentalist Christian parents and teachers have been successful in establishing an equal-time doctrine in the classroom, in obtaining creationist textbook adoptions, in getting creationist books into the library, and in downplaying evolution in the teaching of biology. Much of the problem centers around the fact that a teacher's beliefs influence how he or she teaches a subject, and a substantial proportion of high school teachers believe in creationism and believe that it should be taught in the classroom.

A number of studies (summarized in Eve and Harrold, 1991, p.163) found that the proportion of public science teachers who agree that creationism should be taught in the classroom varied between 30 and 69 percent. Related studies show the proportion of teachers who report teaching creationism in the classroom varies from 22 to 30 percent (p.165). Moreover, a study of college students in Texas, California, and Connecticut revealed that between 33 and 83 percent said they had been taught the equal-time or two-model doctrine in high school; that is, evolution and creationism were presented alongside one another. In short, in spite of defeats at legislative and judicial levels, on the grassroots, local, or instructional level, students are most likely to receive a heavy dose of creationism.

Summary. The infiltration of creationism into the public classroom represents the triumph of populism over the hegemony of scientific elitism. In fact, the teaching of creationism in public schools is a victory for a biblical account that scientists argue is all but impossible. The fact that nearly all scientists see the creationist claim as lacking in factual foundation is secondary. What counts is that it is believed and acted upon. Creationism, a paranormal belief system, is appealing to much of the public and is validated by a kind of folk epistemology that is convincing as a result of a selective yet emotionally persuasive reading of the evidence. The beliefs are real, they have real-world consequences, and they are not going to disappear through mere exhortation or debunking. In fact, it is almost impossible to imagine what manner of evidence would persuade a creationist that his or her beliefs are wrong. To quote the author of a high school biology textbook designed for Christian schools, if scientific conclusions "contradict the Word of God, the conclusions are wrong no matter how many scientific facts may appear to back them" (Pinkston, 1980, p.vii).

Part Five

Conclusions

Why paranormalism? What is it that believers find compelling and convincing about an extra-scientific way of looking at reality? Does it offer something a strict mechanistic or materialistic interpretation does not? To turn the question around, what does science offer to its believers that a more spiritual interpretation fails to provide? The appeals of each system of thought demand investigation.

At the end of our journey, what have we learned about the human condition? Where has our investigation taken us? What can we say about who we are that we didn't know before? In what ways is a study of paranormalism a worthwhile endeavor?

Chapter Fourteen

WHY PARANORMALISM?

What generates and sustains paranormalism? Given the dominance of science, a perspective that is promulgated in the educational system, in the most prestigious and influential media, and in the mainstream, secular, ecumenical religious bodies how do alternative views arise? If evolution is taught in the schools, why isn't that view the most widespread one in the United States? Indeed, why do *any* Americans believe in creationism? Why is the American population so evenly split on the evolution-creationism issue? If the nation's most credible media sources are more likely to make fun of than endorse the idea of "little green men" in our skies and in our midst, why, again, does nearly half the public embrace the extraterrestrial hypothesis as valid? Why is belief in ghosts, ESP, lucky numbers, the devil, and angels held by a majority of Americans? Why isn't the *dominant* interpretation of reality also the most *popular* view? Why is paranormalism so widespread?

Even though much of my focus has delineated the position of science as dominant or hegemonic and paranormalism as counter-hegemonic, we also have to consider the fact that each belief system fits into and resonates with people's lives in distinctly different ways. That is, belief systems should not be examined *solely* or even *mainly* from the point of view of their prestige and influence. A given belief may seem to *work*—that is, from a psychological and sociological point of view. Independent of where it stands on one or another hierarchy, it may serve personal or social functions. Certain beliefs are more appealing than others because they make "common sense." Within a given widely accepted framework, a belief may be perceived to be true simply because it resonates with the way we and others like us think in our everyday lives. A practice may be believed to be effective in achieving a given goal, again, because it *seems* to work; we imagine that good things happen when we engage in it. To repeat: power and prestige are part of the picture, but they are far from the whole picture.

At this point, then, the question becomes, *why?* Why do paranormal claims, ideas, beliefs, and narratives catch on? What propagates them, what sustains them? Why are the audiences for these two approaches—the paranormal and the scientific—as disproportionate as they are? Where is the debunking, skeptical, or scientific equivalent of *The X-Files, Touched by an Angel, Men in Black*, and *Independence Day?* Why are books, films, television programs, and newspaper and magazine stories about paranormal phenomena so much more popular than scientific theories, descriptions, and explanations? In short, *why paranormal beliefs?*

DIVERSITY

Before we address the *why* question, we must remind ourselves that there is enormous diversity in the universe of paranormal beliefs. Hence, a somewhat different explanation may be necessary to account for different forms of paranormal thinking.

Some, like the belief that the earth is flat, are held by an extremely minuscule proportion of the population. Others, such as the belief in creationism or that aliens from outer space are visiting Earth are, as we've seen, believed by nearly half of the entire population. Beliefs in ESP and that angels are real and intervene in our lives are supported by a strong majority of the American public.

Some paranormal beliefs have a religious origin or generate communities of believers and serve functions very similar to those of conventional religions. Others are endorsed by those segments of the population that are most alienated from traditional religious beliefs.

Some paranormal beliefs form the basis of fads. They are little more than hobbies in the lives of adherents. They are accepted simply because their adherents have not thought very rigorously, systematically, or empirically about the issue at hand. Some, in fact, are little more than harmless, escapist entertainment. It must be emphasized that the vast majority of the advocates of most paranormalisms are marginally and superficially involved with those beliefs.

But the same cannot be said for every adherent of every belief I've discussed or mentioned. In fact, as we've seen, some paranormal beliefs form the basis of social movements and hold a potential for profoundly influencing the political process. Certainly creationism provides an outstanding example of this. Will Native American creation myths be invoked to induce the white majority to recognize Indian claims to their traditional lands? Are white supremacist narratives sufficiently contrary to what scientists regard as the laws of nature to qualify as paranormal in nature? Will other cult-like quasi-movements centered around UFOs emerge after the collective suicide of Heaven's Gate? While these examples remind us that paranormal beliefs generate collectivities whose members are so committed to their interpretation of reality that they are willing to die for them, we also have to keep in mind that there is a continuum in degrees of commitment from marginal and superficial to central and intense.

Some systems of paranormal beliefs (such as creationism and astrology) are rejected by the overwhelming majority of credentialed practicing scientists on the planet. Others (such as parapsychology and alternative medicine) are regarded by these scientists as not altogether implausible; the evidence contradicting their claims, some scientists would say, is far from definitive. Moreover, diverse categories in the population may support altogether different paranormal beliefs. In principle, creationists tend to reject the validity of astrology but are extremely likely to accept the physical reality of angels. Belief in astrology is embraced by more women than men; the belief that UFOs are alien aircraft is more likely to be held by men than women. Westerners (mainly Californians) are less likely to accept creationism than southerners but more likely to believe in nearly all other forms of paranormalism.

In short, it is crucial not to lump all paranormal beliefs together and simply assume the dynamics behind their acceptance are all the same. Although they are united by a common thread, their diversity is as important as their unity.

CHANGING THE WAY WE THINK?

With the qualification that different paranormalisms are likely to have a somewhat different set of appeals, we nonetheless need explanations that account for these belief systems. At this point it should be clear the author's position is that paranormal thinking is a fundamental sociological fixture of the way that certain members of major segments of the population view reality. It is not a thinking process that will disappear with this or that gimmick of social tinkering. Presenting a more scientific and less paranormal approach in the media or in the educational system will not transform many paranormalists into scientific thinkers, as many debunkers seem to believe. To the extent that the media and the educational system promulgate unscientific ideas, they are more likely to reinforce than to be independent causes of our major beliefs, and many media sources can be found that affirm belief in paranormal powers.

Paranormalism grows out of a general worldview that entails reasoning about how the world works, notions of causality, what constitutes evidence, how one draws conclusions, what in one's life is important and what is secondary, and what it all means. And these fundamental epistemological building blocks of thinking tend to be a product of one's early socialization, especially with respect to religion and the spiritual/material dimension, educational background, social class position, the social networks in which one is involved and interacts, major life commitments and emotional investments, and life situation—crises, threats, traumas, and consequent fears, insecurities, and anxieties.

These features of one's life shape how we think about material reality and the role that spiritual forces play. They are not about to change with a bit of exhortation from experts, spokespersons, gurus, authorities, illuminati, masters, pedagogues, guides, visionaries, or cognoscenti. Adult "converts" in this area tend to be relatively rare. A single factor alone (for instance, having sat through a one-year high school biology course) is unlikely to sway one's thinking about such a crucial issue. (More accurately, a high school biology course may influence a student with a fundamentalist Christian background to believe in evolution for a year or two, after which time, the beliefs acquired during childhood often reassert themselves.) In principle, as we saw, the media do seem to have something of an impact in an audience's belief in paranormal phenomena. But convincing media moguls to present a more scientific approach in their programs, thereby accepting leaner profits—or substantial losses—is not going to be an easy sell.

WHY SCIENCE?

Let's turn the question around: *Why science?* The question, "*Why paranormalism?*" assumes that there's something problematic, something that needs explaining, something that's not quite right about paranormal beliefs. It assumes that science is the norm and paranormalism a departure from the norm. If we ask, "Why science?", we take the belief in traditional scientific reasoning as peculiar and in need of explaining. To repeat, therefore, "Why science?"

Scientific reasoning has a great many drawbacks. As I pointed out earlier, one type of paranormal reasoning or another has been around since the dawn of humanity. Belief in paranormal reasoning is so ancient and widespread—trans-historical and trans-cultural—that it seems to border on being a human instinct. If left to their own devices, humans almost naturally turn to some form of extra-scientific thinking.

What is more natural than to imagine that there are ghosts and goblins lurking in the forest? That gods control forces that human powers are too weak to influence? That prayers, magic, witchcraft, and animal sacrifice will influence the gods to give humans what they want? That dreams predict the future? That life has a purpose? That, when our body dies, our soul will live forever in a wonderful place? And that, one day, just a few thousand years ago, a huge, gray-bearded man rose up, issued a command, and created the universe out of nothing? These beliefs offer a meaningful narrative, explaining what life is all about, a "sacred canopy" (Berger, 1967), an apparent refuge from the terror of meaninglessness.

For instance, the fact that almost every culture in the world has a scientifically implausible account of how the world came into being is important and meaningful. Clearly humans have something of a hunger to account for origins. The fact that these accounts bear no relationship to the scientist's accounts is crucial. The scientist's account is emotionally barren and culturally unsatisfying. In contrast, folk, tribal, or traditional narratives are plausible specifically because they are emotionally meaningful.

All these extra-scientific creation beliefs appeal to common sense. They appeal to the yearning in all of us to make sense of the events of the world. In contrast, science is *not* intuitively appealing; it does not resonate with common sense. Strict materialists have no comforting beliefs in an afterlife; indeed, they must confront the terror of death as the end; such contemplation can lead people to believe that life is meaningless, absurd, and purposeless. In many ways, belief in science seems to make no intuitive sense whatsoever.

"In inspecting modern occultisms," say psychologists Singer and Benassi (1981, p.52), "we find that most offer an alleged ability to increase predictability and control, especially under uncertain circumstances. Thus, Tarot cards, clairvoyance, or astrology allow us to 'know' the future; biorhythms and psychic healing allow us to regulate our often capricious bodies and health." How can we wipe out pseudoscientific beliefs, asks science writer Isaac Asimov (1986, p.212)

> when those beliefs warm and comfort human beings? Do you enjoy the thought of dying, or having someone you love die? Can you blame anyone for convincing himself that there is such a thing as life-everlasting and that he will see all those he [or she] loves in a state of perpetual bliss? Do you feel comfortable with the daily uncertainties of life; with never knowing that the next moment will

bring? Can you blame anyone for convincing himself [or herself] he [or she] can forewarn and forearm himself [or herself] against these uncertainties by seeing the future clearly through the configuration of planetary positions, or the fall of cards, or the pattern of tea-leaves, or the events in dreams? Inspect every piece of pseudo-science and you will find a security blanket, a thumb to suck, a skirt to hold. What do we [scientists] offer in exchange? Uncertainty! In-security!

In short, almost everything science tells us is something "we do not want to hear" (Anderson, 1998, p.44).

A great deal of science also violates conventional wisdom or "common sense." Much of it is distinctly odd, almost literally unbelievable. To accept the tenets of science we have to believe that solid objects are mostly empty space; that we are standing on the surface of an immense ball that is hurtling through space at an unimaginably high speed; that old, collapsed stars are so dense that light cannot escape from their gravitational field; and that many of our most cherished beliefs are simply wrong. What earthly motives would induce anyone to reject what seem to be the data of the senses and accept notions that violate them?

Traditional positivistic scientists would argue that they believe in science because that's the way the universe is put together; science offers an explanation for how things are. They would argue that the evidence for paranormal claims is extremely weak while that for the scientific point of view is strong. "Everything we know," they claim, argues against the validity of paranormalism and for that of traditional science (Westrum, 1977, p.272).

This is far too simplistic an explanation, however. Science is compelling for a segment of the population for a variety of reasons. For one thing, science is the dominant belief system. The higher up one climbs on the prestige-and-power hierarchy, the more dominant and entrenched scientific beliefs are. As we saw, evolution is taught in the university system. Moreover, the more prestigious the institution, the more hegemonic evolutionary thinking is and the more contempt the faculty has for creationism. When mavericks come along and challenge the dominant scientific paradigm, as Velikovsky did in the 1950s, as John Mack did in the 1990s, that paradigm's proponents react with hostility. And the more education one has, the less likely one is to believe in creationism and the more likely one is to believe in evolution. As we saw, high-prestige and high-impact media, such as *The New York Times*, do not carry a horoscope column; low-prestige and low-impact media, such as the supermarket tabloids, not only carry horoscopes, they devote a substantial amount of attention to astrology. Hence, the higher prestige and influence of science as opposed to paranormal thinking might appear to be a major incentive to embrace the former and to reject the latter. Paranormal thinking might very well condemn one to marginality and powerlessness.

To the extent that paranormal beliefs are accorded prestige, legitimacy, and credibility, this undermines the prestige, legitimacy, and credibility of the scientific establishment and hence poses a threat to it (Westrum, 1977, pp.271–272). In a sense, then, debates about science and anti-science become "turf wars," with representatives of competing interest groups courting the public in order to protect scarce resources. Scientific training represents a kind of investment—an investment with respect to time, emotional energy, career, livelihood, worldview, and so on. Challenges to that investment are met with dismissal or a counter-response.

Science is a *worldview*; it offers a satisfying and coherent accounting for why things are the way they are. Science holds out the enticement of intellectual mastery that places the human mind and its cognitive powers at center stage and relegates the spiritual realm to irrelevancy. It also promises not only an understanding of nature but control over it as well. For someone who seeks rational, mechanistic, and materialistic explanations for why things are the way they are, science presents an extremely appealing account of the universe.

A corollary to this worldview is the sense of satisfaction (bordering on smugness) that comes with being *right*. Read the science-oriented journals whose job it is to debunk paranormal beliefs; the *Skeptical Inquirer* is a good place to start. The sentiment of self-righteousness fairly leaps off its pages. (Mind you, this sentiment is not unique to scientists; many of the creationists' critiques of evolution harbor it, too.) Listen as James Randi offers a million dollars to anyone who can demonstrate a paranormal power, exposes another paranormal charlatan, or skewers another paranormal belief. Sanctimoniousness might be part of the inducement to embrace the scientific worldview.

THE ENTERTAINMENT FACTOR

The strictly scientific approach to reality is not for everyone. Indeed, I would argue, if left to our own devices, most of us would naturally gravitate to paranormal thinking. As we saw, paranormal beliefs are a great deal more *interesting* and *entertaining* than scientific beliefs. The fact that a snake bit a man and the man died is mildly interesting. The story that a snake tattoo materialized into an actual snake and crawled up the man's arm and choked him to death (Frick, 1986), well, that's *wildly* interesting! Of course, being entertained by the story and believing it are—theoretically—two different things, but the story is *far* more interesting if true than if a fabrication.

The fact that a number of people saw bright lights in the night sky and believed that they were spaceships is a fairly routine story (Schmatz, 1984). The fact that people were captured by space creatures and subjected to bizarre experiments (Mack, 1995) is far more likely to stir up the interest of a wide range of audiences. The fact that an archaeologist uncovered an ancient tomb in Egypt and found some artifacts is not without interest. But the fact that an ancient pharaoh put a curse on anyone who entered his tomb, and persons who violated that curse died, one by one, of mysterious causes—well, *that's* a story that captures our attention! The fact that an archaeologist opened a tomb and was attacked by a cat "the size of a small leopard" that had been sealed inside for 4,000 years (Shifflett, 1990) is *very* entertaining. Most paranormal descriptions of events or supposed events tell one hell of a good story. They are dramatic and contain folkloric elements that have a strong narrative appeal.

In the *Dialogues* of Plato, composed in the fourth century B.C.E., a character named Critias mentions an island called Atlantis, larger than Libya and Asia combined, lying beyond Gibraltar (that is, in the Atlantic Ocean), whose residents lived in a utopia, a kind of Golden Age. At some point, 9,000 years before Critias, the people of Atlantis became ugly and "base," and presumably the god Zeus decided to destroy them. The island's people perished in an earthquake and a flood, and the island sank beneath the waves.

Over the years, according to one count, roughly 2,000 books have been written on Atlantis (Ellis, 1998), nearly all of them endorsing the view that this island physically existed at one time. Not one shred of geological or archaeological evidence has ever been located that suggests that Atlantis was anything more than a myth, a tale fabricated and told by Plato to make a philosophical point. Which is more interesting—that is, which is more *entertaining?* That Atlantis once existed in the literal, material sense? Or that it was a myth narrated for a pedagogical purpose? There is no competition; most people would choose the former, and the position adopted by the authors of the many books that have been published on the subject over the centuries testifies to that fact.

There is a saying, "Truth is stranger than fiction," which is, of course, completely fallacious if examined carefully. What is usually meant by the statement is that *some* truth is stranger than *some* fiction. But the strangest truth is never as strange as the strangest fiction. It can't be. Fiction is bound by no rules whatsoever except those of drama and audience response, whereas fact is bound by rules of evidence, causality, and logic. In fact, in many ways, the rules of drama and those of fact are almost entirely contradictory: often what's true is boring, while what's fascinating and amazing is untrue. Truth is sometimes strange *because* it is acknowledged as true; because it is bound by the rules and constraints of the material world, we are amazed when it sometimes is odd, unlikely and strange. But this is very different from saying that it is *stranger* than fiction (Goode, 1992, p.329).

In other words, we have a double standard. The strangeness of fact and fiction are judged by entirely different standards. To put things another way, imagine that a given book, which you thought was a literally true account of concrete events, was a novel, a work of fiction. Would it seem less (or more) remarkable? Most people would find it less so. Richard de Mille (1980, pp.17–18) opines that Carlos Castaneda's "Don Juan" works were presented as nonfiction because they were *remarkable* if judged by the standards of fact but *unremarkable* by the standards of fiction (Goode, 1992, p.329; de Mille, p.18).

Even people who do not believe such fanciful tales find them entertaining. Paranormal beliefs appeal to the child in us. Like science fiction, they mystify the world, create a sense of awe, mystery, wonderment, adventure, romance (Ben-Yehuda, 1985, p.77). They create opportunities for encounters with the unknown. Most of us find an "anything is possible" approach to reality a great deal more entertaining than the view that "the world is governed by forces that place limits on what is likely or possible."

The foundation of paranormal thinking is that, somewhere, on land, in the sea, in the air, or just around the corner, hidden in the house next door, in our backyard, in the grass we step on or the shrubs we walk by—*or even deep within ourselves*—some wild, mysterious, and esoteric event or phenomenon will cause us to gasp in astonishment. Actualizations of that idea are much more fun, more appealing, and more entertaining to listen to, read about, or watch for many of us than are the difficult, complicated, factually and theoretically-based explanations of why all of this just isn't, and can't be, so. In a way, traditional, mainstream, "core" science does almost exactly the opposite. It *demystifies* the world, attempts to make it clear, understandable, mundane—and, to many observers, *boring!* There is no real competition between the two. Only a very unusual person would prefer detailed, sober, empirical accounts of how the world works to the enchantment and magic of paranormalism. It is very difficult to make scientific accounts exciting, if one is being complete and honest.

POPULISM

A strong populist "underdog" streak pervades many (although not all) forms of paranormalism. In fact, a common thread running throughout most perspectives that challenge the dominant scientific institution is an awareness of that challenge, combined with an antiestablishment appeal. Most parananormalists are antielitist in their orientation. (Interestingly, this is also often combined with a strong conservative streak, as we saw with supermarket tabloids.) It is a major reason for their popularity (Stiebing, 1984, pp.169–170).

The sharp-eyed logician might object: "Hey, wait a minute! Didn't you *define* paranormalism by its opposition to one or more scientific laws? Now you're trying to *explain* paranormalism by that same opposition. Isn't that called a tautology? Isn't your explanation true *by definition?*"

My answer is, no, not exactly. Not all viewpoints that challenge scientific assertions attempt to question or undermine scientific hegemony. In fact, some paranormal belief systems are *not* explained by the populism factor, but they *do* challenge assertions that scientists make. For instance, as we saw, parapsychology rejects the traditional scientist's assumption that mind-to-mind or mind-to-matter communication violates the laws of nature. But parapsychology adopts very much the same research methods and the same elitist notions of acceptable research as mainstream scientists do. It is not the scientist's worldview the parapsychologist rejects, but a limited number of very specific assumptions.

Moreover, rejecting scientific conclusions or assumptions does not necessarily entail rejecting the establishment or the powers that be. The adherents of a number of paranormal belief systems see themselves as the "underdog" struggling against an oppressive, manipulative, and deceitful political structure. Scientists are simply a relatively small part of a very big picture. Clearly ufologists fit into this characterization . Science is not the ufologist's specific target; the entrenched power structure is the enemy. These forms of paranormalism construct the government as the establishment. They see a high-level cover-up of the truth running all the way up to the president. Most ufologists believe there is a government conspiracy hide the fact that alien spaceships are circling the globe and kidnapping humans. In fact, a fundamental axiom of ufology is that a government conspiracy covers up significant information about UFOs.

Science is not merely an institution located in a specific spot in the power-and-prestige hierarchy. It is also an enterprise that entails thinking and acting in certain ways about how we know what we know. Populism represents a more "romantic" notion of knowing than is true of scientific reasoning. By that I mean the populist view of things is not constrained by as many rules or regulations as science is; it does not require as many credentials, it is based more on freedom from constraint and on individual interpretations of things. Achieving successful validation of a scientific assertion is extremely tedious, technical, and confining. In contrast, a social circle or segment of the population can be found who will valorize almost any conceivable paranormal claim. In this sense, as we've already seen, science is an elitist enterprise, while paranormalism is a far more grass-roots and populist endeavor. The fact that many paranormal claims are interwoven with a critique of "the establishment" provides a clue to their appeal.

Other paranormal claimants see the scientific establishment as the enemy. It is scientists who are hidebound, dogmatic, and closed-minded. As we saw, this position may be found in the works of "cranks." Cranks, like all antiestablishment paranormalists, "see themselves as believers in the Truth that dogmatic scholars won't accept." For them, "rejection of their favorite theory by the scholarly establishment is not a problem to be overcome, it is a mark of honor to be borne proudly. It proves that they are part of a small elect [who are] persecuted because of their superior insight" (Stiebing, 1984, p.172).

Creationism views mainstream culture as having lost its religious anchor, as having been secularized to the point of corruption. This entire process is taking place from the top down. The upper reaches of the power structure are debasing and defiling a Christian way of life. Since evolution posits a purposeless universe guided by random material processes, it is the key to the corruption. At the same time, all the major social institutions of contemporary society are handmaidens to this wicked degradation. The courts have legalized abortion and, hence, are accomplices to murder; they release drug addicts and murderers back onto the street to victimize righteous citizens. Politicians pass one indecent law after another, undermining Christian virtues. The public educational system teaches evolution and bans prayer. The mass media broadcast pornography, tolerate homosexuality, and foster blasphemy and godlessness. The decent Christian must fight against these powerful monsters of secular evil while, at the same time, seeking sanctuary from their corrupting influence. It is David against Goliath, St. George against the dragon, Jesus against the Pharisees.

COGNITIVE BIASES AND HEURISTICS

A great deal of research has been conducted by social psychologists on the ways in which people think about how the world works and their explanations concerning why others do what they do (for instance, Nisbett and Ross, 1980; Kahneman, Slovic, and Tversky, 1982; Hewstone, 1983; Gilovich, 1991; Piatelli-Palmarini, 1994). Many of the findings of these studies are consistent and point more or less in the same direction. They reveal that human reasoning displays some serious deficiencies.

As a general rule, people tend to see more patterning and order in events than exist in real life. They see more purposiveness and intentionality in phenomena and in people's actions than really exist. They overestimate the degree of control that actors—including themselves—have in a given situation, and underestimate situational constraints. They fail to conceive of or seriously entertain explanations that contradict their own pet theories; are far too confident about the validity of their views; and have a selective memory concerning whether past events verify what they think is true. They overestimate their own centrality and importance in a given event or phenomenon, especially if it is positively valued. They jump to conclusions before all the evidence is in; ignore evidence that is contrary to their beliefs, and use any and all information that seems to confirm their views. They have an extremely erroneous conception of probability and misinterpret the likelihood of chance or random events; rely far too heavily on personal experience and testimony and far too little on rigorous, objective, systematic data; have an unrealistic faith in eyewitness testimony; strongly resist changing their beliefs.

Many phenomena or events people regard as astounding or paranormal can be accounted for with the use of perfectly ordinary processes. Among believers in the paranormal, the tendency to attribute extraordinary forces to ordinary processes is strong. Indeed, it can be said that paranormal belief depends *heavily* on these cognitive biases.

Consider the fact that, when only 23 people get together, the statistical odds that at least two of them will share a birthday are 50/50; to get an 85 percent likelihood, we need only 35 people. The tendency is to imagine that the odds are vastly more improbable than this; many of us will attribute special, even paranormal significance when this occurs (Paulos, 1988, pp.26–28; Gilovich, 1991, p.175; Piatelli-Palmarini, 1994, pp.129, 207). The trick is, most of us don't distinguish between *any* two people having the same birthday and two people having a birthday on a *specific* date. We think the occurrence of both is remarkable, but the odds are quite different. For a 50/50 chance that at least one person has a birthday on a specific date, we'd need 253 people, and for at least two, we'd need 613 (Martin, 1998, p.25).

Many people find it "spooky" that there are so many remarkable parallels between John F. Kennedy's and Abraham Lincoln's lives. But similar, coincidental parallels may be found in the lives of presidents William McKinley and James Garfield; William Henry Harrison and Zachary Taylor; Martin van Buren and Franklin Roosevelt; and so on (Leavy, 1992). In fact, the journal, *Skeptical Inquirer* ran a "Spooky Presidential Coincidences Contest" and the winner was Arturo Magidin (Frazier, 1993), a math major at a Mexican university, who found more than a dozen coincidences in the lives of Kennedy and Mexican president Alvaro Obregon. (The contest didn't state that they had to be U.S. presidents.) But since Kennedy and Lincoln were both heroes and both assassinated—and hence were, presumably, martyrs for a cause—we regard the parallels between their lives as especially remarkable, indeed, "spooky." But if you search far and wide enough for different facts about their lives, you can find "amazing coincidences" between any two people.

People tend to recall similar events or to remember characteristics that fall together; they imagine that the co-occurrence is highly meaningful. In truth, they forget about or discount the many thousands of times that a given event or phenomenon was *not* followed by a similar or corresponding one (Kolata, 1990). Audiences regard the fact that psychics can occasionally guess certain events, conditions, or objects, but they discount the cases when these psychics are wrong.

The Bible Code, an extremely popular book, is a bestseller in a dozen countries, (Drosnin, 1997). It is based on arbitrary formulas to reveal hidden prophetic messages in the Hebrew Bible. Millions of readers take its findings as proof of the existence of God or a godlike intelligence. These people seem unaware of the fact that exactly the same gimmick, given enough words, could yield similar messages in a stack of comic books, a row of cereal boxes, or a pornographic novel. In *Newsweek*, *The Bible Code*'s author challenged anyone to come up with predictions in any other text, for example, *Moby Dick*. Accepting the challenge, mathematician Brendan McKay found assassination predictions in *Moby Dick* for Indira Gandhi, Leon Trotsky, Martin Luther King, Jr., and Robert Kennedy (Begley, 1997). In April 1998, one skeptic found a prediction that the Chicago Bulls would win their sixth National Basketball Association championship encoded in the novel *War and Peace*. He concluded that either the "Bible Code" theory is nonsense or "Leo Tolstoy is the Supreme Being who created the universe" (Thomas, 1998, p.17).

In ancient magic and religion, members of nearly all societies believed in the "representativeness" bias, which is "like goes with like" (Kahneman, Slovic, and Tversky, 1982, pp.23–98; Gilovich and Savitsky, 1996). This principle is also called "homeopathy," or magic based on similarity. Voodoo is based on representativeness: if a pin is stuck in a doll that resembles someone, serious harm will come to that person. In Asia, many men believe that a rhinoceros horn will cure impotence.

The belief is based on the similarity between the horn, which is hard and erect, and the penis of a sexually aroused man. Likewise, many societies believe that eating the testicles of a bull will produce much the same effect.

The principle of representativeness survives to this day. Most of us believe that "big" events must have "big" causes, another "like causes like" manifestation. For instance, because it was such a "big" event, John F. Kennedy cannot have been assassinated by a lone gunman. Indeed, his death must have been the result of a vast and powerful conspiracy. Astrological signs are based on representativeness. Cancers are crabby; Leos are proud and forceful; Virgos are shy and virtuous; and so on. Extraterrestrials have big, bulbous heads because they are so smart. (And the ones who want to destroy us must look like malignant, ravenous beasts.) In point of fact, most forms of paranormal thinking lean heavily on the representativeness bias.

We place a great deal of confidence in our own personal sighting of a UFO and are disappointed, or angry, or incredulous when hard, concrete evidence is turned up revealing the craft to have been a weather balloon. "Yes," we will often acknowledge, "a weather balloon *did* travel directly above my house last night, but what *I* saw wasn't a weather balloon!" (Sagan, 1980, p.55; Klass, 1981). In fact, as research consistently shows, eyewitness testimony is extremely unreliable (Loftus, 1977), an "imperfect interface between stimuli and story" (Reich, 1993). Over and over again, in both experiments and naturalistic situations, people who *were there* describe events and features that didn't happen or don't exist—and fail to notice those that did. What is even more remarkable, there is no relationship between the *certainty* that witnesses have that they are right and their actual likelihood of being right (Ross, Read, and Toglia, 1994).

In sum, I am suggesting that the vast majority of paranormal belief systems are heavily dependent on thinking processes such as coincidence, recall, or representativeness (Singer and Benassi, 1981, pp.50–51). Empirical evidence supporting the operation of these biases or "heuristics" in paranormal reasoning is robust and independently derived (or so social psychologists argue.). However, this is not to say that paranormal beliefs can be entirely accounted for by these perceptual and cognitive psychological processes. Indeed, it could be that paranormal forces nonetheless operate and, *in addition*, we are subject to such biases. Moreover, some paranormal belief systems may have been born in such reasoning processes, but some of their proponents may very well not be subject to them. (And here, possibly, parapsychologists represent a good example.) While the mystery of the ultimate validity of paranormal forces may never be solved, it is clear that many general *pat-*

terns of paranormal beliefs can be explained or accounted for by invoking perceptual and cognitive biases.

COMPARTMENTALIZATION

Hardly anyone would entrust a psychic, a medium, an astrologer, or anyone else who relies strictly on occult powers to fly an airplane or program a computer. (Yes, some supplicants do rely on "psychic surgeons" or weeping statues to heal their illnesses, but usually only after conventional medicine has already failed, usually repeatedly.) And yet, millions of Americans are willing to place their spiritual, intellectual, or psychological fate in the hands of individuals and belief systems that, scientists believe, have virtually no contact with how the material world works. Why the discrepancy? It is entirely possible that paranormal thinking may not so much supplant rational, empirical thinking as *complement* it.

The anthropologist Bronislaw Malinowski (1954) discovered that, among the inhabitants of the Trobriand Islands in the Pacific, there were no magical or superstitious beliefs when it came to efforts that were safe and whose outcome was likely or certain, such as harvesting yams or fishing in lagoons. On the other hand, a great deal of magic was associated with enterprises that were dangerous and whose outcome was uncertain, such as fishing in the open sea. Trobrianders did not imagine they could conjure up yams or fish with an amulet or an incantation. However, where necessary, the requisite action plus a judicious application of magic, they believed, increased the odds of survival and a bountiful yield.

George Gmelch (1978), a social scientist and former professional baseball player, documented an abundance of magical practices associated with hitting and pitching (uncertain activities with a high rate of failure) and very little in fielding (an activity where, most of the time, success is assured with the application of skill and experience). Early in the twentieth century, mothers tied a lump of camphor around the necks of their children to ward off polio. When the Salk vaccine was developed in the 1950s, they took their children to the doctor's office to receive shots (Carlson, 1998). If science, medicine, or technology produces results, many people tend to use it; if it doesn't, they seek out the special powers of magic.

In these cases, the sphere of technical expertise and that of superstition exist side by side. These two contrary ways of thinking are compartmentalized. When the outcome is uncertain, the risk great, and no amount of skill can guarantee results, humans often turn to the world of the paranormal. Where clear-thinking and systematic process is strategic and yields a desired goal, people are far more likely to think and act that way. In a sense, then, many of us operate according to a two-track or two-tiered system; much of the time, the two modes of thinking may not even conflict with one another.

Moreover, paranormal forces—forces that scientists, including medical scientists, believe do not and cannot cause the results some believe them to produce—can *seem* to help us. This is the case for two reasons.

First, most of us do not take a careful tally of when we appeal to magical forces, when we don't, and then compare the results of both conditions. Does baseball magic work? Ideally, a pitcher or a batter would add up all the times when he used a rabbit's foot, when he didn't, and then determine if he struck out the batter or got a hit under each condition. Most people are not careful or systematic about comparing the two conditions. When something good happens, they attribute the outcome to magic and conveniently forget about those times when it didn't work. Even if we tried to be systematic about it, the random variation of chance events can produce a pattern we may attribute to other forces.

Secondly, it is possible, *even within the scientific framework*, that magical forces might actually work, at least more often than *not* resorting to magic. In medicine, there's a phenomenon known as the "placebo effect." A placebo is a pharmacologically inactive substance that is administered to patients to make them feel better. The interesting thing about placebos is they often, work. Physicians are discovering "mechanisms that can turn belief into an agent of biological change" (Blakeslee, 1998, p.F1). If we look at three groups of patients who are in pain—those administered a narcotic, those administered a placebo, and those administered nothing—the likelihood that the placebo patients will feel better is somewhere in between the first and the last of these groups. In other words, placebos will work significantly better than nothing; they will seem to do *some* good, though not as much as the most effective substance. It is entirely possible that if the patient *believes* that he or she is being administered the appropriate substance, pathways in the nerves will be activated and hormones will be released that produce effects similar to those of pharmacologically active substances. In other words, the placebo reaction is "real" (that is, it has a neurological and biochemical basis), it is not just "in the mind." To put the matter another way, what is in the mind can sometimes produce physical effects that are "real."

The same applies to believing in and using paranormal techniques to achieve a certain end. Resorting to prayer is more effective than not resorting to prayer. Patients who pray, or whose friends and relatives pray, for a medical recovery are more likely to survive than patients who do not pray and whose friends and relatives do not pray. Why? Is it because God or a guardian angel intervenes and produces the desired outcome? Possibly, but traditional materialistic medicine does not admit the possibility. Conventional physicians would refer to that type of reasoning as paranormal. But they would say there is such a thing as *the biology of hope*. Prayer indicates optimism for the desired outcome, and believing that outcome is not only possible but likely may in fact *produce* neurological and hormonal changes in the patient's body that are conducive to healing. Hence, resorting to what traditional scientists refer to as magic may not be so paranormal after all. In fact, it may have a material basis and be understandable within the framework of conventional, mainstream science. In other words, a great deal of magic may be used because it is effective, because it really does "work" after all. Religionists and traditional medical scientists will agree on the fact of the efficacy of prayer but disagree on its interpretation.

In addition, we have to consider the role of cost. In areas of life where there is no clear-cut payoff one way or another, magical, nonscientific, extra-scientific, paranormal, or superstitious beliefs do not *cost* the believer much or anything at all—or, at any rate, does not *appear* to—with respect to losing out on valued ends. It's a bit like taking chicken soup when you are sick. It may not cure an illness, but "it can't hurt." In addition, in many realms of life the failure of occult beliefs is not clear-cut, and therefore, holding them is not seen as costly or punishing. "What can I lose?" is often the reasoning that is used here. In such low-cost, possibly high-yield situations, it is understandable that people often resort to magical or paranormal techniques.

Chapter Fifteen

SUMMARY AND CONCLUSION

Although the many paranormal belief systems we've explored come in varied and assorted hues, they contain several common threads. All are bound together by their defining quality: each one asserts that a force or power that science regards as next to impossible operates in the material world. Paranormalism is made up of beliefs that scientists say violate, sidestep, abrogate, or subsume a law of nature. Paranormalists argue that science is wrong in at least some of its theories or explanations.

Science is one way of thinking about the material world. Scientists reason, think, evaluate evidence, and reach conclusions in ways that differ not only from paranormalists but also from the way most people picture how the everyday world works. Scientists believe common sense is a poor guide to drawing conclusions about the material world. Most of us believe common sense is a good thing and is accurate about guiding us to correct observations. Many features of paranormal thinking are drawn from this faith or confidence in common sense, for instance, a belief in fate, spirits, angels, an afterlife, reincarnation, and so on.

Belief systems vary with respect to the social grouping that generates and sustains them. Some adherents of paranormal belief systems are innovators, theorists, and researchers; others are professional practitioners who offer a service to a paying clientele; others are members of one or more religious or spiritual organizations; while still others are part of a broader, more amorphous grassroots public.

Why paranormalism? Clearly, the paranormal orientation offers many appeals not found in the secular, materialistic, scientific approach to life and the world. It cannot be denied that paranormal accounts are more interesting and entertaining than scientific narratives. It is even possible that the entertainment factor has something to do with why such accounts are more believable to much of the public. Paranormalism, the "underdog" perspective, is also appealing in some quarters for its populist streak.

Whither paranormalism? Is paranormalism entering the mainstream? Is Western society shedding its materialistic, traditional scientific stance and turning back to a more spiritual, more paranormal way of thinking, as some argue (Simmons, 1990)? Will either side win the other over?

Kurt Wise, a creationist paleontologist and geologist, seeks to destroy evolutionary theory and replace it with a perspective consistent with biblical accounts of the creation (Hitt, 1996). If he is right, demonstrating his view might represent a turn to a more spiritual way of thinking about the emergence of the species.

Parapsychologists insist that the effects they observe in their experiments are real and are caused not by mysterious, spiritual forces, but by agents explicable through the principles of conventional physics and biology (Radin, 1997). Does parapsychology represent the wave of the future, as some of its practitioners believe?

At bottom, science represents a faith in the preeminence of the material realm. The only way faith *in* the material realm can be tested is *through* the material realm. Although some scientists have a spiritual side, as a general rule they tend to be less attuned, and in many cases even indifferent, to the spiritual dimension. "What you see is what you get" is their motto. Max Weber (1864–1920), the great early twentieth-century German sociologist, referred to himself as "religiously unmusical." In a like fashion, most scientists are "spiritually unmusical"—they cannot "hear" the angels singing, the devil growling, the whisper of mind-to-mind communication, the whoosh of alien space ships across the night sky. Most scientists would argue that scientific theories possess beauty, elegance, and symmetry, and that these offer a motivating principle for most scientists. But such appeals tend to be a bit too subtle, complex, and difficult for the average scientific layperson to appreciate. The "music" savored by the scientist sounds very different from that which appeals to the religionist, the layperson or the paranormalist. All too often, scientists imagine that paranormal thinking is a simple delusion, a failure in rationality that needs a good, stiff dose of pedagogy. The fact is, some of us are attuned to the spiritual dimension while some of us remain spiritually "unmusical."

Will the third millennium witness something of a rapprochement or coming together of science and spiritualism, science and paranormalism, science and religion? In October, 1998, Pope John Paul II issued an encyclical, "Faith and Reason," denouncing the "fateful separation" between these two realms, and calling for a reconciliation. Will the Pope's message be heeded? At the news conference announcing the encyclical, a spokesperson explained that great philosophical questions that were asked in the past have been replaced by "a naive faith in U.F.O.'s, astrology and the New Age" (Stanley, 1998, p.A10).

Given the enormous and growing popularity of paranormal beliefs, their connections with the major social institutions, and the magnitude of the issues they raise, it is remarkable, even peculiar, that sociologists and other social scientists have largely ignored paranormal beliefs as a subject of investigation. The vast majority of writings on the subject by non-sociologists have been devoted to affirming the validity and efficacy of paranormal powers; the bulk of the remainder is dedicated to debunking them. Only a tiny fraction of this material attempts to understand the appeal of paranormal reasoning, who adopts it and why, and with what consequences, both for the lives of believers and for the cultural and social life of the society as a whole. I sincerely hope this book represents at least some small contribution to this kind of effort. Perhaps it will inspire current or future social scientists to explore the subject in greater detail.

Appendix
PERSONAL ACCOUNTS

Paranormalism
What I Believe

☙☙

During the fall semester of 1998, 1 taught a seminar on the sociology of the paranormal. Each student was asked to write a brief paper entitled "What I Believe," a personal account describing what he or she believes to be true about paranormal phenomena. The accounts that follow are slightly edited versions of most of these papers. While the students who wrote them do not represent a random sampling of undergraduates generally, or even students who have taken courses on paranormalism, their accounts nonetheless offer a rough cross-section of undergraduate views on the subject. These accounts raise interesting questions. Do you agree with any of them? Is their reasoning plausible to you? What about their conclusions? If so, why? If not, why not? And *which* accounts are more plausible? Which ones are less so? What do these accounts tell us about some of the principles discussed in this book?

CRISTAL JIMENEZ

I was born into a family that migrated from Puerto Rico in 1952. My grandparents were humble people who wanted a better life for their children. My mother confided in her parents her own paranormal experiences of seeing ghosts, spirits, visions, dreams of coming events, and sensations of a trance-like state. Instead of validating these experiences, my mother was told she has a vivid imagination. She grew up confused, and began searching for answers in different religions, becoming a kind of religious gypsy, wandering from one denomination to another. She was disappointed to find that these religions opened the door to even more unanswered questions. She began to read one book after another on the subject of paranormalism.

My mother had a male friend, a widower. Once, about 20 years ago, she had the experience of leaving a room her friend was in and, from the other room, hearing conversations between him and other people. When she confronted her friend about it, he denied talking to anyone. Soon after that, she felt and heard the presence of something in the house. Again, she confronted her friend. Finally, he told her, yes, her suspicions were correct, he was gifted with ESP. He was born with a veil on his head. In folklore, having a saclike veil or caul over a neonate's head meant the baby was gifted and special. My mother's friend told her of the many paranormal experiences he had had, like talking with ghosts, out of body sensations, and so on. My mother's friend validated her own paranormal experiences.

She would hear the phone ringing before it did, she knew when her friend was about to show up, where he was without him telling her, things like that. At the time, I was five and my sisters were nine and seven. One night, when we were all asleep, my mother began hearing loud noises in the apartment. The sounds were eerie groans and the dragging of feet throughout the house. My mother sensed a ghost entering our room. My youngest sister sensed the ghost, became frightened, and began screaming and crying. My uncle and some of my mother's friends told her that they saw an apparition of a woman. Later, my mother found out that her house was being haunted by my uncle's former wife, whose ghost wanted to be close to her husband through my mother. These visitations continued for several weeks, draining my mother of all her energy. It drove us out of our apartment; we moved to my grandmother's house, which was located in the same building.

Our move didn't really work. My mother could hear the ghost leave our apartment, come down the stairs, crawl into her bed, and enter her body. My mother became paralyzed and fell asleep; she realized the ghost had taken possession of her.

The next day, she consulted a spiritualist, who made a special bath to rid her of the ghost. As soon as my mother poured the bath water over her body, she felt a kind of cold energy whoosh out of her pores in an upward discharge. After the bath, she stomped all over the house, demanding that the ghost get out. It worked; she was finally rid of the ghost.

This experience had a profound impact on me. It happened when I was young and impressionable. At the same time, by itself, it was not the cause of my belief in the reality of paranormal phenomena because I have seen and felt the presence of ghosts on my own, beginning at the age of five. I was afraid of these ghosts, but as hard as I tried to push them away, the stronger they became. I was plagued with something I did not want. This was something I was born with, not something I sought out. My whole family is prone to having paranormal experiences. My nephew and my daughter have the gift of seeing visions. (I never imparted any of this to my daughter, since she is only three years old; she came to it on her own.) Once, when I was living with my mother, we felt uneasy in my bedroom, so we went to hers, only to see my cat literally running across the walls. We figured this was the work of ghosts. One night, my mother heard singing coming from my room. When she tried to open the door, it was locked. I never sleep with the door closed, let alone locked. My mother claims these paranormal occurrences only take place when I'm around. She feels I never travel alone, I'm always accompanied by a spirit or a ghost. The fact is, because of this, I am never fully accepted by members of my immediate family.

As I grew older, I experienced and felt things that most of this society would label as deviant. Today, I have no choice other than to accept it and call it a gift, a gift in the form of sight, communication with spirits and ghosts, and psychic abilities, such as knowledge of future events. Growing up, I had dreams that warned me of future hardships and major events in the lives of family members and close friends.

Not long ago, we had a poltergeist experience in our house. When we moved in, we were not aware that the house was haunted. As it turns out, it was inhabited by seven ghosts. They became noisy, letting us know they were there. Once, I saw a baby in diapers at the top of the stairs who ran from me when I approached her. I assumed it was my daughter, although she was already potty trained at the time. I went into her room and found her fast asleep in her bed. I continued to hear noises throughout the house; eventually, even my husband heard them, too. I began communicating with ghosts through automatic writing. A few months ago, I met and made friends with a woman, Lauren, who has psychic abilities; I told her about the ghostly inhabitants in our house. She told me that there were seven of them, five males and two females. My friend advised me that these ghosts needed to be moved on. Moving a ghost on means instructing it to find the light of the holy spirit and to walk into it to reach the afterlife.

Two of these ghosts refused to cooperate; they became angry when I tried to make them leave. They shook my bed at night, knocked on the walls, and created traffic in and out of my bedroom. The evening before Halloween, I spoke to the ghosts in anger. A half hour later, just minutes after I passed directly under it, a chandelier located near the front door came crashing down. I was scared for my children's safety. While I was fixing the chandelier, I heard a knock on the dining room table nearby, confirming that it was the ghosts that had brought the fixture down. The message was clear: They had no intention of leaving.

I decided to try to communicate with the ghosts by practicing automatic writing. First I was contacted by Henry; he was one of the mischievous ones who brought the chandelier down. His first words to me were, "Hi, bitch." I got straight to the point and asked if Henry would like to be moved on. He said no, because he was afraid. In his life, he was abusive to his female partner, killed her in a fit of rage, and then killed himself, he was fearful of what might lie in wait for him in the next life. The second ghost who came through was named Michael, Henry's partner in crime in the chandelier incident. Michael had the same fears as Henry, since he was cruel to people, although he did not kill anyone. I did not ask for the details of his life. The rest of the gang was made up of Melanie, Mary, Luke, David, and William. Melanie was the baby I saw at the top of the stairs; she died in a fire. William was a passenger in a car that was hit by a drunk driver. The rest were lost souls; I did not ask about their deaths. Melanie, Mary, Luke, David, and William were ready to move on, but were waiting for Henry and Michael.

At this point, I consulted my psychic friend, and we devised a plan to convince the two reluctant ghosts to move on. Henry would have to go to Purgatory to re-experience the pain of the two lives he took. His next step would have to be intense prayer and healing before he could pass into the light. Michael needed to repent of the cruelty he had inflicted on people before he could pass into the light. It took a couple of weeks to convince Henry and Michael to move on; after that, I did not experience any more problems with ghosts in my house.

I have had many such experiences. My belief in the power of paranormal forces does not stem exclusively from childhood socialization, since I have had real-world experiences that validate the reality of otherworldly beings. My spiritualist friend, Lauren, has had no childhood history of paranormal socialization, and yet she believes because these things happen to her. Most of mainstream society does not believe in or accept paranormal occurrences. Many non-believers can be cruel and condemnatory, often stigmatizing the minority of believers. But I don't have any choice. Do I want to be labeled a deviant? No. Do I want to be average and fit into the mainstream? Yes. Has it been difficult to sustain a normal life, believing what I believe and experiencing what I have experienced? Yes. But unfortunately, these experiences are a fact of life for me. I believe only because of my experiences. Had I not had these experiences, I would not be a believer. I believe in them because they happened to me. In my life, they were all too real.

TINA CONTORNO

I was raised to be a Roman Catholic. I was forced to attend religion classes and to go to Church every Sunday. I hated it. The only thing I liked about going to Church was when we went to the bagel store afterwards. From the very beginning, I felt that none of Catholicism's so-called divinities existed. Here and there I prayed, mostly to be forgiven for the bad things I did. But no feelings or emotions of devotion or love ever arose inside me when God's name was spoken. I had no revelation of any kind. One can say that my religious experiences were entirely negative.

Today, I am an atheist. I feel that there is no supreme being above and beyond us. This may or may not be because of my negative religious experiences. One reason for my disbelief is my awareness that there are many varieties of religion. How can there be such a huge assortment of religions, each one claiming to be the right one? Who is to say which one is the right one? To me, it makes more sense to believe in none of these religions than to believe in the wrong one. Many contradictions exist even within a single religious tradition. For example, there are two creation stories in the Bible, one saying that woman came from Adam's rib, the other claiming that man and woman were created at the same time.

Submission to a religious belief is a difficult concept for me. To believe in something requires conviction in the reality that something is true. Yet, accepting something as true depends on the environment in which you grew up. Take the fact that I was raised as a Roman Catholic. This means that I was brought up to believe in a particular religion. It didn't work with me, but it does with most people. You were not born with the predisposition to be Protestant, Catholic, Jewish, or Islamic; instead, you learn to believe in a particular religion. Religion is simply yet another institution that was made up by humans as a result of being creative social beings. People always seem to be in search of meaning, especially ultimate meaning. In my view, people created religion to comfort themselves into believing that their lives have some meaning. To me, this is a plausible explanation for the existence of religion.

I believe in the theory of evolution. I see human life as the result of a game of chance. It seems to be a great deal more plausible explanation for how we got here than the Bible's account. To believe in the claims of religion, I need more material proof, and I do not have that. I do not see the tangible results of godly powers; to me, religion's only power is the power to convince believers to have faith in it. In contrast, I do see the material confirmation of organic evolution; that is why I believe in evolution. Organized religion does not and never did appeal to me as offering an explanation for anything. This is independent of my tendency to believe in science as an explanation for events in the world. Even if the scientific way of thinking did not exist, I feel I still would not turn to religion to answer my questions about our origin.

What I do believe in is the right to hold what I consider a benevolent system of morality. This is a belief system I cannot prove empirically. In a sense, this is my equivalent of a religious belief. I also believe in the possibility of life on other planets. I cannot prove that it is true except through the principle of probability. And, chances are, if life does exist elsewhere, it is very different from the way it is depicted here on earth, for example, in the movies. Life on other planets is likely to be extremely far away and may be in a form we can't even comprehend.

I watched a tape of *Contact* to write a paper for a course on paranormal beliefs. The movie reminded me of the controversy between science and religion. It draws a parallel between religious belief and the belief that there is life on other planets. It seems to be saying that belief in aliens is equivalent to belief in God. It made me feel that there is the possibility that God could be just one big alien.

In the movie, Palmer is a deeply religious character who likes Ellie, the main character, who is a scientist. Palmer argues that humans are putting too much faith in science and, as a consequence, we are losing a sense of meaning; we are becoming empty. Ellie, an astronomer, is searching for little green men. Even though she is searching for something that is presumably paranormal in nature, she represents the scientific side of human thinking; an atheist, she has all of her faith invested in a strictly scientific way of looking at things. Palmer and Ellie argue about things. Ellie says she needs proof to believe in something. Palmer asks her, "Did you love your dad?" She responds that, indeed, she did love her dad, who is now dead. Palmer then asks her to prove it. Ellie is at a loss for words because one cannot provide tangible evidence for an emotion such as love. At the end of the movie, she asks other people to believe, on faith, her experience of meeting an alien, since she has no material evidence to prove it.

As a result of watching this movie, I gained a better understanding of how people can have a religious faith. This does not change my atheistic stance one bit, but the movie did provide me with some insight on what it means to accept a system of belief in the absence of any material proof that it is valid.

NADYNE SCHNEIDER

I have not always been a believer in paranormalism. In the past, paranormal beliefs did not appeal much to me. More of a logical, purely-the-facts type of person, I was skeptical of anything that did not conform to known or demonstrable fact. Thus, I had no reason to be a believer in the occult. I was not an avid fan of science fiction, which deals a lot with the unknown. I guess you would have called me a radical skeptic. As a teenager, when I encountered paranormal claims, I took each one on a case-by-case basis. I didn't think much about the beliefs of others, and I had no reason to ponder larger or more cosmic concepts or definitions of life. All four of my grandparents were alive, and I experienced a supportive family life; I was just a regular teenager who wanted to fit in with the crowd. As a consequence, my belief system was dependent mainly on the thoughts of others. You might say I had succumbed to peer approval. This carried into my freshman year of college. At the time, everything seemed picture-perfect. I had a wonderful boyfriend, I was on the dean's list, and I was away from home. It was not until this protected world began to fall apart that my beliefs in the paranormal came to the surface.

Trauma, whether it is emotional or physical, causes the person who is experiencing it to. reevaluate his or her own identity. At some point, I realized I had no identity to call my own. My boyfriend began dating my only friend, my grades slipped to below the minimum GPA, and I had no nearby family support. I was left alone to contemplate my own beliefs. I tried to grasp some meaning in what was happening to me. I began to search into the unknown for answers to deal with the pain and to heal my psychic wounds.

On a recommendation from a therapist, I began reading a book by James Redfield, *The Celestine Prophecy*. This book seemed to address all the questions I needed answered, and the answers the author gave were in the spiritual realm. This book replaced my tears with a new-found longing for discovery. After I read my fourth book adopting a paranormal perspective, I decided I was a believer; I accepted the notion of paranormalism in principle and accepted the validity of certain specific paranormal claims. For me, paranormal thinking had become a positive coping technique for problems in my life. It promoted thought and generated notions I had come to accept. This new spiritual world became the basis for my identity.

As I learned more about coincidence and fate, I was able to see them working in my life. The more I believed, the more I was able to relate to the unknown. Each new day, I would come into contact with someone new who accompanied me on my journey into the paranormal. It was as if each of these different people had been placed in my life for a specific reason. Either each person I encountered had a message for me or I had one for him or her. I developed the idea that the circumstances in our lives happen for a reason. When we grasp the truth that everything happens for a reason, we can move more closely to the development of a meaningful lifestyle. We must find the silver lining in each cloud, for it is there. Once we get a clear idea of fate, we can see that all our past experiences occurred to lead us to where we are in the present. It can be visualized as a chain reaction, with each experience imparting knowledge that carries us through to the next experience. We can determine the meaning of our own life by making use of this basic principle.

For instance, synchronicity is the simultaneous occurrence of seemingly separate events. Some people call them coincidences. They often happen in our lives, but some of us rarely take note of them. These co-occurrences are so statistically unlikely that, when they do happen, there must be some significance to them. I feel that accepting this principle is necessary for anyone who craves an understanding of how things work. I realize that we are more likely to remember events that are vivid and are relevant to our lives. Still, their significance is central to us for a reason. Why do we recall some things more than others? Such events stir up something we consider important, and the reason for this has to be investigated. Certain paranormal assertions may very well be psychological necessities, and may demonstrate psychological functioning. Such beliefs may prompt us to make ourselves into better people by getting at the psychological root of our difficulties. Belief in coincidence may very well be one element in this process.

When there's no apparent explanation or reason for an event, we search around for its meaning. I do this when a death occurs. I've been fortunate; my entire family is still alive. However, last summer, a friend of mine committed suicide. This was my first close experience with death, and with the realization of its finality. It also challenged my acceptance of purpose. If everything occurred for a reason, what would push a young man only 22 years old to terminate his life? I decided to try to understand the role of the afterlife as a possible explanation for death. After reading up on the subject, I became better able to cope with my feeling of loss. This new sense of comfort made me realize that people only begin to become believers when they endure a hardship of some kind. My newfound beliefs made me contented with events around me. I was able to make sense of the world in which I live. Even if an afterlife does not exist in the natural or material world, belief in it provided me with a sense of well-being.

I am certain in my conviction that paranormal phenomena take place, even though they contradict what scientists believe are the laws of nature. I recognize that a believer in the paranormal, such as myself, becomes one-sided. Books and arguments supporting paranormalism tend to dismiss scientific arguments. Perhaps they prey on the vulnerable, many of whom are lower on the ladder of success. This reinforces the generalization that the higher up one goes on the ladder of success, the less of a believer in the paranormal one will become. At a time when I was struggling with my own identity, I found that I enjoyed reading books spelling out paranormal arguments. At the same time, I recognize that I was susceptible to these arguments. In addition, I see that being female has something to do with my belief system. As the world becomes more complicated for women, we are constantly forced to search for alternate meanings in life. In many societies of the world, women are healers and spiritual leaders. Perhaps there is a connection between being female and the tendency toward paranormal beliefs.

At present, I do not consider myself a true believer. I both agree and disagree with certain paranormal claims. Who am I to say that a given assertion is false? Many things can happen that some people have said were impossible. Our ancestors used the spiritual realm to gain certain powers. In my view, if someone creates a belief system that is harmless to others, it should be regarded as acceptable. If I choose to seek a deeper meaning in my life, I should not be discouraged from that path by others. We should be aware of the-other side, however much we embrace our own personal beliefs. If our beliefs create harmony within our own psyches and maintain balance in our world, why should this be considered unacceptable?

Part of living in this vast, tumultuous world is cultivating the capacity to see the many ways of looking at a phenomenon. The paranormal is one way of doing this. Dismissing occult beliefs in their entirety makes us ignorant. To close our minds is to close our eyes. We must remain open to any possibility, for if we do not, one may just pass us by.

CHRIS DLUGOZIMA

I had a faith-healing, invisible friend with psychic powers who came from the planet Schlobotnick before settling in Loch Ness. My possessed invisible friend and I belonged to a cult that is centered around the belief that the reincarnated King Tut created the universe in seven days. The cult meets in a crop circle on those days in which the planets are aligned in the correct fashion. On our well-deserved breaks from the mundane world, we teleport ourselves to our vacation home in the Bermuda Triangle. But then I had to go and take this course in the sociology of the paranormal, and suddenly my fantasy world was destroyed. Science. Why do scientists always have to explain everything? Why does everything have to make sense? Can't a guy just live his life believing that the reason he keeps failing that calculus quiz is that his pen is haunted?

The world would be a boring place if it weren't for paranormal beliefs. Let's take the following scenario. You are driving in your car and you are about to call, on your car phone, a friend with whom you have not spoken in years. As you are dialing, you crash into the car in front of you—a car that is being driven by the very friend you are calling. What explanation is one likely to hear? Did the supernatural play a role? Or is someone more likely to say: "Wow! How about that application of the laws of chance!" While the latter might very well be true, I really hope it isn't. And that's basically where I stand. I am skeptical about 99 percent of the paranormal claims I encounter. But there's something in me that hopes I'm too damn logical, that life is a little more mysterious and exciting than science would have us believe.

I immediately dismiss many paranormal beliefs. Before I studied it, I thought that ESP might have been possible. But after learning that it has been systematically studied for years without having been demonstrated to be true, I grew more skeptical. People with ESP look very believable on talk shows, but unless I was right there when it was supposed to have happened, I won't be convinced. Psychic hotlines just make me laugh. The commercials say—in microscopic print on the bottom corner of the screen for about a tenth of a second—that they are for entertainment purposes only. Yet in those same commercials, we see people who are so moved by their psychic reading that they are in tears. One woman was shocked when the psychic correctly predicted she was moving to Tallahassee. Maybe the psychic was tipped off by the "I Love Tallahassee" T-shirt she was wearing. Real psychics would not become involved with cheesy television commercials. Nope—they want to take your money in person. It's not as fun to steal on the phone. There are psychics who honestly believe that they have mystical powers. You can't blame them. If people were constantly giving me money to read their minds, I'd begin believing that I had those powers, too. How do I explain the seemingly inexplicable in the psychic world? I attribute most of the success of psychics to their ability to read body language and make broad generalizations appear personal. It may seem as if you are the only person with a sick relative, but doesn't that describe everyone? I think that psychics are believed because people want to believe them. If psychics didn't give people hope about their lives, people would realize what their true motives are.

I used to think that true prophecy was possible. I based this belief on what I had heard about Nostradamus as well as some present-day prophets. That view quickly changed when I saw what Nostradamus had actually written. I doubt if he was even trying to see into the future. The man was a poet! People who believe that he could see into the future are etching meaning into the meaningless. It is absolute nonsense to think that he foresaw the rise and fall of Hitler. You hear about supposed seers like Jeanne Dixon and you think that psychic powers are being exercised. Then you hear that she could not even predict a presidential election! I think the word prophet should be spelled p-r-o-f-i-t. And making a profit is hardly a paranormal phenomenon.

I used to think that time travel was one of those phenomena that would be discovered in the future. Then logic had to ruin things for me! I could travel back in time and make it so that my parents never met, which would mean that I was never born. (And if I had never been born, would I just evaporate?) And if it happens, how could I have arranged things so that my parents never met? Time travel is a logical impossibility, not just a scientifically or technically difficult enterprise.

Astrology brings a smile to my face. We read an astrological prediction and say, "Wow! That describes me exactly!" But they are so vague and general that they could apply to a lot of us. I want to come across an astrology column that gets really specific. "Today, you will eat a chicken salad sandwich with a side of cole slaw with a left-handed man named Larry who weighs 209 pounds." But what does a typical column say? "You will enjoy a meal with someone who is close to you." A few years ago, a column did seem to describe me. It said I would make a major purchase that I had wanted for a long time. Sure enough, earlier in the day, I had shelled out 200 bucks for a portable video game system. But one accurate prediction out of hundreds of columns I've read hardly convinces me. Some people need to feel secure in thinking that something else controls their lives. If astrological columns give people confidence, that's hardly a bad thing.

Of all paranormal beliefs, psychic surgeons are the most dangerous. Stealing money is one thing, risking lives is quite another. I don't
doubt that a psychic surgeon can make some people feel better. A positive attitude is vital to physical health. The medical profession is far from
perfect and more profit-driven than they should be. But psychic surgeons prey on people who are desperate and will try anything. The false
sense of hope they give prevents patients from taking the very action that
can cure them. I would like to find out where psychic surgeons go when
they are threatened with a life-threatening illness.

I make a conscious effort not to spend too much time thinking
about life after death. I do believe in life after death, but not for logical
reasons. I have to believe in it. I'd just depress the hell out of myself if I
believed otherwise. I'm scaring myself now just writing about it. It is
noteworthy to point out that I am always the most certain that there is
a heaven after a close relative has just passed away. How can we know
what happens when we expire? People are not just snuffed out like a candle. After all, you can smell the smoke after it has been extinguished. At
the very least, people still have an influence long after they are gone.

I don't know if any of the UFOs that have been spotted in the sky
are space ships from another planet. I think they might exist. The reasons UFO skeptics cite against their reality do not always convince me.
One reason used against their presence is that there are many reports
of noiseless, hovering saucers, something that is supposedly scientifically impossible. How conceivable was it a hundred years ago that we
could have sent a man to the moon? How miraculous would television
have seemed several hundred years ago? How could we have explained
to our ancestors our ability to send invisible waves through the air that,
somehow, magically, become moving pictures on a television screen?
Another reason UFO skeptics give is that the nearest planet is light years
away. Well, first of all, how do we know that UFOs have aliens on board?
Couldn't they be similar to humanly-built satellites? And the fact that it
would take light years for the aliens to get here doesn't convince me. How
do we know what the life span of an alien is? It's possible that a hundred
years is a blink of an eye on another planet. I think scientists close the
door too quickly when it comes to UFOs. The reasons they give render
the reality of alien space ships unlikely but not impossible.

Doesn't this skeptic believe in anything? Absolutely! I know there's
something out there. Not all coincidences can be explained entirely by
chance. I believe in some form of fate. Not everything is set in stone or
necessarily has a reason, but I certainly do believe that some things happen for a reason. For example, my little brother is handicapped and
mentally retarded. He could have been born into any family. Most families would see him as a liability and a major obstacle, but we see him as

a blessing. At this very moment, his laughter is making it very difficult for me to stay in this chair and write these words; I want to get up and hug him. I know there are plenty of caring families out there, but I think it's more than a coincidence that my mom worked with diseases in a lab before she had him. Her background proved vital when he was disease-stricken early in his life.

I believe in God, but I don't believe in an active one. I don't think He controls people's lives. I think He gives us strength. I was always amused when I watched a football game when I saw players from both teams genuflect after a touchdown; I wondered how God could be helping both teams win. What He is doing is giving both teams the strength to play their best. I also believe that if God does not exist, it would not really matter, in the material world, at least. Whether the fortitude that people acquire comes from within or is a gift from God, it is the strength itself that is the most important thing.

Paranormalism is quite normal if you think about it. We live in such a complicated world that, if we tried to make logical sense of everything, our minds would just explode.

The supernatural world doesn't just make life more interesting. It gives people hope and makes them feel as if there is something watching over them. The laws of science are supposed to make nature predictable. But experience tells us that life is not predictable. People are not predictable. There has to be an explanation for all this randomness. I still think that most paranormal claims are bogus. I would love to be wrong. And if I am wrong, I just hope the aliens don't abduct me.

JENNIFER ROBERTS

It has been said that prayer is able to heal the sick through the "biology of hope." I feel that prayer is very valuable in treating the ill. It allows positive energy to flow from one person through to another. Creating positive energy may not be the main factor in healing the individual exclusively. It works as a placebo to raise the spirits of the ill, let them know we care, and believe that they may become well again. My mother and I attend church every morning. We hear sermons on hope and healing and love from the pastor. We listen to the word of God, a higher being than ourselves, and realize that there is hope in having a spiritual guide in our lives. The pastor tells a story from the Bible and interprets it within a particular value system. We may not be able to touch or see the higher being that guides us, but God is there in our souls. This higher being helps heal my mother and other terminally ill patients.

Another way in which spirits can touch our lives is through angels. Throughout everyone's life, we lose loved ones. When this happens, some of us find resolution in believing that those loved ones are in heaven and become our own personal angels on earth. I believe that these angels watch over us and help us through tough times, just as our belief in a higher being helps us as well. My cousin passed away several months ago. When he died, I was devastated, but I later found out that he was still with me in spirit. I felt he was the guiding force in the changes I've made this year.

For instance, at the beginning of the school year, I rejoined the university's swimming team. Last year, he knew I was miserable on the team; this year, his spirit helped me make a choice about whether or not to remain on the team for another year. His voice recounted the advice he had given me in the past on the subject of swimming. After two practice sessions into the season, I decided to quit the team. Shortly after my decision, I was offered a coaching position on a local swimming team in town. Because of the NCAA rules, had I remained on the team, I could not have taken that position. I believe that my cousin was helping me move away from something that was upsetting me toward a situation that was better for me. His help guided me to make that decision because I was never strong enough to give up the sport I have been involved in for the past fifteen years. I never had the courage to tell my parents that I didn't want to compete on the college level and end my swimming career. But Derek knew my fear of telling them; it was he who helped make me strong enough to get out of something I no longer enjoyed. Angels may not hover over us in long white gowns and wings, but I believe they are there.

There is also some truth in people having the will to live; it's mind over matter. If your mind is willing, your body can follow. Religion can help this process along. I have found this to be true by watching the people around my mother in her battle against cancer.

Women who are sick with cancer, whom my mother has befriended while she has been ill, have carried themselves differently and been surrounded by different types and levels of support networks and groups. Those women who don't trust doctors and don't believe in prayer or religion to help them through the rough times have simply withered away instead of fighting to the end. Others, like my mother, who have decided that this disease isn't going to take them from their families and friends and who, in addition, had people around them to help pray for them, have stayed in the fight and haven't given up when their lives have become almost unbearable. I believe that a religion, or a belief that some entity larger than human beings, is trying to help them through an illness or through difficult times in their lives to ease their burden.

Some people claim to have seen visions of the Virgin Mary or Jesus or other religious figures. I believe that they did see that vision, but to a nonbeliever, what they saw would have been just a vague, ambiguous image. Believers may have seen that vision because they were in a state of crisis or need; they may have been losing or lost faith in their religion, and this was a way of finding their way back to the faith. It may have been a creation all their own or perhaps it was directed by a higher being for a specific purpose.

I don't accept all the paranormal claims I've heard. I do think there is intelligent life outside of our galaxy; however, it is debatable as to whether aliens have flown in a space craft to visit us. It would be an awful waste of space if we were the only intelligent beings in the universe. I do not believe it to be impossible for intelligent aliens to visit earth. Just because scientists don't see how it is possible for them to come here doesn't mean that they haven't figured out how to travel light years away from their home planet. There is something to be said in support of things we deem unreal or impossible. Many things that are part of our everyday life today were once considered impossible. Sometimes scientists figure out a way of making what was once thought to be impossible possible. Years ago, taking a craft into space was a far-off idea, but today it is not only possible but safe enough for women, and in John Glenn's case, a 77-year-old man, to make the trip.

Paranormal phenomena include powers that scientists say are all but impossible, such as psychics, levitation, psychokinesics, or mind over matter. I have decided not to rule out the possibility of any these paranormal powers. I haven't had the chance to see a psychic and see for myself whether such things are possible. I have read many horoscopes in my time, and I even wrote a column for my junior high school newspaper. I find most of them to be very vague. Sometimes, I enjoy reading them for laughs. A horoscope could lift your spirits in the morning if it said that you are going to meet a tall, dark, handsome man at some point in the day or have fabulous financial good fortune during the course of the week. Where horoscopes become vague is in the readers' notion of what these words are saying specifically to them. Financial good fortune means different things to different people. I might consider it good fortune to stumble on a $100 bill; the next person might think it means winning a $40 million jackpot in the lottery. So I think it's all crockery. A warning label should be attached to all horoscopes saying, "For entertainment purposes only."

The full and ultimate truth will never be revealed about the spiritual world. Still, it makes it easier for us to survive each and every day if we feel that there is a higher being watching over us. Even crystals could have healing powers if we believe they do. The mind can definitely flourish over matter. If you believe in yourself, you can triumph.

TAE SOP CHOE

I'm a strong believer in "Seeing is believing." I find I have to see or experience something to be convinced that it is true. I feel I am an open-minded skeptic. My beliefs about paranormal phenomena conform to this principle: If I see it, I believe it; if I see it disproved, I can't believe it. Still, in spite of being a skeptic, I am intensely curious about all aspects of paranormalism, including the afterlife and other religious matters, UFO sightings, psychic powers and abilities, ghosts and spirits.

When I was a child, I was typical; I believed in Santa Claus, the tooth fairy, the boogie man, ghosts, and all of the rest of it. As I grew older, I found out that most of these beliefs were not true; learning that Santa Claus did not exist was a heartbreaking experience for me. This realization came when I was unable to see for myself that these things were true. Still, though I hold most paranormal claims to be false, I do have some beliefs that are based not on experience but on faith, on a "what if" kind of hope.

I have had a few paranormal experiences in my life. They have shaped my beliefs. Some of them were extremely personal.

As far as religion is concerned, I was not born into a religious family and when I was a child, I never attended church, aside from weddings and funerals. During high school, some friends attempted to convert me to Christianity. For a time, I even attended religious services. Eventually, I realized that I was going along with it simply because I wanted to meet girls. Realizing that I was going to church for the wrong reason, I became aware that it was difficult for me to attend for the sole purpose of embracing God. My life was oriented to a materialistic, secular world; I was not willing to convert my entire lifestyle. When I expressed doubts about certain things, the answers I got were along the lines of, "You must have faith," or "That's not an appropriate question." I was left with more doubt rather than faith.

I came to the conclusion that Jesus was either truly the Son of God or a raving lunatic who, like leaders of some of today's cults, find enough followers who support them. I also struggled with the idea that, if God really were an almighty being who could control everything that happens in the universe, then why would He permit such much suffering? Is this just a test of Christian faith? It seems to me a cruel joke rather than a means of determining who is worthy of entering the gates of heaven. Thoughts such as these led me to the doubts I currently have rather than the faith some wanted me to have. I consider myself an agnostic rather than a Christian.

In spite of my doubts about the teachings of Christianity, I have accepted the idea of some form of an afterlife. I feel—or rather hope— that there is something more to this life than just what appears in physical form. I hold this view as a result of the realization that everyone as well as every living thing on earth will eventually die. Having a sense of hope or a feeling that there is something beyond the material world gives me a sense of reassurance. Believing in an afterlife is kind of an insurance policy. I wouldn't want to take this too far, though. Think of all the people who have devoted their entire lives on earth to the next life— priests, nuns, monks, and so on. I would feel great pity toward these people if their majestic faith were nothing but a huge hoax.

I had an experience about two years ago that made me realize that there could be an afterlife. It also tied in with the significance of coincidence. My grandmother fell ill with an aneurysm which in turn led to a series of strokes. While she was recovering, I did not have a chance to visit her in the hospital. The doctors had given us a false prognosis, and so, we thought that my grandmother was on her way to recovery.

About two weeks after the operation, I had a dream in which my grandmother called me on the phone. She informed me, in Korean, that she was all right and that I shouldn't worry about her condition. In the dream, I felt peace of mind. The dream seemed very real. I woke up, startled, and thought about what had happened in the dream. A few minutes after waking up, I received a call from my mother telling me that my grandmother had fallen into a coma, and her chances of recovery were slim. She advised me to come home immediately so that all of us could go to the hospital to see my grandmother while she was still alive. I narrated my dream to my mother, and we both burst into tears. She interpreted the dream as a message about her dying; it was an indication, she said, that she is following the right path in the afterlife.

For me, one of the most startling aspects of the dream was that it took place in Korean. Since I speak English better than Korean, I always dream in English. When we got to the hospital, I described my dream to my relatives, both as a way of reassuring them that my grandmother was passing on to a better place and as a way of soliciting an interpretation of the dream. Two of my cousins revealed that they also had a dream relating to my grandmother.

I still don't know whether these dreams, mine and my cousins', were just a result of chance or had profound significance. What are the chances that three relatives would have dreams incorporating his or her grandmother, all three of whom were under the impression that she would recover from an illness? This experience provided evidence that convinced me that more than mere chance was operating. At the same time, it was a if I had seen something that wasn't there, or I had smelled something that had no scent, tasted something that had no flavor. It left me restless for answers. I read a book on interpreting dreams, but it provided no help.

This dream of my grandmother has been the strongest indication in my life that there may actually be some validity in the claims made by the advocates of paranormal phenomena. Despite the fact that I have no concrete evidence, I feel that the evidence I have gathered is enough to convince my mind as well as my heart that there is an afterlife and that my grandmother's soul is resting in peace. Some may say that my beliefs are based solely on my hope or wish for my grandmother's soul to rest, but chances are, I'll never find out until the day comes for my own passing.

Science has answered many of the questions that have plagued humankind over the centuries. But some questions may never be answered. Despite not having answers, we can always hope and believe in what is true in our hearts and minds.

ROBERT HORN

I believe that the sciences are vital to gaining objective knowledge of ourselves and the universe in which we live. At the same time, I believe that people who ignore the spiritual side simply because it cannot be demonstrated or proven empirically are neglecting aspects of their own humanity. For instance, I would argue that a feeling of oneness and a connection to the earth is essential to being human. If we don't see the sublime in nature and feel a connection to the earth, we are isolating ourselves from the outside word.

One might say that the scientific way of looking at the world and the beliefs of paranormalists are contradictory, that you can't combine them into a single system of beliefs. I would argue not only that this is possible but that everyone does it, and in a variety of ways. For example, even the most rigid scientist would say he loves his wife and mother. The concept of love has paranormal elements. There is something in love that is beyond a functional and a sexual partnership; it can't be explained scientifically. Paranormal beliefs provide essential human satisfactions; hence, as humans, we all have some measure of paranormal beliefs. Another example of a nearly universal paranormal belief is the belief that human life has real value, that we are not merely biological organisms. This belief cannot be proven scientifically.

To turn the equation around, paranormalists incorporate scientific ways of reasoning into their belief systems. When ufologists investigate a UFO claim, they usually check to make sure that the observation was not of a satellite or the planet Venus. When the more ordinary possible sources for the sighting have been discounted, ufologists will then seek out explanations centering around alien spacecraft. So I would argue that there is a great deal of overlap between paranormal and scientific belief systems.

A discussion of beliefs usually involves an answer to the question: Do I believe in God? Yes, I believe in God, but it is my own personal concept of God. God for me is the maker of me and my surroundings. For me, a belief in God is essentially the belief that the world is not a big accident or a mere random occurrence. I choose not to understand myself as a collection of random genetic components. On one level that is true, because my physical features are consistent with my genetic pattern, which was randomly created when I was conceived. However, I do not see my physical makeup as intrinsically and essentially me. I believe that there is a spiritual dimension to me which cannot be understood in terms of random genetic patterns. Because I see myself as more than an accident, I therefore believe in God, which means that there is design to my creation.

I believe in purpose. If my existence is not ultimately a random occurrence, my life must therefore have some kind of purpose. I see the purpose in life in the context of the world and the people around me. Since all things are interconnected—the physical world, the metaphysical world, the human world—therefore, I am connected to a living world. Humans perceive more than the physical or sensory dimension. It is important not to neglect the non-physical dimension of your existence.

In this sense, I believe in a soul. My soul exists on my non-physical dimension. It is as real to me as is my physical shape and the color of my hair. It is of no consequence to me that my soul cannot be observed, measured, or labeled. Life is more than the sum of the biological features of a human body. Therefore, humans must have a soul or inner identity.

I choose not to formulate my beliefs into an established religion, with practice, dogma, and rituals. To me, belief is personal; religions which attempt to establish an exclusive claim to truth are totalitarian. A religion which claims truth and attempts to convert others to this truth is an insult to me because it does not allow for my own spiritual input into the belief system. To convert to an established religion would be to adopt what someone else has decided for me. Throughout human history, conflict has arisen when groups have differing religious beliefs which claim exclusivity to truth. For example, the Crusades resulted from one group deciding they have religious authority to attack another group with differing beliefs. This was because the Crusaders believed that from on high, God was passing down orders to humans on earth. To me, this is a very deferential attitude. It is also a very arrogant attitude, for it assumes that only certain people are able to interpret and carry out God's message. For me, God is part of ourselves and should be found within each one of us.

In this sense, one might say I have an affinity with many paranormal beliefs, such as belief in the soul or in spirits. However, on many other issues, such as the question of whether extraterrestrial life exists on earth, I am quite indifferent. I would be open to an idea if I experienced it personally, but I would not say that UFOs are real until I experienced one personally. I am in part persuaded by the scientific argument that the laws of physics cannot be broken, and the flight to earth by an extraterrestrial craft within the lifespan of any conceivable being would violate the laws of physics. However, I also appreciate that the laws of physics do not represent the only dimension that should be considered.

I am also indifferent on the issue of ghosts. I believe that humans have a spiritual dimension, but I would not go so far as to say that the apparitions some people see in the middle of the night are necessarily dead spirits trying to communicate with their loved ones. This may be true, but again, I am persuaded partly by the skeptical and partly by the paranormalists argument. If someone believes that they have seen a ghost, this may be a very real and meaningful spiritual experience for them which should not be scoffed at. I personally would not criticize a person for making such a claim. However, I am also mindful that there are very persuasive psychological reasons why someone would need to experience such a vision.

I believe in telepathy to some extent. This is because, on many occasions, I have experienced a sense of communicating with someone on a deeper level than merely verbal communication. In close relationships, such as with family members, close friends or partners, I often feel a sense of being connected to them in a spiritual dimension. I believe my mother communicates to me more than mere words or thoughts. She communicates love, care, and the intimate connection that exists between us. This communication takes place on a spiritual, perhaps even a paranormal level. In this sense, I would argue that telepathy exists between some individuals.

In sum, I regard myself as appreciating both the physical and the spiritual dimensions of our universe. There is more to the universe than can be recorded scientifically, and spiritual dimensions to the universe do exist. In this universe, spiritual forces, which are those focused on by paranormalists, interplay with physical forces, which are the ones in which scientists are interested. To disregard either is to close one's eyes to a broader truth. To lose contact with your sense of spirituality is to lose contact with an inherent part of your humanity, because the human spirit is the driving force behind the physical body.

Elisabeth Manners

My beliefs about paranormal phenomena change from one time to another. There have been periods when I strongly believed in astrology, but after becoming aware of the Forer effect, my beliefs have changed. Like most people, I am influenced by the media's presentation of paranormal. events; it is easy to become swept up by a television show, but later, one realizes that many of them are mostly fictional. Books and personal experience have more of an impact on my beliefs. When reading, especially scholarly works, it is more difficult to find fault with an argument; I often find myself persuaded by what I read.

I believe in angels, the kind that watch over and guard us. I feel I have a guardian angel. I do not see guardian angels as chubby and child-like, but as divine and powerful. My sister, Jessica, was murdered ten years ago. She is my guardian angel and she watches over and protects me while I am here on earth. I do not believe that her violent death was without reason or purpose. I feel that there was a need for her to be in heaven, that God had His reasons for taking her. She is present with me in spirit; her encounters with me have made this obvious to me. Since her murder, she has appeared to me several times. Once, at night, when I was walking past her former bedroom, I saw her standing near the window. There was a glow to her I had never seen before. She did not speak, but reassured me that she was happy. Afterwards, I had an overwhelming sense of joy. I do not feel that a camera would have captured her image. She appeared before me momentarily, and I feel her appearance was for me alone to see. I think it was done to reassure me of what her present existence is like.

Jessica has appeared to me in dreams many times to reassure me of her presence. I believe dreams tell us things that we cannot understand while we are awake. During sleep, we gain knowledge that surpasses what is given to us by science.

I believe both in reincarnation of the soul as well as in heaven. These two beliefs contradict one another, but I still hold them both. I began holding these convictions two years after my sister Michelle was born. She was conceived before Jessica died, but she claimed to have known Jessica. When I showed Michelle Jessica's pictures, she told me that she knew Jessica and that she does not look like those pictures. Michelle told me that Jessica is beautiful and with God. I believe that what Michelle told me was true because of the childlike innocence young children of two have. She had never been exposed to the ideas she was expressing. They must have come from somewhere.

I also believe in ghosts. I feel there are souls that are trapped on earth who cannot find their way to where they belong, wherever that may be. They reside in the houses they lived in when they were alive. These ghosts are miserable because they cannot escape the misery of knowing they are dead. They are alone; nobody can help them. They do not sleep because they are dead; they are awake with nothing to do. They feel trapped, and they are. Ghosts like this are rare because most people who die are called to heaven or sent to hell. I do not believe that the existence of these ghosts is because of God's imperfections. Maybe they exist because they could not accept the fact that they are dead. Or maybe they felt they had a reason to stay on earth. After a period of time, I feel, they regret having stayed. They want to move on, but some do not know how. I hope God helps them.

I agree with the notion that hell is an actual place where the afterlife is lived. The souls who go there can never be reborn. They lie morbid due to their violence and bad nature during their life on earth. They suffer in the same ways they made others suffer. The damage they inflicted on others is inflicted on them in retaliation, only many times over. They spend all eternity there with no chance to make up for their crimes. I am not sure how fair it is to make souls agonize for all eternity, but I feel it is God's will. I believe there are not many souls in hell. Most people are forgiven for their sins, but those who commit murder, especially mass murder, are doomed to eternal hell. I believe that this is appropriate.

I do not believe that witches are real. I do believe that there are people who hold powers that are greater than the average human, but not in the way those powers are depicted in movies or television shows about witches or other people with super paranormal powers. I do feel that some people possess telepathic powers or ESP. But I do not believe that people can burn things with the use of their mind, as in Stephen King's *Fire Starter*. I feel telekinesis is a stretch beyond what humans are capable of, as is clairvoyance.

As I said above, in my view, psychics are usually false. The Forer effect comes into play: statements are so broad that they inevitably relate to each one of us in some fashion. My mother took off her wedding band and went to a psychic, who told her she would soon meet the man she will spend the rest of her life with. I do not think that the psychic would have said that if she had left her wedding band on. I also don't believe in palm reading or tarot cards.

Many of my beliefs in the paranormal help me deal with the issue of death. While I accept some of science's debunking of many paranormal beliefs, there are still some unexplained phenomena I accept. I know that my experiences are true because I had them. I also accept the fact that others had similar experiences as well. It is always difficult to lose a loved one, especially one so young as my sister. Perhaps such a loss would have had a different impact on different people. Some lose faith in God or in the goodwill of others. But others pick up spiritual belief patterns to help them cope. Initially, after the death of my sister, I lost faith altogether. Later on, I began to accept belief in an afterlife, in God, angels, and ghosts. I realize that what I believe is related to my life history, but I know these things are true because I have seen them and experienced them.

ZAIRA LUZ SERRANO

I was born a Catholic and converted to evangelical Christianity. God is the ultimate force in my life; He helps me make the right decisions. Without Him, my existence would not be possible, your existence would not be possible, and humanity would never have been created. Because I believe that God created the world, I also believe that when you die, your spirit goes to heaven. I believe in Purgatory and hell as well. As a matter of fact, Purgatory is where we live now; it is a place we call earth. On the other hand, heaven is a place where good people go when they die. These people are true believers who repented of their sins before they passed on. The people who become angels watch over us, guide us, and protect us from evil. Hell is a place where non-believers go when they die, people who were evil when they were here on earth.

I believe that everyone has a guardian angel, believers as well as nonbelievers. These angels are God's assistants who want to help us to be saved from an eternal existence in hell. I believe this because my grandmother is my guardian angel. She passed away in 1992 of diabetes. Prior to her death, her hands and legs had been amputated. While she was in the hospital, my mother asked our priest why God was taking her away from us in such a cruel manner. He responded that when she died, she would get a new body once she reached heaven. When I dream of my grandmother, her arms and legs are not amputated; she looks like the grandmother I knew as a child. My grandmother always appears to me during the hardest times of my life. She often guides me to the right path and tells me what I should or should not do.

In addition to angels, I also believe in ghosts. However, they are not like the ghosts you see on television that look like white sheets over a person's head with holes cut out where the eyes are supposed to be. Ghosts are spirits that have yet to lie to rest. They are lost souls; some are evil and some are good. I believe that they just couldn't say goodbye to us on earth yet, or didn't feel it was their time to die, so they linger around as spirits.

My uncle claims to have seen the ghost of my grandfather Miguel, who passed away almost 20 years ago. On Christmas day, my uncle entered my mother's house and saw my grandfather sitting on the couch. My uncle said hello to my grandfather without realizing who he was or that he was speaking to a dead man. When he finally realized he said hello to my dead grandfather, he ran downstairs to my parents' room to tell everyone who he had seen. We were told by a spiritualist that my grandfather's spirit lives in my mother's house to protect us from evil. My grandmother, Miguel's wife, who is still alive, said prayers for him in hopes that his spirit is finally laid to rest.

I also believe in prayer. I pray to thank the Lord for waking me up in the morning, for gracing me with the food I eat, and for guiding and protecting me through the day. I also pray when I need the Lord to provide me with something I need, for example, my health or the strength to take an exam. I try not to ask for materialistic things because I feel that if I am selfish in my requests, eventually God will not answer my prayers. My prayers are almost always answered. I believe that if prayers aren't answered, there is a reason for it. God works in mysterious ways. But God is loving; he wouldn't answer a prayer that would harm someone or not be beneficial in some way.

Many people have lost faith in God because their prayers haven't been answered. They believe God is a hoax. I respond by saying that God puts us through many trials and tribulations. He has ways of testing our faith. But without faith, one cannot please God; if you don't have faith, God will not recognize you. It all begins with faith; if you have it, God will answer your prayers. In Matthew, it says: "Ask, and it shall be given you; seek and ye shall find; knock, and it shall be opened."

If you deny the existence of Jesus Christ, you deny the existence of God, for Jesus is God manifested in the flesh. Jesus was sent to earth in order to save us from our sins. He died carrying all the weight of our evilness on His back. He came, knowing he would suffer for us, but He did so because we are all God's children. Four different prophets gave similar accounts of what happened when Jesus came to Jerusalem.

Since all four gave the same testimony, the events they narrate must be true.

Some people interpret the story of Revelation to mean that the world will end in the year 2000. I don't believe this is true. I can't believe that God would brutally take us off the world. There are different possible interpretations of the Bible, and I don't accept the one that says the coming of the millennium means the end of the earthly world.

Two years ago, a co-worker encouraged me to go to a church called S.O.S. Ministries. I could feel the spirit of the Lord as soon as I walked in. At first, I was skeptical because, as I explained, I was raised a Catholic, and this church was evangelical Christian. To my surprise, I was overwhelmed by what I saw. When the pastor read the scriptures, for once in my life, I understood what was going on. Before we left the church, we said a prayer, and I began to cry. I don't know why I was crying, but it felt good. I felt that God was with me and understood my sorrows.

One can believe without going to church. All one needs is faith and the belief in Jesus Christ. God exists; all you need to do is to let Him in your life and you will see that this is true.

MELANIE MCALLISTER

I do not practice religion and never have. I lean more toward the evolutionist's account of the origin of the world than toward the creationist's. I am an educated person, and believers of creationism tend to be less well-educated. I do not see as plausible that simply because an assertion is made in the Bible, it is necessarily true. There are many different religions in the world which hold many different beliefs about the origin of the world. In addition, not everyone takes the Bible as their religious text. The world could not have begun in different ways, it began in only one way. Instead of holding as true the assertions of a book written several thousand years ago, I believe in evolution. We don't even know if the persons who wrote the Bible were reliable, credible sources. Further, I believe the Supreme Court's decision not to allow the teaching of creationism into the public school classroom is valid and intelligent. Since creationism refers to God and the Bible, it is religious by its very nature.

I believe that there are psychological reasons why people have paranormal experiences. Pareidolia is a psychological phenomenon whereby humans interpret significant meaning into vague assertions or stimuli. A good example is horoscopes. Horoscopes, contain ambiguous statements which could apply to almost anyone. Their claims about marriage, love, finances, the family, and so on, are so general that they will mean something to anyone who reads them. I also believe that when people read them, they are trying to make sense of their lives, and will find something meaningful in them.

Simulacra are similar to pareidolia; they are holy visions that are seen in very ordinary things. One of the most famous examples is the cinnamon bun with the face of Mother Teresa on it. Why Mother Teresa? Why do these visions always come back to Catholicism? Are Allah or Buddha or Moses not good enough to be seen atop a cinnamon bun for the public, and the media, to see? To a non-believer, the notion of Mother Teresa on a cinnamon bun, or the Virgin Mary in a cloud, or a window, or anywhere else, seems ridiculous, completely out of whack. It does not make sense to me at all. If Mother Teresa wanted to show herself, why in the world would she do it on a cinnamon bun? Does it make sense that this is her way of saying to the world, keep the faith? I don't think so. It doesn't make sense to me at all. I agree with science on this issue: These visions are a product of the psychological phenomenon known as pareidolia.

With respect to paranormal claims, I consider myself a skeptic, but I do not close my mind to the possibility that the laws of science can be violated. Such a thing is rare, and these exceptional claims often lack the empirical data to prove their plausibility. A few months ago, I read a book on ESP which stated that persons who close their minds to this type of phenomenon will never see anything. At times, I agree with this statement. Scientists seem to be so hung up on facts that their eyes aren't open enough even to consider that sometimes, things can't be proved.

For instance, about four years ago, I went to a psychic that was said to be able to communicate with the dead. I lost a close family member, and was hoping this would give me the opportunity to find some answers I had been looking for. The psychic's secretary explained that there were no guarantees and that I should tape-record the incident if my family member was contacted. I walked into a medium-sized room with many other people inside, all looking for the same answers. The psychic entered and sat down; he had a pad of paper in his hand. After briefly explaining some rules of etiquette, he proceeded to move his hand in a circular motion while looking downward. Before getting to me, he spoke to a few other people. He began by telling me the name of my family member and how he died. I was amazed because this man had no idea who I was; I gave him a fake name. Then he told me a number of personal things that were not ambiguous or vague at all, specific things about my family, me, and my childhood that he *could not* have known. For example, he knew about specific activities that were taking place in my life.

He told me that I would get a part in a play I was trying out for; two weeks later, I got the part. I tape-recorded this entire session, and will save it forever. I plan to see this psychic again in the future.

Although I do hold a skeptical point of view toward most paranormal phenomena, I will always strongly believe in exceptions to the rule. A scientist would probably tell me that when I saw the psychic, I was vulnerable, and that what I was hearing were vague and ambiguous assertions. But clearly they were not vague or ambiguous. I feel I am using facts and empirical evidence to back up my belief. I saw all I needed to see, I had enough evidence to draw my conclusion; scientists cannot take that away from me no matter how hard they try. This might seem to contradict what I said initially, but in reality, it doesn't. I am skeptical about that which I have not experienced firsthand. I understand that it is the job of the scientist to demonstrate assertions with the use of facts. But I believe that, sometimes, in some cases, there is no evidence. And my firsthand experience with the psychic told me that he had powers that scientists can't explain.

SOONA KIM

Ever since I was little, I always feared sleeping in the dark. My parents tucked me in every night, left my bedroom door half-open, and turned on a night-light so that I would feel safe. But the night-light scared me even more. The light threw shadows on the ceiling and the walls that seemed to me to be horrifying images. These images seemed to change, much the way scenes change in a television show. I interpreted these shadows as evil monsters or the devil, lurking on my ceiling and walls. Eventually my fear of these shadows faded, only to be replaced by a new fear, now, my greatest fear: sleep paralysis.

I am a strong believer in the paranormal. When I am in a bookstore, I go to the paranormal section first. I am also a horoscope junkie; when I flip through the pages of magazines, I usually go to the horoscopes first. And yes, I truly believe that something is "out there," that UFOs exist and are real. I am a Catholic, and I tend to relate my paranormal experiences to religion. For example, if I encounter an amazing paranormal experience, I would relate it to God; if I encounter a truly horrifying experience, the devil would be the obvious culprit. I've been a Catholic all my life, my family is Catholic, and my values and beliefs are Catholic. Therefore, my interpretation of experiences are related to my Catholic upbringing. Religion has taught me to be open, creative, and optimistic about the experiences in my daily life.

I have been a victim of sleep paralysis since the beginning of my freshman year of high school. Actually, I didn't know what sleep paralysis was until I heard a couple of my friends discussing it. That night, I tossed and turned in bed for two hours, wondering why I had never experienced it. I almost wished I had. I eventually fell asleep, only to wake up paralyzed, invisibly chained to my bed. I was awake, but my body was motionless. I felt as if something or someone was sitting on top of me, holding me down. My heart was beating and thumping so fast, I thought it was going to jump right out of my body. I tried to call out for my parents, but I couldn't. Every time I tried to open my mouth or move my body, I couldn't do it. The only movement I could make was to open my eyes, but I was too frightened of encountering my attacker, so I didn't. I recalled my friends saying that the only way of dealing with sleep paralysis was through prayer, so I began praying; within fifteen minutes, it stopped, but those fifteen minutes were the worst I ever experienced.

A couple days later, I had an encounter with my unfriendly night visitor again. I thought by sleeping on my stomach, I would fend off my visitor, but that proved to be a failure. This time, when sleep paralysis struck, I was trapped on my stomach; I felt the odd sensation that nothing was underneath me. I was in shock because I could not feel the soft, feathery pillow that usually presses against my face. Again, I was too frightened to open my eyes. After several minutes, I began to feel the pillow beneath me. I decided to face my adversary and open my eyes. The image of my room that night will never leave my mind. My bedroom did not look familiar at all. The room looked very hazy; it was covered with grayish smoke, accompanied by black shadows circling around. I was terrified because I believe that the black shadows were going to hurt me. I closed my eyes and began to pray. After five minutes, everything came to a halt. I knew deep inside that the culprit behind everything was not stress, illness, or sleep deprivation, but the product of something evil.

My first-hand experience with sleep paralysis has led me to hold stronger beliefs in the paranormal, especially with respect to its religious elements. I found that during the time when I was experiencing sleep paralysis, prayer was the only solution. This experience also exposed me to the evil, dark side of the paranormal. Fortunately, prayer has protected me from that evil and kept me safe from whatever dangers I have encountered in my life. I am able to trace the reason for my belief in the paranormal to one main experience. Though it may be different from the reason most other people have for believing, I feel that it is strong enough to support my position.

ELENA PACE

Until recently, when it came to paranormal phenomena, I was a skeptic. In the past, if you had asked me to write a paper about whether I believed miracles, psychic powers, extraterrestrials, or the earthly influence of angels were possible, I would have explained why they do not and cannot exist in the world. But as a result of my recent experiences and the people I know, the views I held in the past about paranormal phenomena have changed substantially.

A year ago, my grandmother died. I was very close to her. Although she spoke only Italian, and I can speak and understand only the basics, we were always able to converse and have a decent conversation. Though I felt sad when she passed away, I felt as if she never really left me.

A couple of days ago, exactly one year since my grandmother died, some unexplainable things began happening to me. Ever since my childhood, I have been fascinated by the sky, the stars, and the planets; I even bought my own telescope so I could see them more closely and more clearly. Even though I've spent many hours staring at the sky, I have never seen a shooting star; even when someone else sees one, I'm always two seconds too late to see it. But on the first anniversary of my grandmother's death, as I was driving along, thinking about my grandmother, for the first time in the 22 years of my life, I saw a shooting star. Coincidence? Maybe. But I feel it has something to do with my grandmother's angel.

I know that many things happen purely by chance, but most of them have no significance or meaning for our lives. For instance, if you begin singing a song, then turn on the radio and hear that same song playing, that may seem freaky and unusual at the time, but it usually doesn't change your life or have an impact on it in any way. So that type of coincidence has no significance or meaning. But on the very day, a year after my grandmother died, at the exact moment I was looking into the sky and thinking about my grandmother, I saw a shooting star. One might ask why that has special significance to me, why it had anything to do with my grandmother, what led me to believe that the shooting star was sent to me by my grandmother. Normally, I would have blown it off as pure luck, but the background of this event is what gives this coincidence its meaning. When I was young, my grandmother and I used to sit on her porch and stare into the night sky. She used to say to my father in Italian, who would translate it for me into English, "Everyone eventually becomes a star up in the sky to shine down on their loved ones on earth." When I saw that shooting star, I remembered what she said; it gives me reason to believe that she sent me the star I saw.

That same night, another strange thing occurred. As I walked into my house, I heard music playing on a radio. Not just any music, but Italian music. But I knew that nothing was turned on in the house, no radio, no television, nothing. The music was coming from my parents' bedroom. I shut it off, thinking that it had been set for 6:00 P.M. instead of 6:00 A.M., and the radio had gone off instead of the alarm. But it was set for its usual time, 6:00 A.M., and the alarm mode was on, not the radio mode. The other thing that seemed strange to me was that my parents always put the setting on a weather and traffic station, not one that would play music of any kind, let alone Italian music. And yet, that radio played Italian music, the only music my grandmother ever listened to or could even understand. The odds against Italian music playing on a radio that was not left on and not programmed to be on that station, exactly one year to the day of my grandmother's death, are too great to have occurred by chance. I consider that event to be a bit on the supernatural side. It was my grandmother's ways of saying that she is still here with me to watch over me, only in a spiritual form. Perhaps she is my guardian angel.

Some may argue that if everyone has a guardian angel, why do innocent people die? Why are babies brutalized by their parents? Don't they have guardian angels too? Anyone who raises this objection fails to recognize that many people overcome incredible obstacles every day; in spite of the odds, they achieve wonderful things in their lives. An innocent person may be killed in a drunk driving accident, but maybe that person's death will make an impact on someone else and enable them to lead a more fulfilling life. I admit that horrible things happen to some people; one would be foolish not to question what kind of God would allow such things to happen. But one has to look at everything that unfolds after someone's life is suddenly harmed or senselessly ended before anyone can say that they did not have a guardian angel.

Once I began to let my guard down and accept one paranormal belief, other supernatural events seemed to make more sense to me as well. I began to have less confidence in the ability of science to solve the world's problems and explain everything in scientific terms. Though science may not set this task for itself, people are always looking to science for answers to seemingly unexplainable questions. For instance, though many scientists believe that life exists on other planets, most also doubt that these other life forms have the capability to visit earth. A lot of people describe being abducted; they say that they have seen aliens land on earth, that they were lifted up into spaceships, and certain acts were performed on them. In contrast to scientists, I do not dismiss the notion that these beings may actually have the ability to do this. When I hear or read stories told by abductees that aliens beamed them up into a space ship and inserted this into them and poked them with that, my first reaction is, what's the matter with the psyche of these people? But then I also wonder what are the chances that these stories are actually true? How is it that so many people who report these encounters describe the same kinds of events, and describe creatures that look similar from one description to another? Does one story influence the next, or are real events taking place? Or do these people have something in common, say, psychologically, or in their early family experiences? Until I see convincing evidence demonstrating otherwise, I cannot help but give these people the benefit of the doubt.

As far as scientists believing the laws of physics cannot be violated is concerned, it is possible that extraterrestrials can do things we can't because they are more technologically advanced than we are. Many other planets have existed far longer than our solar system; perhaps during this longer period of time, they were able to develop the technology to get to earth. A hundred years ago, the idea that people could communicate with each other through computers or e-mail seemed impossible. In the past, things people thought could exist only in the imagination exist in reality today. If there are other planets out there with life on them, maybe their inhabitants have turned imagination into reality. Perhaps they have achieved the reality of traveling faster than the speed of light, or perhaps they learned how to travel through black holes. Who really knows? What I do know is that scientists shouldn't eliminate the possibility that some UFO sightings might be, true. Scientists believe that the laws of physics are universal and uniform; that is, they are the same everywhere in the universe. But maybe the laws of physics that apply in our galaxy are not the same that apply in theirs. We have never been to another galaxy; we just assume that the laws that apply here also apply everywhere. We have to accept the possibility that there may be a planet or a galaxy that has yet to be discovered that contains forces that can neutralize the basic laws of physics.

Angels and aliens are not the only paranormal phenomena I've changed my opinion about. I also accept the possibility of miracles and visions of Jesus and the Virgin Mary.

Accounts of such events lead me to believe that anything is possible. Many people with no history of trickery have related stories of miracles and visions; many of them were narrated by priests. Visions of statues weeping and miracles of the Virgin Mary coming to one's bedside and healing the sick are laid out in page after page, book after book. Don't things that can't be explained sometimes happen? Even though scientists say no, I tend to think so. They would say we just don't have enough information yet to explain such accounts thoroughly. Nonbelievers will have counterarguments to my assertions. For instance, they would raise the possibility of collective misperception among the people who make such claims. But I too used to be a nonbeliever. Aside from the incident with my grandmother, I have not had any leaps of faith to make me change my opinion and believe what I now believe. I just re-evaluated what scientists know, assessed the possibility of knowing much more than they know, and reached my own conclusion.

I realize that scientists would argue that one can never demonstrate that these supernatural or paranormal events can take place; they would make a claim based on plausibility, not absolutes. Still, I will continue to believe that nothing is known for sure, and anything is possible!

NICOLE PRISCO

I believe in the ability to communicate with the deceased or, as I prefer to phrase it, persons from the "other side." I also believe that there is significance in coincidences. There are many seemingly chance occurrences in life that take place when two similar things take place either simultaneously or within days; many of these occurrences hold a special meaning for me.

My belief in the ability to communicate with the "other side" became apparent to me about eight years ago. A close friend was reading a book she couldn't put down. It is called *We Don't Die* written by George Anderson. As I read the first few pages of this book, it became evident to me why my friend was so intrigued. George Anderson discovered his calling in his youth after he became very ill. Since that time, he was able to communicate with spirits who have "crossed over."

Ten years ago, a close family friend, Andrea, was killed after a drunk driver drove into her car; she was only 19 and she had her whole life ahead of her. My whole family grieved over her death; all of us were struggling to answer the question, "Why?" Why her, and why now? I was only 15 when Andrea died; as we all know, adolescence is an extremely troubling and perplexing period in our lives. Therefore, dealing with such a loss was painful.

The night following the accident, my parents were at the hospital comforting Andrea's parents and providing support. I was at home with my older sister Charlene. All I was told was that she was in the hospital, nothing more. I drifted asleep. A few minutes past 11 P.M., I woke. up. An hour later, the phone rang. My mother called to say that Andrea had passed away a few minutes after 11, just when I had woken up. At the time, I passed it off as a coincidence.

A few nights after her death, I had a dream. Andrea was floating on the ceiling of our basement. She looked at me and said, "I'm OK. I am not hurt, I'm just angry." I awoke from that dream with my heart pounding. I told my mother about that dream. She said it was probably that Andrea had been on my mind. But I knew deep inside that it was a divine message from Andrea. She communicated through me to help ease the minds of the members of our family.

Over the years, I have had a number of dreams about Andrea. I can't fully account for the significance of these dreams. I recall thinking, during the dreams, what is Andrea doing here? Doesn't she know she is dead?

The last time I dreamed about Andrea was about three years ago. It was three days before her sister Renee was to be married. In the dream, I was in Renee's house helping to prepare for her wedding. Everyone was running around trying to get things taken care of. All of a sudden, I looked outside the dining room window, and I saw Andrea, sitting in a tree. I tried to summon her family's attention, but no one answered my calls.

That dream disturbed me because I was unsure of its meaning. Was Andrea trying to say, "Hey, don't forget me?" Or was she simply saying, "I'll always be here, looking out for all of you?"

The day of Renee's wedding, I had an experience I've never had before or since. As Renee's maid of honor, I was to arrive at her house earlier than the bridesmaids. As I was driving down the block to her house, I got a sudden chill; I felt Andrea's presence right there in the car with me. If I had glanced over to the passenger side, I am sure I would have seen her sitting there beside me.

Some people would not regard these events as evidence of paranormal phenomena. They are not believers; I am. I believe just as George Anderson says: We don't die; we are not forgotten; when we die, we merely cross over to the "other side."

When my Aunt Perna was growing up in Brooklyn, she knew an older woman named Santalla, who always made hurtful remarks about my aunt. Eight years passed since Perna had seen Santalla or heard her name. One morning, my aunt awoke at 5 A.M. from what she called a nightmare. In that nightmare, Aunt Perna was floating on the ceiling of a hospital room. She looked down and saw Santalla lying in a hospital bed with her husband and children around her. My aunt said that she was simply witnessing a scene unfolding beneath her.

All of a sudden, Santalla looked up at my aunt and communicated with her. The words, Perna said, were not spoken, but were conveyed through mental telepathy. Santalla said, "I'm sorry," and shed a tear.

My aunt woke my uncle and told him of her dream, Later that day, they were visiting my uncle's mother, who was still in contact with Santalla. My aunt began recalling her nightmare to her mother-in-law. Suddenly, my uncle's mother was beside herself in disbelief. As it turns out, Santalla *did* die earlier that morning, and it was exactly the way my aunt had seen it, with her family around her.

As I said, I also believe in coincidences. I believe in them because of my experiences, because they have happened to me. While dining out with my boyfriend and his family, I was asked, what would your wedding song to be? I responded with the title of the first song that entered my head, "Groovy Kind of Love." This song has no special significance for me, it was simply the first one to pop into my head. Later that evening, as I drove home from the restaurant, I turned on the radio. The song that was playing was "Groovy Kind of Love." What are the chances of that happening? It's an old song; why would that song be playing at that time? Things like this make me think there's more than mere random accident in simultaneous occurrences.

One last example of coincidences. When I was dining out, again, with my boyfriend's family, we were discussing a person's hectic schedule. I made a joke about having to make an appointment with her on May 18th. Someone asked me why I picked that date. I said that's just a date that popped into my head. Then I was told that May I 8th happens to be the birthday of the woman we were talking about. I had no knowledge of the date of her birth.

If I had to write all of the coincidences I have experienced, I'd be writing for days. In fact, I am sure I experience at least one a day.

I feel people are more inclined to believe in something if they can relate it to their own experiences. My beliefs are simply that, *mine.* I would not say that everyone should believe what I believe. Nor would I try to sway others to accept my beliefs. I feel as long as what I believe does not harm anyone else, then it is okay.

PHIL SALAMACHA

I have been going to church pretty much my whole life; I consider myself a pretty religious person. I believe in God as well as the Holy Trinity of the Father, the Son, and the Holy Spirit. I also believe that there has been divine intervention in my life at least a few times when I came fairly close to death.

Once I was alone, in the basement of my house, washing my football uniform after a muddy, rainy practice. Earlier in the day, we were having new windows installed in our house, including in the basement. The installers had disconnected a water line that ran from the washer to outside; I was unaware of this. I turned on the washer and left the basement. Fifteen minutes later, I walked past the basement door and heard a whooshing sound. Checking, I discovered the basement was flooded with a foot of water, and it was rising. I ran down the steps and waded over to the washer and found that the disconnected water line was ejecting water into the basement at a high rate of speed. I grabbed the water line and the connection and, using every ounce of my strength, connected them. By the time the gushing stopped, the water was up to my knees. After a few hours, the water receded. When my parents came home, I told my dad about what had happened. He went into the basement and discovered something that was quite literally shocking: If the water had risen another three inches, it would have made contact with an electrical outlet, and I would have been electrocuted.

Close call? Coincidence? Or was it in fact divine intervention that was looking out for me on that day? If someone told me about escaping a similar situation through sheer luck, I would explain to them that we are taught that God and His angels are watching over you to protect you from harm.

I also believe in the existence of aliens on earth. I realize that this belief seems to contradict my belief in God, because there is no mention of God creating aliens in the Bible. But over the hundreds of years of sightings, testimony, and books written about them, I believe that someone has to be telling the truth.

One reason why I believe extraterrestrials exist is that descriptions of these beings are usually the same: They have large heads, big, black eyes, small mouths, and small, thin bodies. I think this is pretty significant. I also believe that the government is covering something up. Why would they have all those secret bases in the desert that are patrolled 24 hours a day? If you trespass onto them, you will be shot on sight. I think that they must be hiding something that is extraterrestrial in nature. Area 51 is an example.

I am not one hundred percent sure why aliens visit the earth. But after reading and hearing countless testimonies, I believe that the aliens have a problem with reproducing themselves; eventually, their race will die out. This is the reason why they are abducting people and conducting tests on them, to try to create some sort of human-alien hybrid. Even though these aliens have extraordinary powers, I don't think their powers can help them with their problem of reproduction; they need outside help.

I had a dream a couple of years ago that convinces me of an alien presence. I dreamt I was dreaming. In the dream, I woke up, but in reality, I was still dreaming. In the dream, I was lying in bed. All of a sudden, lights began flashing outside my 14th-story window. I tried to move, but I couldn't. I also tried to yell, but again, I couldn't. I became terrified, and woke up. But once again, I didn't really wake up, I only dreamt I did. In the dream, I was relieved that I had woken up, so I tried to get out of bed, and again, I couldn't move. I tried to say something, but nothing came out of my mouth. Then the flashing lights came back on, and again I recall feeling terrified. This time, I actually woke up. I was in a sweat and was really frightened. I jumped out of bed, ran to the window, and saw nothing. When I told the dream to a friend, he told me, in a joking manner, that I had been abducted and my memory of it had been erased. I also believe that it was just a dream. But there is always a slight chance it might not have been. Perhaps it was aliens.

I also believe in the existence of the devil. I believe that the devil is trying to corrupt people on earth through a number of channels such as satanism, devil worship, music, as well as a number of others. I do believe that satan exists and is trying to corrupt people. Aleister Crowley and Anton LaVey are some of the devil's followers. I make a distinction between devil worship and satanism. Satanists don't even believe in the devil; what they believe is that if something makes you feel good, then you should do it, even if it hurts somebody else. Devil worship deals with sacrificing babies and animals to gain power. I recall seeing an interview with one of the former high priests of satan, who claimed he could light a bonfire from 50 feet away by just thinking about it. He said he got his power through human sacrifices for demons; at one point in his life, he claimed, he was possessed by the devil. After years of this practice, this man was able to get away from it and lead a normal life. After ten years, he doesn't even possess the ability to laugh out loud; because of what devil worship did to him, only now is he beginning to learn how to smile. He will not allow anyone to test him for the powers he allegedly had.

The Bible claims that satan will use any means he can to corrupt people, promising them great power if they kill someone. I've heard testimony and seen television programs to this effect. For instance, a while ago, I saw a two-hour Geraldo special that dealt with satanism. It was very moving. Thousands and thousands of followers of satan were exposed on the program, which was scary. After seeing and hearing all this, and connecting it with what I've learned from the Bible, I do feel strongly that satan exists and that he is trying to corrupt humanity.

Some day, my beliefs may be proven. But they might also not ever go past hearsay and folklore.

AMANDA BOWCOCK

I grew up in a very traditional household. My father and mother have no education beyond high school. My dad is a mechanic; he has worked full-time plus second and third jobs to support a family of six. My mom has never had a paying job outside the home; she has stayed at home and cared for the house and the kids. I believe my parents are very intelligent people. I was raised as a born-again Christian. I take my faith very seriously. I believe that, without my faith in Jesus Christ, I would not be where I am today. I work full-time as the head manager of a fast-food restaurant. Throughout my entire college career, I have worked 60 hours a week and have taken at least 15 credits each semester. I do not think that I could have done this without God's help.

I believe in the literal interpretation of the Bible; I take it as the true word of God. In my opinion, everything that is described in the Bible happened just as it says. All the prophecies that were foretold in the Old Testament held true in the New Testament. I do not see any way of disputing this evidence. I know some people who think I am crazy, but I take the Bible as an official historical document, unchanged over time. In order to learn about the past, we read history books which narrate historical events in the past, such as wars. Why don't we have just as much faith in God and in the Bible as a historical text? My family and I have had personal experiences that strengthen our religious faith. Here are three of them.

When I was about seven years old, I became very ill. For about three months, I was in and out of hospitals. I had a continual stomach pain. I lost a significant amount of weight, I was pale, and my face looked drawn all the time. After a month of testing and a month-long stay in the hospital, I overheard the doctors tell my parents that it looked as if leukemia was the cause of my symptoms. All I could think of was that I was going to die. When the hospital could do no more for me, I was sent home.

I remember being in my room that night; it felt good to be home at last. I lay down to go to sleep and closed my eyes, praying to the Lord. I thanked Him for the day I had and asked that, if it was His will, please, to help me get better. I finished my prayer with an "amen," and then opened my eyes. I could not believe what I saw. Jesus Christ was standing right before me. His eyes were so blue, they made me squint and tear. By shaking his head, he told me that I was going to be okay. Being as young as I was, I was frightened of this apparition; I ran upstairs and slept on the floor of my parents' room, next to their bed. When they woke up in the morning, they asked me why I was there, but I hid my secret from them.

As time progressed, my symptoms declined. Eventually, when I went back for more testing, all my blood work came back fine. The doctors never found out what was wrong with me, but they thought it strange that I had become better so quickly. I know what happened. God healed my ailments because He had a plan for my life that I had not yet completed.

When my sister was an infant, she also became very ill. She was bleeding internally and had a 101 degree fever. The doctors could not locate the source of the bleeding and thought they were going to have to do exploratory surgery to find out. When she heard this horrific news, my mother went downstairs to the chapel at St. Charles, the hospital where my sister was being examined. She told me she fell to her knees and wept uncontrollably. She prayed, "Please God, save my baby girl." A few moments later, she heard the clear response, "Whose child is she?" After recalling her promise to the Lord always to remember that her children were His children first and foremost, my mother stopped crying; she continued to pray. "Lord, I am sorry," she said, "please forgive me. I remember that this is your child. Please do Your will in her life." Then my mother dried her eyes and returned upstairs to be with my father and my sick baby sister. When she entered her room, the physicians and nurses told her, "Your daughter's fever has broken."

Her bleeding had stopped and surgery did not have to be performed. The doctors were in awe at this point. They called my sister's improvement a miracle. My family and I know that it was not a miracle, but one example of God's awesome powers.

When I was a small child, perhaps a year or so old, my mother was having recurrent heart and chest pains. She was only 24 at the time, far too young to be having heart problems. I recall being dragged to the hospital every weekend because my mother had to be tested. One weekend in particular is vividly imprinted on my mind. This is what my mother told me:

> The doctors put a long needle in my arm and injected me with iodine. A few minutes later, I began to feel faint. I knew something was very wrong. I told the doctors and nurses of my fear, but they replied that it was just my nerves. I lay down; a few moments later, I heard a nurse screech, "Oh, my God!" I had blown up with hives all over my face and body. I felt as if someone were choking me; I could not breathe. But just a few moments later, everything felt better. I felt as if I were floating. Suddenly, I felt no pain. I saw bright lights; I felt as if I were moving upward, toward heaven. Soon after that, I heard a doctor yelling, "We are losing her!" I fought the sensations

I was feeling because I sensed that I was dying. I told God that I wanted to watch my children grow up. The instant I finished that phrase, I began to feel my body returning to earth. Then I heard, "Code Blue, I hope we see this young woman smile again." At this point, I thought I was dead I opened my eyes and saw all kinds of devices hooked up to my body. I looked at the doctor. "Am I going to die?" I asked him. "Not now!" he replied

At this point, my mother's story ends. I believe that my mother died and began to make her way to heaven. I cannot see any other explanation for what she told me. She had died. All of her vital signs had ceased for over two minutes. The doctors aided in bringing her back to life, but, in my opinion, ultimately, what happened was that God's will was done.

I do not agree with the notion that science explains everything. For instance, science cannot explain the three events I described here. I intend to continue my education beyond college in psychology and sociology. What I have learned so far has not swayed my faith one bit; I do not plan to let it do so. I feel that I have led a fairly decent life; I try my best to follow the Lord's commandments. I am not telling everyone that they must believe in God or the Bible. But if I die and find out that there is no God or heaven, at least my beliefs will have helped me lead a decent, well-rounded life. I will not have lost anything by believing that Jesus died for my sins. In my opinion, without faith in God and heaven, we have nothing to look forward to.

References

Adams, John. 1997. "Gray Matters: The Origin of the 'Gray' Alien Archetype." *Skeptic*, 5 (2): 14–17.

Anderson, Wayne R. 1998. "Why Would People *Not* Believe Weird Things?" *Skeptical Inquirer*, 22 (September/October): 42–45, 62.

Anonymous. 1998. "New Mars Photos Cast Doubt on Speculation on a 'Face.'" *The New York Times*, April 7, p.A24.

Asimov, Isaac. 1986. "The Perennial Fringe." *Skeptical Inquirer*, 10 (Spring): 212–214.

Bainbridge, William Sims, and Rodney Stark. 1980. "Superstitions: New and Old." *Skeptical Inquirer*, 4 (Summer): 18–31.

✓ Baker, Robert A. 1987–88. "The Aliens among Us: Hypnotic Regression Revisited." *Skeptical Inquirer*, 12 (Winter): 147–162.

Balch, Robert W., and David Taylor. 1976. "Salvation in a UFO." *Psychology Today*, October, pp.58–66, 106.

Barber, Bernard. 1961. "Resistance by Scientists to Scientific Discovery." *Science*, 134 (1 September): 596–602.

Barrick, Mac E. 1976. "The Migratory Anecdote and the Folk Concept of Fame." *Mid-South Folklore*, 4 (1): 39–47.

Bartholomew, Robert E. 1990. "The Airship Hysteria of 1896–97," *Skeptical Inquirer*, 14 (Winter): 171–181.

Bartholomew, Robert E., and George S. Howard. 1998. *UFOs and Alien Contact: Two Centuries of Mystery.* Buffalo, NY: Prometheus Books.

Begley, Sharon. 1997. "Seek and Ye Shall Find." *Newsweek*, June 9, pp.66–67.

Begley, Sharon. 1998. "Science Finds God." *Newsweek*, July 20, pp.46–51.

Belfield, Dominic. 1987. "Nessie Keeps Her Head Down." *New Scientist*, 29 October, p.71.

Beloff, John. 1980. "Seven Evidential Experiments." *Zetetic Scholar*, no.6 (July): 91–94.

Benassi, Victor A., Barry Singer, and Craig B. Reynolds. 1980. "Occult Belief: Seeing Is Believing." *Journal for the Scientific Study of Religion*, 19 (4): 337–349.

Ben-Yehuda, Nachman. 1985. *Deviance and Moral Boundaries: Witchcraft, the Occult, Science Fiction, Deviant Sciences and Scientists*. Chicago: University of Chicago Press.

Berger, Peter L. 1967. *The Sacred Canopy: Elements of a Sociological Theory of Religion*. Garden City, NY: Doubleday.

Berger, Peter L., and Thomas Luckmann. 1966. *The Social Construction of Reality*. Garden City, NY: Doubleday.

Bernstein, Jeremy. 1978. "Scientific Cranks: How to Recognize One and What to Do Until the Doctor Arrives." *The American Scholar*, 47 (March): 8–14.

Bird, S. Elizabeth. 1992. *For Enquiring Minds: A Cultural Study of Supermarket Tabloids*. Knoxville, TN: University of Tennessee Press.

Blackmore, Susan. 1986. *The Adventures of a Parapsychologist*. Buffalo, NY: Prometheus Books.

Blakeslee, Sandra. 1998. "Placebos Prove So Powerful Even Experts Are Surprised." *The New York Times*, October 13, pp.F1, F4.

Brackman, Harold. 1996. "Farrakhanspiracy: Louis Farrakhan and the Paranoid Style in African-American Politics," *Skeptic*, 4 (3): 36–43.

Broad, William J. 1994. "Wreckage in the Desert Was Odd but Not Alien." *The New York Times*, September 18, pp.1, 40.

Broad, William J. 1997. "Air Force Details a New Theory in U.F.O. Case." *The New York Times*, June 25, p.B7.

Broad, William J. 1998. "Astronomers Revive Scan of the Heavens for Sign of Life," *The New York Times*, September 29, pp.F1, F5.

Brown, Chip. 1996. "They Laughed at Galileo Too." *The New York Times Magazine*, August 11, pp.41–45.

Brunvand, Jan Harold. 1981. *The Vanishing Hitchhiker: American Urban Legends and Their Meaning*. New York: W. W. Norton.

Brunvand, Jan Harold. 1993. *The Baby Train and Other Lusty Urban Legends*. New York: W. W. Norton.

Callahan, Tim. 1997. *Bible Prophecy: Failure or Fulfillment?* Altadena, CA: Millenium Press.

Carlson, Elof. 1998. "Science Isn't Magic, but We Don't Always Know the Difference." *The Times Beacon Record* (Port Jefferson), September 10, p.C1.

Carlson, Shawn. 1985. "A Double-Blind Test of Astrology." *Nature*, 318 (5 December): 419–425.

Carlson, Shawn. 1988. "Astrology." *Experentia*, 44 (April): 290–297.

Clark, Jerome, and Nancy Pear. 1997. *Strange & Unexplained Phenomena*. Detroit: Visible Ink.

Cole, Henry P., and Eugenie C. Scott. 1982. "Creation-Science and Scientific Research." *Phi Delta Kappan*, 63 (April): 557–558.

Cole, Jonathan R., and Stephen Cole. 1973. *Social Stratification in Science.* Chicago: University of Chicago Press.

Cole, Stephen. 1992. *Making Science: Between Nature and Science.* Cambridge, MA: Harvard University Press.

Cromer, Alan. 1993. *Uncommon Sense: The Heretical Nature of Science.* New York & Oxford, UK: Oxford University Press.

Culver, R. B., and P. A. Ianna. 1984. *The Gemini Syndrome: A Scientific Evaluation of Astrology.* Buffalo, NY: Prometheus Books.

Curran, Douglas. 1985. *In Advance of the Landing: Folk Concepts of Outer Space.* New York: Abbeville Press.

Dawkins, Richard. 1998. *Unweaving the Rainbow: Science, Delusion and the Appetite for Wonder.* Boston: Houghton Mifflin.

Dean, Jodi. 1998. *Aliens in America: Conspiracy Cultures from Outerspace to Cyberspace.* Ithaca, NY: Cornell University Press.

Deloria, Vine, Jr. 1969. *Custer Died for Your Sins: An Indian Manifesto.* New York: Macmillan.

Deloria, Vine, Jr. 1995. *Red Earth, White Lies: Native Americans and the Myth of Scientific Fact.* New York: Scribners.

de Mille, Richard (ed.). 1980. *The Don Juan Papers: Further Castaneda Controversies.* Santa Barbara, CA: Ross-Erikson Publishers.

Drosnin, Michael. 1997. *The Bible Code.* New York: Simon & Schuster.

Duncan, Lois, and William Roll. 1995. *Psychic Connections: A Journey into the Mysterious World of Psi.* New York: Delacorte Press.

Dunne, Brenda J., and John P. Bisaha. 1979. "Precognitive Remote Viewing in the Chicago Area: A Replication of the Stanford Experiment." *Journal of Parapsychology,* 43 (March): 17–30.

Eldridge, Niles. 1982. *The Monkey Business: A Scientist Looks at Creationism.* New York: Pocket Books/Washington Square Press.

Ellis, Richard. 1998. *Imagining Atlantis.* New York: Alfred A. Knopf.

Eve, Raymond A., and Francis B. Harrold. 1991. *The Creationist Movement in Modern America.* Boston: Twayne.

Feder, Kenneth L. 1997. "Indians and Archaeology: Conflicting Views of Myth and Science." *Skeptic,* 5(3): 74–80.

Ferguson, Marilyn. 1980. *The Aquarian Conspiracy.* Los Angeles: Jeremy P. Tarcher.

Forer, Bertram R. 1949. "The Fallacy of Personal Validation: A Classroom Demonstration of Gullibility." *Journal of Abnormal and Social Psychology,* 44 (January): 118–123.

Foster, Mike. 1998. "New 'Face on Mars' Photo Is Phony!" *Weekly World News,* June 2, p.19.

Frazier, Kendrick. 1993. "Our 'Spooky Presidential Coincidences Contest' Winners." *Skeptical Inquirer,* 17 (Winter): 212–214.

Frick, Joe. 1986. "Snake Tattoo Chokes Man." *Sun,* September 16, p.15.

Friedlander, Michael W. 1995. *At the Fringes of Science.* Boulder, CO: Westview Press.

Friedman, Stanton T., and Don Berliner. 1992. *Crash at Corona: The U.S. Military Retrieval Cover-Up of a UFO.* New York: Paragon House.

Futuyma, Douglas J. 1983. *Science on Trial: The Case for Evolution*. New York: Pantheon Books.

Gallup, George, Jr. 1988. *Public Opinion 1987*. Wilmington, DE: Scholarly Resources.

Gallup, George, Jr. 1997. *Public Opinion 1996*. Wilmington, DE: Scholarly Resources.

Gallup, George, Jr., and Frank Newport. 1991. "Belief in Paranormal Phenomena Among Adult Americans," *Skeptical Inquirer*, 15 (Winter): 137–146.

Gardner, Martin. 1957. *Fads and Fallacies in the Name of Science* (2nd rev. ed.). New York: Dover.

Geertz, Clifford. 1973. *The Interpretation of Cultures*. New York: Basic Books.

Gildenberg, Bernard D., and David E. Thomas. 1998. "Case Closed: Reflections on the 1997 Air Force Roswell Report." *Skeptical Inquirer*, 22 (May/June): 31–36.

Gilovich, Thomas. 1991. *How We Know What Isn't So: The Fallibility of Human Reason in Everyday Life*. New York: Free Press.

Gilovich, Thomas, and Kenneth Savitsky. 1996. "Like Goes with Like: The Role of Representativeness in Erroneous and Pseudoscientific Beliefs." *Skeptical Inquirer*, 20 (March/April): 34–40.

Gish, Duane. 1978. *Evolution? The Fossils Say No!* San Diego: Creation-Life Publishers.

Gmelch, George. 1978. "Baseball Magic." *Human Nature*, 1 (August): 32–39.

Goode, Erica. 1997. "The Eternal Quest for a New Age." *U.S. News & World Report*, April 7, pp.32–34.

Goode, Erich. 1992. *Collective Behavior*. Ft. Worth, TX: Harcourt Brace.

Goode, Erich. 1999. "Two Paranormalisms or Two and a Half? An Empirical Examination," *Skeptical Inquirer*, 23 (November/December).

Gould, Stephen Jay. 1984. *Hen's Teeth and Horses' Toes: Further Reflections on Natural History*. New York: W. W. Norton.

Gray, Thomas. 1995. "Educational Experiences and Belief in Paranormal Phenomena." In Francis B. Harrold and Raymond A. Eve (eds.), *Cult Archaeology and Creationism: Understanding Pseudoscientific Beliefs About the Past* (exp. ed.). Iowa City: University of Iowa Press, pp.21–33.

Gray, William D. 1991. *Thinking Critically About New Age Ideas*. Belmont, CA: Wadsworth.

Green, Mark, and Gail MacColl. 1983. *There He Goes Again: Ronald Reagan's Reign of Error*. New York: Pantheon Books.

Grinspoon, Lester, and Alan D. Persky. 1974. "Psychiatry and UFO Reports." In Carl Sagan and Thornton Page (eds.), *UFO's—A Scientific Debate*. New York: W. W. Norton, pp.233–246.

Handy, Bruce. 1997. "Roswell or Bust." *Time*, June 23, pp.62–67.

Harrold, Francis B., and Raymond A. Eve. 1986. "Noah's Ark and Ancient Astronauts: Pseudoscientific Beliefs About the Past Among a Sample of College Students." *Skeptical Inquirer*, 11 (Fall): 61–75.

Harrold, Francis B., and Raymond A. Eve. 1995. "Patterns of Creationist Belief Among College Students." In Francis B. Harrold and Raymond A. Eve (eds.), *Cult Archaeology and Creationism: Understanding Pseudoscientific*

Beliefs About the Past (exp. ed.). Iowa City: University of Iowa Press, pp.68–90.

Hedges, Stephen J. 1997. "www.masssuicide.com." *U.S. News & World Report,* April 7, pp.26–30.

Hess, David J. 1993. *Science in the New Age: The Paranormal, Its Defenders and Debunkers, and American Culture.* Madison: University of Wisconsin Press.

Hewstone, Miles, 1989. *Causal Attribution: From Cognitive Processes to Collective Beliefs.* Oxford, UK: Basil Blackwell.

Hines, Terence. 1988. *Pseudoscience and the Paranormal: A Critical Examination of the Evidence.* Buffalo, NY: Prometheus Books.

Hitt, Jack. 1996. "On Earth As It Is In Heaven." *Harper's Magazine,* November, pp.51–60.

Hoggart, Simon, and Mike Hutchinson. 1995. *Bizarre Beliefs.* London: Richard Cohen Books.

Hogshire, Jim. 1997. *Grossed-Out Surgeon Vomits inside Patient! An Insider's Look at Supermarket Tabloids.* Venice, CA: Feral House.

Honorton, Charles. 1985. "Meta-Analysis of Psi Ganzfeld Research." *Journal of Parapsychology,* 49 (March): 51–91.

Honorton, Charles, and Diane C. Ferrari. 1989. "Future Telling: A Meta-Analysis of Forced–Choice Precognition Experiments." *Journal of Parapsychology,* 53 (December): 281–308.

Hopkins, Bud, David M. Jacobs, and Ron Westrum. 1991. *Unusual Personal Experiences: An Analysis of the Data from Three National Surveys.* Las Vegas, NV: Bigelow Holding Corporation.

Howard, Jane M. 1992. *Commune with the Angels: A Heavenly Handbook.* Virginia Beach, VA: A.R.E Press.

Hufford, David J. 1982. *The Terror That Comes in the Night: An Experience-Centered Study of Supernatural Assault Traditions.* Philadelphia: University of Pennsylvania.

Hyman, Ray. 1977. "'Cold Reading': How to Convince Strangers that You Know All About Them." *The Zetetic,* 1 (Spring/Summer): 18–37.

Hyman, Ray. 1981. "Scientists and Psychics." In George O. Abell and Barry Singer (eds.). *Science and the Paranormal: Probing the Existence of the Paranormal.* New York: Charles Scribner's Sons, pp.119–141.

Irwin, H. J. 1994. *An Introduction to Parapsychology* (2nd ed.). Jefferson, NC: McFarland.

Jacobs, David M. 1992. *Secret Life: Firsthand Documented Accounts of UFO Abductions.* New York: Simon & Schuster/Fireside.

James, George. 1987. "Death of a Passer-By: Legend Grows." *The New York Times,* July 24, p.B3.

Jaroff, Leon. 1997. "Did Aliens Land?" *Time,* June 23, pp.68–71.

Jorgensen, Danny L., and Lin Jorgensen. 1982. "Social Meaning of the Occult." *The Sociological Quarterly,* 23 (Summer): 373–389.

Kahneman, Daniel, Paul Slovic, and Amos Tversky (eds.). 1989. *Judgment Under Certainty: Heuristics and Biases.* Cambridge, UK: Cambridge University Press.

Kelly, Ivan. 1979. "Astrology and Science: A Critical Examination." *Psychological Reports*, 44 (February–June): 1231–1240.

Kelly, Ivan. 1980. "The Scientific Case Against Astrology." *Astrology*, 9 (November–December): 135–142, 157.

Kennedy, Donald. 1998. "Helping Schools to Teach Evolution." *The Chronicle of Higher Education*, August 7, p.A48.

Kitcher, Philip. 1982. *Abusing Science: The Case Against Creationism*. Cambridge, MA: MIT Press.

Klass, Philip J. 1981. "UFOs." In George O. Abell and Barry Singer (eds.), *Science and the Paranormal: Probing the Existence of the Supernatural*. New York: Charles Scribner's Sons, pp.310–328.

Klass, Philip J. 1997. *The Real Roswell Crashed-Saucer Coverup*. Buffalo, NY: Prometheus Books.

Kluth, Rose, and Kathy Munnell. 1997. "The Integration of Scientific Knowledge on the Leech Lake Reservation." In Nina Swidler et al. (eds.), *Native Americans and Archaeologists: Stepping Stones to Common Ground*. Walnut Creek, CA: Altamira Press, pp.112–119.

Kolata, Gina. 1990. "1-in-a-Trillion Coincidence, You Say? Not Really, Experts Find." *The New York Times*, February 27, pp.C1, C2.

Kossey, Donna. 1994. *Kooks: Guide to the Outer Limit of Human Belief*. Venice, CA: Feral House.

Kuhn, Thomas S. 1962. *The Structure of Scientific Revolutions*. Chicago: University of Chicago Press.

Kurtz, Paul. 1978. "Is Parapsychology a Science?" *Skeptical Inquirer*, 3 (Winter): 14–32.

Larson, Bob. 1989. *Straight Answers on the New Age*. Nashville, TN: Nelson, 1989.

Larson, Edward J., and Larry Witham. 1997. "Scientists Are Still Keeping the Faith." *Nature*, 386 (3 April): 435–436.

Leavy, John. 1992. "Our Spooky Presidential Coincidences Contest." *Skeptical Inquirer*, 16 (Spring 1992): 316–320.

Leuba, James H. 1916. *The Belief in God and Immortality: A Psychological, Anthropological, and Statistical Study*. Boston: Sherman, French.

Leir, Roger K. 1998. *The Aliens and the Scalpel: Scientific Proof of Extraterrestrial Implants in Humans*. Columbus, NC: Granite Publishing, LLC.

Lippert, Dorothy. 1997. "In Front of the Mirror: Native Americans and Academic Archaeology." In Nina Swidler et al. (eds.), *Native Americans and Archaeologists: Stepping Stones to Common Grounds*. Walnut Creek, CA: Altamira Press, pp.120–127.

Loftus, Elizabeth F. 1977. *Eyewitness Testimony*. Cambridge, MA: Harvard University Press.

Logan, Rhett. 1998. "Ghost Chases Couple Across America," *Sun*, June 23, p.24.

Losh-Hasselbart, Susan. 1988. "Religion in the Public Schools: A Study of Attitudes Among Florida Residents." *Florida Public Opinion*, 3 (Winter): 2–12.

Lyons, Arthur, and Marcello Truzzi. 1991. *The Blue Sense: Psychic Detectives and Crime*. New York: Mysterious Press/Warner Books.

MacAndrew, James. 1997. *The Roswell Report: Case Closed.* Washington, DC: U.S. Government Printing Office.

Mack, John. 1994. *Abductions: Human Encounters with Aliens.* New York: Scribner.

Mack, John. 1995. *Abductions: Human Encounters with Aliens* (rev. ed.). New York: Bantam Books.

Malinowski, Bronislaw. 1954. *Magic, Science, and Religion.* Garden City, NY: Doubleday/Anchor.

Marks, David, and Richard Kammann. 1980. *The Psychology of the Psychic.* Buffalo, NY: Prometheus Books.

Martin, Bruce. 1998. "Coincidences: Remarkable or Random?" *Skeptical Inquirer,* 22 (September/October): 23–28.

McClenon, James. 1984. *Deviant Science: The Case of Parapsychology.* Philadelphia: University of Pennsylvania Press.

McClenon, James. 1994. *Wondrous Events: Foundations of Religious Belief.* Philadelphia: University of Pennsylvania.

McGowan, Chris. 1984. *In the Beginning . . . A Scientist Shows Why the Creationists Are Wrong.* Buffalo, NY: Prometheus Books.

Melton, J. Gordon. 1995. "The Contactees: A Survey." In James R. Lewis (ed.), *The Gods Have Landed: New Religions from Other Worlds.* Albany: State University of New York Press, pp.1–13.

Melton, J. Gordon, Jerome Clark, and Aidan Kelly. 1990. *New Age Encyclopedia.* Detroit: Gale Research.

Menzel, Donald H. 1972. "U.F.O.'s—The Modern Myth." In Carl Sagan and Thornton Page (eds.), *UFO's—A Scientific Debate.* New York: W. W. Norton, pp.123–182.

Meyer, Philip. 1986. "Ghostboosters: The Press and the Paranormal." *Columbia Journalism Review,* March/April, pp.38–41.

Miller, David. 1985. *An Introduction to Collective Behavior.* Belmont, CA: Wadsworth; Prospect Heights, IL: Waveland Press.

Miller, Jon D. 1987. "The Scientifically Illiterate." *American Demographics,* 9 (June): 26–31.

Miller, Kenneth. 1998. "Psychics: Science or Seance? Our Reporter Visits the Twilight Zone." *Life,* June, pp.88–90, 93, 96, 98, 101, 103.

Morris, Henry M. 1963. *The Twilight of Evolution.* Grand Rapids, MI: Baker.

Morris, Henry M. 1970. *Biblical Cosmology and Modern Science.* Nutley, NJ: Craig Press.

Morris, Henry M. 1974. *The Troubled Waters of Evolution.* San Diego: Creation-Life.

Morris, Henry M. 1977. *The Scientific Case for Creationism.* San Diego: Creation-Life Publishers.

Morris, Henry M. 1984. *A History of Modern Creationism.* San Diego: Master Books.

Morris, Henry M., and Duane T. Gish (eds.). 1976. *The Battle for Creation.* San Diego: Creation-Life.

Mumford, Michael D., Andrew M. Rose, and David A. Goslin. 1995. *An Evaluation of Remote Viewing: Research and Applications*. Washington, DC: American Institutes for Research.

Nardi, Peter M. 1984. "Toward a Social Psychology of Entertainment Magic (Conjuring)." *Symbolic Interaction*, 7 (1): 25–41.

Nietzsche, Friedrich. 1974. *The Gay Science*. New York: Random House.

Nisbet, Matt. 1998. "New Poll Points to Increase in Paranormal Beliefs." *Skeptical Inquirer*, 22 (September/October): 8, 12.

Nisbett, Richard, and Lee Ross. 1980. *Human Inference: Strategies and Shortcomings of Social Judgment*. Englewood Cliffs, NJ: Prentice-Hall.

Paulos, John Allen. 1988. *Innumeracy: Mathematical Illiteracy and its Consequences*. New York: Hill & Wang.

Peebles, Curtis. 1994. *Watch the Skies! A Chronicle of the Flying Saucer Myth*. Washington, DC: Smithsonian Institution Press.

Piatelli-Palmarini, Massimo. 1994. *Inevitable Illusions: How Mistakes of Reason Rule Our Minds* (trans. Massimo Piatelli-Palmarini and Keith Botsford). New York: John Wiley & Sons.

Pinkston, William S. 1980. *Biology for Christian Schools*. Greenville, SC: Bob Jones University Press.

Plamann, Steve. 1990. "Predictions for the Rip-Roaring 90s!" *National Enquirer*, January 2, p. 30.

Polanyi, Michael. 1958. *Personal Knowledge*. Chicago: University of Chicago Press.

Popper, Karl R. 1959. *The Logic of Scientific Discovery*. New York: Basic Books.

Radin, Dean. 1997. *The Conscious Universe: The Scientific Truth of Psychic Phenomenon*. New York: HarperEdge.

Radin, Dean, and Diane C. Ferrari. 1991. "Effects of Consciousness on the Fall of Dice." *Journal of Scientific Exploration*, 5 (1): 61–83.

Rae, Stephen. 1994. "John Mack." *The New York Times Magazine*, March 20, 30–33.

Randi, James. 1993. *The Mask of Nostradamus: The Prophecies of the World's Most Famous Seer*. Buffalo, NY: Prometheus Books.

Reich, James R., Jr. 1993. "The Eyewitness: Imperfect Interfact Between Stimuli and Story." *Skeptical Inquirer*, 17 (Summer): 394–399.

Rhine, J. B. 1934. *Extra-Sensory Perception*. Boston: Boston Society for Psychic Research.

Rhine, J. B. 1937. *Frontiers of the Mind: The Story of the Duke Experiments*. New York: Farrar & Reinhart.

Rosen, Ruth. 1997. "The Sinister Image of 'The X-Files.'" *The Chronicle of Higher Education*, July 11, p.B7.

Ross, David Frank, J. Don Read, and Michael P. Toglia (eds.). 1994. *Adult Eyewitness Testimony: Current Trends and Developments*. Cambridge, UK: Cambridge University Press.

Rothman, Milton. 1989. "Myths About Science. . . . And Belief in the Paranormal." *Skeptical Inquirer*, 14 (Fall): 25–34.

Sagan, Carl. 1980. *Cosmos*. New York: Random House.

Sagan, Carl. 1995. *The Demon-Haunted World: Science as a Candle in the Dark.* New York: Random House.

Saler, Benson. 1997. "Roswell and Religion." In Benson Saler, Charles A. Ziegler, and Charles B. Moore, *UFO Crash at Roswell: The Genesis of a Modern Myth.* Washington, DC: Smithsonian Institution Press, pp.115–149.

Saler, Benson, Charles A. Ziegler, and Charles B. Moore. 1997. *UFO Crash at Roswell: The Genesis of a Modern Myth.* Washington, DC: Smithsonian Institution Press.

Schechter, Harold. 1988. *The Bosom Serpent: Folklore and Popular Art.* Iowa City: University of Iowa Press.

Schlitz, Marilyn, and Elmer Gruber. 1980. "Transcontinental Remote Viewing." *Journal of Parapsychology,* 44 (December): 305–318.

Schmatz, Jeffrey. 1984. "Strange Sights Brighten the Night Skies Upstate." *The New York Times,* August 25, pp.25, 41.

Scott, Eugenie C., and Henry P. Cole. 1985. "The Elusive Basis of Creation 'Science.'" *Quarterly Review of Biology,* 60 (1): 21–30.

Segraves, Kelly. 1977. *The Creation Report.* San Diego: Creation-Science Research Center.

Shermer, Michael. 1997. *Why People Believe Weird Things: Pseudoscience, Superstition, and Other Confusions of Our Time.* New York: W. H. Freeman.

Shifflett, Francis. 1990. "4,000-Year-Old Cat Found Alive in Ancient Tomb." *Sun,* February 27, p.11.

Simmons, Jerry L. 1990. *The Emerging New Age.* Santa Fe, NM: Bear & Co.

Singer, Barry, and Victor A. Benassi. 1980–1981. "Fooling Some of the People All of the Time." *Skeptical Inquirer,* 5 (Winter): 17–24.

Singer, Barry, and Victor A. Benassi. 1981. "Occult Beliefs." *American Scientist,* 69 (January–February): 49–55.

Singh, Simon. 1998. "Mathematics 'Proves' What the Grocer Already Knew." *The New York Times,* August 25, p.F3.

Slater, Candace. 1982. "The Hairy Leg Strikes: The Individual Artist and the Brazilian *Literatura de Cordel.*" *Journal of American Folklore,* 95 (January–March): 51–89.

Spanos, Nicholas P., Patricia A. Cross, Kirby Dickson and Susan DuBreuil. 1993. "Close Encounters: An Examination of UFO experiences." *Journal of Abnormal Psychology,* 102 (4): 624–632.

Sparks, Glenn G. 1998. "Paranormal Depictions in the Media: How Do They Affect What People Believe?" *Skeptical Inquirer,* 22 (July/August): 35–39.

Sparks, Glenn G., Tricia Hansen, and Rani Shah. 1994. "Do Televised Depictions of Paranormal Events Influence Viewers' Beliefs?" *Skeptical Inquirer,* 18 (Summer): 386–395.

Stanley, Alessandra. 1998. "Pope Calls on World to Reunite Faith and Reason." *The New York Times,* October 16, pp.A1, A10.

Stiebing, William H. 1984. *Ancient Astronauts, Cosmic Collisions, and Other Popular Theories About Man's Past.* Buffalo, NY: Prometheus Books.

Targ, Russell, and Harold E. Puthoff. 1974. "Information Transmission Under Conditions of Sensory Shielding." *Nature,* 251 (October 18): 602–607.

Taylor, John H., Raymond A. Eve, and Francis B. Harrold. 1995. "Why Creationists Don't Go to Psychic Fairs." *Skeptical Inquirer*, 19 (November/December): 23–28.

Terry, Randall A. 1988. *Operation Rescue*. Binghamton, NY: Operation Rescue.

Thomas, David E. 1997. "Hidden messages and the Bible Code." *Skeptical Inquirer*, 21 (November/December): 30–36.

Thomas, David E. 1998. "Tolstoy Predicts Bulls' Sixth Championship (in Code of Course)." *Skeptical Inquirer*, 22 (November/December): 16–17.

Tierney, John. 1987. "Fleecing the Flock." *Discover*, November, pp.51–58.

Toumey, Christopher P. 1994. *God's Own Scientists: Creationists in a Secular World*. New Brunswick, NJ: Rutgers University Press.

Truzzi, Marcello. 1972. "The Occult Revival as Popular Culture: Some Random Observations on the Old and the Nouveau Witch." *Sociological Quarterly*, 13 (Winter): 16–36.

Truzzi, Marcello. 1977. "On Pseudo-sciences and Proto-sciences." *The Zetetic*, 1 (Spring–Summer): 3–8.

Truzzi, Marcello. 1980. "A Skeptical Look at Paul Kurtz's Analysis of the Scientific Status of Parapsychology." *Journal of Parapsychology*, 44 (March): 35–55.

Truzzi, Marcello. 1982. "J. B. Rhine and Pseudoscience: Some Zetetic Reflections on Parapsychology." In K. Ramakrishna Rao (ed.), *J. B. Rhine: On the Frontiers of Science*. Jefferson, NC: McFarland, pp.177–191.

Truzzi, Marcello. 1987. "Introduction." In Stanley Krippner (ed.), *Advances in Parapsychological Research*, 5. Jefferson, NC: McFarland, pp.4–8.

Truzzi, Marcello. 1997. "Reflections on the Sociology and Social Psychology of Conjurers and Their Relations with Psychical Research." In Stanley Krippner (ed.), *Advances in Parapsychological Research*, 8. Jefferson, NC: McFarland, pp.221–271.

Truzzi, Marcello. 1998. "The Skeptic/Proponent Debate in Parapsychology: Perspectives from the Social Sciences." In Nancy L. Zingrone et al. (eds.), *Research in Parapsychology, 1993*. Landham, MD: Scarecrow Press, pp.147–151.

Turner, Patricia A. 1993. *I Heard It Through the Grapevine: Rumor in African-American Culture*. Berkeley: University of California Press.

Turner, Richard. 1998. "A Tabloid Shocker." *Newsweek*, October 12, pp.70–72.

Wallechensky, David, Amy Wallace, and Irving Wallace. 1981. *The Book of Predictions*. New York: William Morrow.

Ward, Bernie. 1997. *Nostradamus: The Man Who Saw Tomorrow*. Boca Raton, FL: Globe Communications.

Weaver, Richard, and James MacAndrew. 1995. *The Roswell Report: Fact vs. Fiction in the New Mexico Desert*. Washington, DC: HQ United States Air Force.

Weber, Max. 1963 (orig. pub. 1922). *The Sociology of Religion* (trans. Ephraim Fischoff). Boston: Beacon Press.

Westrum, Ron. 1977. "Social Intelligence About Anomalies: The Case of UFOs." *Social Studies of Science*, 7 (2): 271–302.

Westrum, Ron. 1978. "Science and Social Intelligence About Anomalies: The Case of Meteorites." *Social Studies of Science*, 8 (4): 461–493.

Whitmore, John. 1995. "Religious Dimensions of the UFO Abductee Experience." In James R. Lewis (ed.), *The Gods Have Landed: New Religions from Other Worlds*. Albany: State University of New York Press, pp.65–84.

Wilson, Robert Anton. 1998. *Everything Is Under Control: Conspiracies, Cults, and Cover-ups*. New York: HarperPerennial.

Wilson, S. C., and Theodore X. Barber. 1983. "The Fantasy-Prone Personality: For Understanding Imagery, Hypnosis, and Parapsychological Phenomena." In A. A. Sheikh (ed.), *Imagery: Current Theory, Research, and Application*. New York: John Wiley & Sons.

Wolpert, Lewis. 1993. *The Unnatural Nature of Science: Why Science Does not Make (Common) Sense*. Cambridge, MA: Harvard University Press.

Woolgar, Steve, and Dorothy Pawluch. 1985. "Ontological Gerrymandering: The Anatomy of Social Problems Explanations." *Social Problems*, 32 (February): 214–227.

Wysong, R. L. 1976. *The Creation-Evolution Controversy*. Midland, MI: Inquiry.

Ziegler, Charles A. 1997. "Mythogenesis: Historical Development of the Roswell Narratives." In Benson Saler, Charles A. Ziegler, and Charles B. Moore, *UFO Crash at Roswell: The Genesis of a Modern Myth*. Washington, DC: Smithsonian Institution Press, pp.1–29.

Zuckerman, Harriet. 1977. "Deviant Behavior and Social Control in Science." In Edward Sagarin (ed.), *Deviance and Social Change*. Beverly Hills, CA: Sage, pp.87–138.

Index